THE SILENT INVASION
THE GREAT FEAR

 GRAPHIC NOVELS

Nantier • Beall • Minoustchine

NEW YORK

NBM Publishing
160 Broadway, Ste. 700, East Wing
New York, NY 10038

We have over 200 graphic novels.
See more at **www.nbmpub.com**
Catalogue available upon request.

ISBN 978-1-68112-206-9
Library of Congress Control Number: 2019935196
Available as an electronic book.
First printing: May 2019.

MICHAEL CHERKAS AND LARRY HANCOCK

THE SILENT INVASION

THE GREAT FEAR

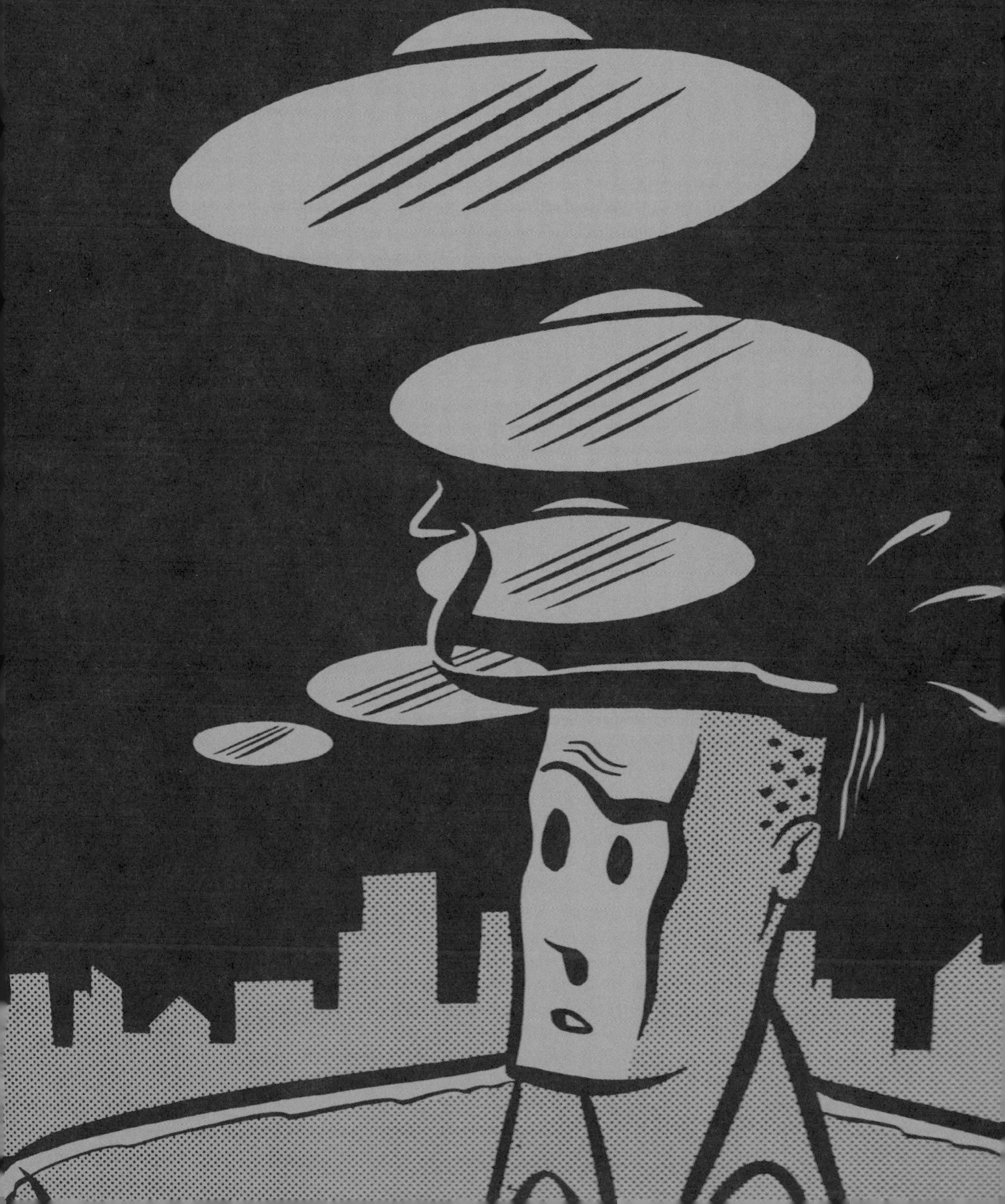

INTRODUCTION
UFOS, CONSPIRACIES AND THE DEEP STATE
(THERE ARE 187 ALIENS IN CONGRESS! WHO DID YOU VOTE FOR?)

A long time ago in a land far, far away, *The Silent Invasion* was originally released as a series of floppy comics by Deni Loubert's fondly-remembered Renegade Press, a publisher of black and white "indie" comics. Just as Deni was setting up shop in Long Beach, California, she asked us to develop a series for her new line.

We jumped at the opportunity. All Michael had ever wanted to do was draw comic books and he knew there was a snowball's chance in hell of him ever working in mainstream comics (take a look at the art in this book and you'll see why). We were just a couple of crazy kids (well, in our early thirties, but feeling young) with a crazy idea of mashing together UFO sightings, 1950s Communist witch hunts and a huge dollop of paranoia into what we termed a "science-fiction mystery." It was a crazy dream, but before you could say Jack Robinson we had a comic book series starring the doggedly-earnest reporter Matt Sinkage and a whole host of supporting characters straight out of a 1950s-era B-movie.

The first issue of the initial twelve part mini-series was published in April of 1986. We had a bi-monthly schedule and in order to meet the deadlines, Michael quit his day job as a graphic designer and art director and committed himself to the project. And, by God, he was going to learn how to ink with a Number 5 Winsor & Newton water colour brush! Larry, being the accountant of the pair, was far more practical and stuck with accounting, and moonlighted/moonlit/moondabbled as a comic book writer.

The Silent Invasion was fun, fast, a little spooky, a little dark, and a little satirical. It featured flying saucers, new-age cults, double agents, conspiracies and very, very, very top secret government organizations (early manifestations of the deep-state?). And it was all made up! Or was it?

The series was well-received, garnering a Kirby-award nomination in the black and white category, and was named by *Amazing Heroes* magazine as one of the 10-best comics of 1986. *The Silent Invasion* almost became a cult classic (two sales short of breaking even, as said by our friend Max Allan Collins). It was reprinted a few years later in several graphic albums which sold well, and then was quickly lost to the mists of time.

Our original run predated *The X-Files* television series (which drew upon common source materials) by several years. There were many similarities—a paranoid protagonist, possible aliens lurking in the shadows, powerful clandestine organizations, again, lurking in the shadows, smoking men lurking in the shadows and a healthy distrust of government and other authorities.

In re-reading the original series prior to these new editions being released, it became increasingly apparent at how *The Silent Invasion*—originally based on our imagined childhood memories of the the 1950s and 1960s—could be interpreted as a warning of a disturbing near future that is no longer the future, but is indeed our very own Gong Show of a present day. A delusional reality-TV star is President of the United States (something straight out of a Phillip K. Dick novel). Las Vegas has an NHL ice-hockey team. In New England, there are some who believe a certain football quarterback is a "strange visitor from another planet who came to earth with powers and abilities far beyond those of mortal men." And apparently Qatar(!!) will be hosting the World Cup of soccer (as that particular type of football is called here).

The internet is home to "Big Brother." We really are being watched. And not just by the CIA, FBI, NSA, DIA, DEA, CSIS, MI5, SVR, FSB and the other usual suspects. Large and insidious multi-national corporations that trade in information want to know your every move, your every desire and your every secret, no matter how dark.

We are now bombarded by massaged and slanted "news stories" from all political persuasions intended to confuse, confound and obfuscate. Outlandish conspiracy theories are now the norm—not the exception. "They" (whoever "they" are) claim the "deep state" orchestrates major events to take away our "god-given" freedoms.

Populism is on the rise in many parts of the world. People are voting against their own best interests. It appears that democracy is being manipulated by mysterious men and women from the shadowy corners of our collective imagination.

Matt Sinkage would feel right at home in today's world. He would not be the lone wolf crying in the wilderness; rather he'd be just one of many.

But if people only knew... they have it all wrong. The "deep state" isn't behind the chaos. Matt Sinkage was right! Aliens from space invaded long ago and insinuated themselves into every aspect of our lives. The game is rigged. And it's been rigged for a long time!

Life imitates art (or low art as the case may be). This may be the perfect era for *The Silent Invasion*. Enjoy it while you can.

Stay tuned and watch the skies!
MICHAEL CHERKAS and LARRY HANCOCK
Toronto, Ontario, May 2019

WHAT HAS GONE BEFORE...

In May 1952, investigative reporter Matt Sinkage chases a UFO into the woods and reappears six hours later with no memory of what has happened to him. Over the weeks that follow, he is driven to recover those lost memories. When his editor kills his investigations into the UFOs, and then he is branded as a communist sympathizer, Sinkage concludes that there are secret organizations actively opposing him. With mounting pressures from family, friends and unseen foes, he starts to believe that his own girlfriend may have been possessed by an alien! Reluctantly, Matt turns to his nemesis, FBI agent Phil Housley for aid. Housley is, in fact, also working for The Council, a secret government agency, which is very interested in what Matt has discovered. Matt's spiraling paranoia leads to a final fatal confrontation, which results in Sinkage—and his secrets—being locked away in an institution.

Now, three years have passed and Matt Sinkage is trying to rebuild his life in the idyllic community of Rockhaven. But his destiny still awaits…

CHAPTER ONE

NO SECRETS

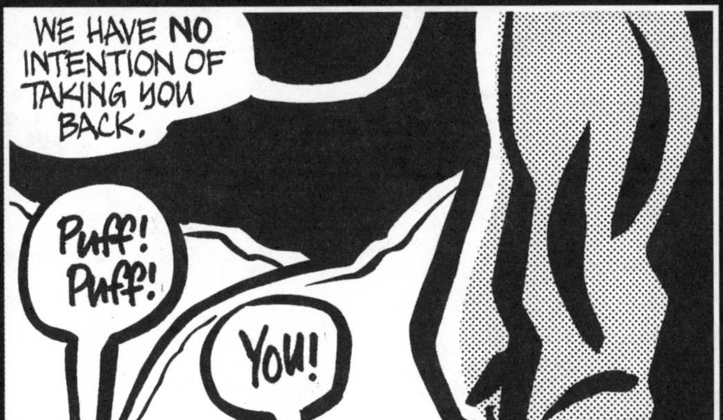
WE HAVE NO INTENTION OF TAKING YOU BACK.
Puff! Puff!
YOU!

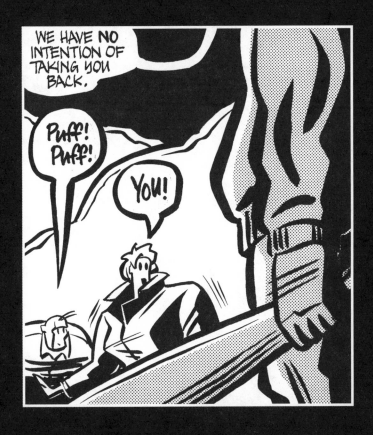

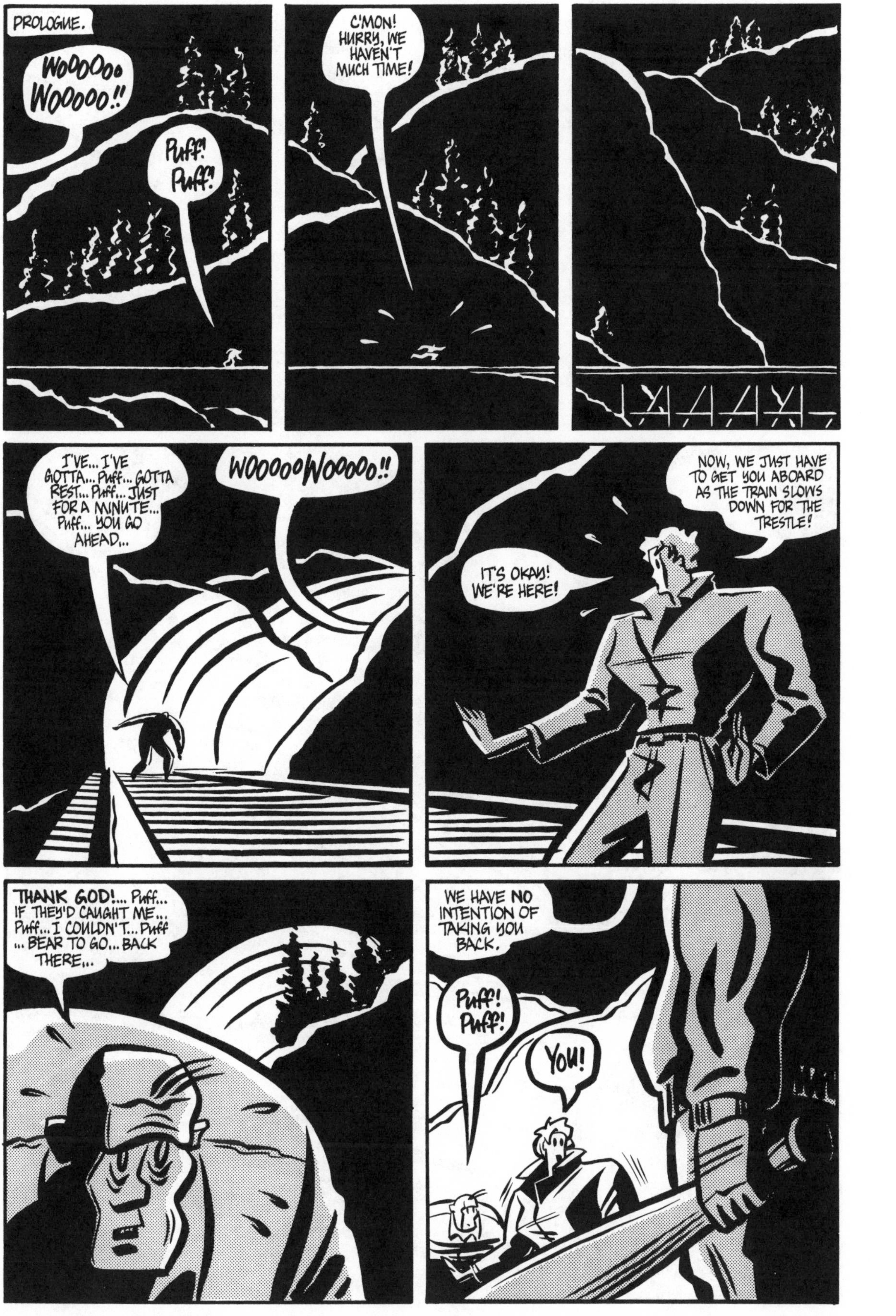
PROLOGUE.
WOOOOOO WOOOOO!!
PUFF! PUFF!
C'MON! HURRY, WE HAVEN'T MUCH TIME!
I'VE... I'VE GOTTA... PUFF... GOTTA REST... PUFF... JUST FOR A MINUTE... PUFF... YOU GO AHEAD...
WOOOOOWOOOOO!!
NOW, WE JUST HAVE TO GET YOU ABOARD AS THE TRAIN SLOWS DOWN FOR THE TRESTLE!
IT'S OKAY! WE'RE HERE!
THANK GOD!... PUFF... IF THEY'D CAUGHT ME... PUFF... I COULDN'T... PUFF ... BEAR TO GO... BACK THERE...
WE HAVE NO INTENTION OF TAKING YOU BACK.
PUFF! PUFF!
YOU!

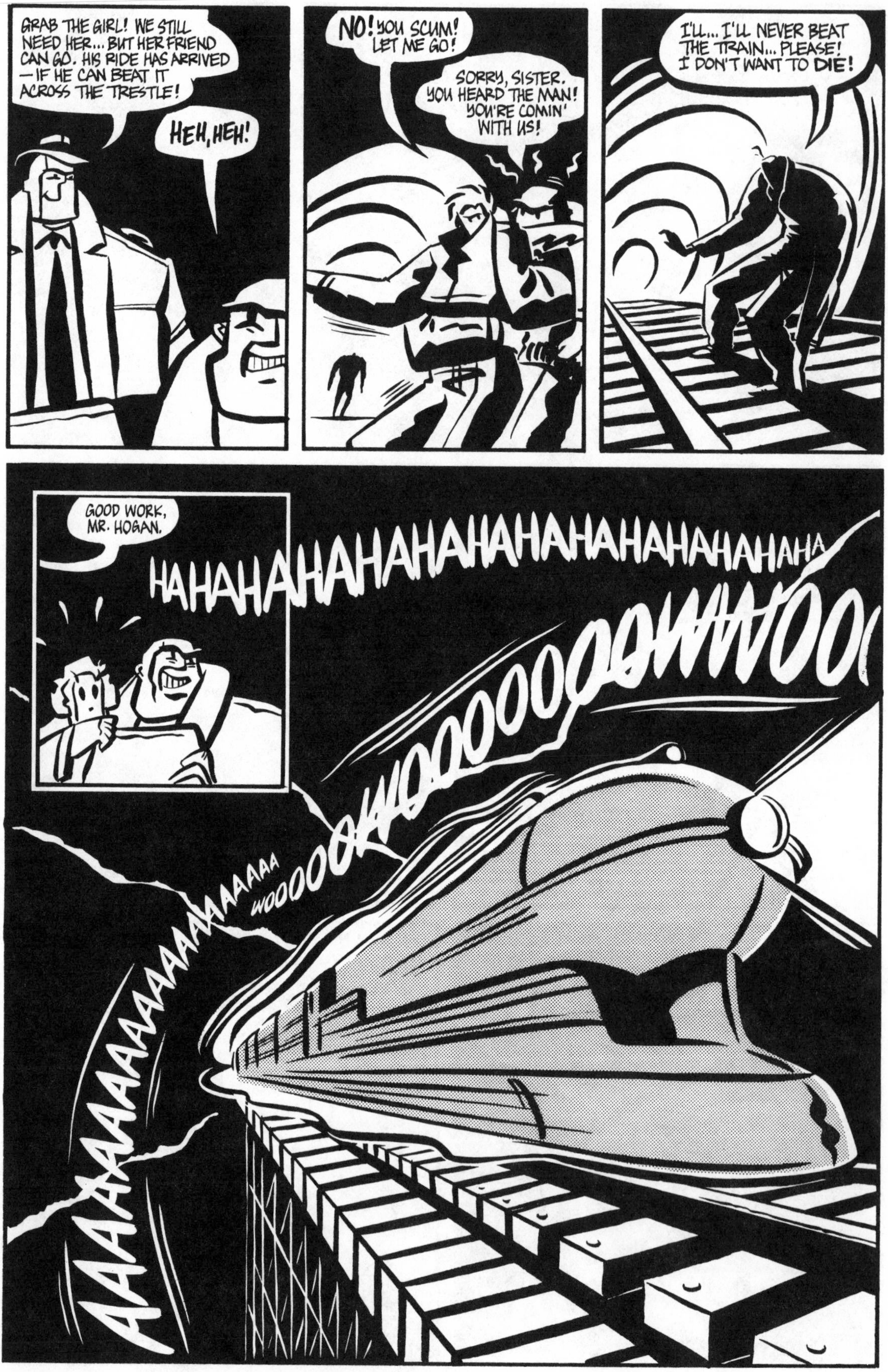
GRAB THE GIRL! WE STILL NEED HER... BUT HER FRIEND CAN GO. HIS RIDE HAS ARRIVED —IF HE CAN BEAT IT ACROSS THE TRESTLE!
HEH, HEH!
NO! YOU SCUM! LET ME GO!
SORRY, SISTER. YOU HEARD THE MAN! YOU'RE COMIN' WITH US!
I'LL... I'LL NEVER BEAT THE TRAIN... PLEASE! I DON'T WANT TO DIE!
GOOD WORK, MR. HOGAN.
HAHAHAHAHAHAHAHAHAHAHAHAHAHAHA
WOOOOOOWOOOOOOOOOOOOWWOO
AAAAAAAAAAAAAAAAAAAA

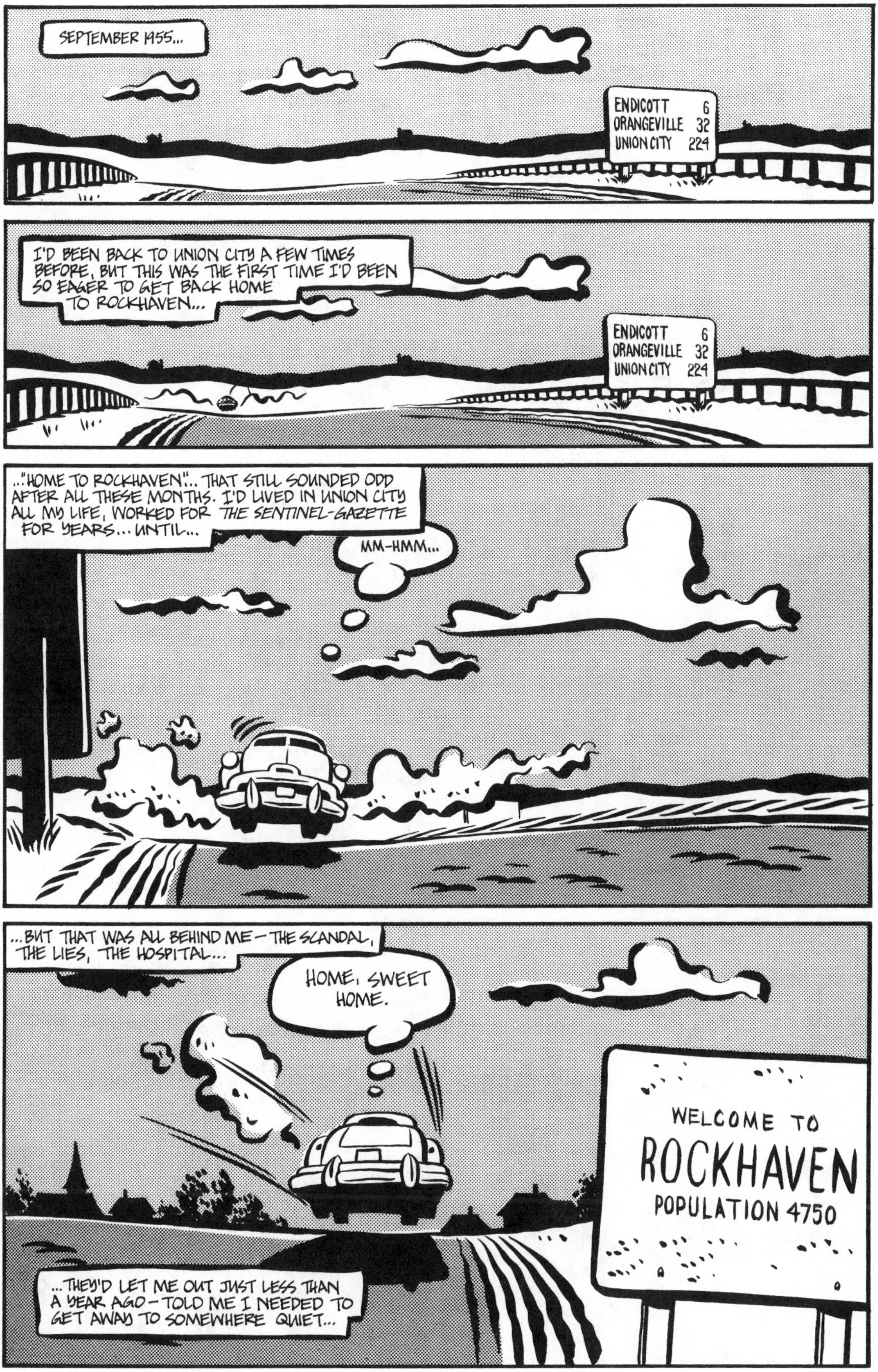
SEPTEMBER 1955...
ENDICOTT 6
ORANGEVILLE 32
UNION CITY 224
I'D BEEN BACK TO UNION CITY A FEW TIMES BEFORE, BUT THIS WAS THE FIRST TIME I'D BEEN SO EAGER TO GET BACK HOME TO ROCKHAVEN...
ENDICOTT 6
ORANGEVILLE 32
UNION CITY 224
..."HOME TO ROCKHAVEN"... THAT STILL SOUNDED ODD AFTER ALL THESE MONTHS. I'D LIVED IN UNION CITY ALL MY LIFE, WORKED FOR THE SENTINEL-GAZETTE FOR YEARS... UNTIL...
MM-HMM...
...BUT THAT WAS ALL BEHIND ME—THE SCANDAL, THE LIES, THE HOSPITAL...
HOME, SWEET HOME.
WELCOME TO
ROCKHAVEN
POPULATION 4750
...THEY'D LET ME OUT JUST LESS THAN A YEAR AGO—TOLD ME I NEEDED TO GET AWAY TO SOMEWHERE QUIET...

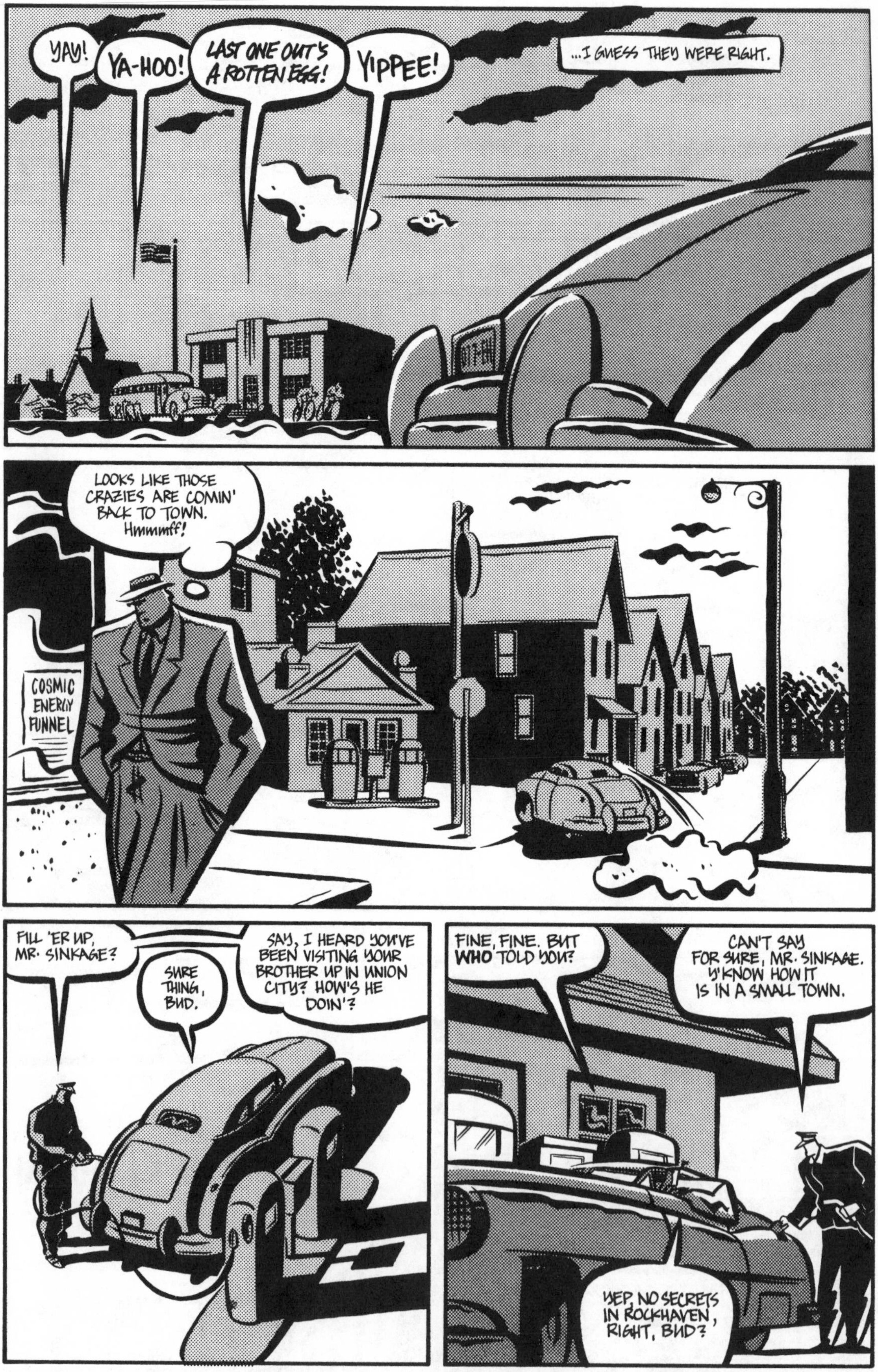
YAY!
YA-HOO!
LAST ONE OUT'S A ROTTEN EGG!
YIPPEE!
...I GUESS THEY WERE RIGHT.
LOOKS LIKE THOSE CRAZIES ARE COMIN' BACK TO TOWN. Hmmmff!
COSMIC ENERGY FUNNEL
FILL 'ER UP, MR. SINKAGE?
SURE THING, BUD.
SAY, I HEARD YOU'VE BEEN VISITING YOUR BROTHER UP IN UNION CITY? HOW'S HE DOIN'?
FINE, FINE. BUT **WHO** TOLD YOU?
CAN'T SAY FOR SURE, MR. SINKAGE. Y'KNOW HOW IT IS IN A SMALL TOWN.
YEP, NO SECRETS IN ROCKHAVEN, RIGHT, BUD?

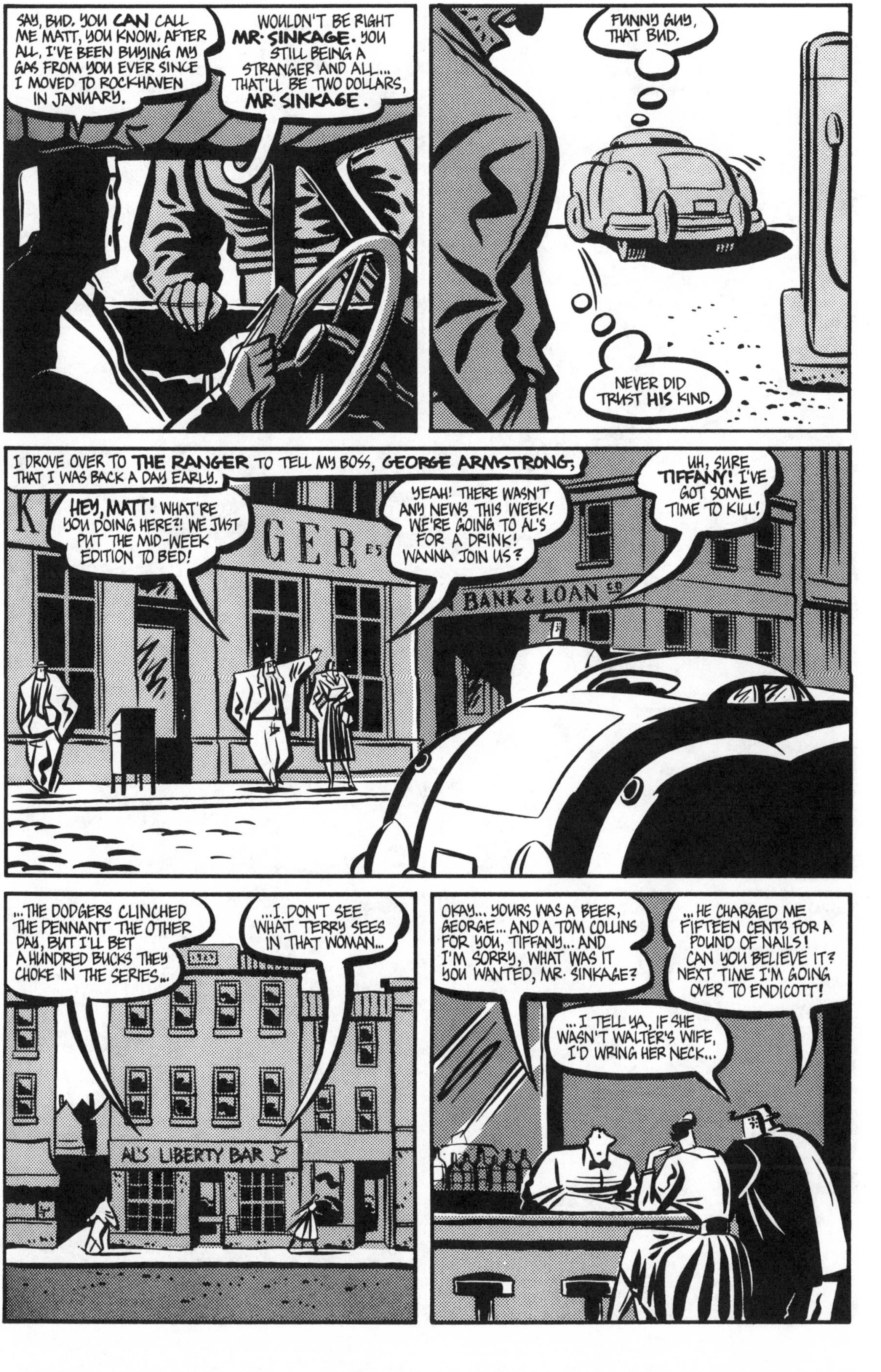
SAY, BUD. YOU CAN CALL ME MATT, YOU KNOW. AFTER ALL, I'VE BEEN BUYING MY GAS FROM YOU EVER SINCE I MOVED TO ROCKHAVEN IN JANUARY.
WOULDN'T BE RIGHT MR. SINKAGE. YOU STILL BEING A STRANGER AND ALL... THAT'LL BE TWO DOLLARS, MR. SINKAGE.
FUNNY GUY, THAT BUD.
NEVER DID TRUST HIS KIND.
I DROVE OVER TO THE RANGER TO TELL MY BOSS, GEORGE ARMSTRONG, THAT I WAS BACK A DAY EARLY.
HEY, MATT! WHAT'RE YOU DOING HERE?! WE JUST PUT THE MID-WEEK EDITION TO BED!
YEAH! THERE WASN'T ANY NEWS THIS WEEK! WE'RE GOING TO AL'S FOR A DRINK! WANNA JOIN US?
UH, SURE TIFFANY! I'VE GOT SOME TIME TO KILL!
GER
BANK & LOAN CO
...THE DODGERS CLINCHED THE PENNANT THE OTHER DAY, BUT I'LL BET A HUNDRED BUCKS THEY CHOKE IN THE SERIES...
...I DON'T SEE WHAT TERRY SEES IN THAT WOMAN...
AL'S LIBERTY BAR
OKAY... YOURS WAS A BEER, GEORGE... AND A TOM COLLINS FOR YOU, TIFFANY... AND I'M SORRY, WHAT WAS IT YOU WANTED, MR. SINKAGE?
...HE CHARGED ME FIFTEEN CENTS FOR A POUND OF NAILS! CAN YOU BELIEVE IT? NEXT TIME I'M GOING OVER TO ENDICOTT!
...I TELL YA, IF SHE WASN'T WALTER'S WIFE, I'D WRING HER NECK...

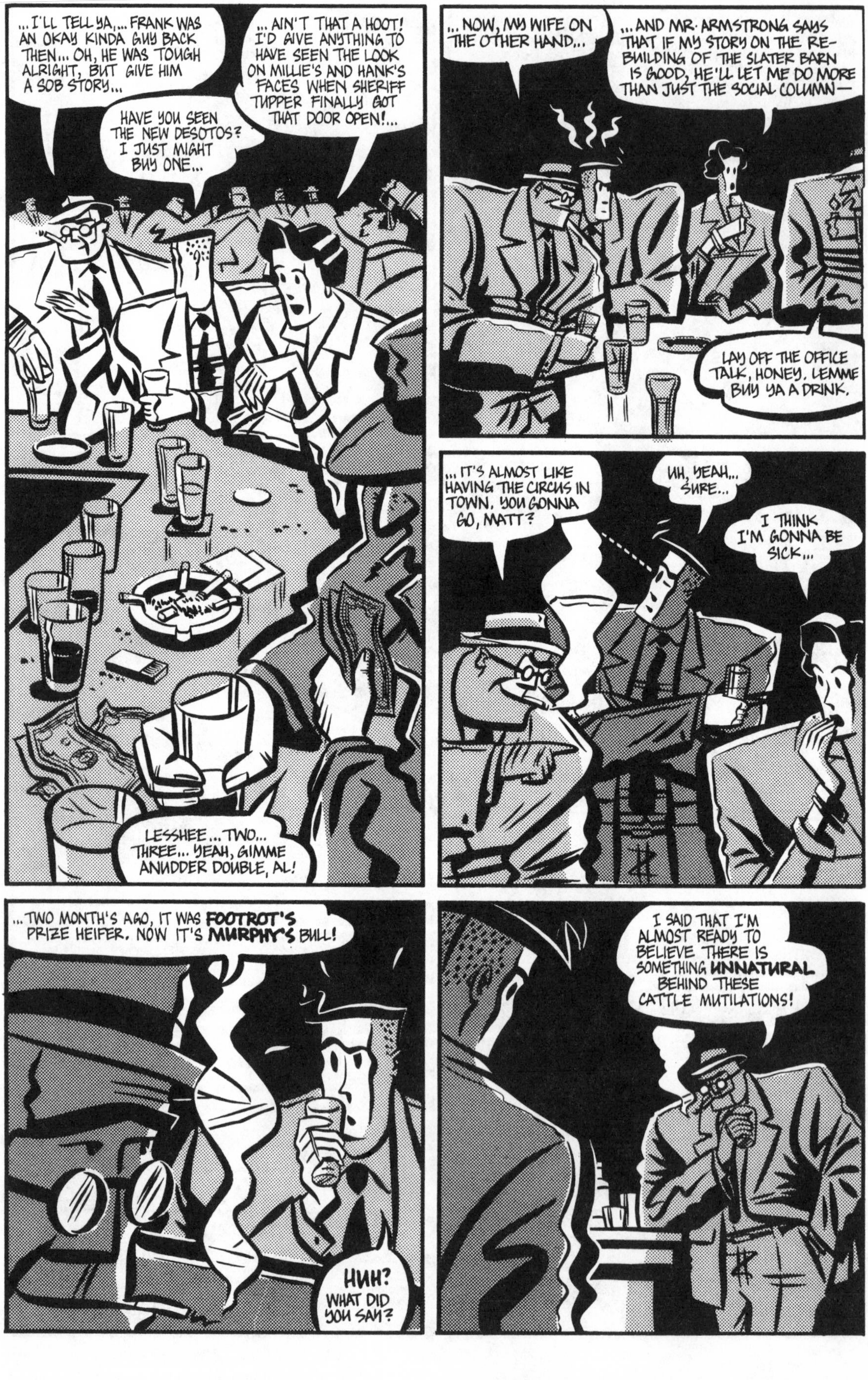
...I'LL TELL YA,... FRANK WAS AN OKAY KINDA GUY BACK THEN... OH, HE WAS TOUGH ALRIGHT, BUT GIVE HIM A SOB STORY...
HAVE YOU SEEN THE NEW DESOTOS? I JUST MIGHT BUY ONE...
...AIN'T THAT A HOOT! I'D GIVE ANYTHING TO HAVE SEEN THE LOOK ON MILLIE'S AND HANK'S FACES WHEN SHERIFF TUPPER FINALLY GOT THAT DOOR OPEN!...
LESSHEE... TWO... THREE... YEAH, GIMME ANUDDER DOUBLE, AL!
...NOW, MY WIFE ON THE OTHER HAND...
...AND MR. ARMSTRONG SAYS THAT IF MY STORY ON THE RE-BUILDING OF THE SLATER BARN IS GOOD, HE'LL LET ME DO MORE THAN JUST THE SOCIAL COLUMN—
LAY OFF THE OFFICE TALK, HONEY. LEMME BUY YA A DRINK.
...IT'S ALMOST LIKE HAVING THE CIRCUS IN TOWN. YOU GONNA GO, MATT?
UH, YEAH... SURE...
I THINK I'M GONNA BE SICK...
...TWO MONTH'S AGO, IT WAS FOOTROT'S PRIZE HEIFER. NOW IT'S MURPHY'S BULL!
HUH? WHAT DID YOU SAY?
I SAID THAT I'M ALMOST READY TO BELIEVE THERE IS SOMETHING UNNATURAL BEHIND THESE CATTLE MUTILATIONS!

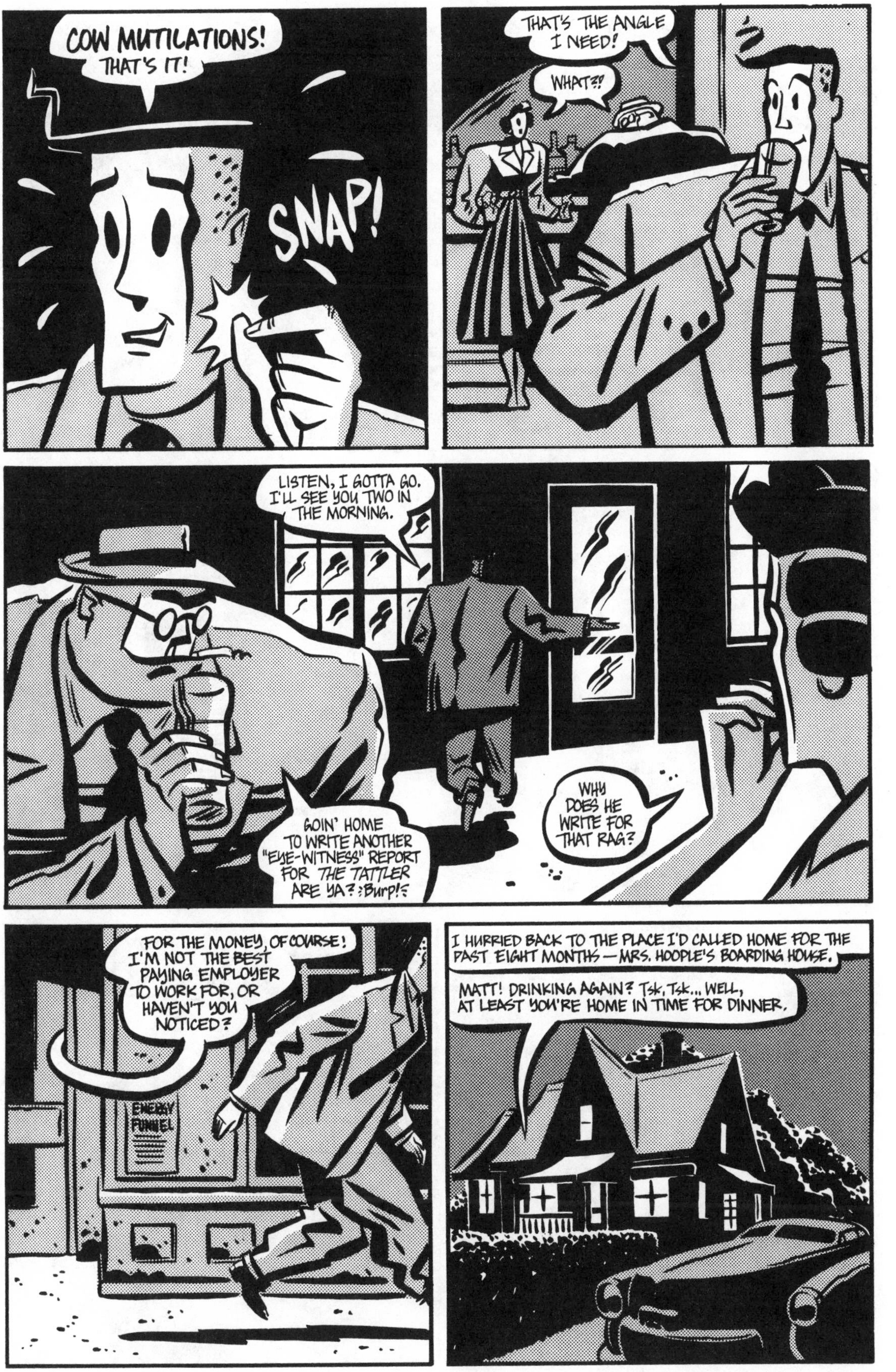
COW MUTILATIONS! THAT'S IT!
SNAP!
THAT'S THE ANGLE I NEED!
WHAT?!
LISTEN, I GOTTA GO. I'LL SEE YOU TWO IN THE MORNING.
GOIN' HOME TO WRITE ANOTHER "EYE-WITNESS" REPORT FOR THE TATTLER ARE YA? Burp!
WHY DOES HE WRITE FOR THAT RAG?
FOR THE MONEY, OF COURSE! I'M NOT THE BEST PAYING EMPLOYER TO WORK FOR, OR HAVEN'T YOU NOTICED?
ENERGY FUNNEL
I HURRIED BACK TO THE PLACE I'D CALLED HOME FOR THE PAST EIGHT MONTHS — MRS. HOOPLE'S BOARDING HOUSE.
MATT! DRINKING AGAIN? Tsk, Tsk... WELL, AT LEAST YOU'RE HOME IN TIME FOR DINNER.

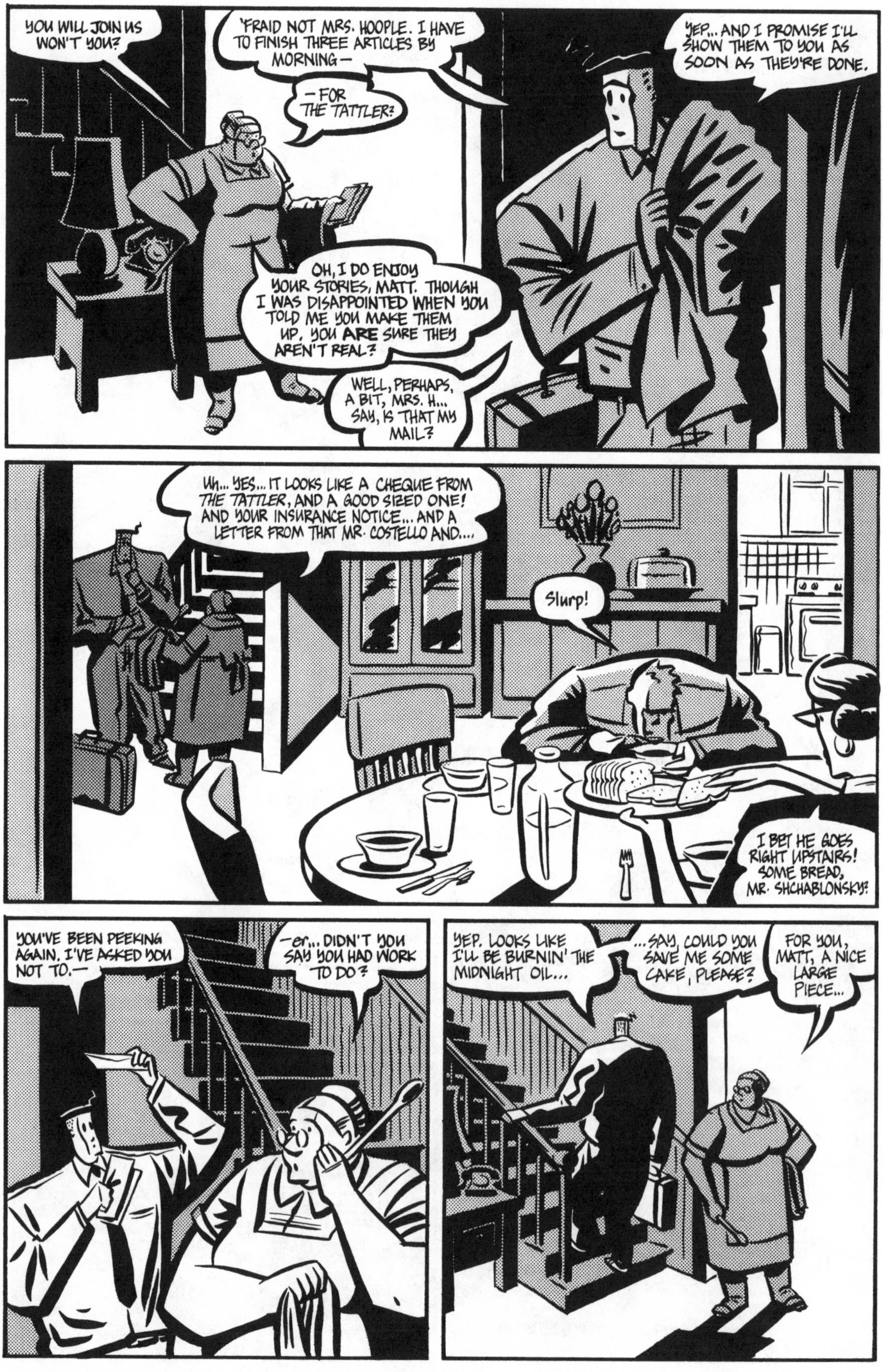
YOU WILL JOIN US WON'T YOU?
'FRAID NOT MRS. HOOPLE. I HAVE TO FINISH THREE ARTICLES BY MORNING—
—FOR THE TATTLER?
YEP... AND I PROMISE I'LL SHOW THEM TO YOU AS SOON AS THEY'RE DONE.
OH, I DO ENJOY YOUR STORIES, MATT. THOUGH I WAS DISAPPOINTED WHEN YOU TOLD ME YOU MAKE THEM UP. YOU ARE SURE THEY AREN'T REAL?
WELL, PERHAPS, A BIT, MRS. H... SAY, IS THAT MY MAIL?
UH... YES... IT LOOKS LIKE A CHEQUE FROM THE TATTLER, AND A GOOD SIZED ONE! AND YOUR INSURANCE NOTICE... AND A LETTER FROM THAT MR. COSTELLO AND....
Slurp!
I BET HE GOES RIGHT UPSTAIRS! SOME BREAD, MR. SHCHABLONSKY?
YOU'VE BEEN PEEKING AGAIN. I'VE ASKED YOU NOT TO.—
—er... DIDN'T YOU SAY YOU HAD WORK TO DO?
YEP. LOOKS LIKE I'LL BE BURNIN' THE MIDNIGHT OIL...
...SAY, COULD YOU SAVE ME SOME CAKE, PLEASE?
FOR YOU, MATT, A NICE LARGE PIECE...

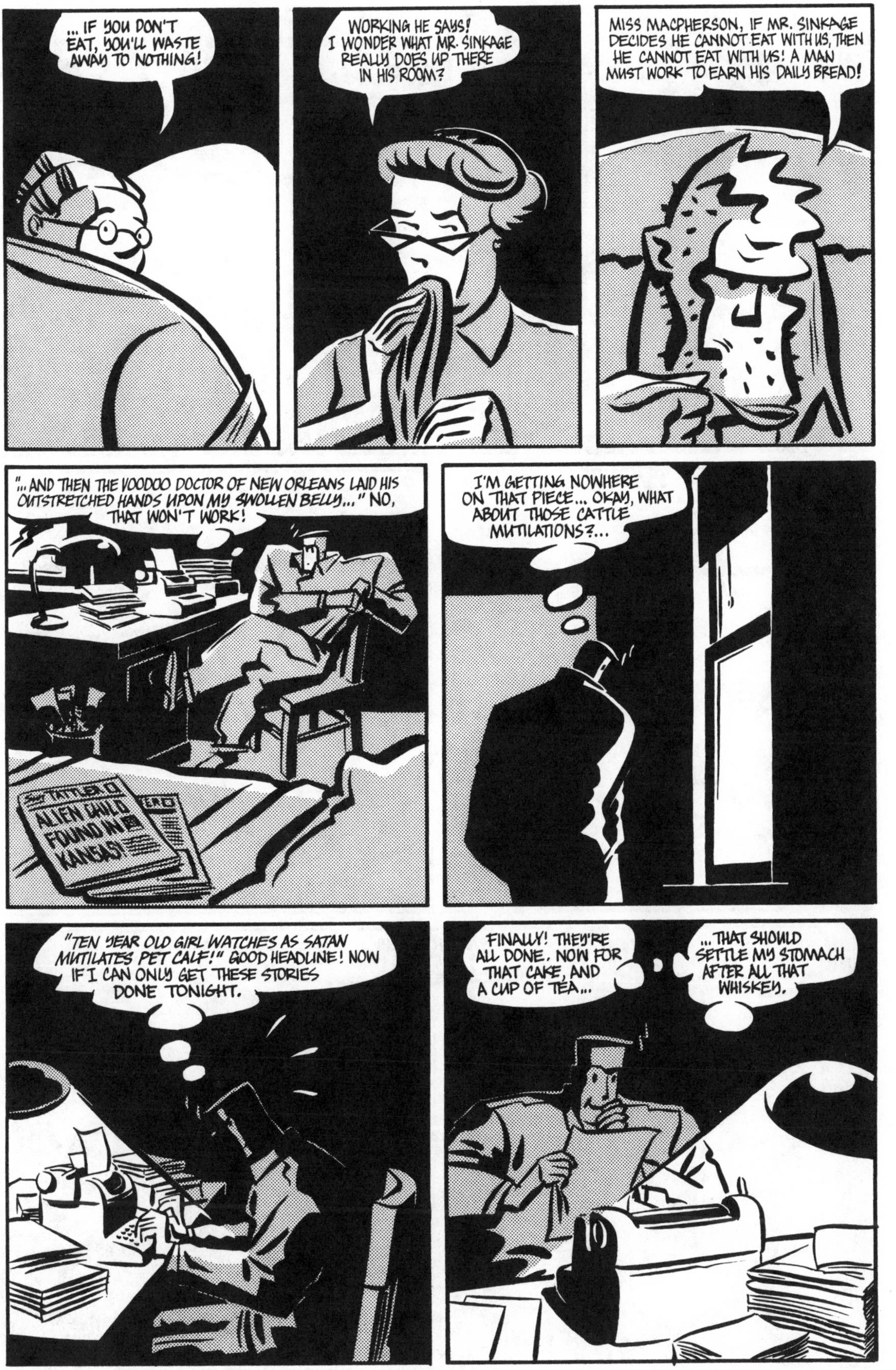

... IF YOU DON'T EAT, YOU'LL WASTE AWAY TO NOTHING!
WORKING HE SAYS! I WONDER WHAT MR. SINKAGE REALLY DOES UP THERE IN HIS ROOM?
MISS MACPHERSON, IF MR. SINKAGE DECIDES HE CANNOT EAT WITH US, THEN HE CANNOT EAT WITH US! A MAN MUST WORK TO EARN HIS DAILY BREAD!
"... AND THEN THE VOODOO DOCTOR OF NEW ORLEANS LAID HIS OUTSTRETCHED HANDS UPON MY SWOLLEN BELLY..." NO, THAT WON'T WORK!
TATTLER
ALIEN CHILD FOUND IN KANSAS!
I'M GETTING NOWHERE ON THAT PIECE... OKAY, WHAT ABOUT THOSE CATTLE MUTILATIONS?...
"TEN YEAR OLD GIRL WATCHES AS SATAN MUTILATES PET CALF!" GOOD HEADLINE! NOW IF I CAN ONLY GET THESE STORIES DONE TONIGHT.
FINALLY! THEY'RE ALL DONE. NOW FOR THAT CAKE, AND A CUP OF TEA...
... THAT SHOULD SETTLE MY STOMACH AFTER ALL THAT WHISKEY.

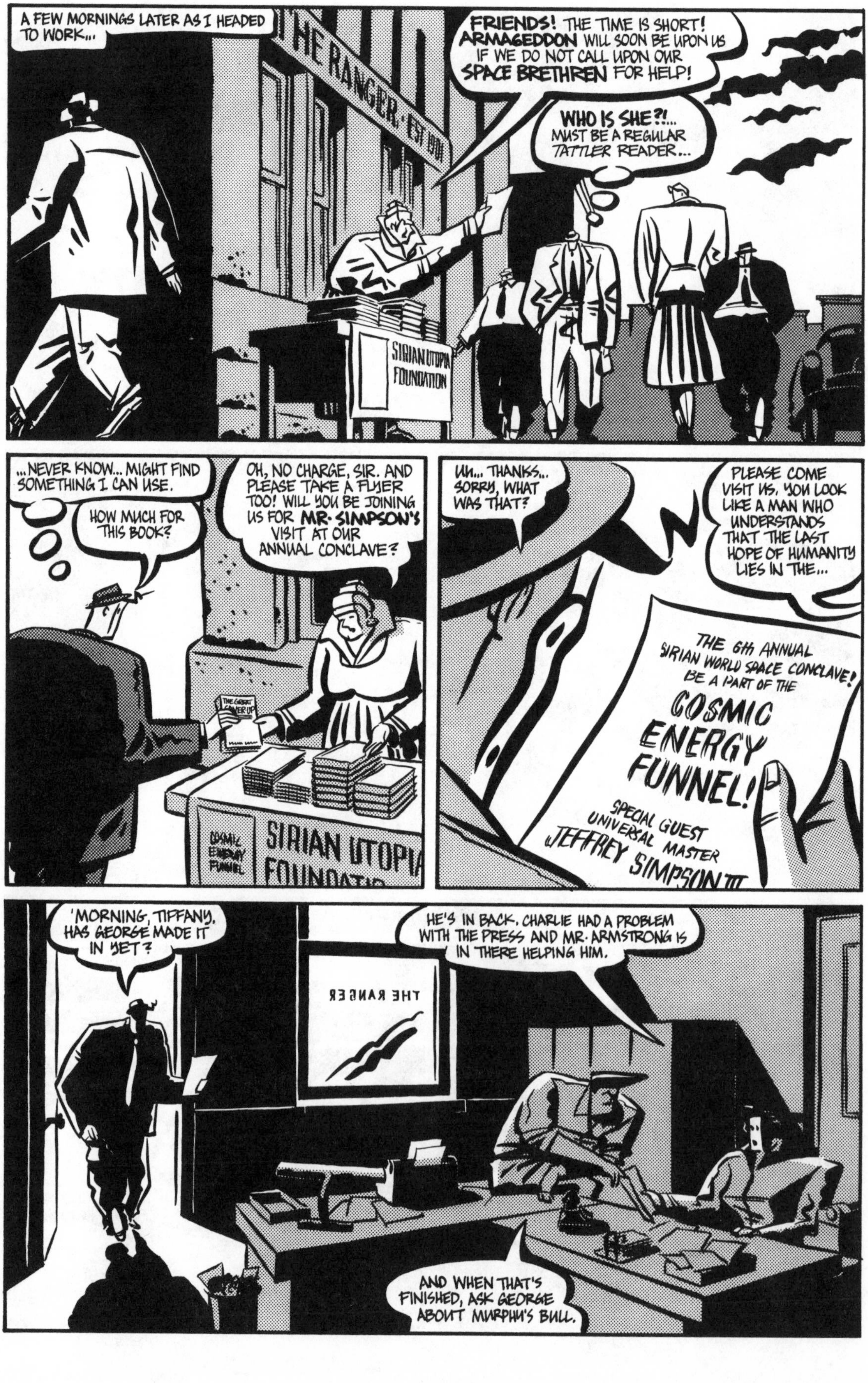
A FEW MORNINGS LATER AS I HEADED TO WORK...
THE RANGER · EST 1904
FRIENDS! THE TIME IS SHORT! ARMAGEDDON WILL SOON BE UPON US IF WE DO NOT CALL UPON OUR SPACE BRETHREN FOR HELP!
WHO IS SHE?!... MUST BE A REGULAR TATTLER READER...
SIRIAN UTOPIA FOUNDATION
...NEVER KNOW... MIGHT FIND SOMETHING I CAN USE.
HOW MUCH FOR THIS BOOK?
OH, NO CHARGE, SIR. AND PLEASE TAKE A FLYER TOO! WILL YOU BE JOINING US FOR MR. SIMPSON'S VISIT AT OUR ANNUAL CONCLAVE?
COSMIC ENERGY FUNNEL
SIRIAN UTOPIA FOUNDATIO
UH... THANKS... SORRY, WHAT WAS THAT?
PLEASE COME VISIT US. YOU LOOK LIKE A MAN WHO UNDERSTANDS THAT THE LAST HOPE OF HUMANITY LIES IN THE...
THE 6th ANNUAL SIRIAN WORLD SPACE CONCLAVE! BE A PART OF THE
COSMIC ENERGY FUNNEL!
SPECIAL GUEST UNIVERSAL MASTER JEFFREY SIMPSON III
'MORNING, TIFFANY. HAS GEORGE MADE IT IN YET?
HE'S IN BACK. CHARLIE HAD A PROBLEM WITH THE PRESS AND MR. ARMSTRONG IS IN THERE HELPING HIM.
THE RANGER
AND WHEN THAT'S FINISHED, ASK GEORGE ABOUT MURPHY'S BULL.

MATT, WHY SO FRAZZLED? THOSE ARTICLES YOU'RE WRITING FOR THAT SCANDAL SHEET GIVING YOU NIGHTMARES?

NOT AS BAD AS THE ONE'S I GET AFTER LOOKING AT YOUR UGLY PUSS!... BUT SERIOUSLY...

...WHO'S THE WOMAN OUT FRONT IN THE STRANGE GET-UP?

THAT'S GLADYS TANNER. SURELY YOU MUST HAVE SEEN HER AROUND TOWN BEFORE THIS?

Uh-uh... WHAT'S EATING HER?

FUNNY YOU SHOULD ASK. IT SO HAPPENS I WANT YOU TO DO A STORY ON HER AND THE SPACE CONCLAVE OUT AT HER FARM IN TWO WEEKS.

SPACE CONCLAVE?

HAVE YOU READ THAT FLYER? YOU KNOW ABOUT THE COSMIK ENERGY FUNNEL?

SOUNDS LIKE SOMETHING I SHOULD BE WRITING FOR THE TATTLER — NOT A HIGH-CLASS OPERATION LIKE THE RANGER.

TAKE IT EASY ON THE SARCASM, MATT. ONE DAY IT MAY BITE BACK...

...BUT BACK TO MRS. TANNER. SHE MIGHT APPEAR TO BE ONE BRICK SHY OF A FULL LOAD...

...BUT SHE IS RESPECTED HERE IN ROCKHAVEN. SO DO A NICE BACK-GROUND PIECE ON HER AND HER GROUP UP AT THE FARM — THE SIRIAN UTOPIA FOUNDATION —

—THE WHA..?

YOU HEARD ME...

"...WHEN HER HUSBAND DIED ABOUT EIGHT YEARS BACK, HE LEFT HER A PRETTY HEFTY CHUNK OF MONEY PLUS THE FARM. THEN ABOUT A YEAR LATER GLADYS STARTED COMING INTO TOWN DRESSED AS IF IT WAS HALLOWE'EN. SHE'D GET UP ON HER SOAP BOX AND START TALKING ABOUT UFO'S, ALIENS, AND SOME ORGANISATION CALLED 'THE SIRIAN UTOPIA FOUNDATION'. IT SEEMS LIKE A NEW, WACKO RELIGION..."

SHE'S CRAZY! HAHAHAHAHA!

LOONEY TUNES!!

AT LEAST LISTEN TO WHAT SHE HAS TO SAY!!

BLAHBLAH BLAHBLAH BLAHBLAHFLYINGSAUCERTD SPACEBLAHBLAHATOMIC WARBLAHBLAHBLAH...

YOU'RE NUTS LADY!!

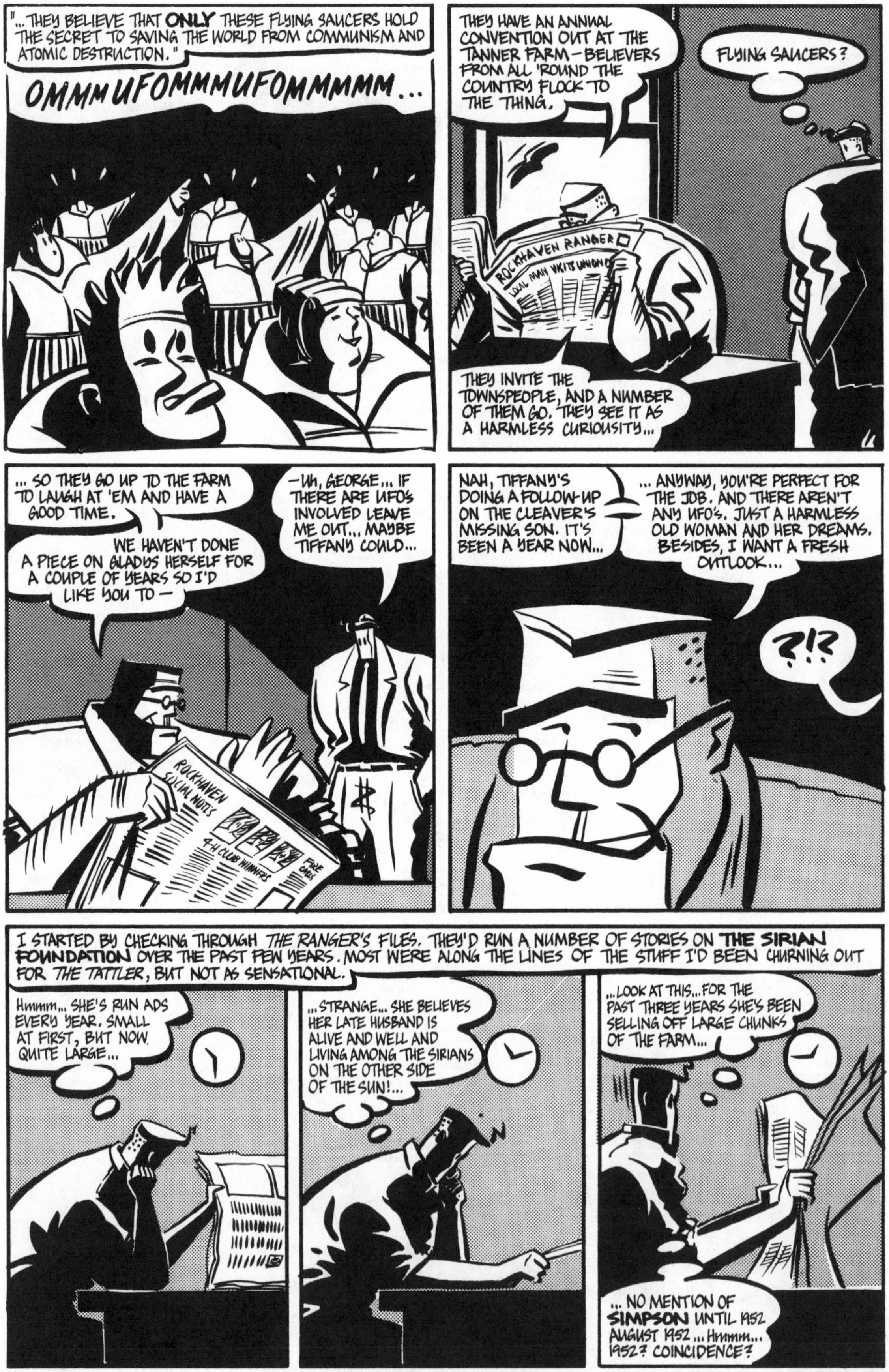
"... THEY BELIEVE THAT ONLY THESE FLYING SAUCERS HOLD THE SECRET TO SAVING THE WORLD FROM COMMUNISM AND ATOMIC DESTRUCTION."
OMMMUFOMMMUFOMMMMM...
THEY HAVE AN ANNUAL CONVENTION OUT AT THE TANNER FARM — BELIEVERS FROM ALL 'ROUND THE COUNTRY FLOCK TO THE THING.
FLYING SAUCERS?
ROCKHAVEN RANGER
LOCAL MAN VISITS UNION
THEY INVITE THE TOWNSPEOPLE, AND A NUMBER OF THEM GO. THEY SEE IT AS A HARMLESS CURIOUSITY...
... SO THEY GO UP TO THE FARM TO LAUGH AT 'EM AND HAVE A GOOD TIME.
WE HAVEN'T DONE A PIECE ON GLADYS HERSELF FOR A COUPLE OF YEARS SO I'D LIKE YOU TO —
—UH, GEORGE... IF THERE ARE UFO'S INVOLVED LEAVE ME OUT... MAYBE TIFFANY COULD...
ROCKHAVEN SOCIAL NOTES
4-H CLUB WINNERS
NAH, TIFFANY'S DOING A FOLLOW-UP ON THE CLEAVER'S MISSING SON. IT'S BEEN A YEAR NOW...
... ANYWAY, YOU'RE PERFECT FOR THE JOB. AND THERE AREN'T ANY UFO'S. JUST A HARMLESS OLD WOMAN AND HER DREAMS. BESIDES, I WANT A FRESH OUTLOOK...
?!?
I STARTED BY CHECKING THROUGH THE RANGER'S FILES. THEY'D RUN A NUMBER OF STORIES ON THE SIRIAN FOUNDATION OVER THE PAST FEW YEARS. MOST WERE ALONG THE LINES OF THE STUFF I'D BEEN CHURNING OUT FOR THE TATTLER, BUT NOT AS SENSATIONAL.
Hmmm... SHE'S RUN ADS EVERY YEAR. SMALL AT FIRST, BUT NOW QUITE LARGE...
...STRANGE... SHE BELIEVES HER LATE HUSBAND IS ALIVE AND WELL AND LIVING AMONG THE SIRIANS ON THE OTHER SIDE OF THE SUN!...
...LOOK AT THIS... FOR THE PAST THREE YEARS SHE'S BEEN SELLING OFF LARGE CHUNKS OF THE FARM...
... NO MENTION OF SIMPSON UNTIL 1952 AUGUST 1952 ... Hmmm... 1952? COINCIDENCE?

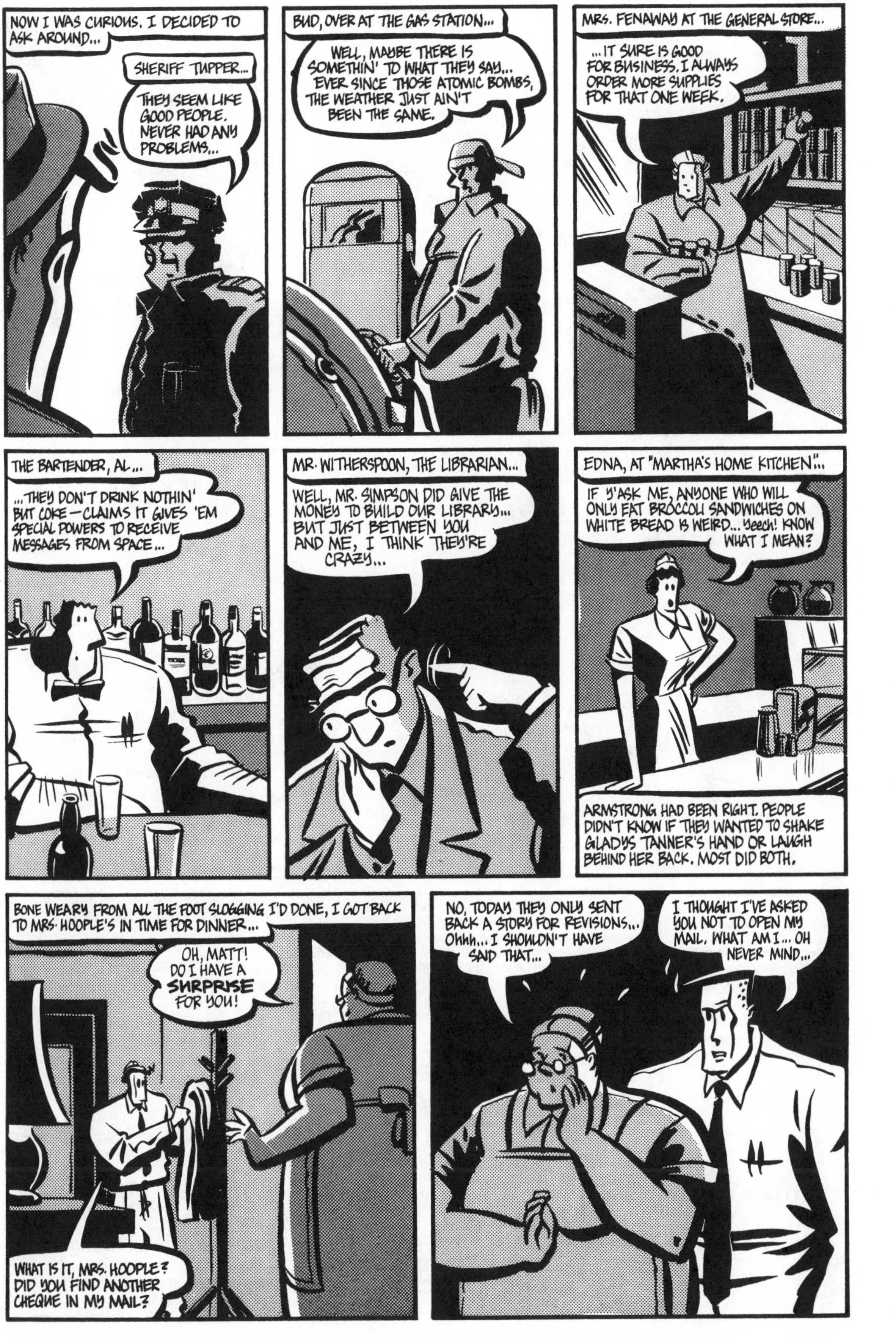
NOW I WAS CURIOUS. I DECIDED TO ASK AROUND...
SHERIFF TUPPER...
THEY SEEM LIKE GOOD PEOPLE. NEVER HAD ANY PROBLEMS...
BUD, OVER AT THE GAS STATION...
WELL, MAYBE THERE IS SOMETHIN' TO WHAT THEY SAY... EVER SINCE THOSE ATOMIC BOMBS, THE WEATHER JUST AIN'T BEEN THE SAME.
MRS. FENAWAY AT THE GENERAL STORE...
...IT SURE IS GOOD FOR BUSINESS. I ALWAYS ORDER MORE SUPPLIES FOR THAT ONE WEEK.
THE BARTENDER, AL...
...THEY DON'T DRINK NOTHIN' BUT COKE—CLAIMS IT GIVES 'EM SPECIAL POWERS TO RECEIVE MESSAGES FROM SPACE...
MR. WITHERSPOON, THE LIBRARIAN...
WELL, MR. SIMPSON DID GIVE THE MONEY TO BUILD OUR LIBRARY... BUT JUST BETWEEN YOU AND ME, I THINK THEY'RE CRAZY...
EDNA, AT "MARTHA'S HOME KITCHEN"...
IF Y'ASK ME, ANYONE WHO WILL ONLY EAT BROCCOLI SANDWICHES ON WHITE BREAD IS WEIRD... YEECH! KNOW WHAT I MEAN?
ARMSTRONG HAD BEEN RIGHT. PEOPLE DIDN'T KNOW IF THEY WANTED TO SHAKE GLADYS TANNER'S HAND OR LAUGH BEHIND HER BACK. MOST DID BOTH.
BONE WEARY FROM ALL THE FOOT SLOGGING I'D DONE, I GOT BACK TO MRS. HOOPLE'S IN TIME FOR DINNER...
OH, MATT! DO I HAVE A SURPRISE FOR YOU!
WHAT IS IT, MRS. HOOPLE? DID YOU FIND ANOTHER CHEQUE IN MY MAIL?
NO, TODAY THEY ONLY SENT BACK A STORY FOR REVISIONS... OHHH... I SHOULDN'T HAVE SAID THAT...
I THOUGHT I'VE ASKED YOU NOT TO OPEN MY MAIL. WHAT AM I... OH NEVER MIND...

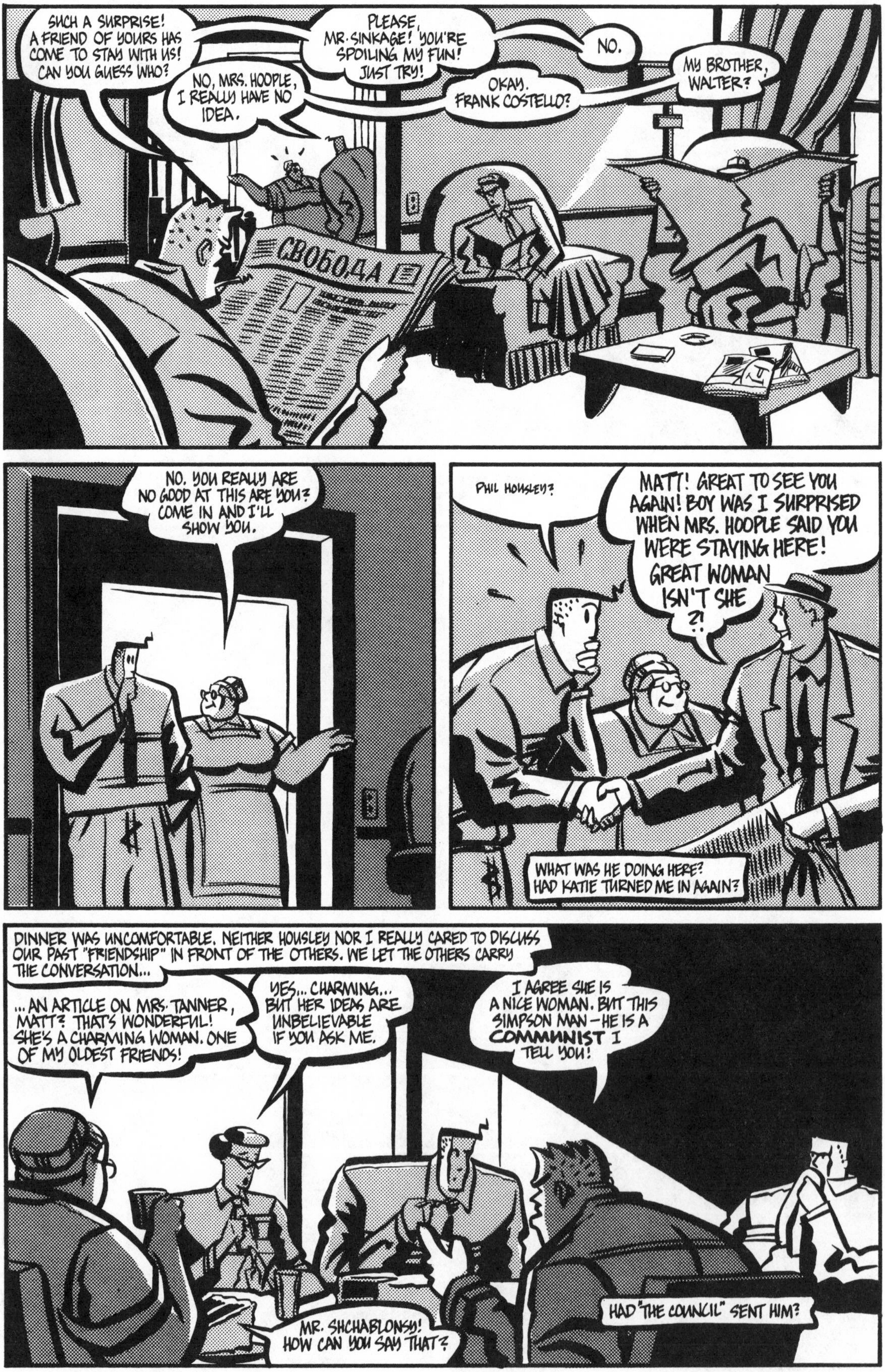

SUCH A SURPRISE! A FRIEND OF YOURS HAS COME TO STAY WITH US! CAN YOU GUESS WHO?
NO, MRS. HOOPLE, I REALLY HAVE NO IDEA.
PLEASE, MR. SINKAGE! YOU'RE SPOILING MY FUN! JUST TRY!
OKAY. FRANK COSTELLO?
NO.
MY BROTHER, WALTER?
СВОБОДА
NO. YOU REALLY ARE NO GOOD AT THIS ARE YOU? COME IN AND I'LL SHOW YOU.
PHIL HOUSLEY?
MATT! GREAT TO SEE YOU AGAIN! BOY WAS I SURPRISED WHEN MRS. HOOPLE SAID YOU WERE STAYING HERE! GREAT WOMAN ISN'T SHE ?!
WHAT WAS HE DOING HERE? HAD KATIE TURNED ME IN AGAIN?
DINNER WAS UNCOMFORTABLE. NEITHER HOUSLEY NOR I REALLY CARED TO DISCUSS OUR PAST "FRIENDSHIP" IN FRONT OF THE OTHERS. WE LET THE OTHERS CARRY THE CONVERSATION...
...AN ARTICLE ON MRS. TANNER, MATT? THAT'S WONDERFUL! SHE'S A CHARMING WOMAN. ONE OF MY OLDEST FRIENDS!
YES... CHARMING... BUT HER IDEAS ARE UNBELIEVABLE IF YOU ASK ME.
I AGREE SHE IS A NICE WOMAN. BUT THIS SIMPSON MAN — HE IS A COMMUNIST I TELL YOU!
MR. SHCHABLONSKY! HOW CAN YOU SAY THAT?
HAD "THE COUNCIL" SENT HIM?

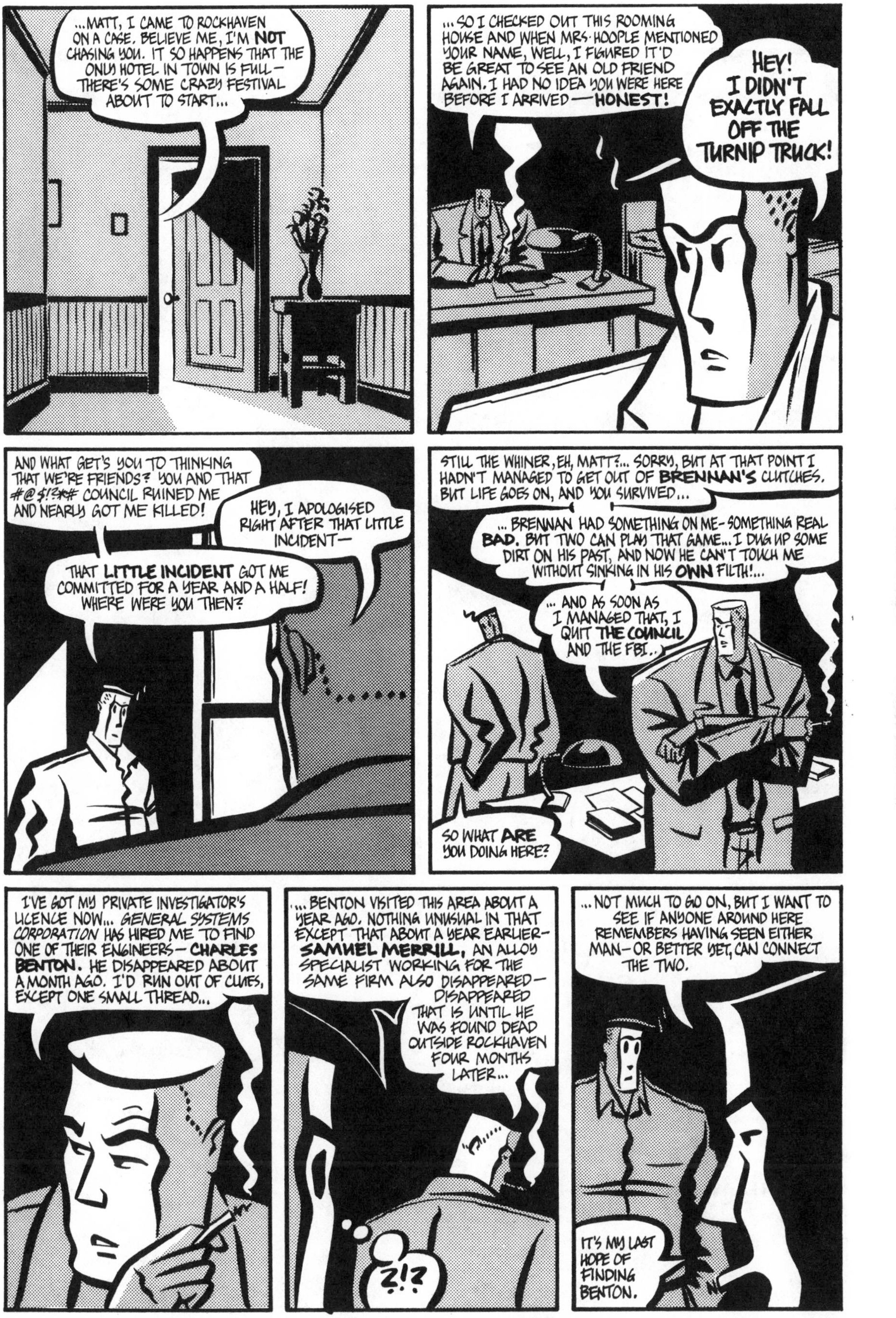
...MATT, I CAME TO ROCKHAVEN ON A CASE. BELIEVE ME, I'M NOT CHASING YOU. IT SO HAPPENS THAT THE ONLY HOTEL IN TOWN IS FULL—THERE'S SOME CRAZY FESTIVAL ABOUT TO START...
...SO I CHECKED OUT THIS ROOMING HOUSE AND WHEN MRS. HOOPLE MENTIONED YOUR NAME, WELL, I FIGURED IT'D BE GREAT TO SEE AN OLD FRIEND AGAIN. I HAD NO IDEA YOU WERE HERE BEFORE I ARRIVED—HONEST!
HEY! I DIDN'T EXACTLY FALL OFF THE TURNIP TRUCK!
AND WHAT GET'S YOU TO THINKING THAT WE'RE FRIENDS? YOU AND THAT #@$!?*# COUNCIL RUINED ME AND NEARLY GOT ME KILLED!
HEY, I APOLOGISED RIGHT AFTER THAT LITTLE INCIDENT—
THAT LITTLE INCIDENT GOT ME COMMITTED FOR A YEAR AND A HALF! WHERE WERE YOU THEN?
STILL THE WHINER, EH, MATT?... SORRY, BUT AT THAT POINT I HADN'T MANAGED TO GET OUT OF BRENNAN'S CLUTCHES. BUT LIFE GOES ON, AND YOU SURVIVED...
... BRENNAN HAD SOMETHING ON ME- SOMETHING REAL BAD. BUT TWO CAN PLAY THAT GAME... I DUG UP SOME DIRT ON HIS PAST, AND NOW HE CAN'T TOUCH ME WITHOUT SINKING IN HIS OWN FILTH!...
... AND AS SOON AS I MANAGED THAT, I QUIT THE COUNCIL AND THE FBI..
SO WHAT ARE YOU DOING HERE?
I'VE GOT MY PRIVATE INVESTIGATOR'S LICENCE NOW... GENERAL SYSTEMS CORPORATION HAS HIRED ME TO FIND ONE OF THEIR ENGINEERS—CHARLES BENTON. HE DISAPPEARED ABOUT A MONTH AGO. I'D RUN OUT OF CLUES, EXCEPT ONE SMALL THREAD...
...BENTON VISITED THIS AREA ABOUT A YEAR AGO. NOTHING UNUSUAL IN THAT EXCEPT THAT ABOUT A YEAR EARLIER- SAMUEL MERRILL, AN ALLOY SPECIALIST WORKING FOR THE SAME FIRM ALSO DISAPPEARED— DISAPPEARED THAT IS UNTIL HE WAS FOUND DEAD OUTSIDE ROCKHAVEN FOUR MONTHS LATER...
?!?
...NOT MUCH TO GO ON, BUT I WANT TO SEE IF ANYONE AROUND HERE REMEMBERS HAVING SEEN EITHER MAN—OR BETTER YET, CAN CONNECT THE TWO.
IT'S MY LAST HOPE OF FINDING BENTON.

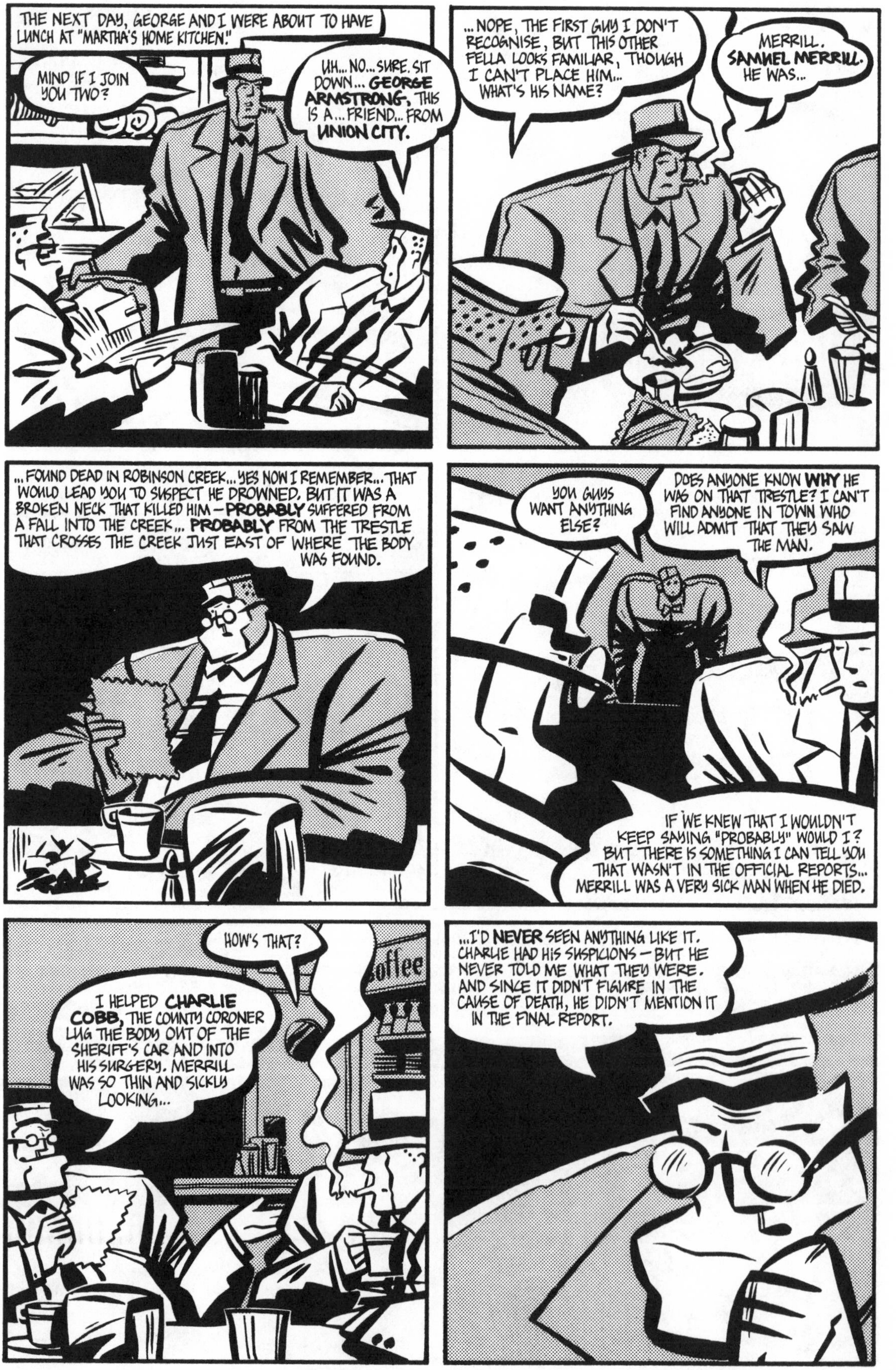
THE NEXT DAY, GEORGE AND I WERE ABOUT TO HAVE LUNCH AT "MARTHA'S HOME KITCHEN."
MIND IF I JOIN YOU TWO?
UH... NO... SURE. SIT DOWN... GEORGE ARMSTRONG, THIS IS A... FRIEND... FROM UNION CITY.
...NOPE, THE FIRST GUY I DON'T RECOGNISE, BUT THIS OTHER FELLA LOOKS FAMILIAR, THOUGH I CAN'T PLACE HIM... WHAT'S HIS NAME?
MERRILL. SAMUEL MERRILL. HE WAS...
...FOUND DEAD IN ROBINSON CREEK... YES NOW I REMEMBER... THAT WOULD LEAD YOU TO SUSPECT HE DROWNED. BUT IT WAS A BROKEN NECK THAT KILLED HIM — PROBABLY SUFFERED FROM A FALL INTO THE CREEK... PROBABLY FROM THE TRESTLE THAT CROSSES THE CREEK JUST EAST OF WHERE THE BODY WAS FOUND.
YOU GUYS WANT ANYTHING ELSE?
DOES ANYONE KNOW WHY HE WAS ON THAT TRESTLE? I CAN'T FIND ANYONE IN TOWN WHO WILL ADMIT THAT THEY SAW THE MAN.
IF WE KNEW THAT I WOULDN'T KEEP SAYING "PROBABLY" WOULD I? BUT THERE IS SOMETHING I CAN TELL YOU THAT WASN'T IN THE OFFICIAL REPORTS... MERRILL WAS A VERY SICK MAN WHEN HE DIED.
HOW'S THAT?
I HELPED CHARLIE COBB, THE COUNTY CORONER LUG THE BODY OUT OF THE SHERIFF'S CAR AND INTO HIS SURGERY. MERRILL WAS SO THIN AND SICKLY LOOKING...
...I'D NEVER SEEN ANYTHING LIKE IT. CHARLIE HAD HIS SUSPICIONS — BUT HE NEVER TOLD ME WHAT THEY WERE. AND SINCE IT DIDN'T FIGURE IN THE CAUSE OF DEATH, HE DIDN'T MENTION IT IN THE FINAL REPORT.

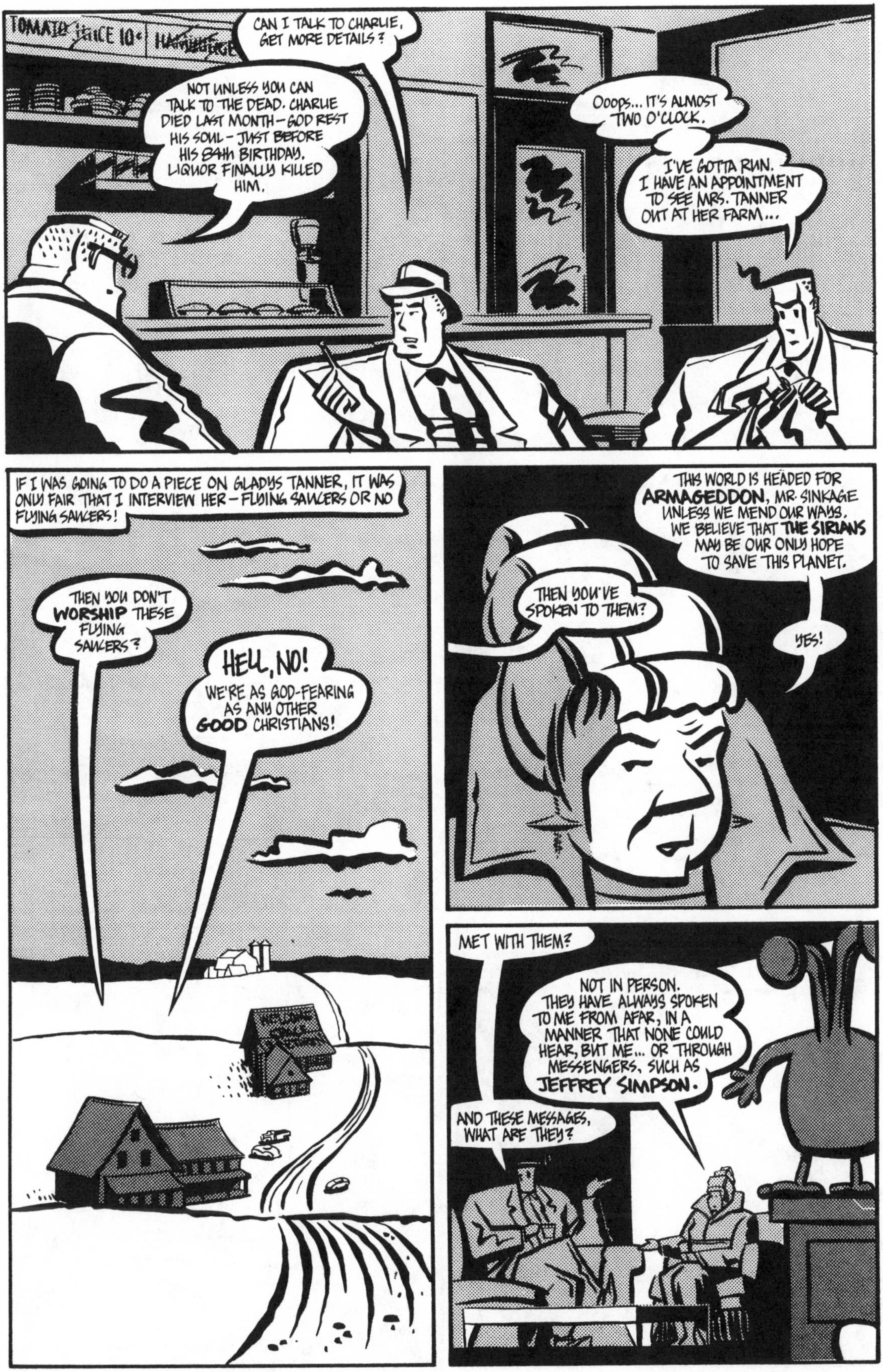
TOMATO JUICE 10¢
CAN I TALK TO CHARLIE, GET MORE DETAILS?
NOT UNLESS YOU CAN TALK TO THE DEAD. CHARLIE DIED LAST MONTH — GOD REST HIS SOUL — JUST BEFORE HIS 84th BIRTHDAY. LIQUOR FINALLY KILLED HIM.
Ooops... IT'S ALMOST TWO O'CLOCK.
I'VE GOTTA RUN. I HAVE AN APPOINTMENT TO SEE MRS. TANNER OUT AT HER FARM...
IF I WAS GOING TO DO A PIECE ON GLADYS TANNER, IT WAS ONLY FAIR THAT I INTERVIEW HER — FLYING SAUCERS OR NO FLYING SAUCERS!
THEN YOU DON'T WORSHIP THESE FLYING SAUCERS?
HELL, NO! WE'RE AS GOD-FEARING AS ANY OTHER GOOD CHRISTIANS!
THIS WORLD IS HEADED FOR ARMAGEDDON, MR. SINKAGE UNLESS WE MEND OUR WAYS. WE BELIEVE THAT THE SIRIANS MAY BE OUR ONLY HOPE TO SAVE THIS PLANET.
THEN YOU'VE SPOKEN TO THEM?
YES!
MET WITH THEM?
NOT IN PERSON. THEY HAVE ALWAYS SPOKEN TO ME FROM AFAR, IN A MANNER THAT NONE COULD HEAR, BUT ME... OR THROUGH MESSENGERS, SUCH AS JEFFREY SIMPSON.
AND THESE MESSAGES, WHAT ARE THEY?

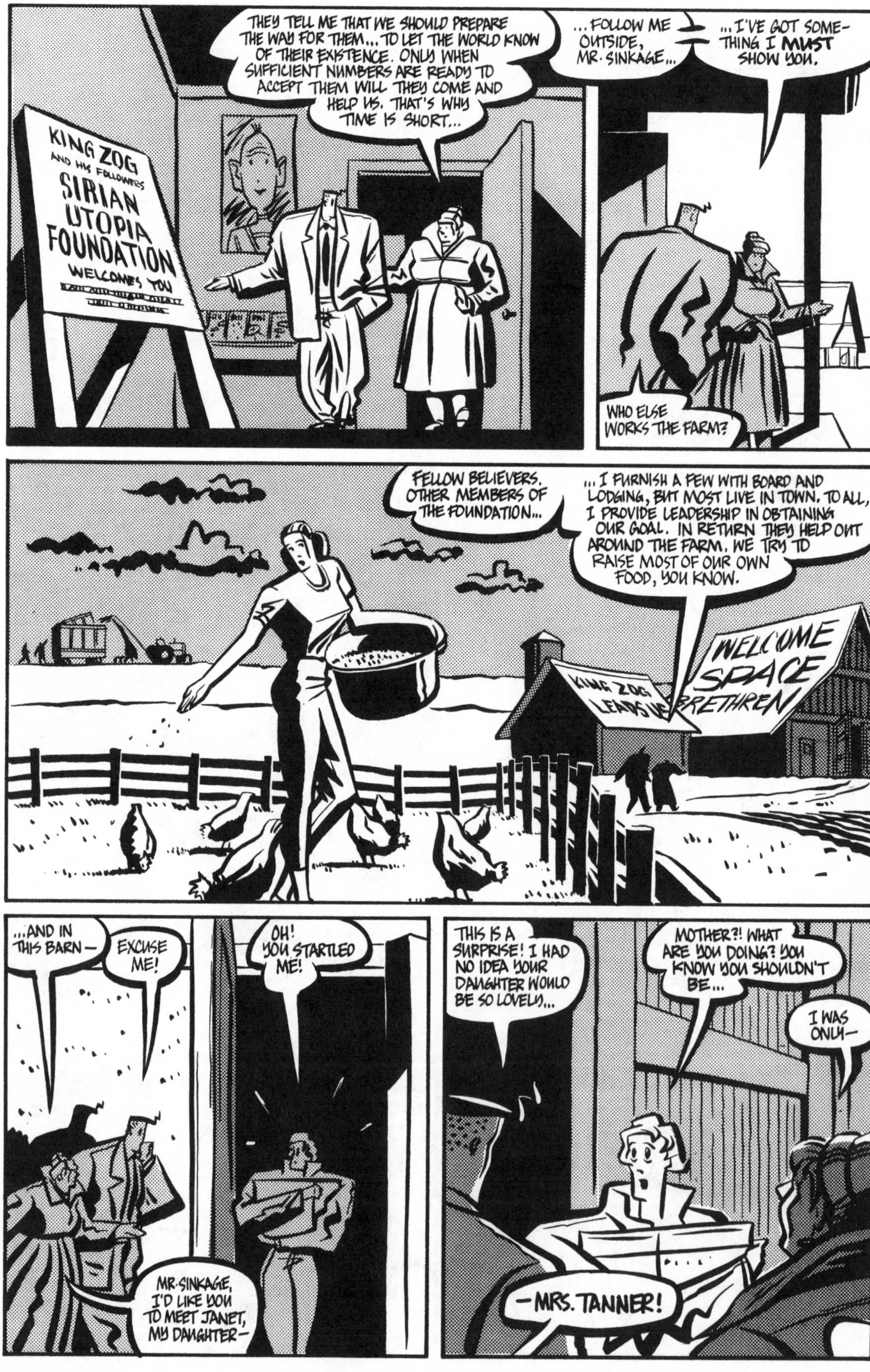
THEY TELL ME THAT WE SHOULD PREPARE THE WAY FOR THEM... TO LET THE WORLD KNOW OF THEIR EXISTENCE. ONLY WHEN SUFFICIENT NUMBERS ARE READY TO ACCEPT THEM WILL THEY COME AND HELP US. THAT'S WHY TIME IS SHORT...
KING ZOG AND HIS FOLLOWERS SIRIAN UTOPIA FOUNDATION WELCOMES YOU
...FOLLOW ME OUTSIDE, MR. SINKAGE...
...I'VE GOT SOME-THING I **MUST** SHOW YOU.
WHO ELSE WORKS THE FARM?
FELLOW BELIEVERS. OTHER MEMBERS OF THE FOUNDATION...
...I FURNISH A FEW WITH BOARD AND LODGING, BUT MOST LIVE IN TOWN. TO ALL, I PROVIDE LEADERSHIP IN OBTAINING OUR GOAL. IN RETURN THEY HELP OUT AROUND THE FARM. WE TRY TO RAISE MOST OF OUR OWN FOOD, YOU KNOW.
KING ZOG LEADS US
WELCOME SPACE BRETHREN
...AND IN THIS BARN—
EXCUSE ME!
OH! YOU STARTLED ME!
MR. SINKAGE, I'D LIKE YOU TO MEET JANET, MY DAUGHTER—
THIS IS A SURPRISE! I HAD NO IDEA YOUR DAUGHTER WOULD BE SO LOVELY...
MOTHER?! WHAT ARE YOU DOING? YOU KNOW YOU SHOULDN'T BE...
I WAS ONLY—
—MRS. TANNER!

MR. SINKAGE, THIS IS **MR. HOGAN.** HE'S **MR. GOLD'S** ASSISTANT. MR. GOLD IS...HE'S...WELL...HE'S IN CHARGE OF EVERYTHING THAT AN OLD LADY LIKE MYSELF DOESN'T WANT TO WORRY ABOUT!

I'M SORRY... BUT I... I HAVE TO GO. I'M LATE.

PLEASED TO MEET YOU...

MR. GOLD SAYS IT'S TIME TO END THE INTERVIEW.

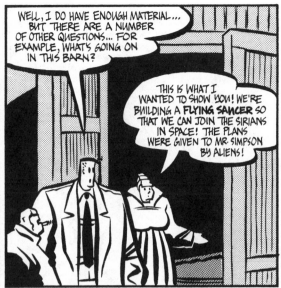

WELL, I DO HAVE ENOUGH MATERIAL... BUT THERE ARE A NUMBER OF OTHER QUESTIONS... FOR EXAMPLE, WHAT'S GOING ON IN THIS BARN?

THIS IS WHAT I WANTED TO SHOW YOU! WE'RE BUILDING A **FLYING SAUCER** SO THAT WE CAN JOIN THE SIRIANS IN SPACE! THE PLANS WERE GIVEN TO MR. SIMPSON BY ALIENS!

I KNEW IT... ARMSTRONG SHOULD'VE LEFT ME OUT OF THIS.

AND IN THOSE NEW BUILDINGS?

THE INTERVIEW IS FINISHED!

RESEARCH SUPPORT FOR THE PROJECT.

COULD WE TAKE A LOOK?

YA DON'T LISTEN TOO GOOD DO YA? **THE INTERVIEW IS FINISHED! GET OUTTA HERE!!**

OKAY, OKAY! SOME PEOPLE!

BACK AT THE BOARDING HOUSE...

LEAVING SO SOON, HOUSLEY?

YEAH. NOBODY RECOGNISED BENTON OR MERRILL FROM THEIR PHOTOS. BUT I DID PICK UP ONE SLIM LEAD THAT I'M GOING TO CHECK OUT BACK IN UNION CITY.

WHAT'S THAT?

THAT BARTENDER, AL, PERKED RIGHT UP WHEN I MENTIONED THAT MERRILL WAS AN ALLOY SPECIALIST. HE REMEMBERS ANOTHER GUY IN THE SAME LINE HAVING A DRINK IN HIS BAR A FEW WEEKS AFTER MERRILL WAS FOUND...

...HE EVEN REMEMBERED THE GUY'S NAME...

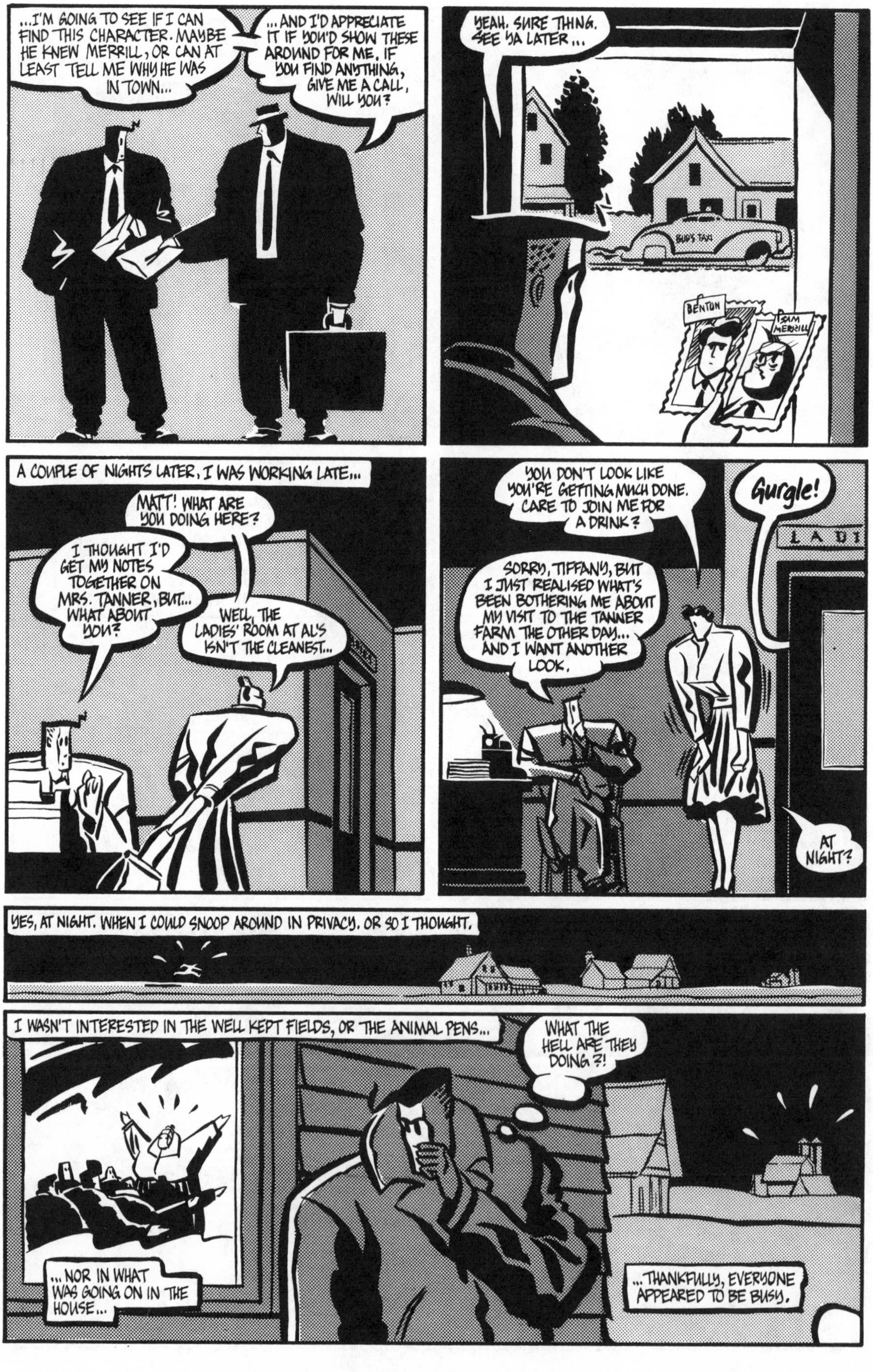
...I'M GOING TO SEE IF I CAN FIND THIS CHARACTER. MAYBE HE KNEW MERRILL, OR CAN AT LEAST TELL ME WHY HE WAS IN TOWN...
...AND I'D APPRECIATE IT IF YOU'D SHOW THESE AROUND FOR ME. IF YOU FIND ANYTHING, GIVE ME A CALL, WILL YOU?
YEAH. SURE THING. SEE YA LATER...
BUD'S TAXI
BENTON
SAM MERRILL
A COUPLE OF NIGHTS LATER, I WAS WORKING LATE...
MATT! WHAT ARE YOU DOING HERE?
I THOUGHT I'D GET MY NOTES TOGETHER ON MRS. TANNER, BUT... WHAT ABOUT YOU?
WELL, THE LADIES' ROOM AT AL'S ISN'T THE CLEANEST...
YOU DON'T LOOK LIKE YOU'RE GETTING MUCH DONE. CARE TO JOIN ME FOR A DRINK?
Gurgle!
SORRY, TIFFANY, BUT I JUST REALISED WHAT'S BEEN BOTHERING ME ABOUT MY VISIT TO THE TANNER FARM THE OTHER DAY... AND I WANT ANOTHER LOOK.
AT NIGHT?
YES, AT NIGHT. WHEN I COULD SNOOP AROUND IN PRIVACY. OR SO I THOUGHT.
I WASN'T INTERESTED IN THE WELL KEPT FIELDS, OR THE ANIMAL PENS...
WHAT THE HELL ARE THEY DOING ?!
...NOR IN WHAT WAS GOING ON IN THE HOUSE...
...THANKFULLY, EVERYONE APPEARED TO BE BUSY.

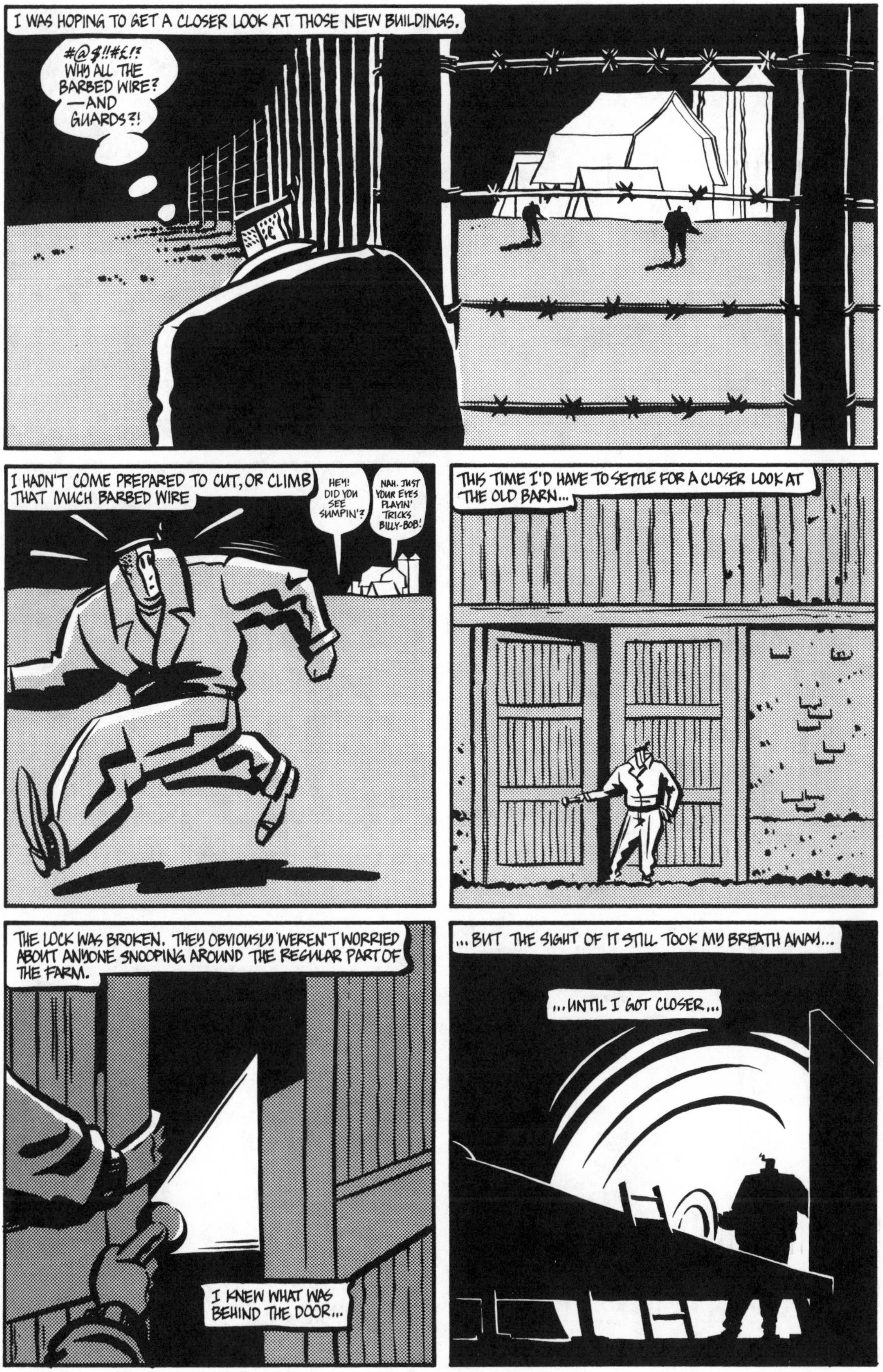
I WAS HOPING TO GET A CLOSER LOOK AT THOSE NEW BUILDINGS.
#@$!!#£!? WHY ALL THE BARBED WIRE? —AND GUARDS?!
I HADN'T COME PREPARED TO CUT, OR CLIMB THAT MUCH BARBED WIRE
HEY! DID YOU SEE SUMPIN'?
NAH. JUST YOUR EYES PLAYIN' TRICKS BILLY-BOB!
THIS TIME I'D HAVE TO SETTLE FOR A CLOSER LOOK AT THE OLD BARN...
THE LOCK WAS BROKEN. THEY OBVIOUSLY WEREN'T WORRIED ABOUT ANYONE SNOOPING AROUND THE REGULAR PART OF THE FARM.
I KNEW WHAT WAS BEHIND THE DOOR...
... BUT THE SIGHT OF IT STILL TOOK MY BREATH AWAY...
...UNTIL I GOT CLOSER...

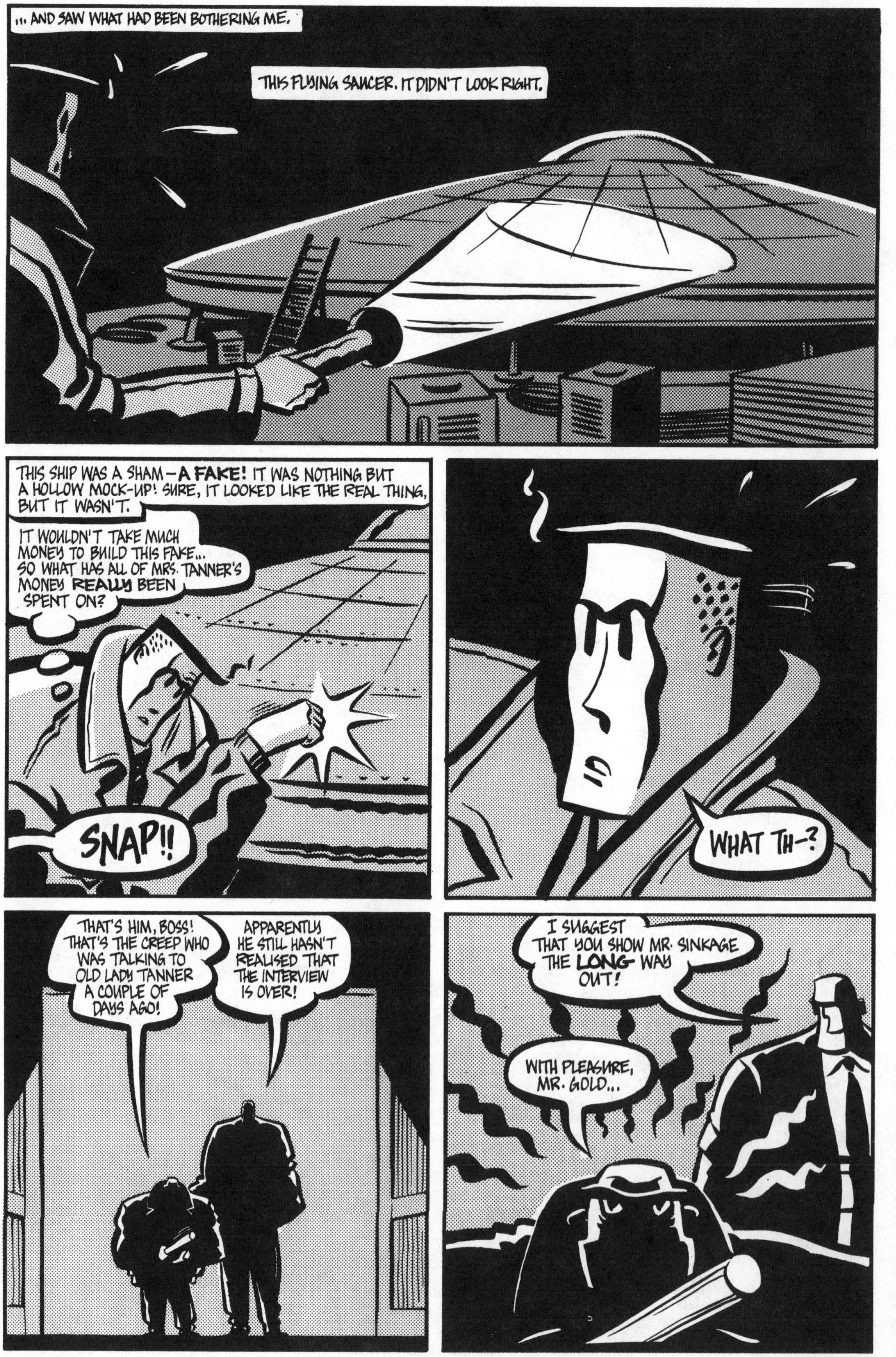
... AND SAW WHAT HAD BEEN BOTHERING ME.
THIS FLYING SAUCER. IT DIDN'T LOOK RIGHT.
THIS SHIP WAS A SHAM — A FAKE! IT WAS NOTHING BUT A HOLLOW MOCK-UP! SURE, IT LOOKED LIKE THE REAL THING, BUT IT WASN'T.
IT WOULDN'T TAKE MUCH MONEY TO BUILD THIS FAKE... SO WHAT HAS ALL OF MRS. TANNER'S MONEY REALLY BEEN SPENT ON?
SNAP!!
WHAT TH-?
THAT'S HIM, BOSS! THAT'S THE CREEP WHO WAS TALKING TO OLD LADY TANNER A COUPLE OF DAYS AGO!
APPARENTLY HE STILL HASN'T REALISED THAT THE INTERVIEW IS OVER!
I SUGGEST THAT YOU SHOW MR. SINKAGE THE LONG WAY OUT!
WITH PLEASURE, MR. GOLD...

CHAPTER TWO

THE ROCKHAVEN CONSPIRACY

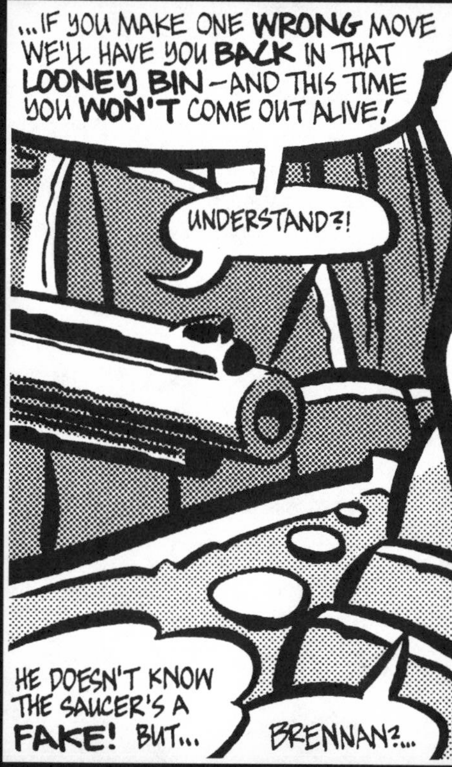
...IF YOU MAKE ONE WRONG MOVE WE'LL HAVE YOU BACK IN THAT LOONEY BIN—AND THIS TIME YOU WON'T COME OUT ALIVE!
UNDERSTAND?!
HE DOESN'T KNOW THE SAUCER'S A FAKE! BUT...
BRENNAN?...

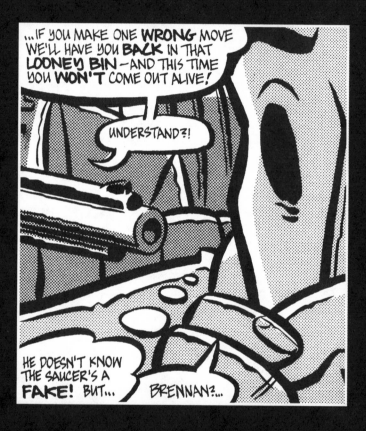

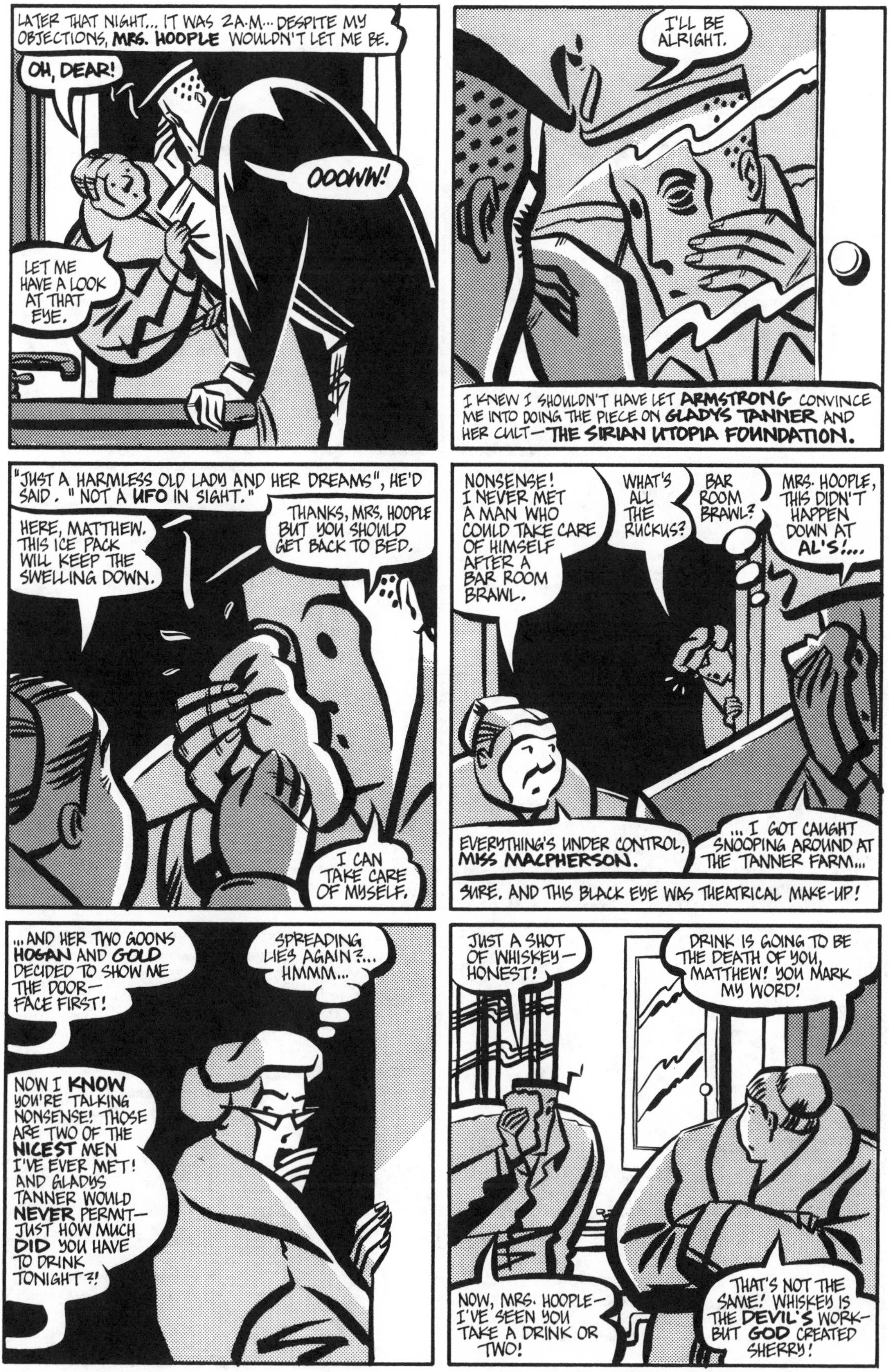
LATER THAT NIGHT... IT WAS 2 A.M... DESPITE MY OBJECTIONS, MRS. HOOPLE WOULDN'T LET ME BE.
OH, DEAR!
OOOWW!
LET ME HAVE A LOOK AT THAT EYE.
I'LL BE ALRIGHT.
I KNEW I SHOULDN'T HAVE LET ARMSTRONG CONVINCE ME INTO DOING THE PIECE ON GLADYS TANNER AND HER CULT—THE SIRIAN UTOPIA FOUNDATION.
"JUST A HARMLESS OLD LADY AND HER DREAMS", HE'D SAID. "NOT A UFO IN SIGHT."
HERE, MATTHEW. THIS ICE PACK WILL KEEP THE SWELLING DOWN.
THANKS, MRS. HOOPLE BUT YOU SHOULD GET BACK TO BED.
I CAN TAKE CARE OF MYSELF.
NONSENSE! I NEVER MET A MAN WHO COULD TAKE CARE OF HIMSELF AFTER A BAR ROOM BRAWL.
WHAT'S ALL THE RUCKUS?
BAR ROOM BRAWL?
MRS. HOOPLE, THIS DIDN'T HAPPEN DOWN AT AL'S!...
EVERYTHING'S UNDER CONTROL, MISS MACPHERSON.
... I GOT CAUGHT SNOOPING AROUND AT THE TANNER FARM...
SURE. AND THIS BLACK EYE WAS THEATRICAL MAKE-UP!
...AND HER TWO GOONS HOGAN AND GOLD DECIDED TO SHOW ME THE DOOR-FACE FIRST!
SPREADING LIES AGAIN?... HMMM...
NOW I KNOW YOU'RE TALKING NONSENSE! THOSE ARE TWO OF THE NICEST MEN I'VE EVER MET! AND GLADYS TANNER WOULD NEVER PERMIT—JUST HOW MUCH DID YOU HAVE TO DRINK TONIGHT?!
JUST A SHOT OF WHISKEY—HONEST!
DRINK IS GOING TO BE THE DEATH OF YOU, MATTHEW! YOU MARK MY WORD!
NOW, MRS. HOOPLE—I'VE SEEN YOU TAKE A DRINK OR TWO!
THAT'S NOT THE SAME! WHISKEY IS THE DEVIL'S WORK—BUT GOD CREATED SHERRY!

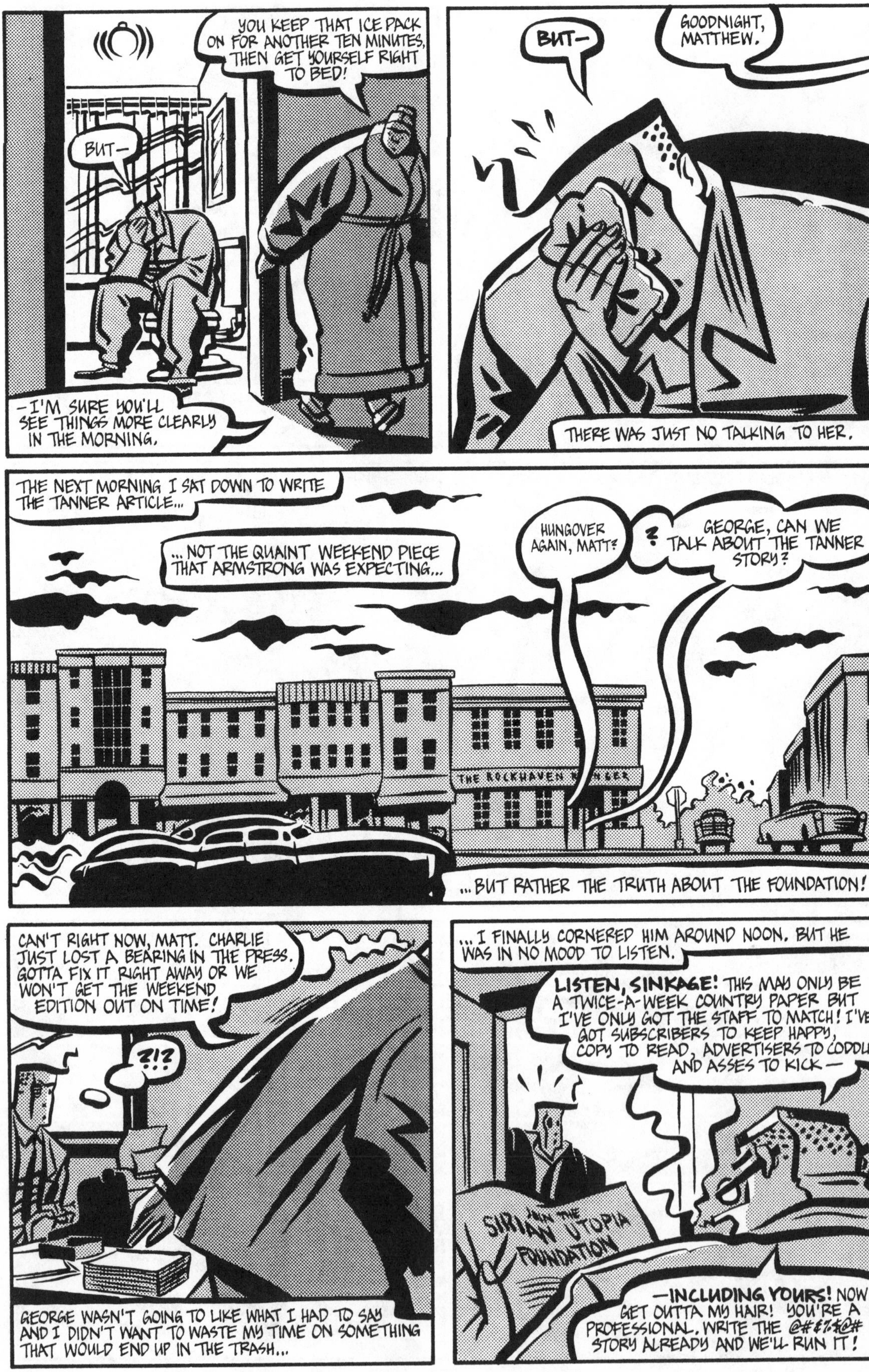

YOU KEEP THAT ICE PACK ON FOR ANOTHER TEN MINUTES, THEN GET YOURSELF RIGHT TO BED!
BUT—
—I'M SURE YOU'LL SEE THINGS MORE CLEARLY IN THE MORNING.
BUT—
GOODNIGHT, MATTHEW.
THERE WAS JUST NO TALKING TO HER.
THE NEXT MORNING I SAT DOWN TO WRITE THE TANNER ARTICLE...
...NOT THE QUAINT WEEKEND PIECE THAT ARMSTRONG WAS EXPECTING...
HUNGOVER AGAIN, MATT?
GEORGE, CAN WE TALK ABOUT THE TANNER STORY?
...BUT RATHER THE TRUTH ABOUT THE FOUNDATION!
CAN'T RIGHT NOW, MATT. CHARLIE JUST LOST A BEARING IN THE PRESS. GOTTA FIX IT RIGHT AWAY OR WE WON'T GET THE WEEKEND EDITION OUT ON TIME!
?!?
GEORGE WASN'T GOING TO LIKE WHAT I HAD TO SAY AND I DIDN'T WANT TO WASTE MY TIME ON SOMETHING THAT WOULD END UP IN THE TRASH...
...I FINALLY CORNERED HIM AROUND NOON. BUT HE WAS IN NO MOOD TO LISTEN.
LISTEN, SINKAGE! THIS MAY ONLY BE A TWICE-A-WEEK COUNTRY PAPER BUT I'VE ONLY GOT THE STAFF TO MATCH! I'VE GOT SUBSCRIBERS TO KEEP HAPPY, COPY TO READ, ADVERTISERS TO CODDLE, AND ASSES TO KICK—
JOIN THE SIRIAN UTOPIA FOUNDATION
—INCLUDING YOURS! NOW GET OUTTA MY HAIR! YOU'RE A PROFESSIONAL. WRITE THE @#$%@# STORY ALREADY AND WE'LL RUN IT!

SO I WROTE THE STORY MY WAY, AND THEN GEORGE READ IT...

HARRUMPH! WE CAN'T RUN THIS...

... NOT ONLY IS IT ALL SPECULATION—

SPECULATION?! WHAT DO YOU CALL THIS?

I CALL IT AN ACCIDENT.

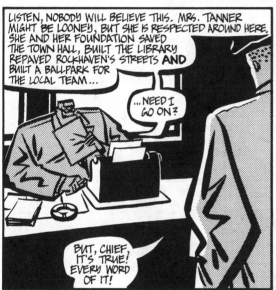

LISTEN, NOBODY WILL BELIEVE THIS. MRS. TANNER MIGHT BE LOONEY, BUT SHE IS RESPECTED AROUND HERE. SHE AND HER FOUNDATION SAVED THE TOWN HALL, BUILT THE LIBRARY REPAVED ROCKHAVEN'S STREETS **AND** BUILT A BALLPARK FOR THE LOCAL TEAM...

... NEED I GO ON?

BUT, CHIEF! IT'S TRUE! EVERY WORD OF IT!

REALLY? WHERE'S YOUR PROOF? YOU'VE GOT A SHINER, BUT SO WHAT! YOU WERE PROBABLY ON A BINGE AT **AL'S** AND WALKED INTO A FENCE ON THE WAY HOME. AL SAID YOU WERE IN THERE LAST NIGHT— PRETTY STEAMED UP, TOO, I HEARD...

?

... MAYBE COSTELLO WAS RIGHT. MAYBE I DID TAKE A BIG CHANCE HIRING YOU?...

HUH?

WHEN HE RECOMMENDED YOU FOR THIS JOB, FRANK WARNED ME. HE SAID YOUR IMAGINATION TENDS TO RUN A LITTLE WILD...

... YOU SEE THINGS THAT AREN'T THERE. MAYBE THAT'S WHY NONE OF THE BIGGER PAPERS WOULD HIRE YOU AFTER YOU GOT OUT OF THE SANITARIUM—

—THAT AND THE COMMIE THING—

—THAT WAS LOW GEORGE! AND UNCALLED FOR!...

... WHAT ABOUT YOU?...

... I HEARD YOU LEFT *THE SENTINEL-GAZETTE* —

I LEFT FOR HEALTH REASONS! MY DOCTOR SAID MY ANXIETY ATTACKS —!

I HEARD YOU COULDN'T TAKE THE HEAT. SOMETHING ABOUT MOB PRESSURE KILLING YOUR EXPOSÉ ABOUT POLICE DEPARTMENT LINKS TO ORGANISED CRIME...

... INSTEAD OF FIGHTING, **YOU QUIT!** YOU MOVED HERE AND BOUGHT *THE RANGER* SO YOU COULD BE YOUR OWN BOSS... SO TELL ME, GEORGE— WHAT'S SO DIFFERENT BETWEEN WHAT THEY DID TO YOU THEN, AND WHAT YOU'RE DOING NOW—

—SINKAGE!

THERE'S SOMETHING ODD GOING ON UP THERE AND **WE** SHOULD **EXPOSE** IT!

—OKAY, SINKAGE.

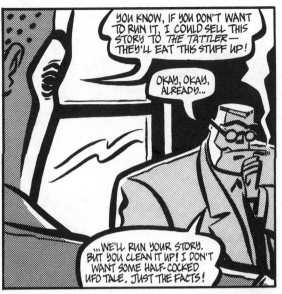

YOU KNOW, IF YOU DON'T WANT TO RUN IT, I COULD SELL THIS STORY TO *THE TATTLER*— THEY'LL EAT THIS STUFF UP!

OKAY, OKAY, ALREADY...

...WE'LL RUN YOUR STORY. BUT YOU CLEAN IT UP! I DON'T WANT SOME HALF-COCKED UFO TALE, JUST THE FACTS!

I'D WON THE BATTLE, SORT OF. BUT ONCE I ELIMINATED THE SPECULATION THERE WASN'T MUCH TO BUILD ON.

ARMSTRONG WANTED THE REVISED COPY ON HIS DESK FIRST THING IN THE MORNING...

... SO I SPENT MOST OF THE NIGHT REWORKING THE STORY...

...AND MY CONSCIENCE.

FINALLY, AROUND THREE IN THE MORNING I MANAGED TO FIND THE RIGHT BLEND OF FACTS...

...AND GOOD CITIZEN'S CONCERN THAT WOULD GET MY POINT ACROSS—

—AND WOULD HOPEFULLY MAKE THE TOWN SIT UP AND TAKE NOTICE.

THERE!

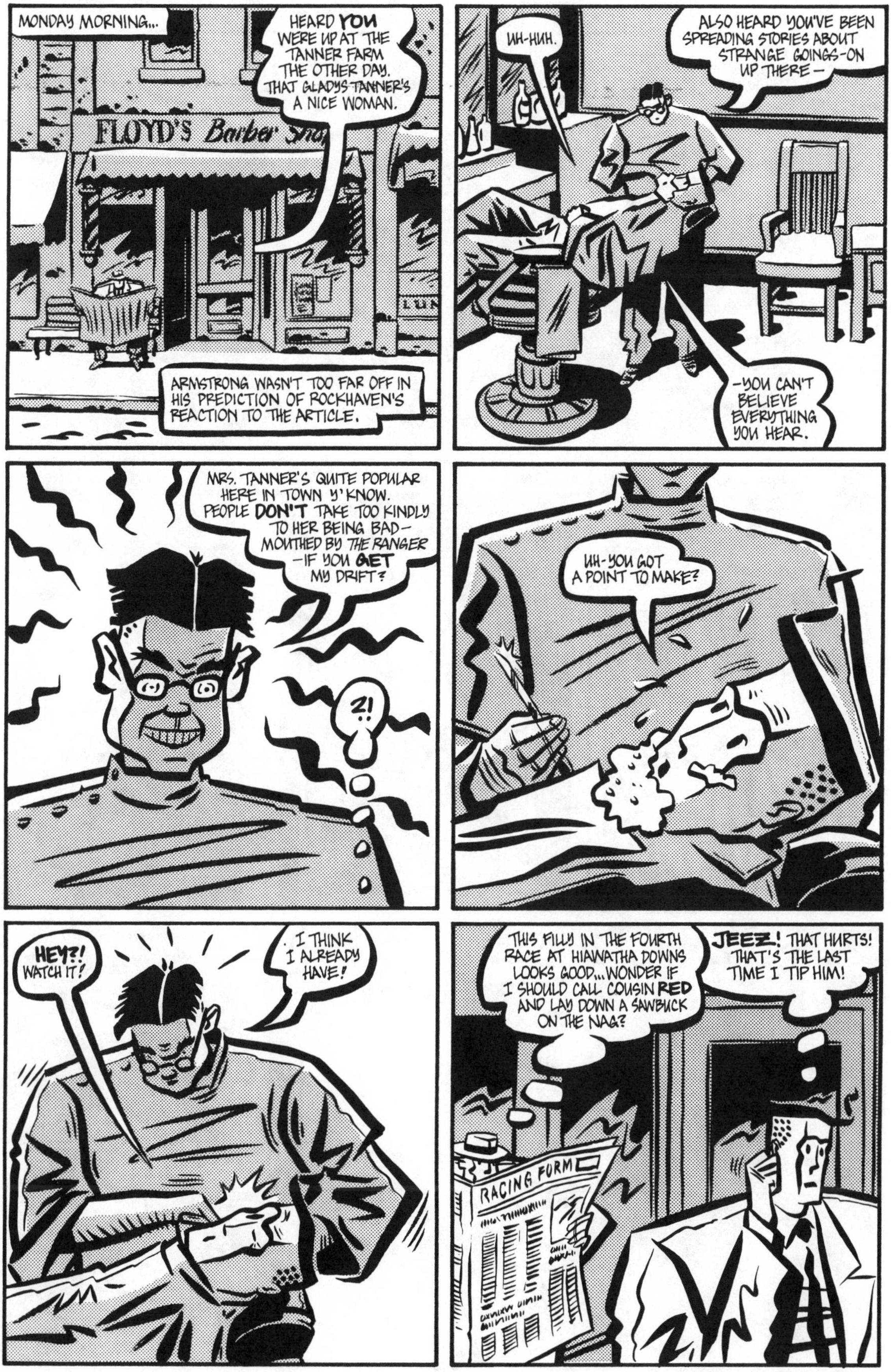
MONDAY MORNING...
HEARD YOU WERE UP AT THE TANNER FARM THE OTHER DAY. THAT GLADYS TANNER'S A NICE WOMAN.
FLOYD'S Barber Shop
ARMSTRONG WASN'T TOO FAR OFF IN HIS PREDICTION OF ROCKHAVEN'S REACTION TO THE ARTICLE.
UH-HUH.
ALSO HEARD YOU'VE BEEN SPREADING STORIES ABOUT STRANGE GOINGS-ON UP THERE —
—YOU CAN'T BELIEVE EVERYTHING YOU HEAR.
MRS. TANNER'S QUITE POPULAR HERE IN TOWN Y'KNOW. PEOPLE DON'T TAKE TOO KINDLY TO HER BEING BAD-MOUTHED BY THE RANGER —IF YOU GET MY DRIFT?
Z!
UH-YOU GOT A POINT TO MAKE?
HEY?! WATCH IT!
I THINK I ALREADY HAVE!
THIS FILLY IN THE FOURTH RACE AT HIAWATHA DOWNS LOOKS GOOD... WONDER IF I SHOULD CALL COUSIN RED AND LAY DOWN A SAWBUCK ON THE NAG?
JEEZ! THAT HURTS! THAT'S THE LAST TIME I TIP HIM!
RACING FORM

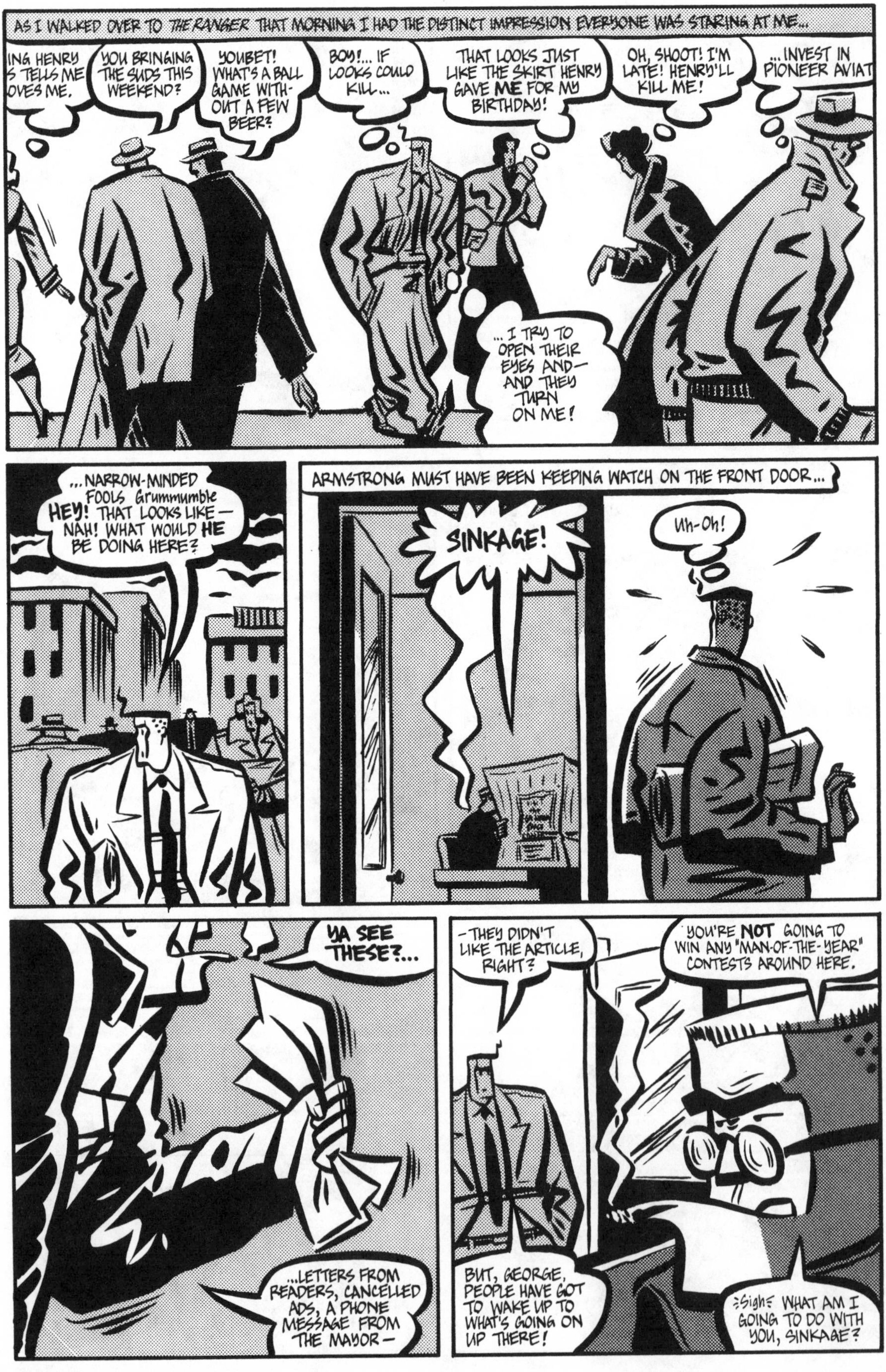
AS I WALKED OVER TO THE RANGER THAT MORNING I HAD THE DISTINCT IMPRESSION EVERYONE WAS STARING AT ME...
ING HENRY S TELLS ME OVES ME.
YOU BRINGING THE SUDS THIS WEEKEND?
YOUBET! WHAT'S A BALL GAME WITH-OUT A FEW BEER?
BOY!... IF LOOKS COULD KILL...
THAT LOOKS JUST LIKE THE SKIRT HENRY GAVE ME FOR MY BIRTHDAY!
OH, SHOOT! I'M LATE! HENRY'LL KILL ME!
...INVEST IN PIONEER AVIAT
...I TRY TO OPEN THEIR EYES AND— AND THEY TURN ON ME!
...NARROW-MINDED FOOLS Grummumble HEY! THAT LOOKS LIKE— NAH! WHAT WOULD HE BE DOING HERE?
ARMSTRONG MUST HAVE BEEN KEEPING WATCH ON THE FRONT DOOR...
SINKAGE!
Uh-Oh!
YA SEE THESE?...
...LETTERS FROM READERS, CANCELLED ADS, A PHONE MESSAGE FROM THE MAYOR—
—THEY DIDN'T LIKE THE ARTICLE, RIGHT?
YOU'RE NOT GOING TO WIN ANY "MAN-OF-THE-YEAR" CONTESTS AROUND HERE.
BUT, GEORGE, PEOPLE HAVE GOT TO WAKE UP TO WHAT'S GOING ON UP THERE!
Sigh WHAT AM I GOING TO DO WITH YOU, SINKAGE?

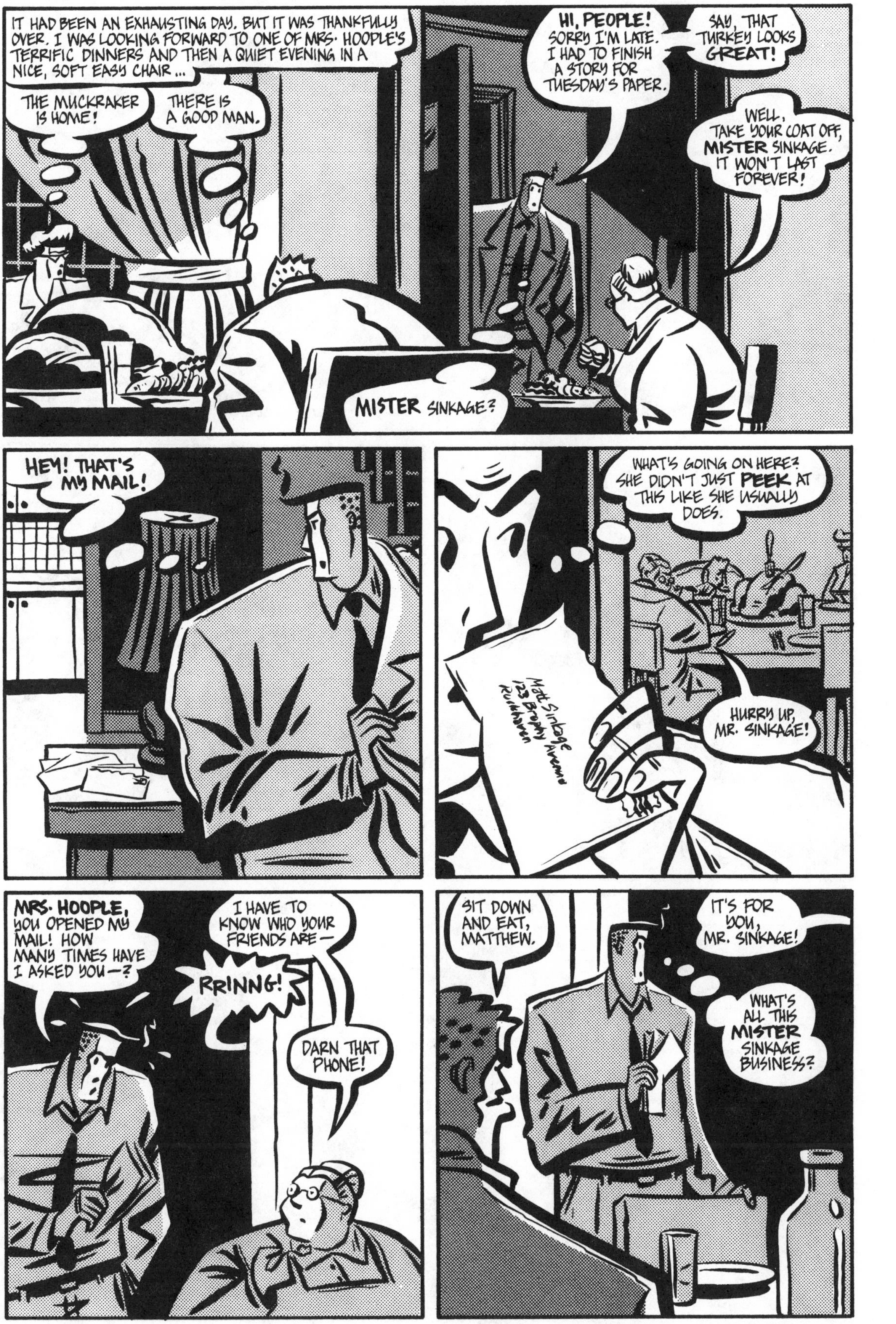
IT HAD BEEN AN EXHAUSTING DAY. BUT IT WAS THANKFULLY OVER. I WAS LOOKING FORWARD TO ONE OF MRS. HOOPLE'S TERRIFIC DINNERS AND THEN A QUIET EVENING IN A NICE, SOFT EASY CHAIR ...
THE MUCKRAKER IS HOME!
THERE IS A GOOD MAN.
HI, PEOPLE! SORRY I'M LATE. I HAD TO FINISH A STORY FOR TUESDAY'S PAPER.
SAY, THAT TURKEY LOOKS GREAT!
WELL, TAKE YOUR COAT OFF, MISTER SINKAGE. IT WON'T LAST FOREVER!
MISTER SINKAGE?
HEY! THAT'S MY MAIL!
WHAT'S GOING ON HERE? SHE DIDN'T JUST PEEK AT THIS LIKE SHE USUALLY DOES.
Matt Sinkage
123 Brophy Avenue
Ruinhaven
HURRY UP, MR. SINKAGE!
MRS. HOOPLE, YOU OPENED MY MAIL! HOW MANY TIMES HAVE I ASKED YOU—?
I HAVE TO KNOW WHO YOUR FRIENDS ARE—
RRINNG!
DARN THAT PHONE!
SIT DOWN AND EAT, MATTHEW.
IT'S FOR YOU, MR. SINKAGE!
WHAT'S ALL THIS MISTER SINKAGE BUSINESS?

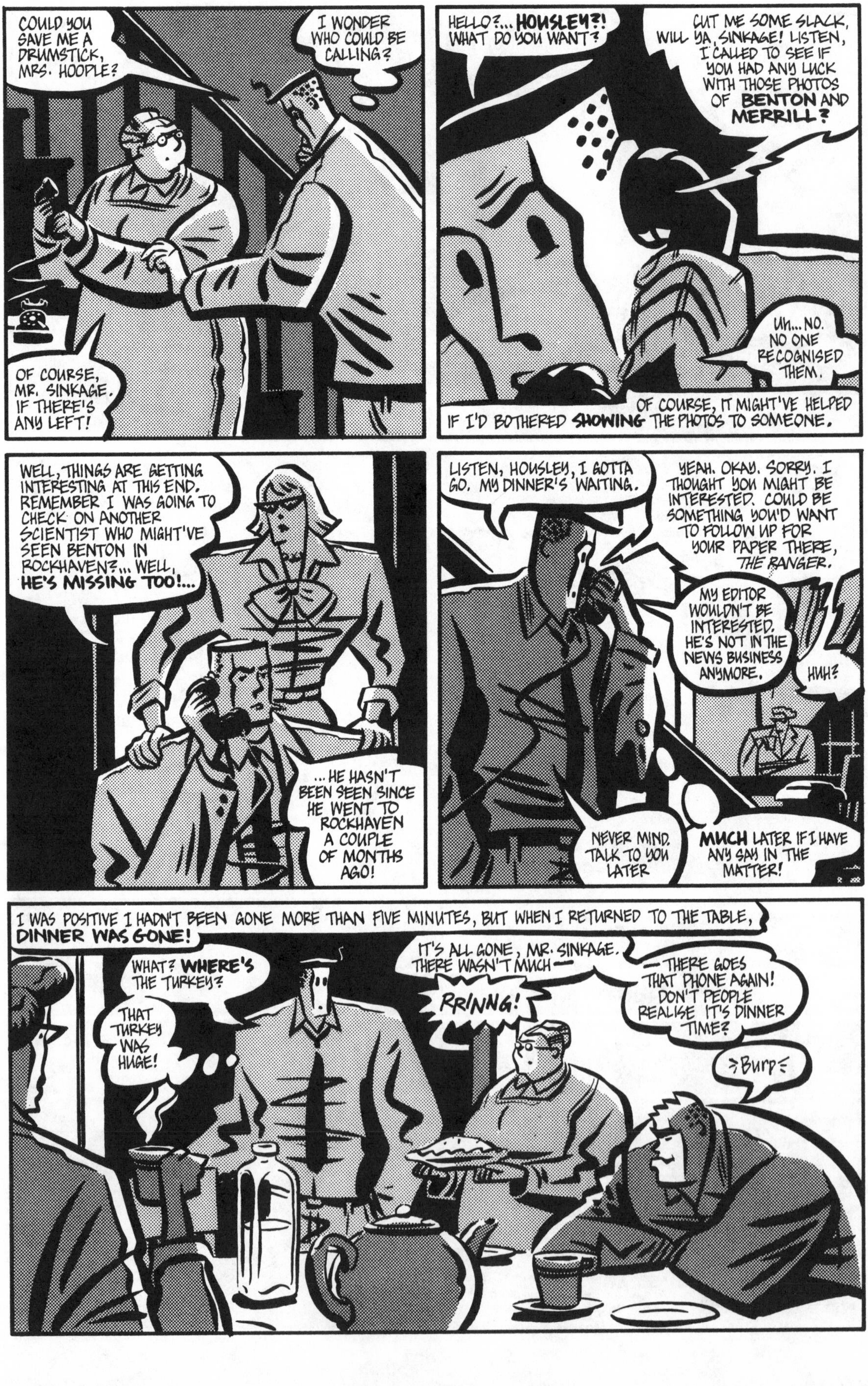
COULD YOU SAVE ME A DRUMSTICK, MRS. HOOPLE?
I WONDER WHO COULD BE CALLING?
OF COURSE, MR. SINKAGE. IF THERE'S ANY LEFT!
HELLO?... HOUSLEY?! WHAT DO YOU WANT?
CUT ME SOME SLACK, WILL YA, SINKAGE! LISTEN, I CALLED TO SEE IF YOU HAD ANY LUCK WITH THOSE PHOTOS OF BENTON AND MERRILL?
UH... NO. NO ONE RECOGNISED THEM.
OF COURSE, IT MIGHT'VE HELPED IF I'D BOTHERED SHOWING THE PHOTOS TO SOMEONE.
WELL, THINGS ARE GETTING INTERESTING AT THIS END. REMEMBER I WAS GOING TO CHECK ON ANOTHER SCIENTIST WHO MIGHT'VE SEEN BENTON IN ROCKHAVEN?... WELL, HE'S MISSING TOO!...
...HE HASN'T BEEN SEEN SINCE HE WENT TO ROCKHAVEN A COUPLE OF MONTHS AGO!
LISTEN, HOUSLEY, I GOTTA GO. MY DINNER'S WAITING.
YEAH. OKAY. SORRY. I THOUGHT YOU MIGHT BE INTERESTED. COULD BE SOMETHING YOU'D WANT TO FOLLOW UP FOR YOUR PAPER THERE, THE RANGER.
MY EDITOR WOULDN'T BE INTERESTED. HE'S NOT IN THE NEWS BUSINESS ANYMORE.
HUH?
NEVER MIND. TALK TO YOU LATER
MUCH LATER IF I HAVE ANY SAY IN THE MATTER!
I WAS POSITIVE I HADN'T BEEN GONE MORE THAN FIVE MINUTES, BUT WHEN I RETURNED TO THE TABLE, DINNER WAS GONE!
WHAT? WHERE'S THE TURKEY?
THAT TURKEY WAS HUGE!
IT'S ALL GONE, MR. SINKAGE. THERE WASN'T MUCH—
RRINNG!
—THERE GOES THAT PHONE AGAIN! DON'T PEOPLE REALISE IT'S DINNER TIME?
Burp

AT LEAST I'LL GET SOME OF YOUR GREAT PIE!

IT'S FOR YOU AGAIN, MR. SINKAGE!

@#7¢#@!!

THIS WAS ONE CALL I WASN'T EXPECTING!

JANET TANNER?

SHALL I HELP YOU CLEAR THE TABLE, MRS. HOOPLE?

OH, WHY, YES. PLEASE DO. THANK YOU! I'LL PUT THE REST OF THIS PIE AWAY FOR TOMORROW.

Munch! Munch! Munch!

I'M CALLING ABOUT YOUR STORY, MR. SINKAGE, Y-YOU DON'T KNOW THE HALF OF W-WHAT'S GOING ON UP HERE! I THINK W-WE SHOULD TALK.

THAT WAS A FINE MEAL, MRS. HOOPLE.

OKAY. HOW ABOUT TONIGHT? I'M FREE RIGHT AFTER DINNER.

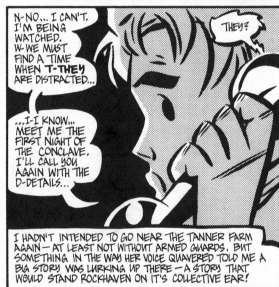

N-NO... I CAN'T. I'M BEING WATCHED. W-WE MUST FIND A TIME WHEN T-THEY ARE DISTRACTED...

THEY?

...I-I KNOW... MEET ME THE FIRST NIGHT OF THE CONCLAVE. I'LL CALL YOU AGAIN WITH THE D-DETAILS...

I HADN'T INTENDED TO GO NEAR THE TANNER FARM AGAIN — AT LEAST NOT WITHOUT ARMED GUARDS. BUT SOMETHING IN THE WAY HER VOICE QUAVERED TOLD ME A BIG STORY WAS LURKING UP THERE — A STORY THAT WOULD STAND ROCKHAVEN ON IT'S COLLECTIVE EAR!

HEY! WHAT HAPPENED TO THE PIE?

I'M SORRY, MR. SINKAGE. THERE IS NO PIE FOR YOU!...

...I DON'T SERVE PIE TO SUSPECTED COMMUNISTS WHO SLANDER MY FRIENDS!!

BUT EVERYTHING IN THE STORY WAS TRUE! AWW, WHAT'S THE USE!? YOU'RE JUST LIKE EVERYONE ELSE IN ROCKHAVEN—

—THERE MAY NOT BE ANY SECRETS IN ROCKHAVEN BUT THERE CERTAINLY ARE A LOT OF SMALL MINDS!

YOU MARK MY WORD, MATTHEW! IF YOU CONTINUE TO SPREAD THESE LIES, THERE COULD BE HELL TO PAY!—

—OH, GOOD GRACIOUS ME!

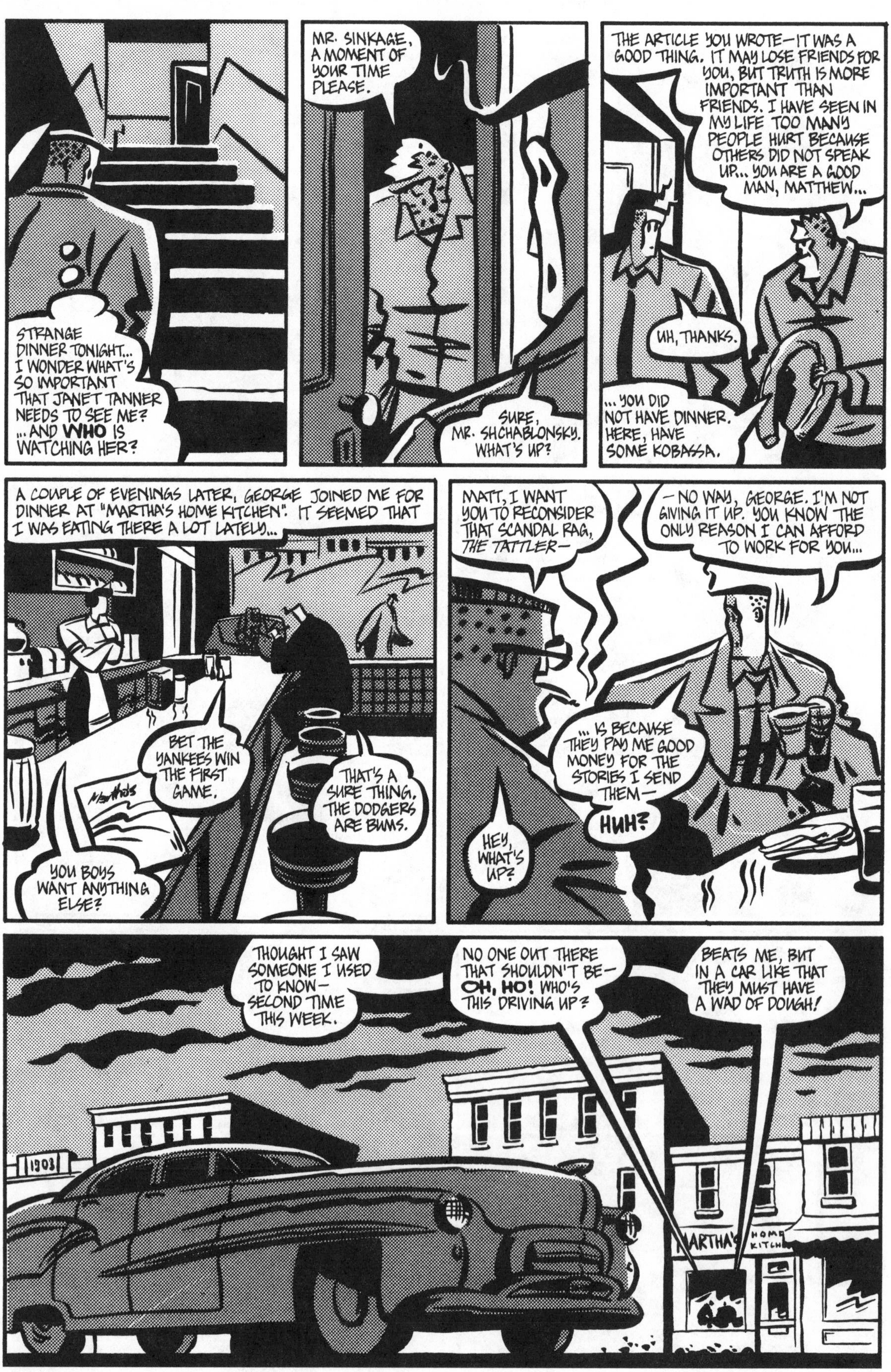
STRANGE DINNER TONIGHT... I WONDER WHAT'S SO IMPORTANT THAT JANET TANNER NEEDS TO SEE ME? ...AND WHO IS WATCHING HER?
MR. SINKAGE, A MOMENT OF YOUR TIME PLEASE.
SURE, MR. SHCHABLONSKY. WHAT'S UP?
THE ARTICLE YOU WROTE—IT WAS A GOOD THING. IT MAY LOSE FRIENDS FOR YOU, BUT TRUTH IS MORE IMPORTANT THAN FRIENDS. I HAVE SEEN IN MY LIFE TOO MANY PEOPLE HURT BECAUSE OTHERS DID NOT SPEAK UP... YOU ARE A GOOD MAN, MATTHEW...
UH, THANKS.
...YOU DID NOT HAVE DINNER. HERE, HAVE SOME KOBASSA.
A COUPLE OF EVENINGS LATER, GEORGE JOINED ME FOR DINNER AT "MARTHA'S HOME KITCHEN". IT SEEMED THAT I WAS EATING THERE A LOT LATELY...
BET THE YANKEES WIN THE FIRST GAME.
THAT'S A SURE THING. THE DODGERS ARE BUMS.
YOU BOYS WANT ANYTHING ELSE?
MATT, I WANT YOU TO RECONSIDER THAT SCANDAL RAG, THE TATTLER—
—NO WAY, GEORGE. I'M NOT GIVING IT UP. YOU KNOW THE ONLY REASON I CAN AFFORD TO WORK FOR YOU...
...IS BECAUSE THEY PAY ME GOOD MONEY FOR THE STORIES I SEND THEM—
HUH?
HEY, WHAT'S UP?
THOUGHT I SAW SOMEONE I USED TO KNOW—SECOND TIME THIS WEEK.
NO ONE OUT THERE THAT SHOULDN'T BE—OH, HO! WHO'S THIS DRIVING UP?
BEATS ME, BUT IN A CAR LIKE THAT THEY MUST HAVE A WAD OF DOUGH!
1903
MARTHA'S HOME KITCHEN

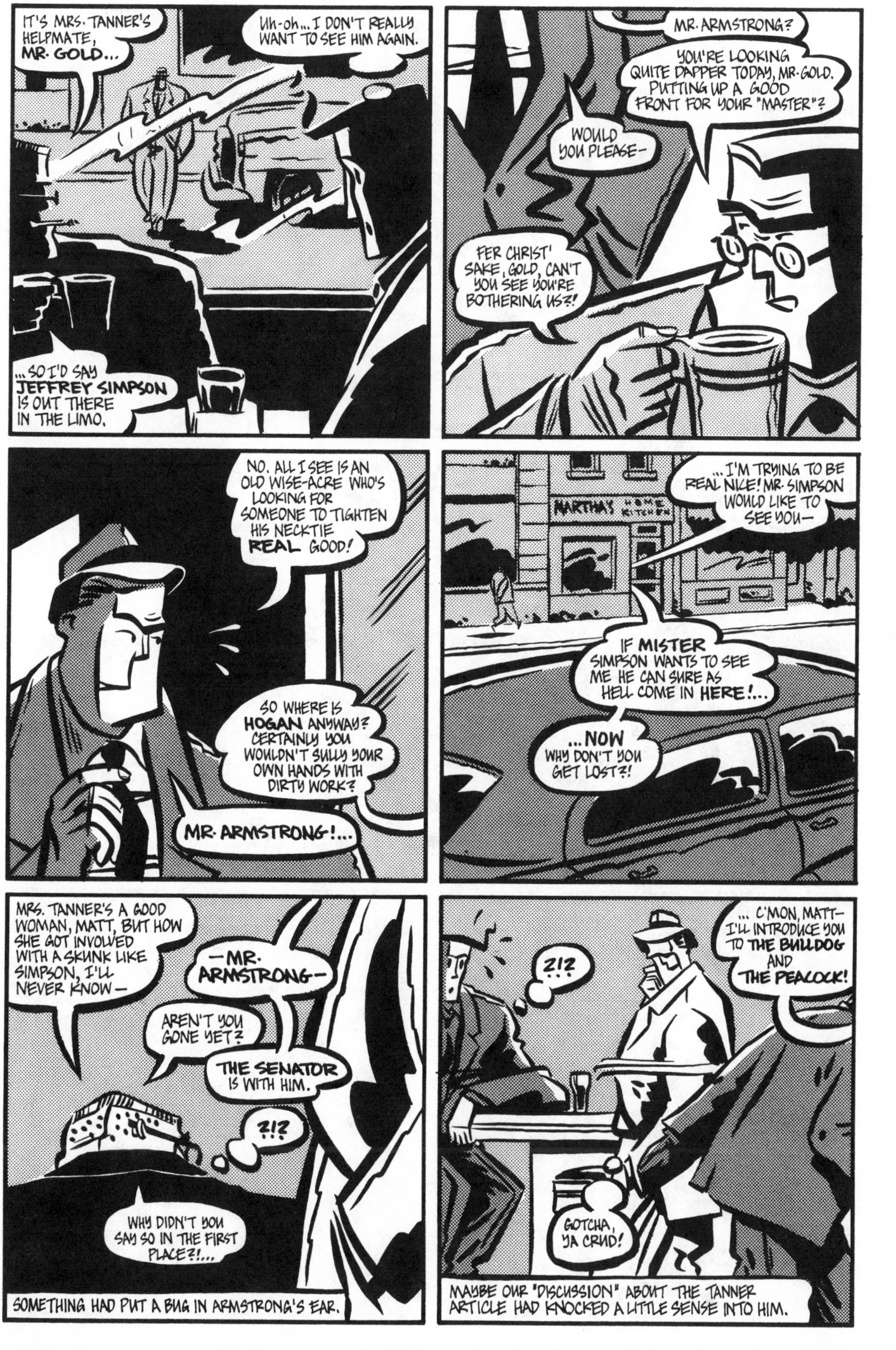
IT'S MRS. TANNER'S HELPMATE, **MR. GOLD...**
Uh-oh... I DON'T REALLY WANT TO SEE HIM AGAIN.
...SO I'D SAY **JEFFREY SIMPSON** IS OUT THERE IN THE LIMO.
MR. ARMSTRONG?
YOU'RE LOOKING QUITE DAPPER TODAY, MR. GOLD. PUTTING UP A GOOD FRONT FOR YOUR "MASTER"?
WOULD YOU PLEASE—
FER CHRIST' SAKE, GOLD, CAN'T YOU SEE YOU'RE BOTHERING US?!
NO. ALL I SEE IS AN OLD WISE-ACRE WHO'S LOOKING FOR SOMEONE TO TIGHTEN HIS NECKTIE **REAL** GOOD!
SO WHERE IS **HOGAN** ANYWAY? CERTAINLY YOU WOULDN'T SULLY YOUR OWN HANDS WITH DIRTY WORK?
MR. ARMSTRONG!...
MARTHA'S HOME KITCHEN
...I'M TRYING TO BE REAL NICE! MR. SIMPSON WOULD LIKE TO SEE YOU—
IF **MISTER** SIMPSON WANTS TO SEE ME HE CAN SURE AS HELL COME IN **HERE!...**
...NOW WHY DON'T YOU GET LOST?!
MRS. TANNER'S A GOOD WOMAN, MATT, BUT HOW SHE GOT INVOLVED WITH A SKUNK LIKE SIMPSON, I'LL NEVER KNOW—
—MR. ARMSTRONG—
AREN'T YOU GONE YET?
THE SENATOR IS WITH HIM.
?!?
WHY DIDN'T YOU SAY SO IN THE FIRST PLACE?!...
SOMETHING HAD PUT A BUG IN ARMSTRONG'S EAR.
?!?
... C'MON, MATT— I'LL INTRODUCE YOU TO **THE BULLDOG** AND **THE PEACOCK!**
GOTCHA, YA CRUD!
MAYBE OUR "DISCUSSION" ABOUT THE TANNER ARTICLE HAD KNOCKED A LITTLE SENSE INTO HIM.

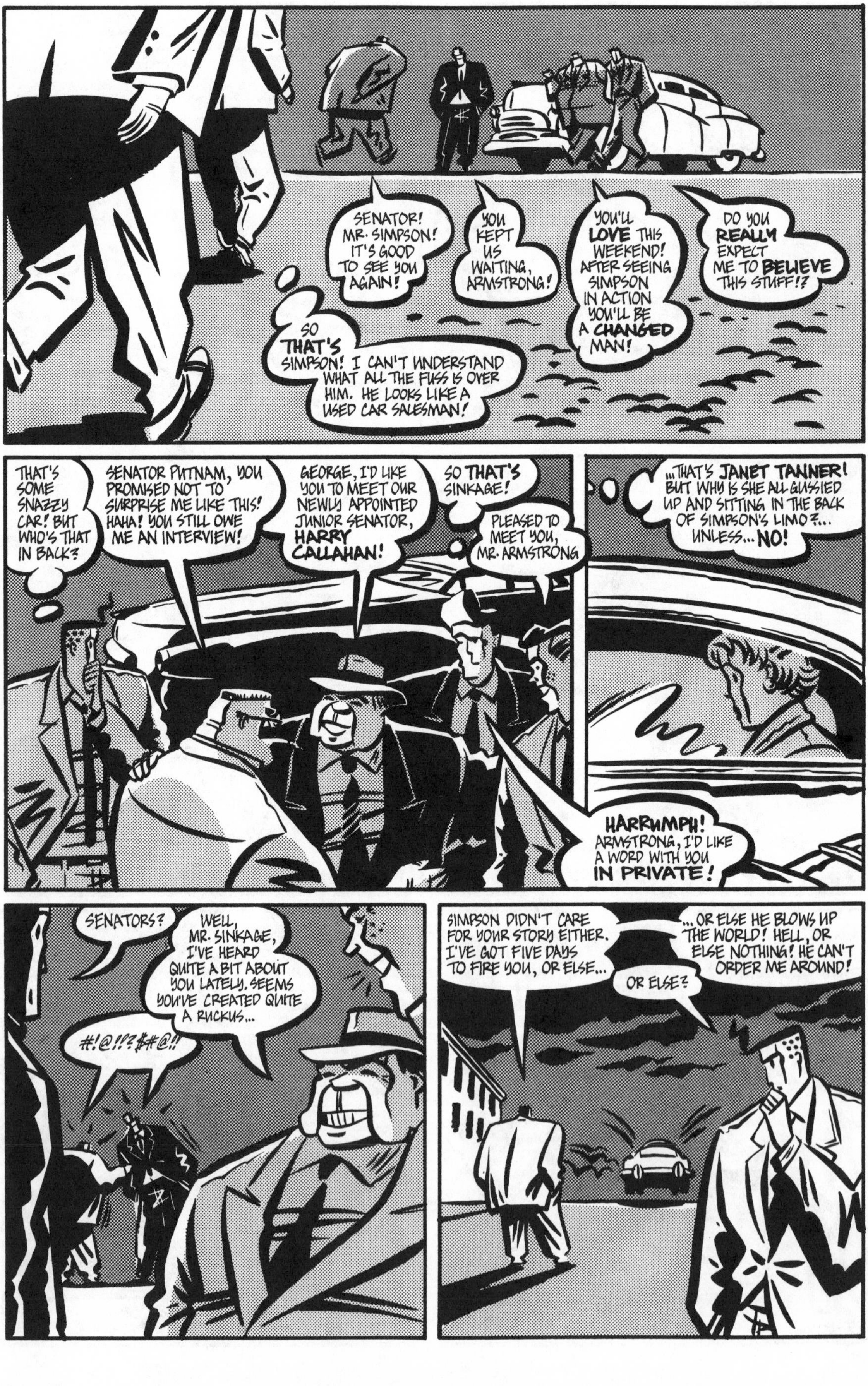
SENATOR! MR. SIMPSON! IT'S GOOD TO SEE YOU AGAIN!
SO THAT'S SIMPSON! I CAN'T UNDERSTAND WHAT ALL THE FUSS IS OVER HIM. HE LOOKS LIKE A USED CAR SALESMAN!
YOU KEPT US WAITING, ARMSTRONG!
YOU'LL LOVE THIS WEEKEND! AFTER SEEING SIMPSON IN ACTION YOU'LL BE A CHANGED MAN!
DO YOU REALLY EXPECT ME TO BELIEVE THIS STUFF!?
THAT'S SOME SNAZZY CAR! BUT WHO'S THAT IN BACK?
SENATOR PUTNAM, YOU PROMISED NOT TO SURPRISE ME LIKE THIS! HAHA! YOU STILL OWE ME AN INTERVIEW!
GEORGE, I'D LIKE YOU TO MEET OUR NEWLY APPOINTED JUNIOR SENATOR, HARRY CALLAHAN!
SO THAT'S SINKAGE!
PLEASED TO MEET YOU, MR. ARMSTRONG
...THAT'S JANET TANNER! BUT WHY IS SHE ALL GUSSIED UP AND SITTING IN THE BACK OF SIMPSON'S LIMO?... UNLESS... NO!
HARRUMPH! ARMSTRONG, I'D LIKE A WORD WITH YOU IN PRIVATE!
SENATORS?
WELL, MR. SINKAGE, I'VE HEARD QUITE A BIT ABOUT YOU LATELY. SEEMS YOU'VE CREATED QUITE A RUCKUS...
#!@!!?$#@!!
SIMPSON DIDN'T CARE FOR YOUR STORY EITHER. I'VE GOT FIVE DAYS TO FIRE YOU, OR ELSE...
OR ELSE?
...OR ELSE HE BLOWS UP THE WORLD! HELL, OR ELSE NOTHING! HE CAN'T ORDER ME AROUND!

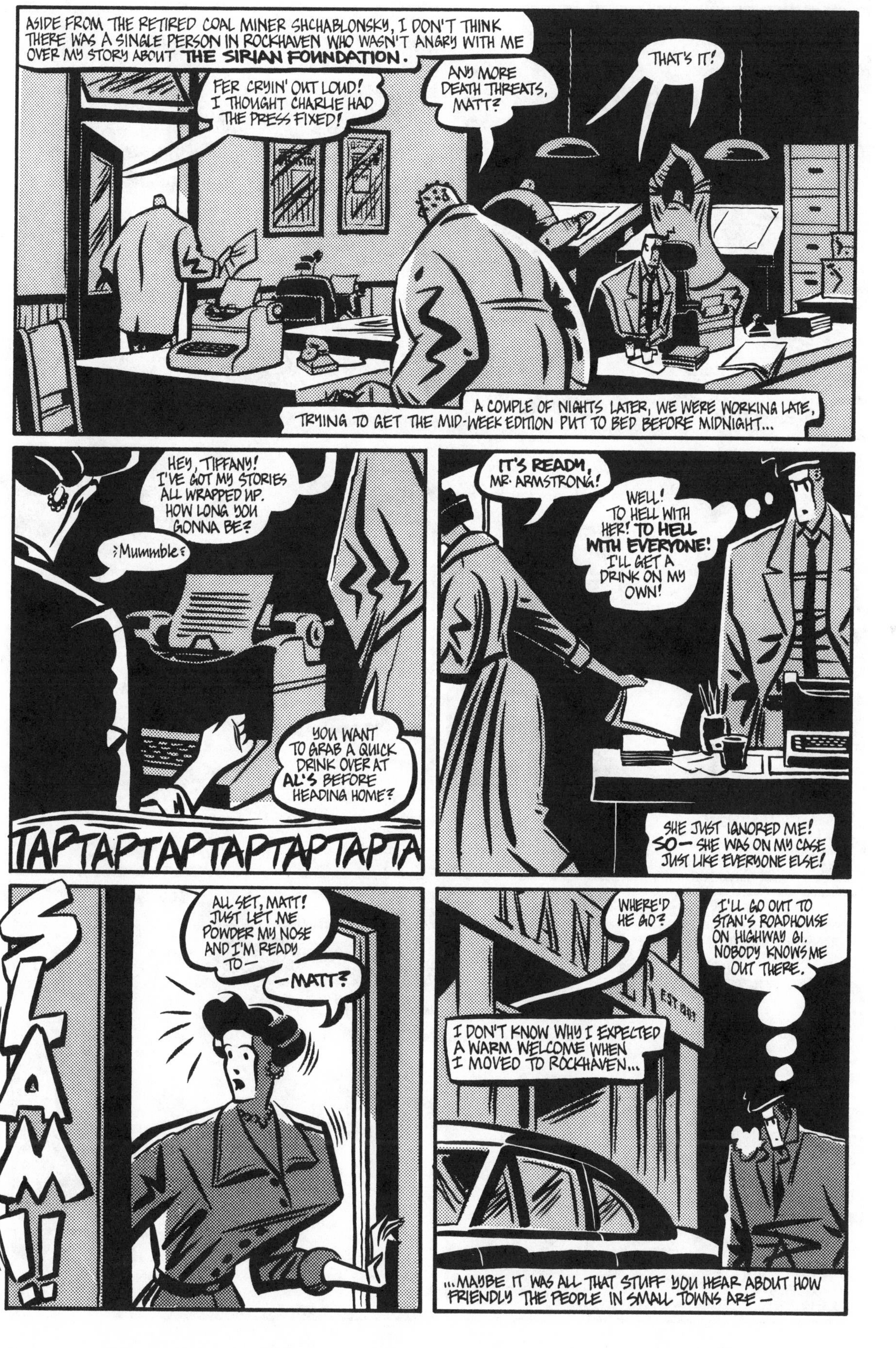

ASIDE FROM THE RETIRED COAL MINER SHCHABLONSKY, I DON'T THINK THERE WAS A SINGLE PERSON IN ROCKHAVEN WHO WASN'T ANGRY WITH ME OVER MY STORY ABOUT THE SIRIAN FOUNDATION.
FER CRYIN' OUT LOUD! I THOUGHT CHARLIE HAD THE PRESS FIXED!
ANY MORE DEATH THREATS, MATT?
THAT'S IT!
A COUPLE OF NIGHTS LATER, WE WERE WORKING LATE, TRYING TO GET THE MID-WEEK EDITION PUT TO BED BEFORE MIDNIGHT...
HEY, TIFFANY! I'VE GOT MY STORIES ALL WRAPPED UP. HOW LONG YOU GONNA BE?
Mummble
YOU WANT TO GRAB A QUICK DRINK OVER AT AL'S BEFORE HEADING HOME?
TAPTAPTAPTAPTAPTAPTAPTA
IT'S READY, MR. ARMSTRONG!
WELL! TO HELL WITH HER! TO HELL WITH EVERYONE! I'LL GET A DRINK ON MY OWN!
SHE JUST IGNORED ME! SO— SHE WAS ON MY CASE JUST LIKE EVERYONE ELSE!
SLAM!!
ALL SET, MATT! JUST LET ME POWDER MY NOSE AND I'M READY TO—
—MATT?
WHERE'D HE GO?
I'LL GO OUT TO STAN'S ROADHOUSE ON HIGHWAY 61. NOBODY KNOWS ME OUT THERE.
I DON'T KNOW WHY I EXPECTED A WARM WELCOME WHEN I MOVED TO ROCKHAVEN...
...MAYBE IT WAS ALL THAT STUFF YOU HEAR ABOUT HOW FRIENDLY THE PEOPLE IN SMALL TOWNS ARE—

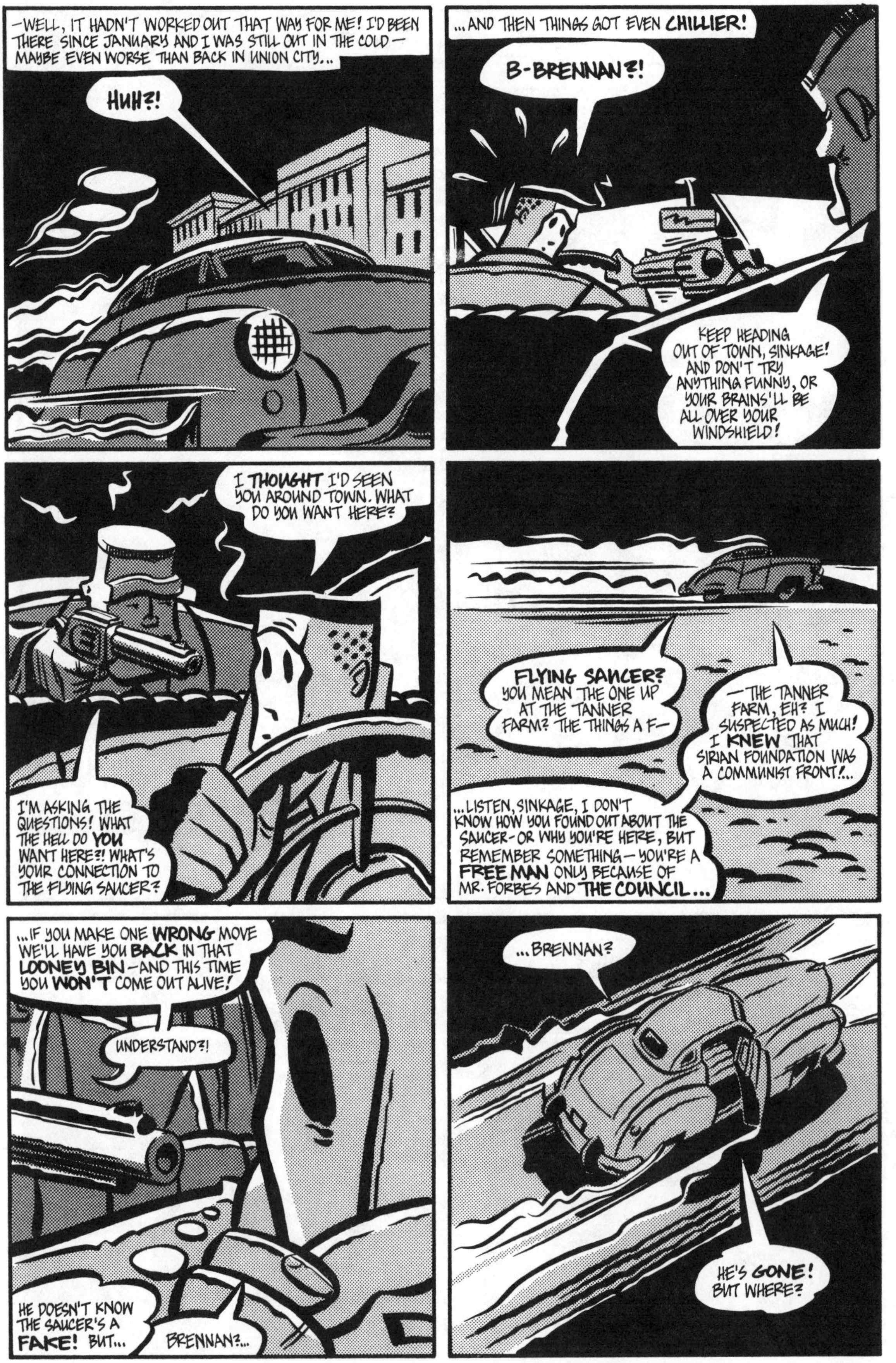

—WELL, IT HADN'T WORKED OUT THAT WAY FOR ME! I'D BEEN THERE SINCE JANUARY AND I WAS STILL OUT IN THE COLD— MAYBE EVEN WORSE THAN BACK IN UNION CITY...
HUH?!
...AND THEN THINGS GOT EVEN CHILLIER!
B-BRENNAN?!
KEEP HEADING OUT OF TOWN, SINKAGE! AND DON'T TRY ANYTHING FUNNY, OR YOUR BRAINS'LL BE ALL OVER YOUR WINDSHIELD!
I THOUGHT I'D SEEN YOU AROUND TOWN. WHAT DO YOU WANT HERE?
I'M ASKING THE QUESTIONS! WHAT THE HELL DO YOU WANT HERE?! WHAT'S YOUR CONNECTION TO THE FLYING SAUCER?
FLYING SAUCER? YOU MEAN THE ONE UP AT THE TANNER FARM? THE THING'S A F—
—THE TANNER FARM, EH? I SUSPECTED AS MUCH! I KNEW THAT SIRIAN FOUNDATION WAS A COMMUNIST FRONT!...
...LISTEN, SINKAGE, I DON'T KNOW HOW YOU FOUND OUT ABOUT THE SAUCER—OR WHY YOU'RE HERE, BUT REMEMBER SOMETHING—YOU'RE A FREE MAN ONLY BECAUSE OF MR. FORBES AND THE COUNCIL...
...IF YOU MAKE ONE WRONG MOVE WE'LL HAVE YOU BACK IN THAT LOONEY BIN—AND THIS TIME YOU WON'T COME OUT ALIVE!
UNDERSTAND?!
HE DOESN'T KNOW THE SAUCER'S A FAKE! BUT...
BRENNAN?...
...BRENNAN?
HE'S GONE! BUT WHERE?

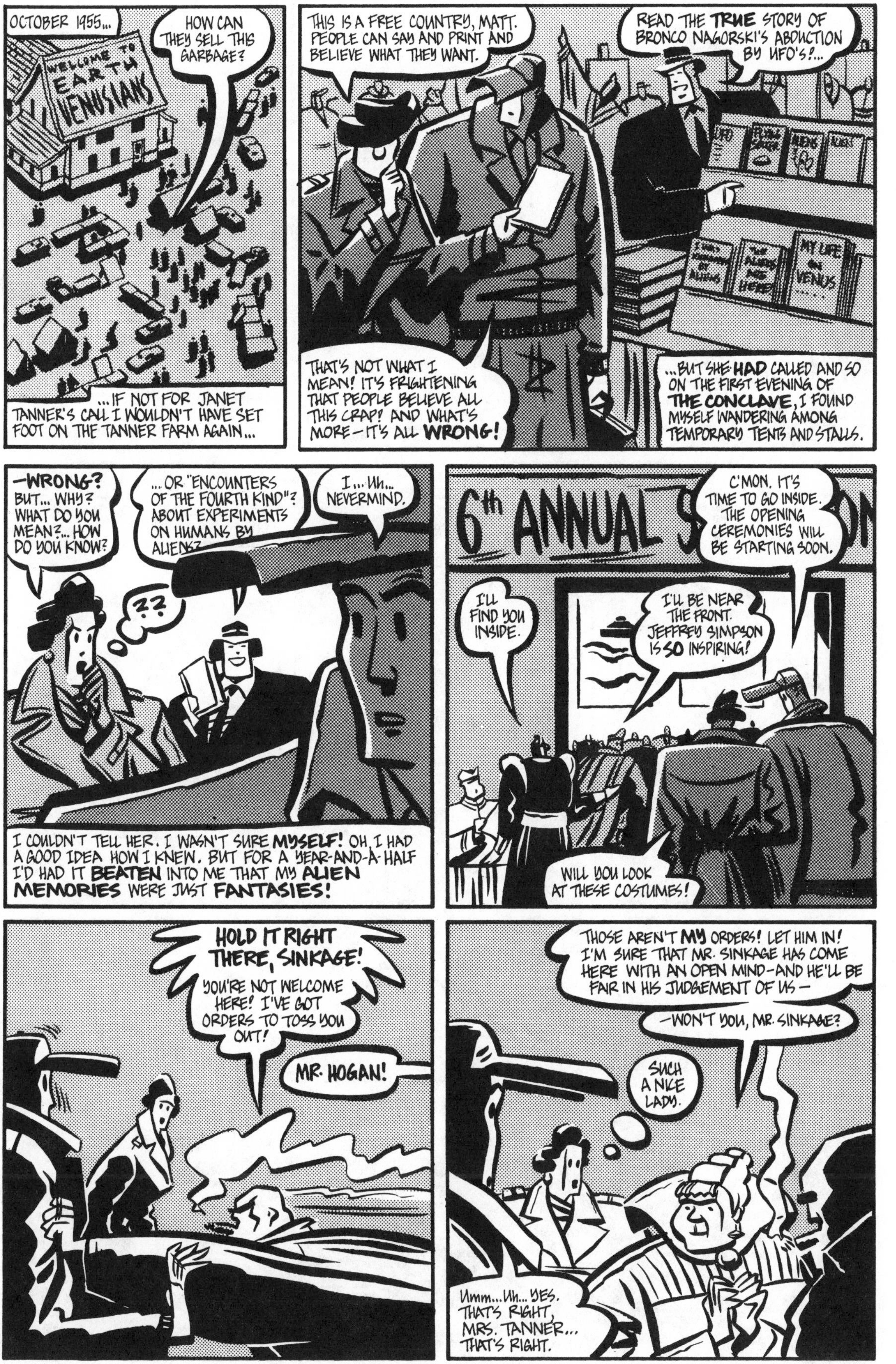
OCTOBER 1955...
HOW CAN THEY SELL THIS GARBAGE?
WELCOME TO EARTH VENUSIANS
...IF NOT FOR JANET TANNER'S CALL I WOULDN'T HAVE SET FOOT ON THE TANNER FARM AGAIN...
THIS IS A FREE COUNTRY, MATT. PEOPLE CAN SAY AND PRINT AND BELIEVE WHAT THEY WANT.
READ THE **TRUE** STORY OF BRONCO NAGORSKI'S ABDUCTION BY UFO'S?...
MY LIFE ON VENUS
THAT'S NOT WHAT I MEAN! IT'S FRIGHTENING THAT PEOPLE BELIEVE ALL THIS CRAP! AND WHAT'S MORE—IT'S ALL **WRONG**!
...BUT SHE **HAD** CALLED AND SO ON THE FIRST EVENING OF **THE CONCLAVE**, I FOUND MYSELF WANDERING AMONG TEMPORARY TENTS AND STALLS.
—**WRONG?** BUT... WHY? WHAT DO YOU MEAN?... HOW DO YOU KNOW?
...OR "ENCOUNTERS OF THE FOURTH KIND"? ABOUT EXPERIMENTS ON HUMANS BY ALIENS?
??
I... UH... NEVERMIND.
I COULDN'T TELL HER. I WASN'T SURE **MYSELF**! OH, I HAD A GOOD IDEA HOW I KNEW. BUT FOR A YEAR-AND-A-HALF I'D HAD IT **BEATEN** INTO ME THAT MY **ALIEN MEMORIES** WERE JUST **FANTASIES**!
6th ANNUAL
C'MON. IT'S TIME TO GO INSIDE. THE OPENING CEREMONIES WILL BE STARTING SOON.
I'LL FIND YOU INSIDE.
I'LL BE NEAR THE FRONT. JEFFREY SIMPSON IS **SO** INSPIRING!
WILL YOU LOOK AT THESE COSTUMES!
HOLD IT RIGHT THERE, SINKAGE!
YOU'RE NOT WELCOME HERE! I'VE GOT ORDERS TO TOSS YOU OUT!
MR. HOGAN!
THOSE AREN'T **MY** ORDERS! LET HIM IN! I'M SURE THAT MR. SINKAGE HAS COME HERE WITH AN OPEN MIND—AND HE'LL BE FAIR IN HIS JUDGEMENT OF US—
—WON'T YOU, MR. SINKAGE?
SUCH A NICE LADY.
UMM... UH... YES. THAT'S RIGHT, MRS. TANNER... THAT'S RIGHT.

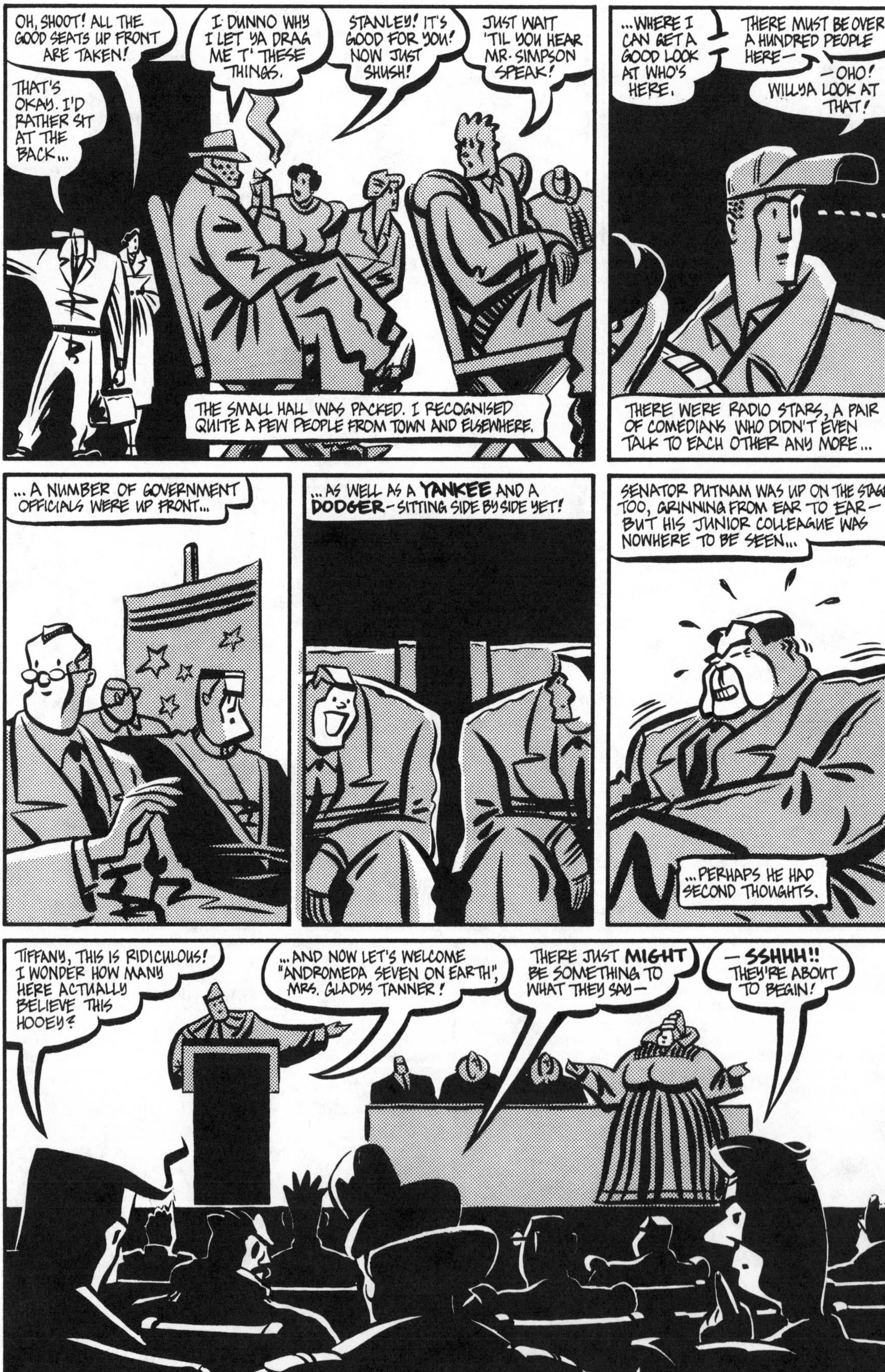
OH, SHOOT! ALL THE GOOD SEATS UP FRONT ARE TAKEN!
THAT'S OKAY. I'D RATHER SIT AT THE BACK...
I DUNNO WHY I LET YA DRAG ME T' THESE THINGS.
STANLEY! IT'S GOOD FOR YOU! NOW JUST SHUSH!
JUST WAIT 'TIL YOU HEAR MR. SIMPSON SPEAK!
THE SMALL HALL WAS PACKED. I RECOGNISED QUITE A FEW PEOPLE FROM TOWN AND ELSEWHERE.
...WHERE I CAN GET A GOOD LOOK AT WHO'S HERE.
THERE MUST BE OVER A HUNDRED PEOPLE HERE—
—OHO! WILLYA LOOK AT THAT!
THERE WERE RADIO STARS, A PAIR OF COMEDIANS WHO DIDN'T EVEN TALK TO EACH OTHER ANY MORE...
...A NUMBER OF GOVERNMENT OFFICIALS WERE UP FRONT...
...AS WELL AS A **YANKEE** AND A **DODGER**—SITTING SIDE BY SIDE YET!
SENATOR PUTNAM WAS UP ON THE STAGE TOO, GRINNING FROM EAR TO EAR—BUT HIS JUNIOR COLLEAGUE WAS NOWHERE TO BE SEEN...
...PERHAPS HE HAD SECOND THOUGHTS.
TIFFANY, THIS IS RIDICULOUS! I WONDER HOW MANY HERE ACTUALLY BELIEVE THIS HOOEY?
...AND NOW LET'S WELCOME "ANDROMEDA SEVEN ON EARTH", MRS. GLADYS TANNER!
THERE JUST **MIGHT** BE SOMETHING TO WHAT THEY SAY—
—**SSHHH!!** THEY'RE ABOUT TO BEGIN!

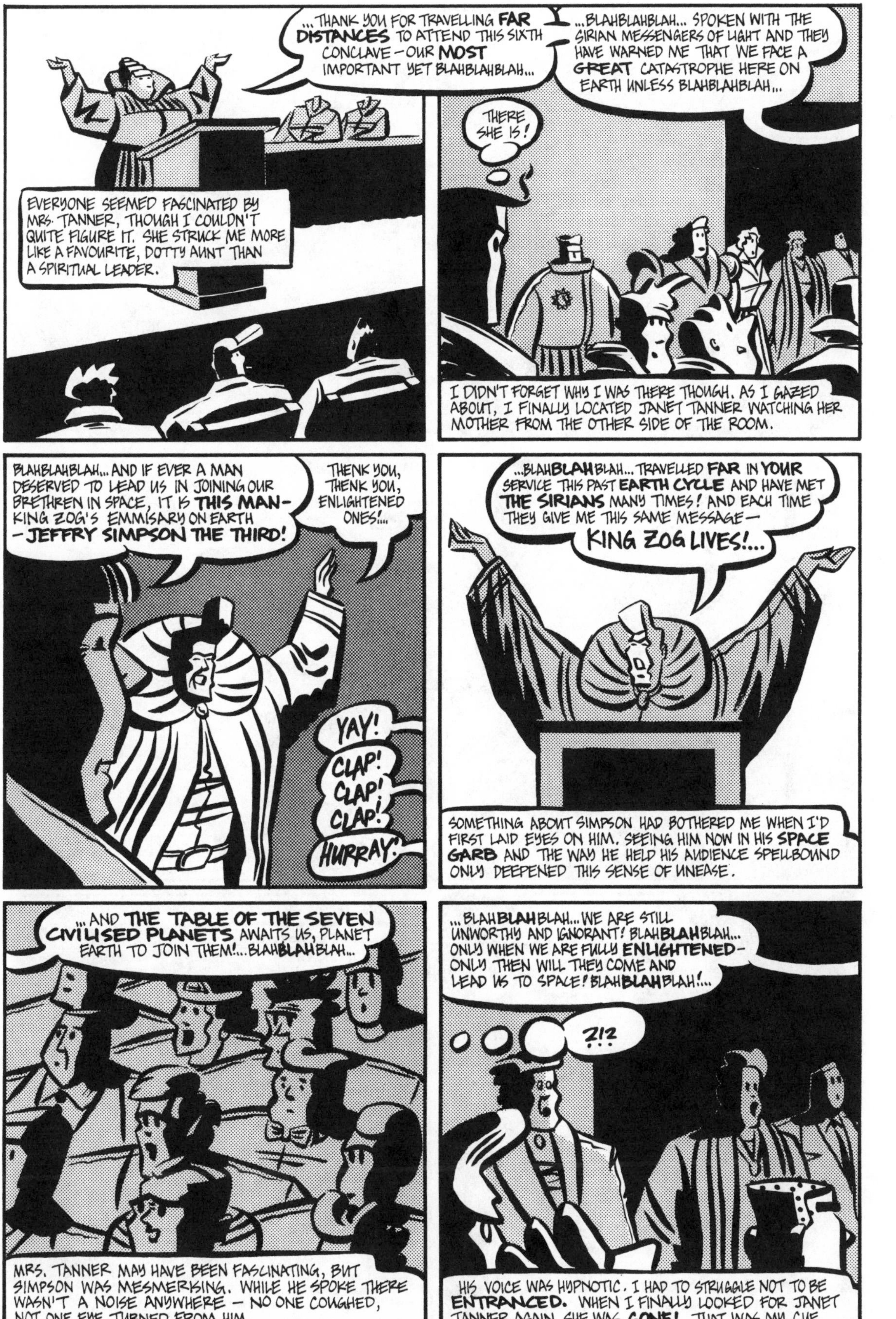
...THANK YOU FOR TRAVELLING FAR DISTANCES TO ATTEND THIS SIXTH CONCLAVE—OUR MOST IMPORTANT YET BLAHBLAHBLAH...
EVERYONE SEEMED FASCINATED BY MRS. TANNER, THOUGH I COULDN'T QUITE FIGURE IT. SHE STRUCK ME MORE LIKE A FAVOURITE, DOTTY AUNT THAN A SPIRITUAL LEADER.
...BLAHBLAHBLAH... SPOKEN WITH THE SIRIAN MESSENGERS OF LIGHT AND THEY HAVE WARNED ME THAT WE FACE A GREAT CATASTROPHE HERE ON EARTH UNLESS BLAHBLAHBLAH...
THERE SHE IS!
I DIDN'T FORGET WHY I WAS THERE THOUGH. AS I GAZED ABOUT, I FINALLY LOCATED JANET TANNER WATCHING HER MOTHER FROM THE OTHER SIDE OF THE ROOM.
BLAHBLAHBLAH... AND IF EVER A MAN DESERVED TO LEAD US IN JOINING OUR BRETHREN IN SPACE, IT IS THIS MAN-KING ZOG'S EMMISARY ON EARTH —JEFFRY SIMPSON THE THIRD!
THENK YOU, THENK YOU, ENLIGHTENED ONES!...
YAY!
CLAP! CLAP! CLAP!
HURRAY!
...BLAHBLAHBLAH... TRAVELLED FAR IN YOUR SERVICE THIS PAST EARTH CYCLE AND HAVE MET THE SIRIANS MANY TIMES! AND EACH TIME THEY GIVE ME THIS SAME MESSAGE— KING ZOG LIVES!...
SOMETHING ABOUT SIMPSON HAD BOTHERED ME WHEN I'D FIRST LAID EYES ON HIM. SEEING HIM NOW IN HIS SPACE GARB AND THE WAY HE HELD HIS AUDIENCE SPELLBOUND ONLY DEEPENED THIS SENSE OF UNEASE.
...AND THE TABLE OF THE SEVEN CIVILISED PLANETS AWAITS US, PLANET EARTH TO JOIN THEM!... BLAHBLAHBLAH...
MRS. TANNER MAY HAVE BEEN FASCINATING, BUT SIMPSON WAS MESMERISING. WHILE HE SPOKE THERE WASN'T A NOISE ANYWHERE — NO ONE COUGHED, NOT ONE EYE TURNED FROM HIM.
...BLAHBLAHBLAH... WE ARE STILL UNWORTHY AND IGNORANT! BLAHBLAHBLAH... ONLY WHEN WE ARE FULLY ENLIGHTENED— ONLY THEN WILL THEY COME AND LEAD US TO SPACE! BLAHBLAHBLAH!...
?!?
HIS VOICE WAS HYPNOTIC. I HAD TO STRUGGLE NOT TO BE ENTRANCED. WHEN I FINALLY LOOKED FOR JANET TANNER AGAIN, SHE WAS GONE! THAT WAS MY CUE.

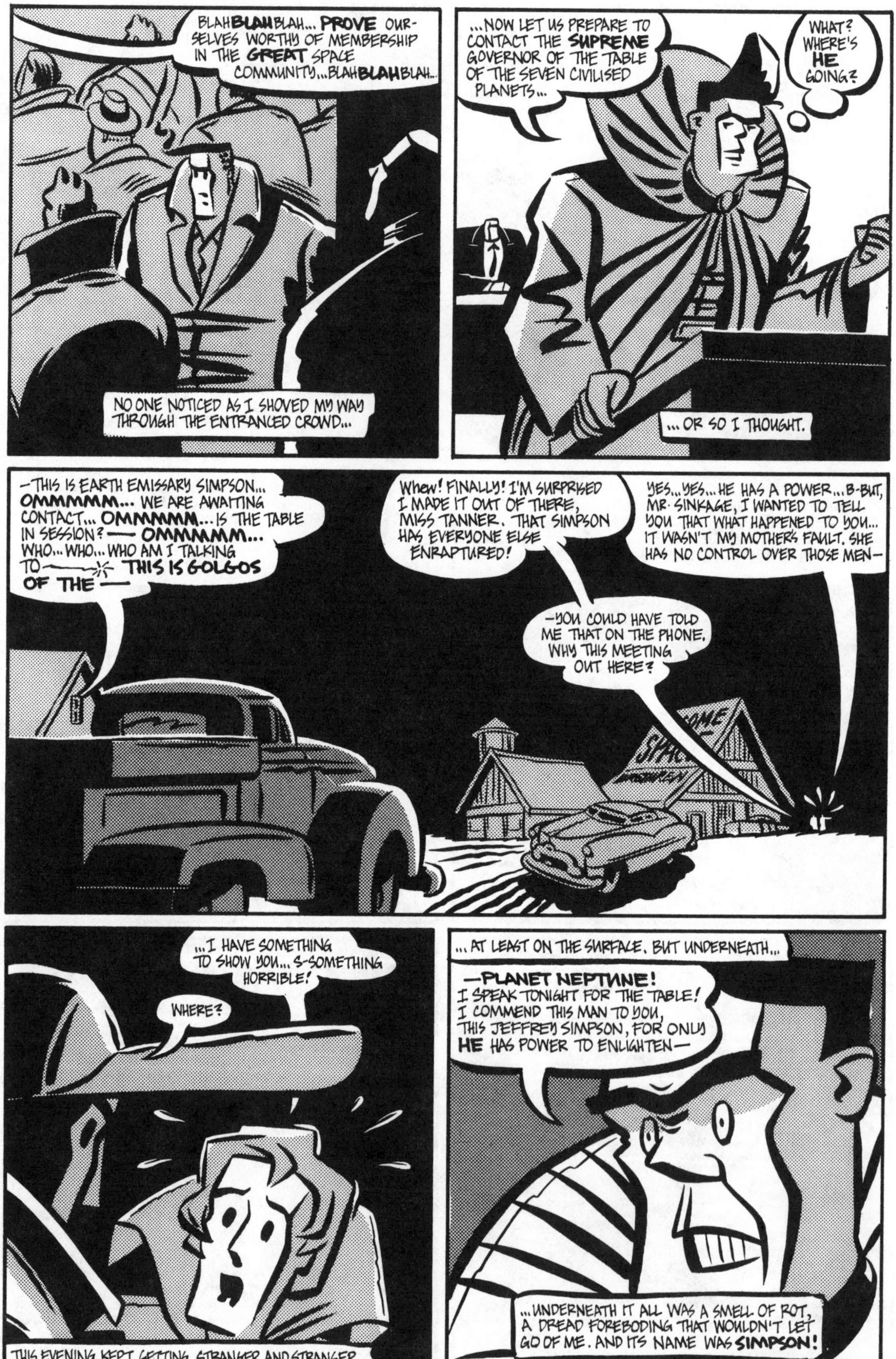
BLAH BLAH BLAH... PROVE OURSELVES WORTHY OF MEMBERSHIP IN THE GREAT SPACE COMMUNITY... BLAH BLAH BLAH...
NO ONE NOTICED AS I SHOVED MY WAY THROUGH THE ENTRANCED CROWD...
...NOW LET US PREPARE TO CONTACT THE SUPREME GOVERNOR OF THE TABLE OF THE SEVEN CIVILISED PLANETS...
WHAT? WHERE'S HE GOING?
...OR SO I THOUGHT.
—THIS IS EARTH EMISSARY SIMPSON... OMMMMM... WE ARE AWAITING CONTACT... OMMMMM... IS THE TABLE IN SESSION? — OMMMMM... WHO... WHO... WHO AM I TALKING TO — THIS IS GOLGOS OF THE —
Whew! FINALLY! I'M SURPRISED I MADE IT OUT OF THERE, MISS TANNER. THAT SIMPSON HAS EVERYONE ELSE ENRAPTURED!
YES... YES... HE HAS A POWER... B-BUT, MR. SINKAGE, I WANTED TO TELL YOU THAT WHAT HAPPENED TO YOU... IT WASN'T MY MOTHER'S FAULT. SHE HAS NO CONTROL OVER THOSE MEN—
—YOU COULD HAVE TOLD ME THAT ON THE PHONE. WHY THIS MEETING OUT HERE?
...I HAVE SOMETHING TO SHOW YOU... S-SOMETHING HORRIBLE!
WHERE?
THIS EVENING KEPT GETTING STRANGER AND STRANGER...
...AT LEAST ON THE SURFACE. BUT UNDERNEATH...
—PLANET NEPTUNE! I SPEAK TONIGHT FOR THE TABLE! I COMMEND THIS MAN TO YOU, THIS JEFFREY SIMPSON, FOR ONLY HE HAS POWER TO ENLIGHTEN—
...UNDERNEATH IT ALL WAS A SMELL OF ROT, A DREAD FOREBODING THAT WOULDN'T LET GO OF ME. AND ITS NAME WAS SIMPSON!

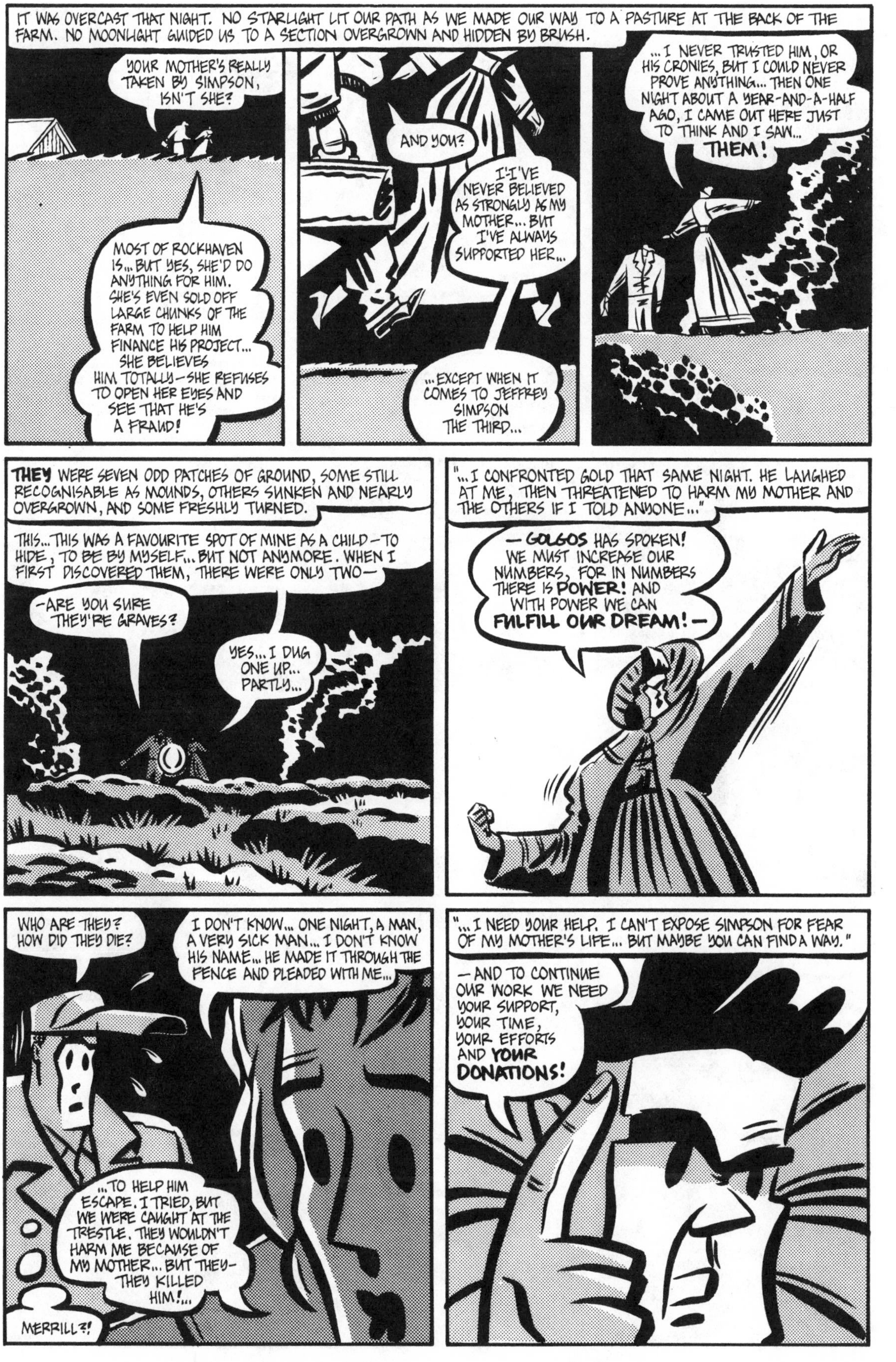
IT WAS OVERCAST THAT NIGHT. NO STARLIGHT LIT OUR PATH AS WE MADE OUR WAY TO A PASTURE AT THE BACK OF THE FARM. NO MOONLIGHT GUIDED US TO A SECTION OVERGROWN AND HIDDEN BY BRUSH.
YOUR MOTHER'S REALLY TAKEN BY SIMPSON, ISN'T SHE?
MOST OF ROCKHAVEN IS... BUT YES, SHE'D DO ANYTHING FOR HIM. SHE'S EVEN SOLD OFF LARGE CHUNKS OF THE FARM TO HELP HIM FINANCE HIS PROJECT... SHE BELIEVES HIM TOTALLY—SHE REFUSES TO OPEN HER EYES AND SEE THAT HE'S A FRAUD!
AND YOU?
I-I'VE NEVER BELIEVED AS STRONGLY AS MY MOTHER... BUT I'VE ALWAYS SUPPORTED HER...
...EXCEPT WHEN IT COMES TO JEFFREY SIMPSON THE THIRD...
... I NEVER TRUSTED HIM, OR HIS CRONIES, BUT I COULD NEVER PROVE ANYTHING... THEN ONE NIGHT ABOUT A YEAR-AND-A-HALF AGO, I CAME OUT HERE JUST TO THINK AND I SAW... THEM!
THEY WERE SEVEN ODD PATCHES OF GROUND, SOME STILL RECOGNISABLE AS MOUNDS, OTHERS SUNKEN AND NEARLY OVERGROWN, AND SOME FRESHLY TURNED.
THIS... THIS WAS A FAVOURITE SPOT OF MINE AS A CHILD—TO HIDE, TO BE BY MYSELF... BUT NOT ANYMORE. WHEN I FIRST DISCOVERED THEM, THERE WERE ONLY TWO—
—ARE YOU SURE THEY'RE GRAVES?
YES... I DUG ONE UP... PARTLY...
"... I CONFRONTED GOLD THAT SAME NIGHT. HE LAUGHED AT ME, THEN THREATENED TO HARM MY MOTHER AND THE OTHERS IF I TOLD ANYONE..."
—GOLGOS HAS SPOKEN! WE MUST INCREASE OUR NUMBERS, FOR IN NUMBERS THERE IS POWER! AND WITH POWER WE CAN FULFILL OUR DREAM!—
WHO ARE THEY? HOW DID THEY DIE?
I DON'T KNOW... ONE NIGHT, A MAN, A VERY SICK MAN... I DON'T KNOW HIS NAME... HE MADE IT THROUGH THE FENCE AND PLEADED WITH ME...
...TO HELP HIM ESCAPE. I TRIED, BUT WE WERE CAUGHT AT THE TRESTLE. THEY WOULDN'T HARM ME BECAUSE OF MY MOTHER... BUT THEY— THEY KILLED HIM!...
MERRILL?!
"... I NEED YOUR HELP. I CAN'T EXPOSE SIMPSON FOR FEAR OF MY MOTHER'S LIFE... BUT MAYBE YOU CAN FIND A WAY."
—AND TO CONTINUE OUR WORK WE NEED YOUR SUPPORT, YOUR TIME, YOUR EFFORTS AND YOUR DONATIONS!

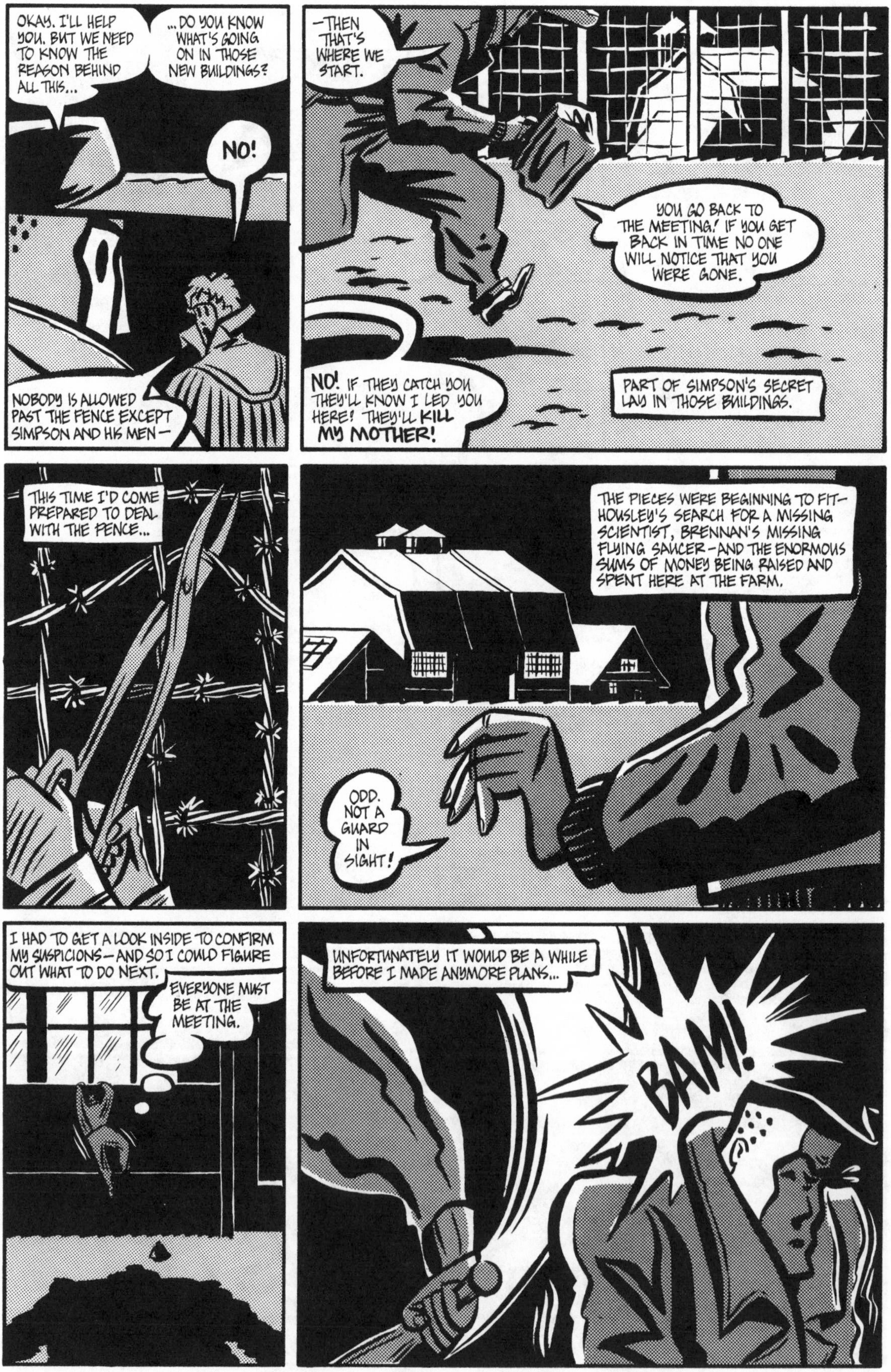
OKAY. I'LL HELP YOU. BUT WE NEED TO KNOW THE REASON BEHIND ALL THIS...
...DO YOU KNOW WHAT'S GOING ON IN THOSE NEW BUILDINGS?
NO!
NOBODY IS ALLOWED PAST THE FENCE EXCEPT SIMPSON AND HIS MEN—
—THEN THAT'S WHERE WE START.
YOU GO BACK TO THE MEETING! IF YOU GET BACK IN TIME NO ONE WILL NOTICE THAT YOU WERE GONE.
NO! IF THEY CATCH YOU THEY'LL KNOW I LED YOU HERE! THEY'LL KILL MY MOTHER!
PART OF SIMPSON'S SECRET LAY IN THOSE BUILDINGS.
THIS TIME I'D COME PREPARED TO DEAL WITH THE FENCE...
THE PIECES WERE BEGINNING TO FIT—HOUSLEY'S SEARCH FOR A MISSING SCIENTIST, BRENNAN'S MISSING FLYING SAUCER—AND THE ENORMOUS SUMS OF MONEY BEING RAISED AND SPENT HERE AT THE FARM.
ODD. NOT A GUARD IN SIGHT!
I HAD TO GET A LOOK INSIDE TO CONFIRM MY SUSPICIONS—AND SO I COULD FIGURE OUT WHAT TO DO NEXT.
EVERYONE MUST BE AT THE MEETING.
UNFORTUNATELY IT WOULD BE A WHILE BEFORE I MADE ANYMORE PLANS...
BAM!

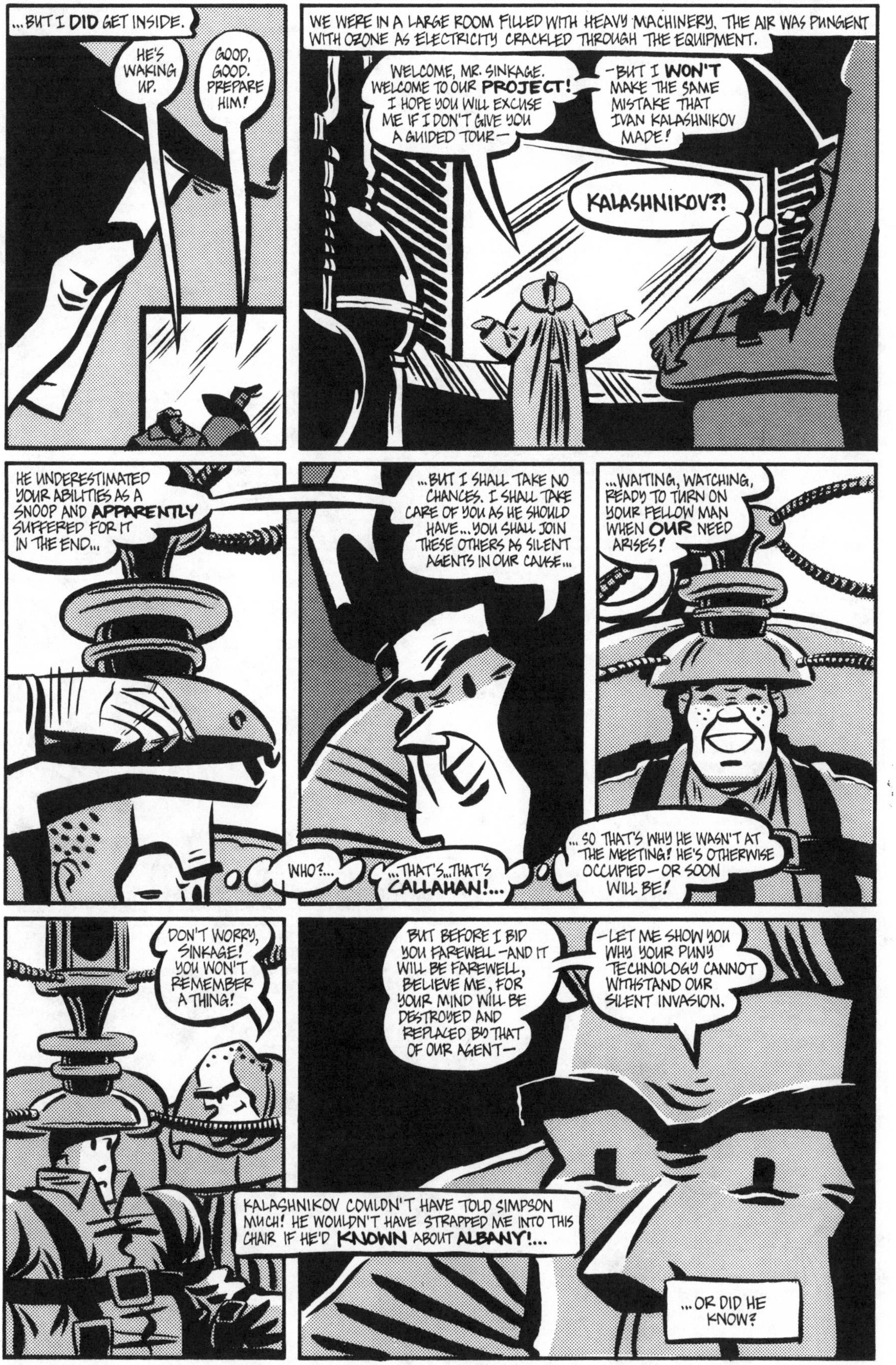
...BUT I DID GET INSIDE.
HE'S WAKING UP.
GOOD, GOOD. PREPARE HIM!
WE WERE IN A LARGE ROOM FILLED WITH HEAVY MACHINERY. THE AIR WAS PUNGENT WITH OZONE AS ELECTRICITY CRACKLED THROUGH THE EQUIPMENT.
WELCOME, MR. SINKAGE. WELCOME TO OUR PROJECT! I HOPE YOU WILL EXCUSE ME IF I DON'T GIVE YOU A GUIDED TOUR—
—BUT I WON'T MAKE THE SAME MISTAKE THAT IVAN KALASHNIKOV MADE!
KALASHNIKOV?!
HE UNDERESTIMATED YOUR ABILITIES AS A SNOOP AND APPARENTLY SUFFERED FOR IT IN THE END...
...BUT I SHALL TAKE NO CHANCES. I SHALL TAKE CARE OF YOU AS HE SHOULD HAVE... YOU SHALL JOIN THESE OTHERS AS SILENT AGENTS IN OUR CAUSE...
...WAITING, WATCHING, READY TO TURN ON YOUR FELLOW MAN WHEN OUR NEED ARISES!
WHO?...
...THAT'S...THAT'S CALLAHAN!...
...SO THAT'S WHY HE WASN'T AT THE MEETING! HE'S OTHERWISE OCCUPIED—OR SOON WILL BE!
DON'T WORRY, SINKAGE! YOU WON'T REMEMBER A THING!
BUT BEFORE I BID YOU FAREWELL —AND IT WILL BE FAREWELL, BELIEVE ME, FOR YOUR MIND WILL BE DESTROYED AND REPLACED BY THAT OF OUR AGENT—
—LET ME SHOW YOU WHY YOUR PUNY TECHNOLOGY CANNOT WITHSTAND OUR SILENT INVASION.
KALASHNIKOV COULDN'T HAVE TOLD SIMPSON MUCH! HE WOULDN'T HAVE STRAPPED ME INTO THIS CHAIR IF HE'D KNOWN ABOUT ALBANY!...
...OR DID HE KNOW?

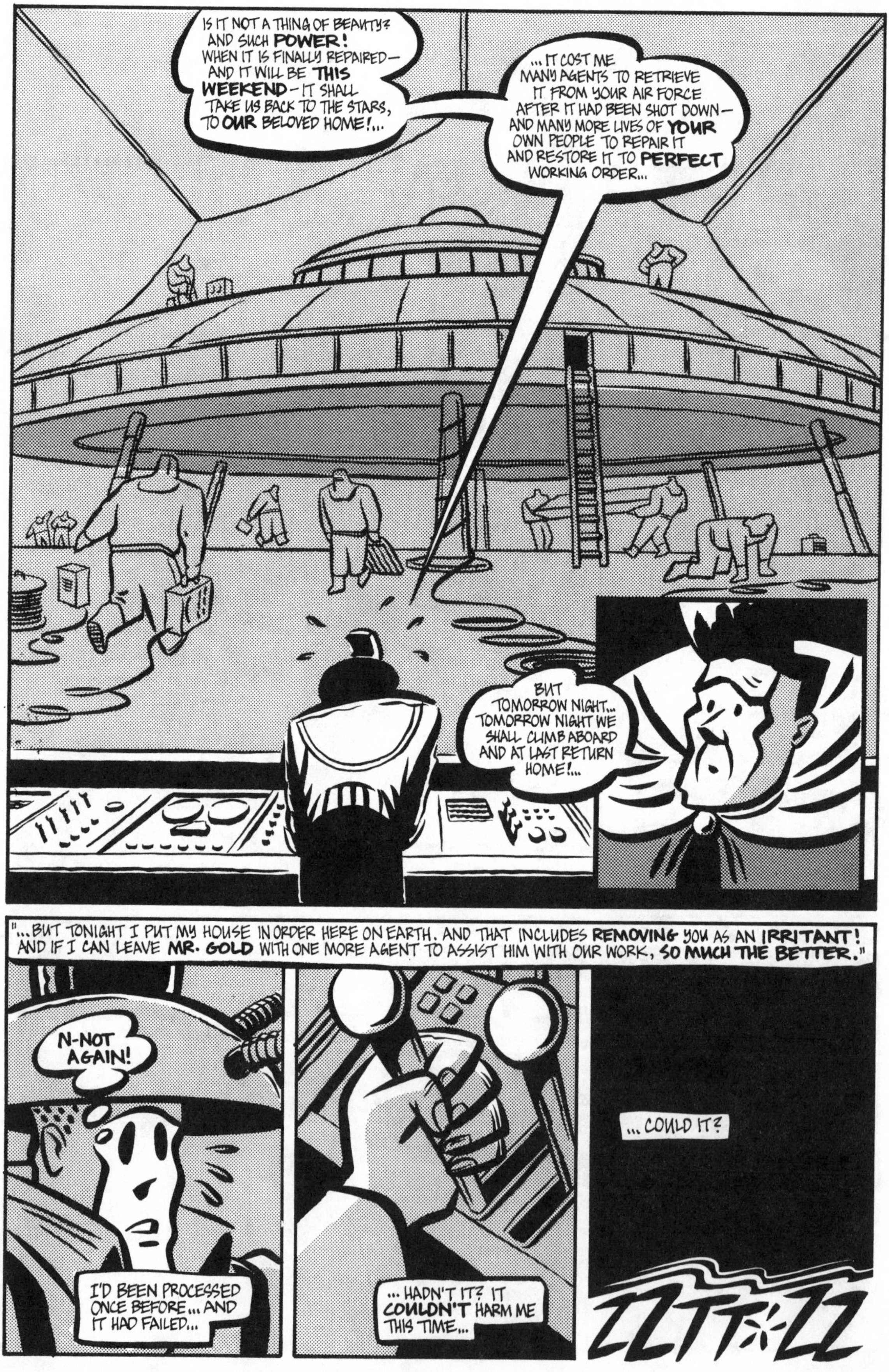
IS IT NOT A THING OF BEAUTY? AND SUCH POWER! WHEN IT IS FINALLY REPAIRED— AND IT WILL BE THIS WEEKEND— IT SHALL TAKE US BACK TO THE STARS, TO OUR BELOVED HOME!...
...IT COST ME MANY AGENTS TO RETRIEVE IT FROM YOUR AIR FORCE AFTER IT HAD BEEN SHOT DOWN— AND MANY MORE LIVES OF YOUR OWN PEOPLE TO REPAIR IT AND RESTORE IT TO PERFECT WORKING ORDER...
BUT TOMORROW NIGHT... TOMORROW NIGHT WE SHALL CLIMB ABOARD AND AT LAST RETURN HOME!...
"...BUT TONIGHT I PUT MY HOUSE IN ORDER HERE ON EARTH. AND THAT INCLUDES REMOVING YOU AS AN IRRITANT! AND IF I CAN LEAVE MR. GOLD WITH ONE MORE AGENT TO ASSIST HIM WITH OUR WORK, SO MUCH THE BETTER."
N-NOT AGAIN!
I'D BEEN PROCESSED ONCE BEFORE... AND IT HAD FAILED...
...HADN'T IT? IT COULDN'T HARM ME THIS TIME...
...COULD IT?
ZZTT*ZZ

CHAPTER THREE
TARNISHED DREAMS

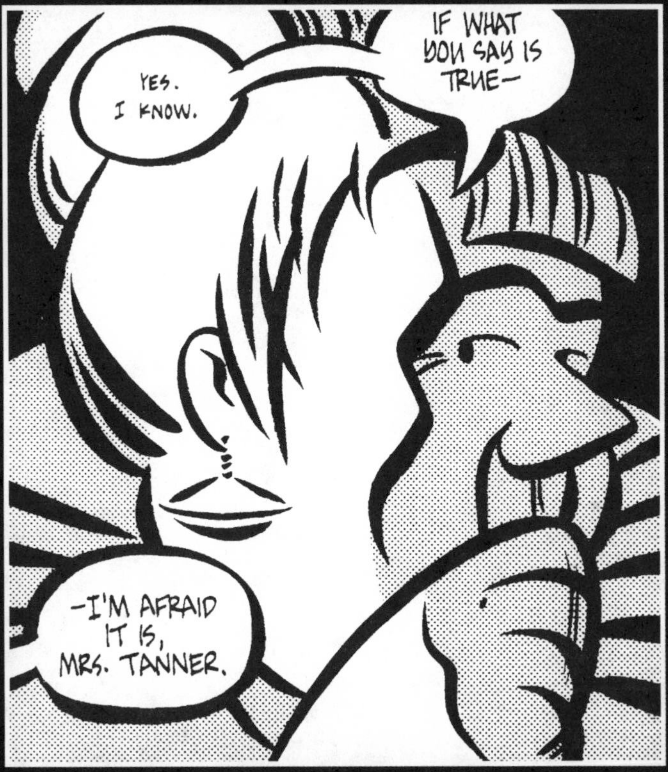
IF WHAT YOU SAY IS TRUE—
YES. I KNOW.
—I'M AFRAID IT IS, MRS. TANNER.

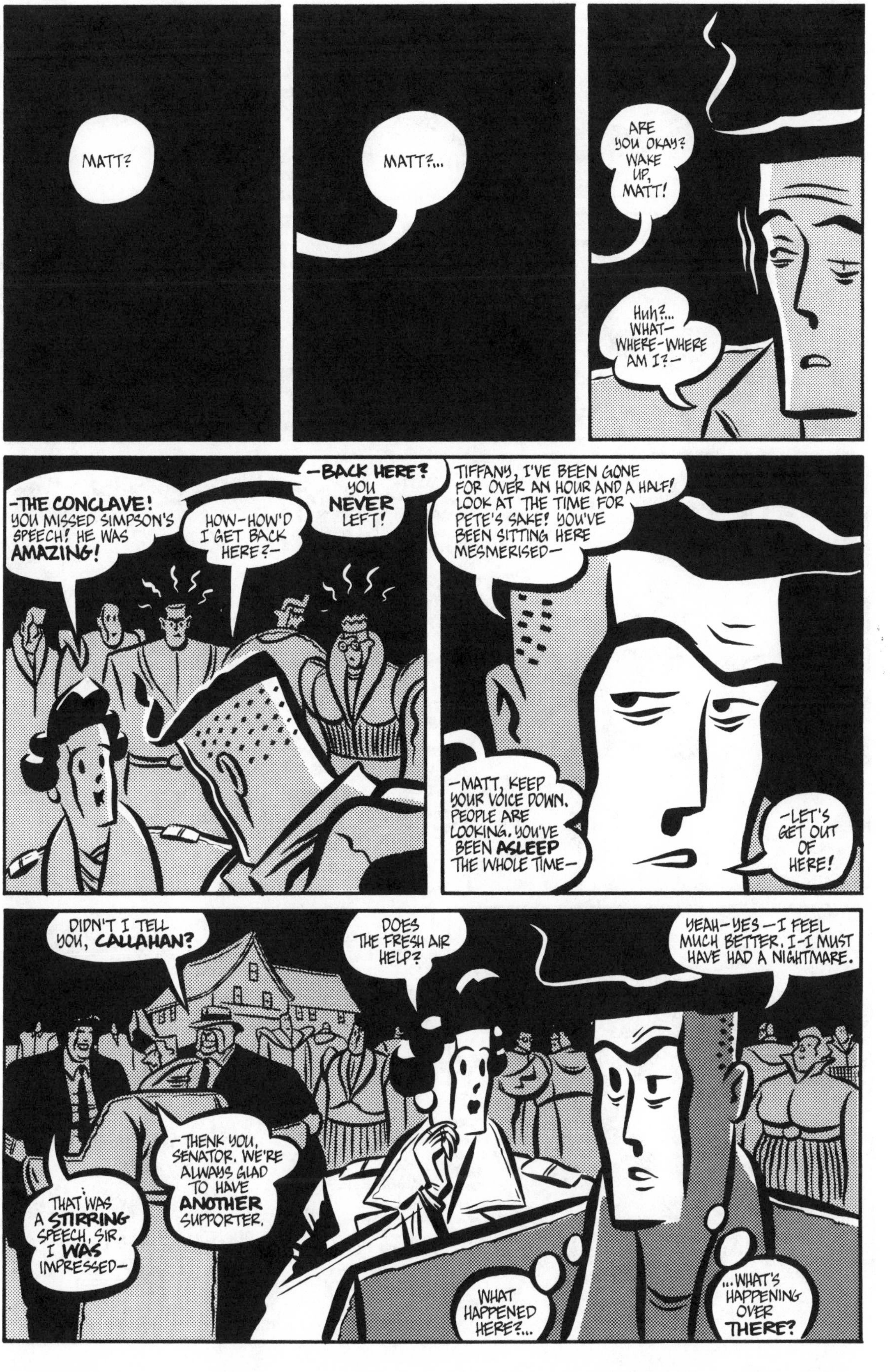
MATT?
MATT?...
ARE YOU OKAY? WAKE UP, MATT!
Huh?... WHAT- WHERE-WHERE AM I?-
-THE CONCLAVE! YOU MISSED SIMPSON'S SPEECH! HE WAS AMAZING!
HOW-HOW'D I GET BACK HERE?-
-BACK HERE? YOU NEVER LEFT!
TIFFANY, I'VE BEEN GONE FOR OVER AN HOUR AND A HALF! LOOK AT THE TIME FOR PETE'S SAKE! YOU'VE BEEN SITTING HERE MESMERISED-
-MATT, KEEP YOUR VOICE DOWN. PEOPLE ARE LOOKING. YOU'VE BEEN ASLEEP THE WHOLE TIME-
-LET'S GET OUT OF HERE!
DIDN'T I TELL YOU, CALLAHAN?
DOES THE FRESH AIR HELP?
YEAH-YES-I FEEL MUCH BETTER. I-I MUST HAVE HAD A NIGHTMARE.
THAT WAS A STIRRING SPEECH, SIR. I WAS IMPRESSED-
-THENK YOU, SENATOR. WE'RE ALWAYS GLAD TO HAVE ANOTHER SUPPORTER.
WHAT HAPPENED HERE?...
...WHAT'S HAPPENING OVER THERE?

THE ROCKHAVEN RANGER. THE NEXT DAY...

WHO WANTS A COFFEE?!

I WAS HAVING A HELL OF A TIME...

?!?

MYRTLE! FIND OUT WHY THAT NEWSPRINT ISN'T HERE YET!

WHAT IS SIMPSON UP TO?

SOME **SHOW** UP AT THE FARM LAST NIGHT, EH, MATT?

NO, SAM! I WON'T GO TO AL'S WITH YOU!

HOW ABOUT YOU, BETSY?

CREEP!

SAME TIME TONIGHT, MATT?

MATT?

GRRRR...

I WASN'T ASLEEP! I'M POSITIVE!

COMIN' TO AL'S AFTER WORK, MATT?

NOT IF I CAN'T GET THIS ARTICLE FINISHED IN TIME!

MATT?

SINKAGE!

THAT MEANS THE GRAVES ARE **REAL**! —UNLESS JANET TANNER IS WRONG...

...BUT IF SHE'S WRONG, THEN WHAT **IS** IN THAT FIELD?

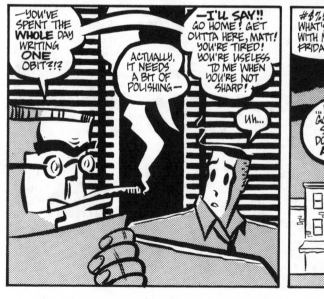

—YOU'VE SPENT THE **WHOLE** DAY WRITING **ONE** OBIT?!?

ACTUALLY, IT NEEDS A BIT OF POLISHING—

—I'LL SAY!! GO HOME! GET OUTTA HERE, MATT! YOU'RE TIRED! YOU'RE USELESS TO ME WHEN YOU'RE NOT SHARP!

Uh...

#$%!!%‡# WHAT'S WRONG WITH ME? IT'S FRIDAY...

...I SHOULD RELAX... UNWIND A BIT... FORGET ABOUT MRS. TANNER...

...WHAT AM I GOING TO DO ABOUT SIMPSON? OR DO I HAVE TO DO **ANYTHING**?

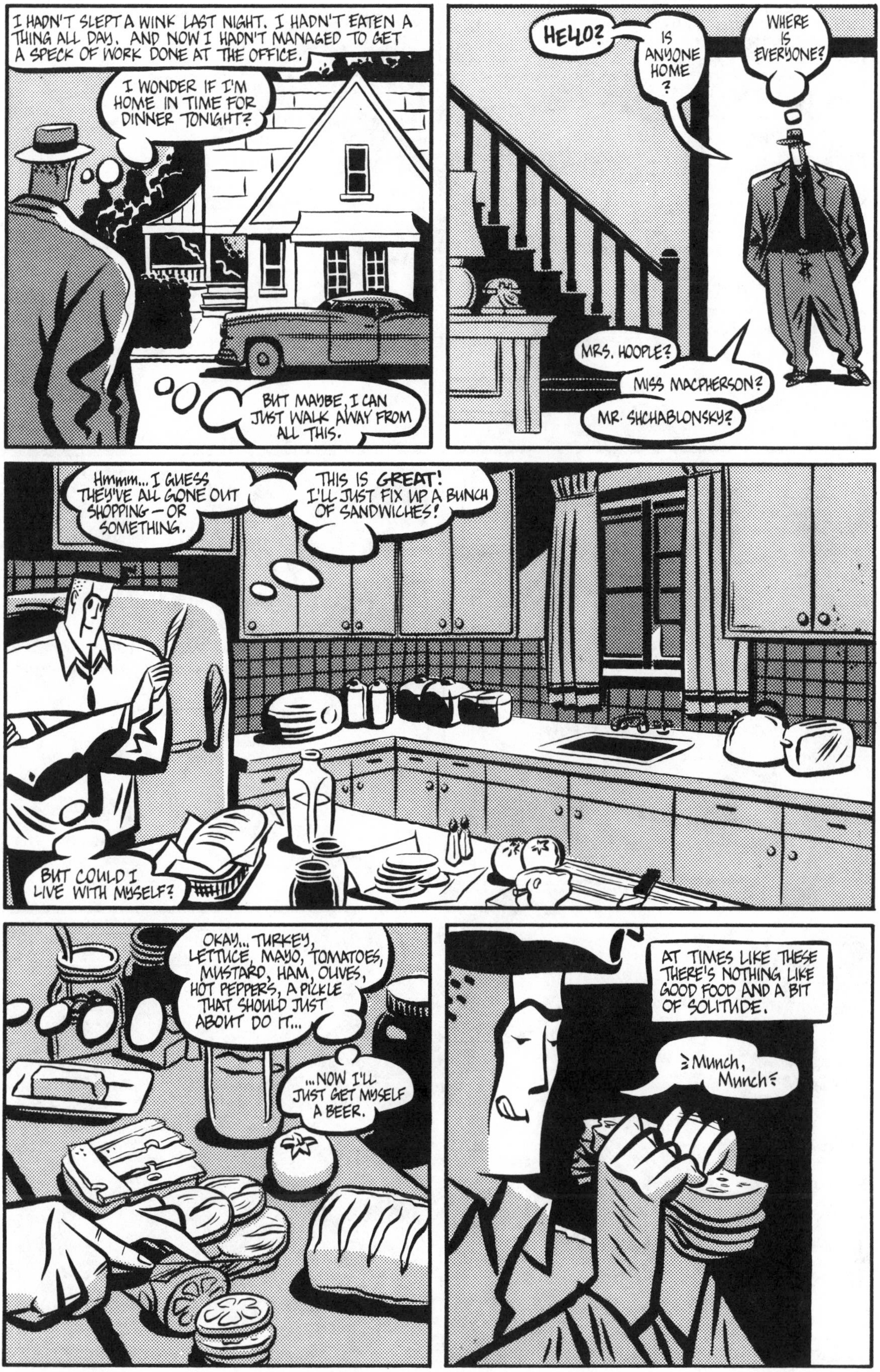

I HADN'T SLEPT A WINK LAST NIGHT. I HADN'T EATEN A THING ALL DAY. AND NOW I HADN'T MANAGED TO GET A SPECK OF WORK DONE AT THE OFFICE.
I WONDER IF I'M HOME IN TIME FOR DINNER TONIGHT?
BUT MAYBE, I CAN JUST WALK AWAY FROM ALL THIS.
HELLO?
IS ANYONE HOME ?
WHERE IS EVERYONE?
MRS. HOOPLE?
MISS MACPHERSON?
MR. SHCHABLONSKY?
Hmmm... I GUESS THEY'VE ALL GONE OUT SHOPPING — OR SOMETHING.
THIS IS GREAT! I'LL JUST FIX UP A BUNCH OF SANDWICHES!
BUT COULD I LIVE WITH MYSELF?
OKAY... TURKEY, LETTUCE, MAYO, TOMATOES, MUSTARD, HAM, OLIVES, HOT PEPPERS, A PICKLE THAT SHOULD JUST ABOUT DO IT...
...NOW I'LL JUST GET MYSELF A BEER.
AT TIMES LIKE THESE THERE'S NOTHING LIKE GOOD FOOD AND A BIT OF SOLITUDE.
Munch, Munch

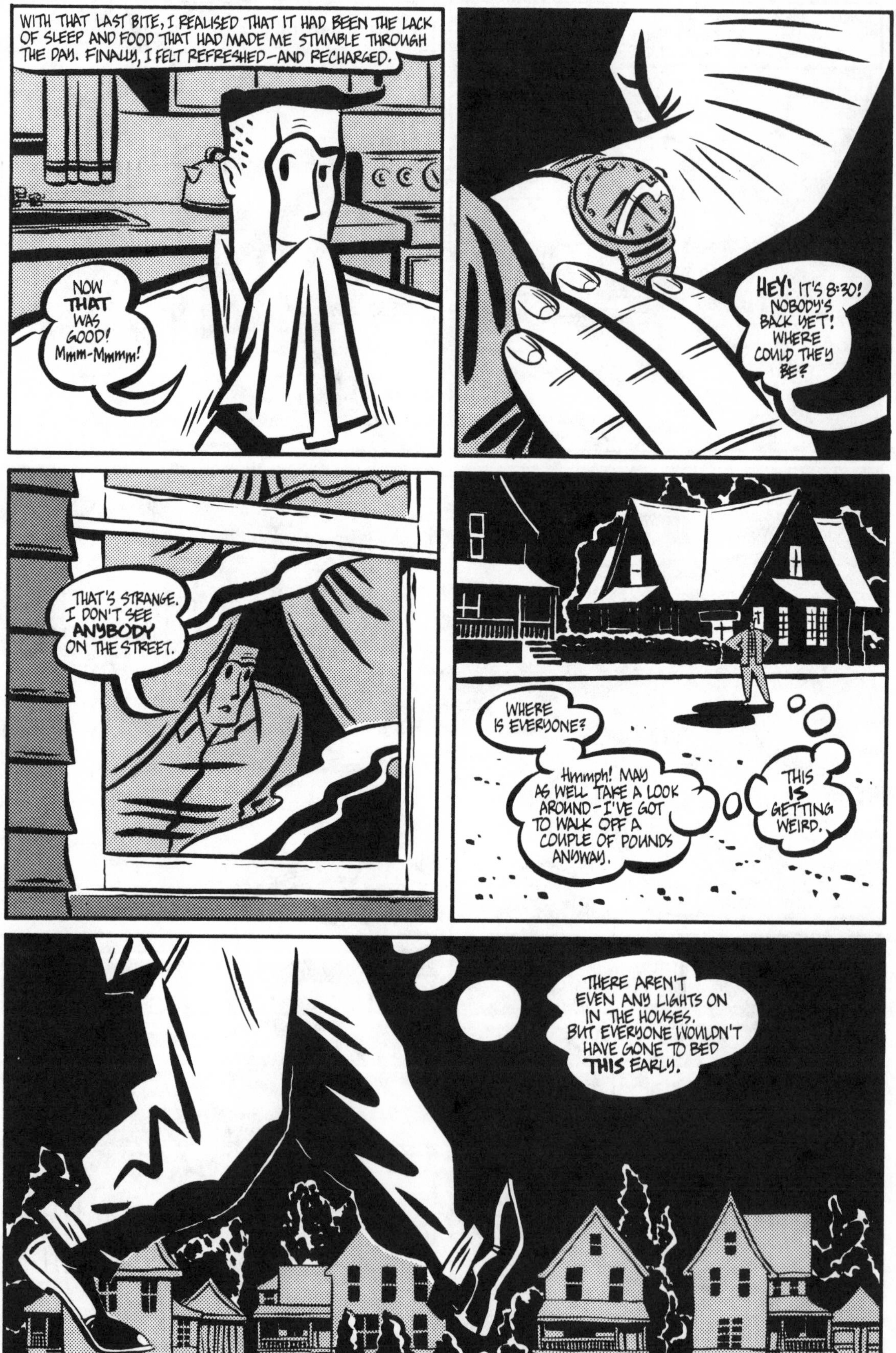
WITH THAT LAST BITE, I REALISED THAT IT HAD BEEN THE LACK OF SLEEP AND FOOD THAT HAD MADE ME STUMBLE THROUGH THE DAY. FINALLY, I FELT REFRESHED—AND RECHARGED.
NOW THAT WAS GOOD! Mmm-Mmmm!
HEY! IT'S 8:30! NOBODY'S BACK YET! WHERE COULD THEY BE?
THAT'S STRANGE. I DON'T SEE ANYBODY ON THE STREET.
WHERE IS EVERYONE?
Hmmph! MAY AS WELL TAKE A LOOK AROUND—I'VE GOT TO WALK OFF A COUPLE OF POUNDS ANYWAY.
THIS IS GETTING WEIRD.
THERE AREN'T EVEN ANY LIGHTS ON IN THE HOUSES. BUT EVERYONE WOULDN'T HAVE GONE TO BED THIS EARLY.

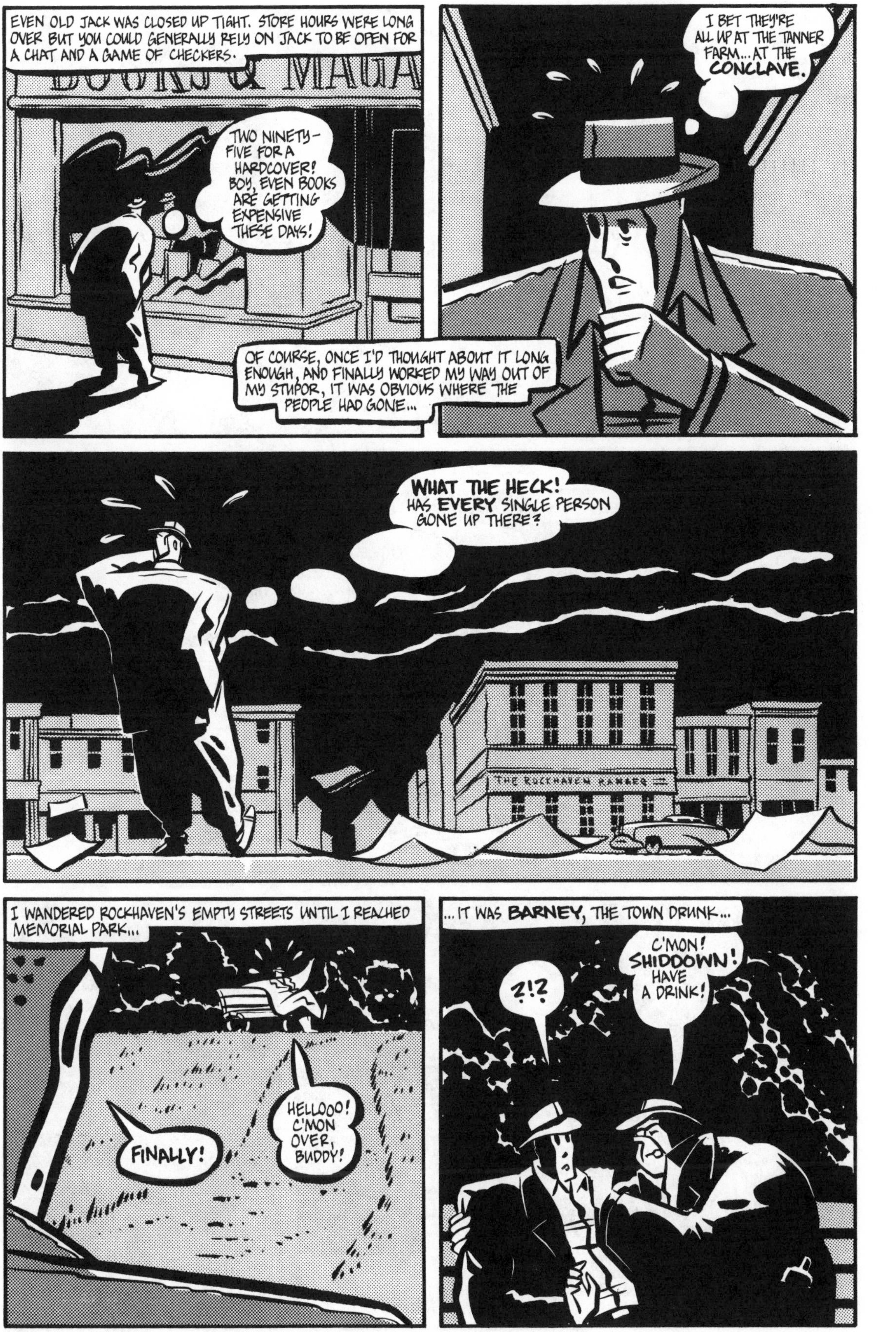
EVEN OLD JACK WAS CLOSED UP TIGHT. STORE HOURS WERE LONG OVER BUT YOU COULD GENERALLY RELY ON JACK TO BE OPEN FOR A CHAT AND A GAME OF CHECKERS.
TWO NINETY-FIVE FOR A HARDCOVER! BOY, EVEN BOOKS ARE GETTING EXPENSIVE THESE DAYS!
I BET THEY'RE ALL UP AT THE TANNER FARM... AT THE CONCLAVE.
OF COURSE, ONCE I'D THOUGHT ABOUT IT LONG ENOUGH, AND FINALLY WORKED MY WAY OUT OF MY STUPOR, IT WAS OBVIOUS WHERE THE PEOPLE HAD GONE...
WHAT THE HECK! HAS EVERY SINGLE PERSON GONE UP THERE?
THE ROCKHAVEN RANGER
I WANDERED ROCKHAVEN'S EMPTY STREETS UNTIL I REACHED MEMORIAL PARK...
HELLOOO! C'MON OVER, BUDDY!
FINALLY!
... IT WAS BARNEY, THE TOWN DRUNK...
?!?
C'MON! SHIDDOWN! HAVE A DRINK!

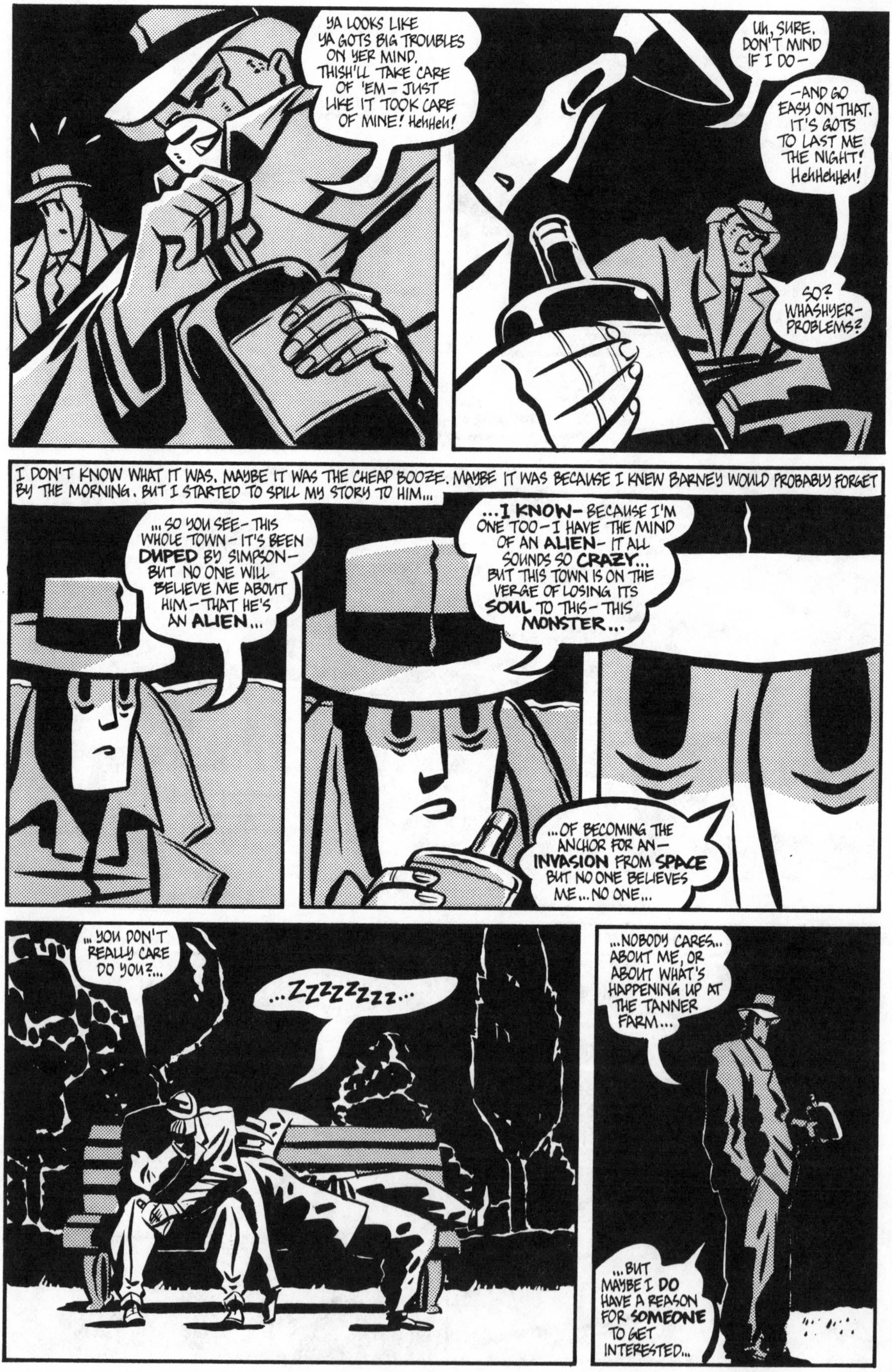
YA LOOKS LIKE YA GOTS BIG TROUBLES ON YER MIND. THISH'LL TAKE CARE OF 'EM— JUST LIKE IT TOOK CARE OF MINE! HehHeh!
Uh, SURE. DON'T MIND IF I DO—
—AND GO EASY ON THAT. IT'S GOTS TO LAST ME THE NIGHT! HehHehHeh!
SO? WHASHYER-PROBLEMS?
I DON'T KNOW WHAT IT WAS. MAYBE IT WAS THE CHEAP BOOZE. MAYBE IT WAS BECAUSE I KNEW BARNEY WOULD PROBABLY FORGET BY THE MORNING. BUT I STARTED TO SPILL MY STORY TO HIM...
... SO YOU SEE— THIS WHOLE TOWN— IT'S BEEN DUPED BY SIMPSON— BUT NO ONE WILL BELIEVE ME ABOUT HIM— THAT HE'S AN ALIEN...
...I KNOW— BECAUSE I'M ONE TOO— I HAVE THE MIND OF AN ALIEN— IT ALL SOUNDS SO CRAZY... BUT THIS TOWN IS ON THE VERGE OF LOSING ITS SOUL TO THIS— THIS MONSTER...
...OF BECOMING THE ANCHOR FOR AN— INVASION FROM SPACE BUT NO ONE BELIEVES ME... NO ONE...
... YOU DON'T REALLY CARE DO YOU?...
...ZZZZZZZZ...
...NOBODY CARES... ABOUT ME, OR ABOUT WHAT'S HAPPENING UP AT THE TANNER FARM...
...BUT MAYBE I DO HAVE A REASON FOR SOMEONE TO GET INTERESTED...

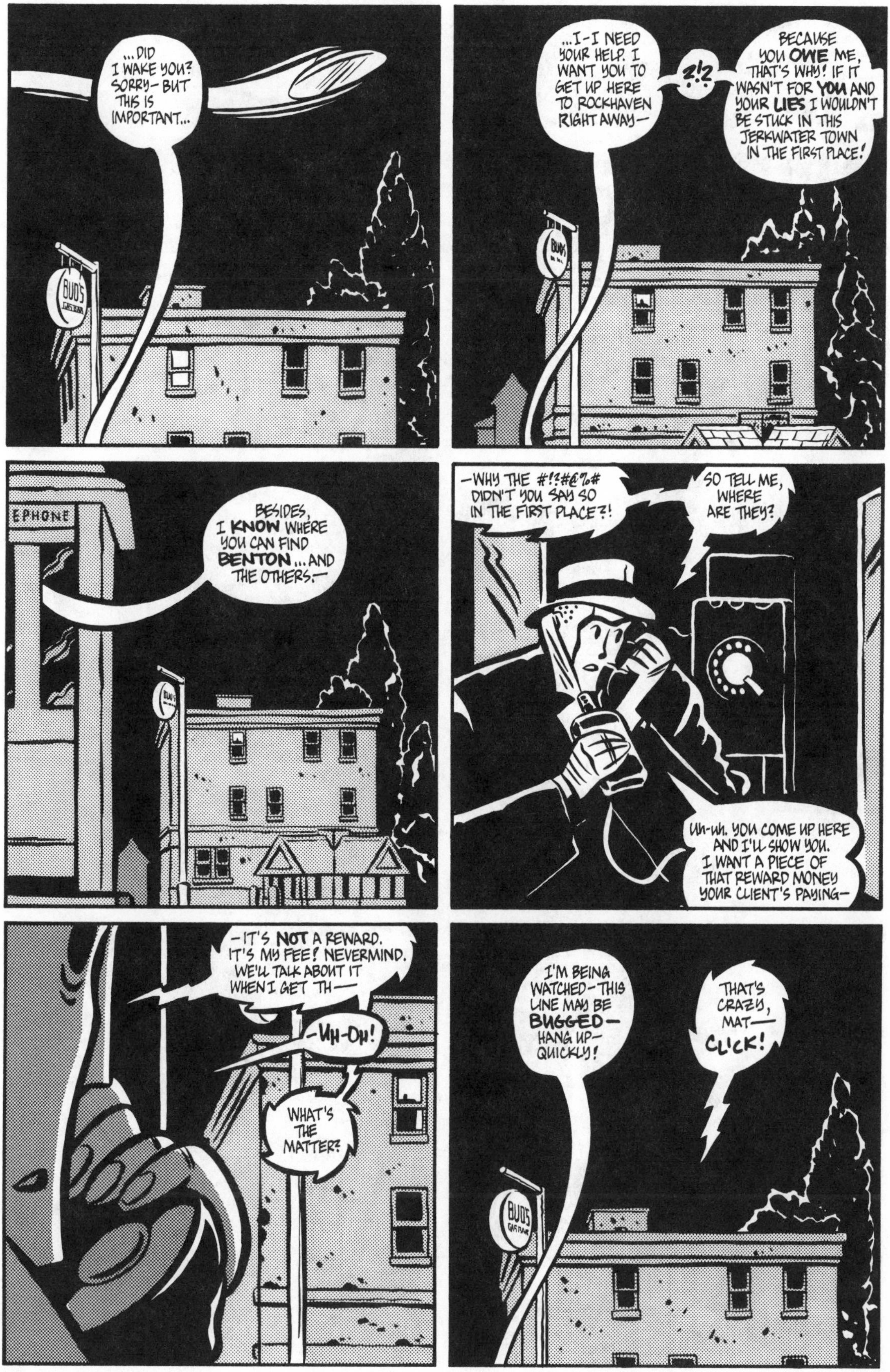
...DID I WAKE YOU? SORRY– BUT THIS IS IMPORTANT...
BUD'S
...I-I NEED YOUR HELP. I WANT YOU TO GET UP HERE TO ROCKHAVEN RIGHT AWAY–
?!?
BECAUSE YOU OWE ME, THAT'S WHY! IF IT WASN'T FOR YOU AND YOUR LIES I WOULDN'T BE STUCK IN THIS JERKWATER TOWN IN THE FIRST PLACE!
EPHONE
BESIDES, I KNOW WHERE YOU CAN FIND BENTON...AND THE OTHERS.–
–WHY THE #!?#@%# DIDN'T YOU SAY SO IN THE FIRST PLACE?!
SO TELL ME, WHERE ARE THEY?
UH-UH. YOU COME UP HERE AND I'LL SHOW YOU. I WANT A PIECE OF THAT REWARD MONEY YOUR CLIENT'S PAYING–
–IT'S NOT A REWARD. IT'S MY FEE! NEVERMIND. WE'LL TALK ABOUT IT WHEN I GET TH—
–UH-OH!
WHAT'S THE MATTER?
I'M BEING WATCHED–THIS LINE MAY BE BUGGED–HANG UP–QUICKLY!
THAT'S CRAZY, MAT—
CLICK!
BUD'S

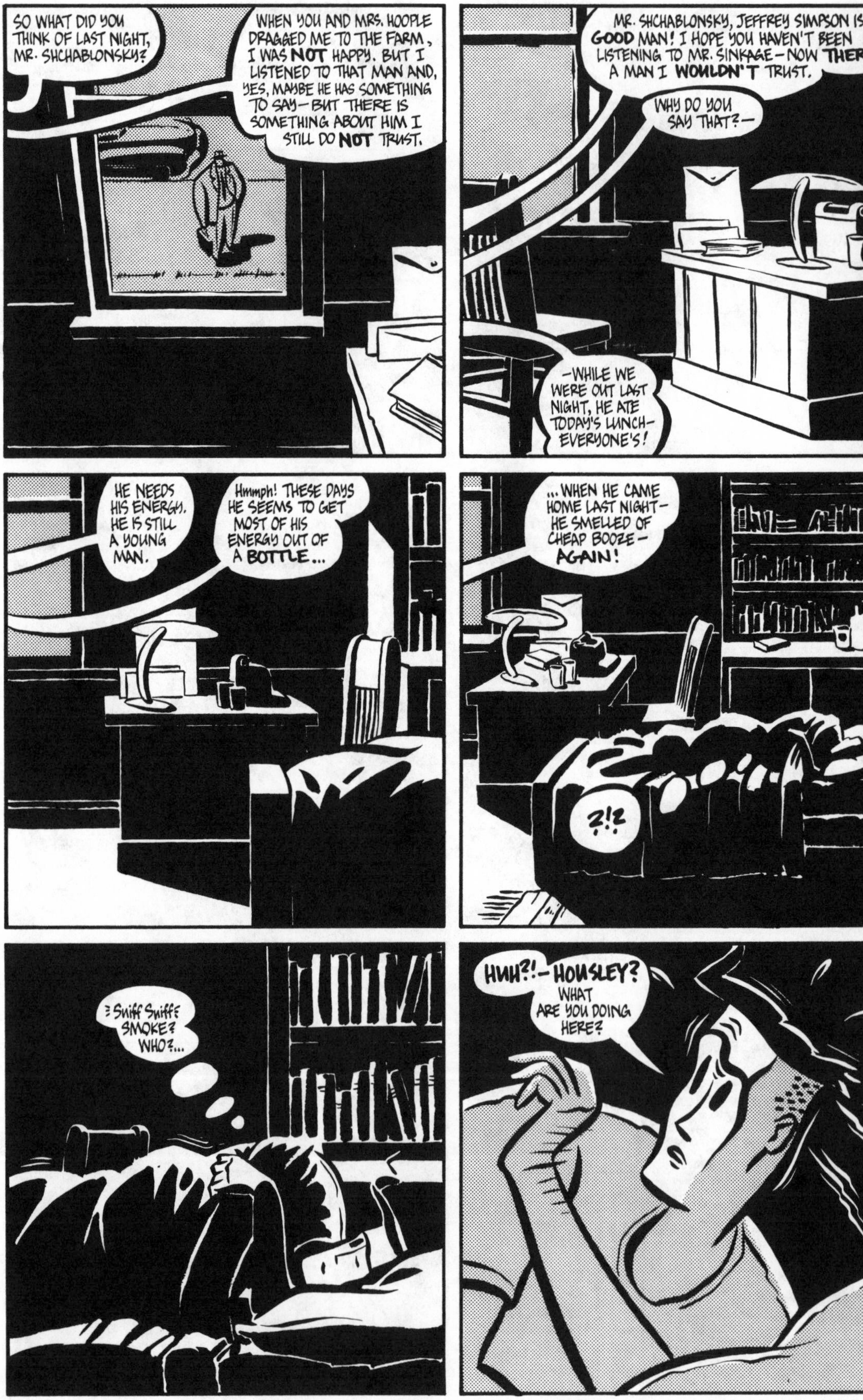
SO WHAT DID YOU THINK OF LAST NIGHT, MR. SHCHABLONSKY?
WHEN YOU AND MRS. HOOPLE DRAGGED ME TO THE FARM, I WAS NOT HAPPY. BUT I LISTENED TO THAT MAN AND, YES, MAYBE HE HAS SOMETHING TO SAY—BUT THERE IS SOMETHING ABOUT HIM I STILL DO NOT TRUST.
MR. SHCHABLONSKY, JEFFREY SIMPSON IS A GOOD MAN! I HOPE YOU HAVEN'T BEEN LISTENING TO MR. SINKAGE—NOW THERE'S A MAN I WOULDN'T TRUST.
WHY DO YOU SAY THAT?—
—WHILE WE WERE OUT LAST NIGHT, HE ATE TODAY'S LUNCH—EVERYONE'S!
HE NEEDS HIS ENERGY. HE IS STILL A YOUNG MAN.
Hmmph! THESE DAYS HE SEEMS TO GET MOST OF HIS ENERGY OUT OF A BOTTLE...
...WHEN HE CAME HOME LAST NIGHT—HE SMELLED OF CHEAP BOOZE—AGAIN!
?!?
Sniff Sniff SMOKE? WHO?...
HUH?!—HOUSLEY? WHAT ARE YOU DOING HERE?

YOU SAID YOU NEEDED MY HELP. HERE I AM.

YOU MUST HAVE DRIVEN ALL NIGHT!—

HELL, NO. LOOK AT YOUR WATCH—IT'S PAST NOON. YOU MUST HAVE TIED ONE ON PRETTY GOOD LAST NIGHT...

...MAYBE I SHOULD LEAVE. YOU WERE OBVIOUSLY DRUNK WHEN YOU CALLED ME—

—NO! WAIT! DON'T GO! I DO KNOW WHERE BENTON IS—AND I NEED YOUR HELP TO PROTECT MRS. TANNER—

—THE CRAZY WOMAN UP AT THE FARM?

SHE'S NO MORE CRAZY THAN I AM.

YOU SAID IT—NOT ME. NOW GET YOUR PANTS ON AND LET'S GO FIND BENTON.

YOU DON'T UNDERSTAND, DO YOU? YOU FIGURE THIS IS A ROUTINE MISSING PERSON CASE...

...IT'S NOT.

I TOLD HOUSLEY WHAT JANET TANNER HAD TOLD ME ABOUT SIMPSON AND THE HOLD THAT HE HAD ON HER MOTHER.

?!?

...BENTON AND MERRILL ARE VICTIMS OF AN INSIDIOUS ALIEN PLOT TO TAKE OVER THE WORLD— DON'T LAUGH—AND MRS. TANNER AND JANET COULD BE THE NEXT VICTIMS. UNLESS WE DO SOMETHING.

I ALSO TOLD HIM ABOUT THE CONCLAVE MEETING ON THURSDAY NIGHT— AND MY MEETING WITH JANET...

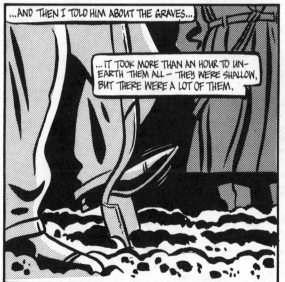

...AND THEN I TOLD HIM ABOUT THE GRAVES...

...IT TOOK MORE THAN AN HOUR TO UN-EARTH THEM ALL—THEY WERE SHALLOW, BUT THERE WERE A LOT OF THEM.

THAT'S THE LAST OF THEM.

WHOEVER BURIED THESE BODIES TOSSED QUICK LIME IN WITH THEM—NO WAY TO TELL WHO THEY WERE...

...EXCEPT FOR THE LAST THREE— THE FRESHEST. I'M SURE THIS ONE IS SELBY FROM UNIVERSAL ELECTRONICS... THE OTHER GUY I DON'T KNOW... YOU RECOGNISE THE KID?

YEAH. TOMMY CLEAVER.

MY STOMACH HEAVED.

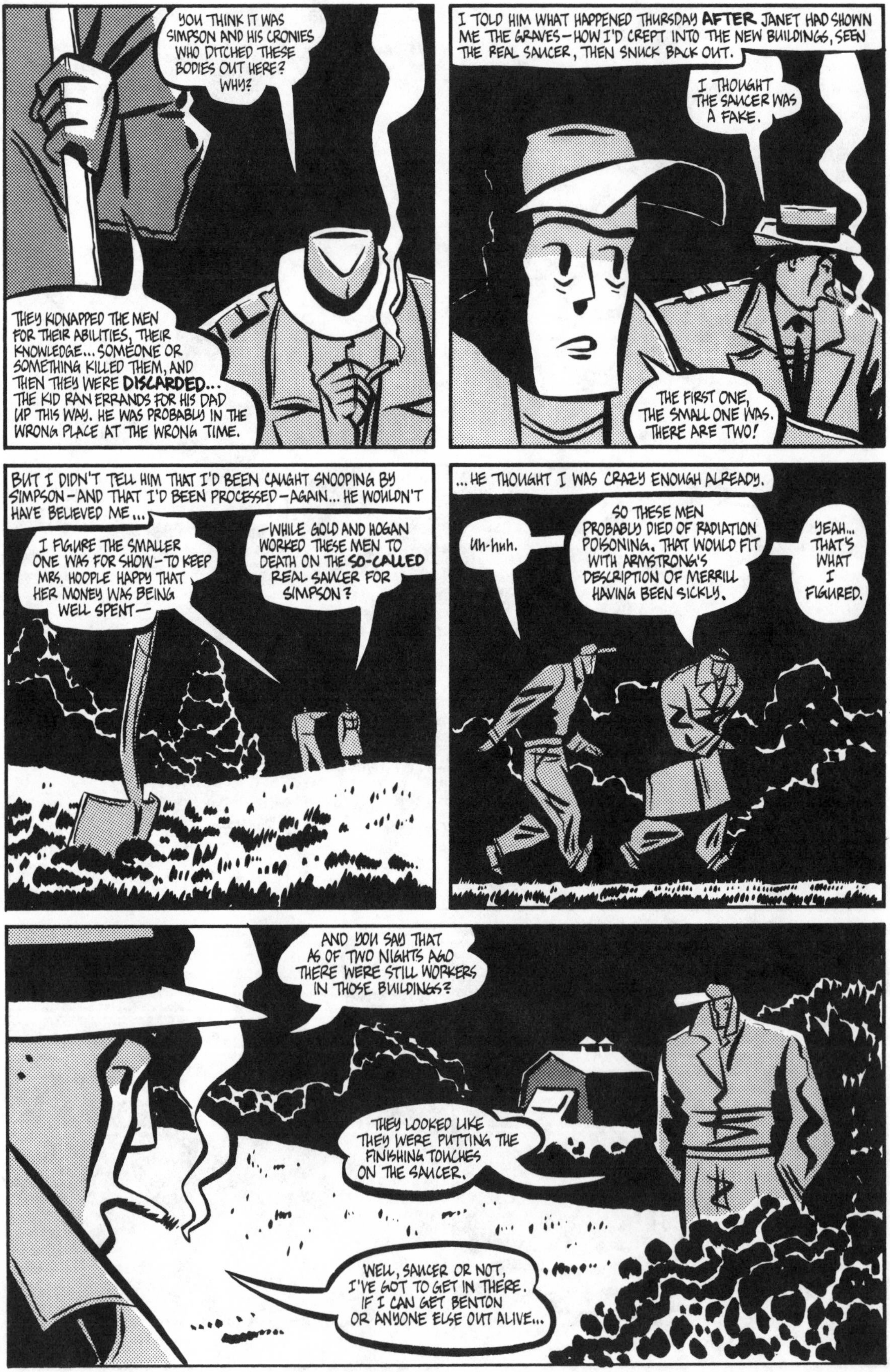
YOU THINK IT WAS SIMPSON AND HIS CRONIES WHO DITCHED THESE BODIES OUT HERE? WHY?
THEY KIDNAPPED THE MEN FOR THEIR ABILITIES, THEIR KNOWLEDGE... SOMEONE OR SOMETHING KILLED THEM, AND THEN THEY WERE **DISCARDED**... THE KID RAN ERRANDS FOR HIS DAD UP THIS WAY. HE WAS PROBABLY IN THE WRONG PLACE AT THE WRONG TIME.
I TOLD HIM WHAT HAPPENED THURSDAY **AFTER** JANET HAD SHOWN ME THE GRAVES—HOW I'D CREPT INTO THE NEW BUILDINGS, SEEN THE REAL SAUCER, THEN SNUCK BACK OUT.
I THOUGHT THE SAUCER WAS A FAKE.
THE FIRST ONE, THE SMALL ONE WAS. THERE ARE TWO!
BUT I DIDN'T TELL HIM THAT I'D BEEN CAUGHT SNOOPING BY SIMPSON—AND THAT I'D BEEN PROCESSED—AGAIN... HE WOULDN'T HAVE BELIEVED ME...
I FIGURE THE SMALLER ONE WAS FOR SHOW—TO KEEP MRS. HOOPLE HAPPY THAT HER MONEY WAS BEING WELL SPENT—
—WHILE GOLD AND HOGAN WORKED THESE MEN TO DEATH ON THE **SO-CALLED** REAL SAUCER FOR SIMPSON?
...HE THOUGHT I WAS CRAZY ENOUGH ALREADY.
Uh-huh.
SO THESE MEN PROBABLY DIED OF RADIATION POISONING. THAT WOULD FIT WITH ARMSTRONG'S DESCRIPTION OF MERRILL HAVING BEEN SICKLY.
YEAH... THAT'S WHAT I FIGURED.
AND YOU SAY THAT AS OF TWO NIGHTS AGO THERE WERE STILL WORKERS IN THOSE BUILDINGS?
THEY LOOKED LIKE THEY WERE PUTTING THE FINISHING TOUCHES ON THE SAUCER.
WELL, SAUCER OR NOT, I'VE GOT TO GET IN THERE. IF I CAN GET BENTON OR ANYONE ELSE OUT ALIVE...

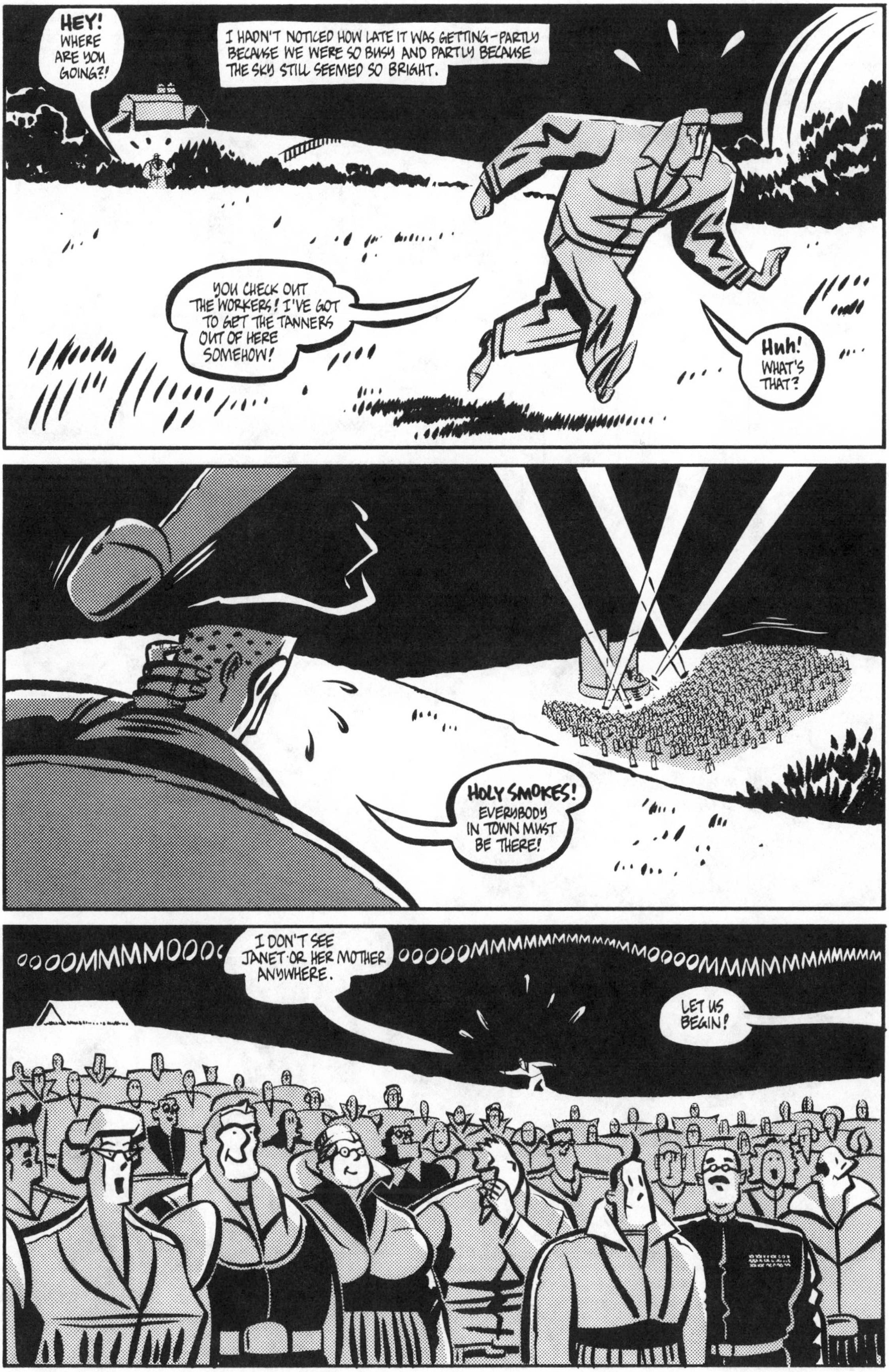
HEY! WHERE ARE YOU GOING?!
I HADN'T NOTICED HOW LATE IT WAS GETTING—PARTLY BECAUSE WE WERE SO BUSY AND PARTLY BECAUSE THE SKY STILL SEEMED SO BRIGHT.
YOU CHECK OUT THE WORKERS! I'VE GOT TO GET THE TANNERS OUT OF HERE SOMEHOW!
Huh! WHAT'S THAT?
HOLY SMOKES! EVERYBODY IN TOWN MUST BE THERE!
OOOOMMMMOOOO
I DON'T SEE JANET OR HER MOTHER ANYWHERE.
OOOOOMMMMMMMMMMMOOOOMMMMMMMMMM
LET US BEGIN!

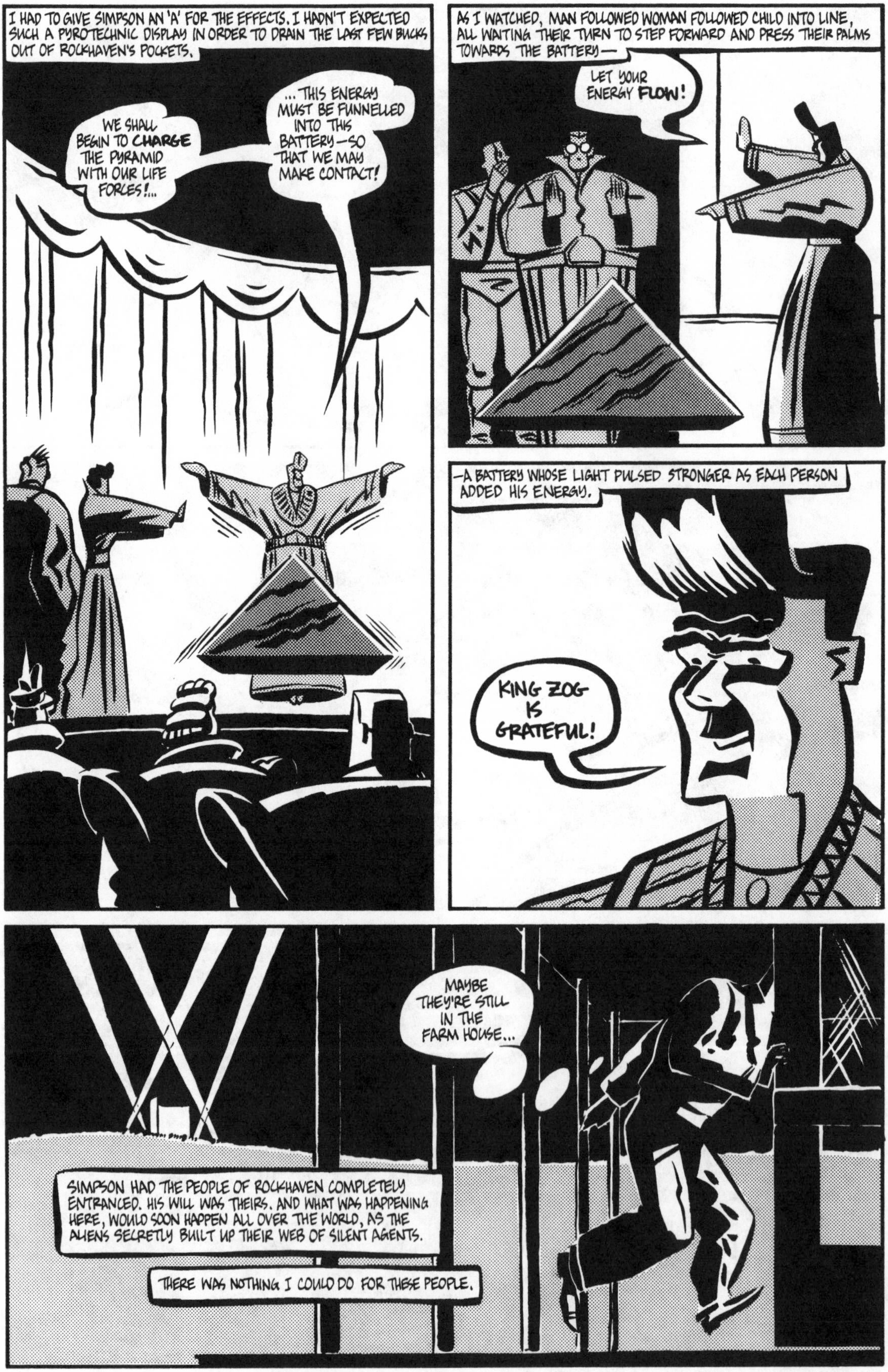
I HAD TO GIVE SIMPSON AN 'A' FOR THE EFFECTS. I HADN'T EXPECTED SUCH A PYROTECHNIC DISPLAY IN ORDER TO DRAIN THE LAST FEW BUCKS OUT OF ROCKHAVEN'S POCKETS.
WE SHALL BEGIN TO CHARGE THE PYRAMID WITH OUR LIFE FORCES!...
... THIS ENERGY MUST BE FUNNELLED INTO THIS BATTERY—SO THAT WE MAY MAKE CONTACT!
AS I WATCHED, MAN FOLLOWED WOMAN FOLLOWED CHILD INTO LINE, ALL WAITING THEIR TURN TO STEP FORWARD AND PRESS THEIR PALMS TOWARDS THE BATTERY—
LET YOUR ENERGY FLOW!
—A BATTERY WHOSE LIGHT PULSED STRONGER AS EACH PERSON ADDED HIS ENERGY.
KING ZOG IS GRATEFUL!
MAYBE THEY'RE STILL IN THE FARM HOUSE...
SIMPSON HAD THE PEOPLE OF ROCKHAVEN COMPLETELY ENTRANCED. HIS WILL WAS THEIRS. AND WHAT WAS HAPPENING HERE, WOULD SOON HAPPEN ALL OVER THE WORLD, AS THE ALIENS SECRETLY BUILT UP THEIR WEB OF SILENT AGENTS.
THERE WAS NOTHING I COULD DO FOR THESE PEOPLE.

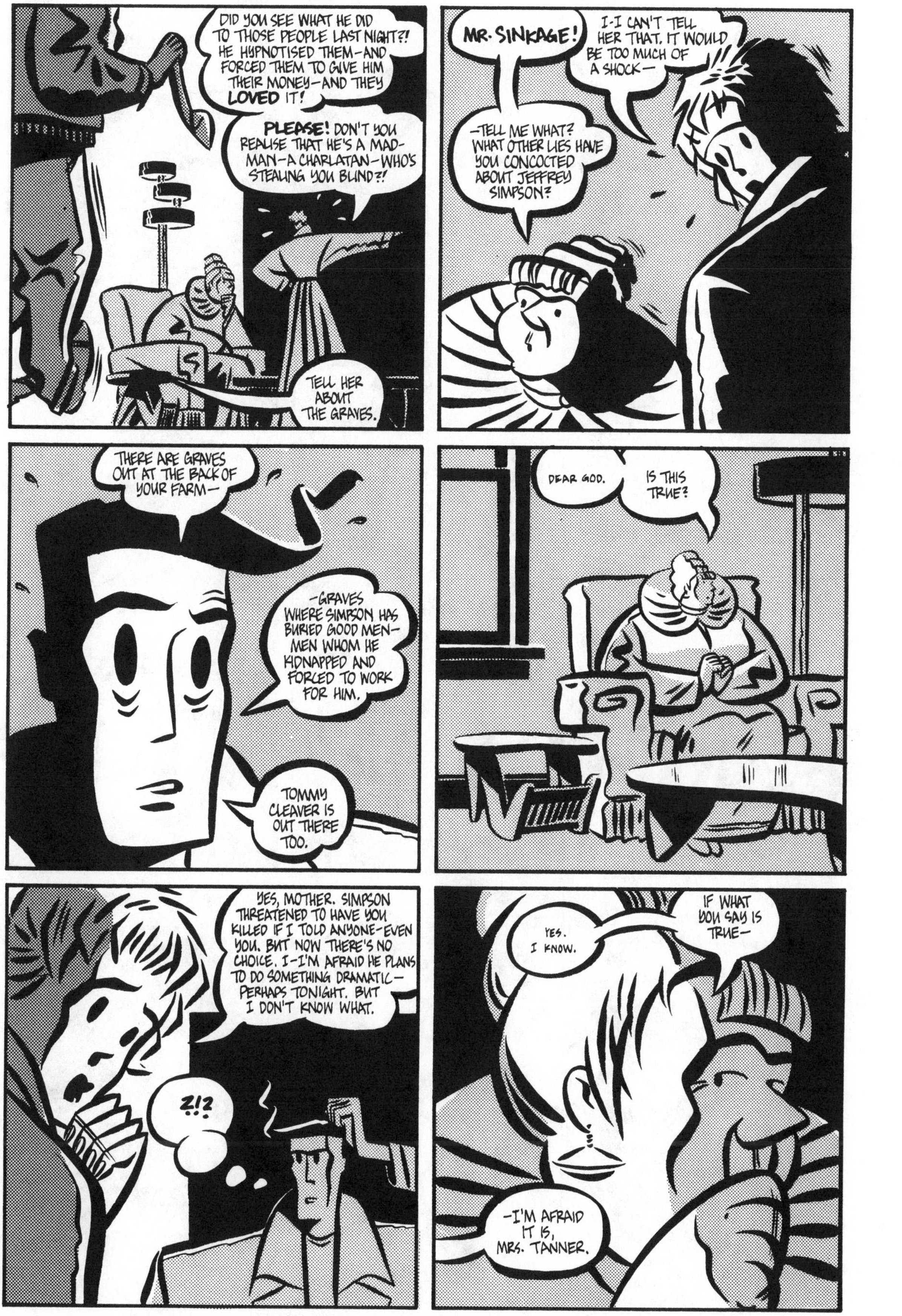
DID YOU SEE WHAT HE DID TO THOSE PEOPLE LAST NIGHT?! HE HYPNOTISED THEM—AND FORCED THEM TO GIVE HIM THEIR MONEY—AND THEY LOVED IT!
PLEASE! DON'T YOU REALISE THAT HE'S A MAD-MAN—A CHARLATAN—WHO'S STEALING YOU BLIND?!
TELL HER ABOUT THE GRAVES.
MR. SINKAGE!
I-I CAN'T TELL HER THAT. IT WOULD BE TOO MUCH OF A SHOCK—
—TELL ME WHAT? WHAT OTHER LIES HAVE YOU CONCOCTED ABOUT JEFFREY SIMPSON?
THERE ARE GRAVES OUT AT THE BACK OF YOUR FARM—
—GRAVES WHERE SIMPSON HAS BURIED GOOD MEN—MEN WHOM HE KIDNAPPED AND FORCED TO WORK FOR HIM.
TOMMY CLEAVER IS OUT THERE TOO.
DEAR GOD.
IS THIS TRUE?
YES, MOTHER. SIMPSON THREATENED TO HAVE YOU KILLED IF I TOLD ANYONE—EVEN YOU. BUT NOW THERE'S NO CHOICE. I-I'M AFRAID HE PLANS TO DO SOMETHING DRAMATIC—PERHAPS TONIGHT. BUT I DON'T KNOW WHAT.
?!?
IF WHAT YOU SAY IS TRUE—
YES. I KNOW.
—I'M AFRAID IT IS, MRS. TANNER.

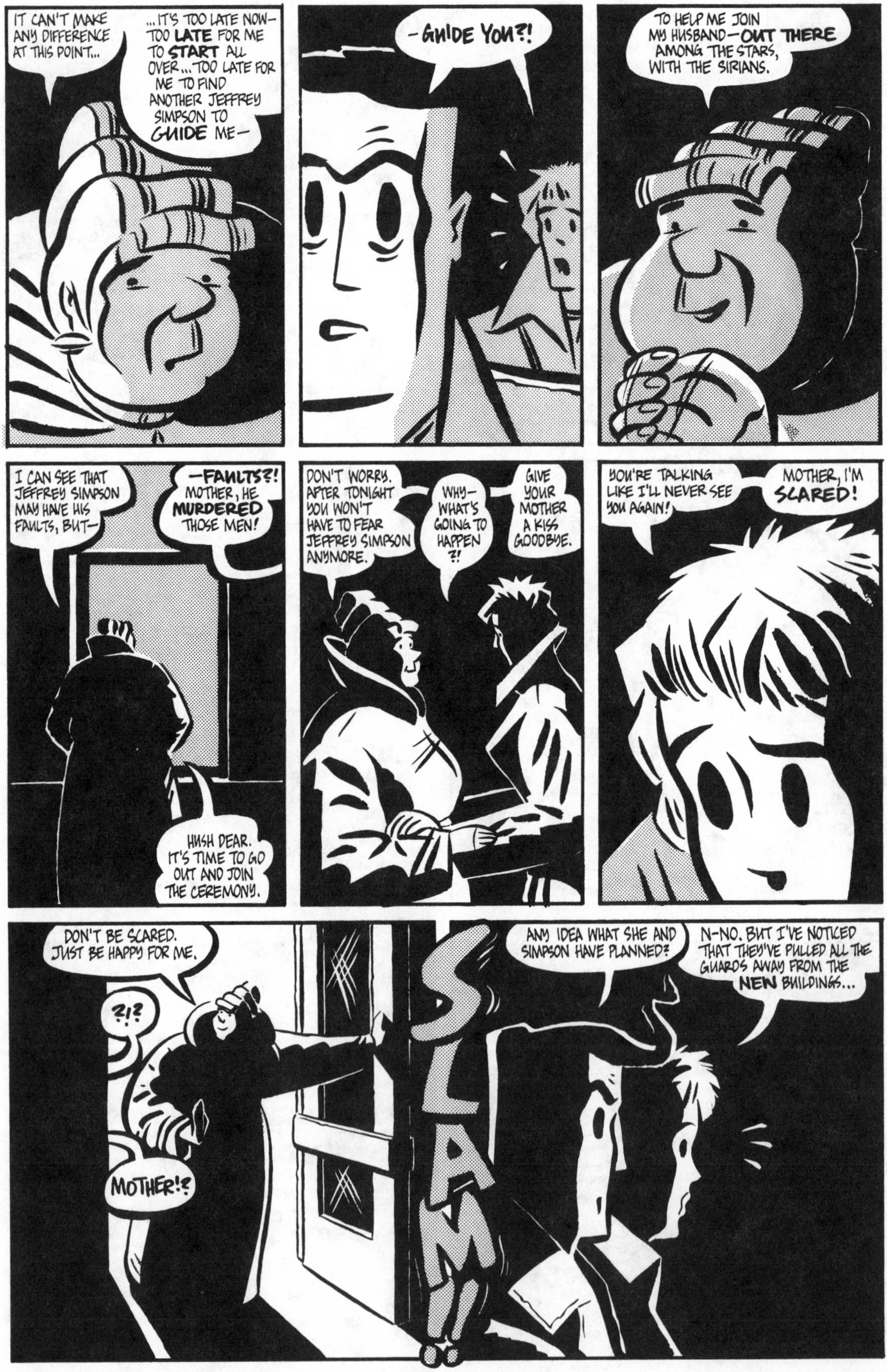
IT CAN'T MAKE ANY DIFFERENCE AT THIS POINT...
...IT'S TOO LATE NOW—TOO LATE FOR ME TO START ALL OVER...TOO LATE FOR ME TO FIND ANOTHER JEFFREY SIMPSON TO GUIDE ME—
—GUIDE YOU?!
TO HELP ME JOIN MY HUSBAND—OUT THERE AMONG THE STARS, WITH THE SIRIANS.
I CAN SEE THAT JEFFREY SIMPSON MAY HAVE HIS FAULTS, BUT—
—FAULTS?! MOTHER, HE MURDERED THOSE MEN!
HUSH DEAR. IT'S TIME TO GO OUT AND JOIN THE CEREMONY.
DON'T WORRY. AFTER TONIGHT YOU WON'T HAVE TO FEAR JEFFREY SIMPSON ANYMORE.
WHY—WHAT'S GOING TO HAPPEN ?!
GIVE YOUR MOTHER A KISS GOODBYE.
YOU'RE TALKING LIKE I'LL NEVER SEE YOU AGAIN!
MOTHER, I'M SCARED!
DON'T BE SCARED. JUST BE HAPPY FOR ME.
?!?
MOTHER!?
SLAM
ANY IDEA WHAT SHE AND SIMPSON HAVE PLANNED?
N-NO. BUT I'VE NOTICED THAT THEY'VE PULLED ALL THE GUARDS AWAY FROM THE NEW BUILDINGS...

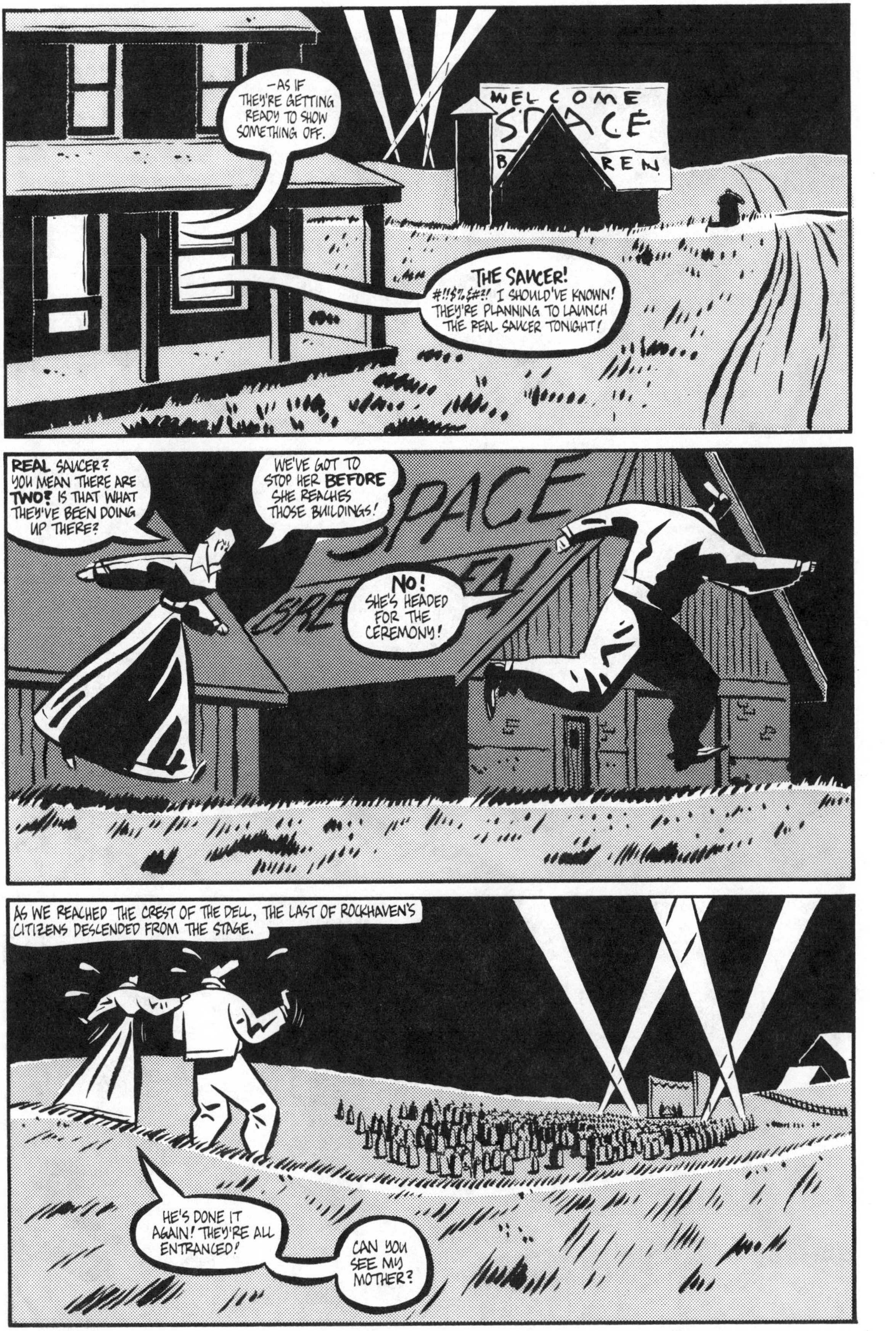

—AS IF THEY'RE GETTING READY TO SHOW SOMETHING OFF.
WELCOME SPACE B REN
THE SAUCER! #!!$%&#?! I SHOULD'VE KNOWN! THEY'RE PLANNING TO LAUNCH THE REAL SAUCER TONIGHT!
REAL SAUCER? YOU MEAN THERE ARE TWO? IS THAT WHAT THEY'VE BEEN DOING UP THERE?
WE'VE GOT TO STOP HER BEFORE SHE REACHES THOSE BUILDINGS!
SPACE
NO! SHE'S HEADED FOR THE CEREMONY!
AS WE REACHED THE CREST OF THE DELL, THE LAST OF ROCKHAVEN'S CITIZENS DESCENDED FROM THE STAGE.
HE'S DONE IT AGAIN! THEY'RE ALL ENTRANCED!
CAN YOU SEE MY MOTHER?

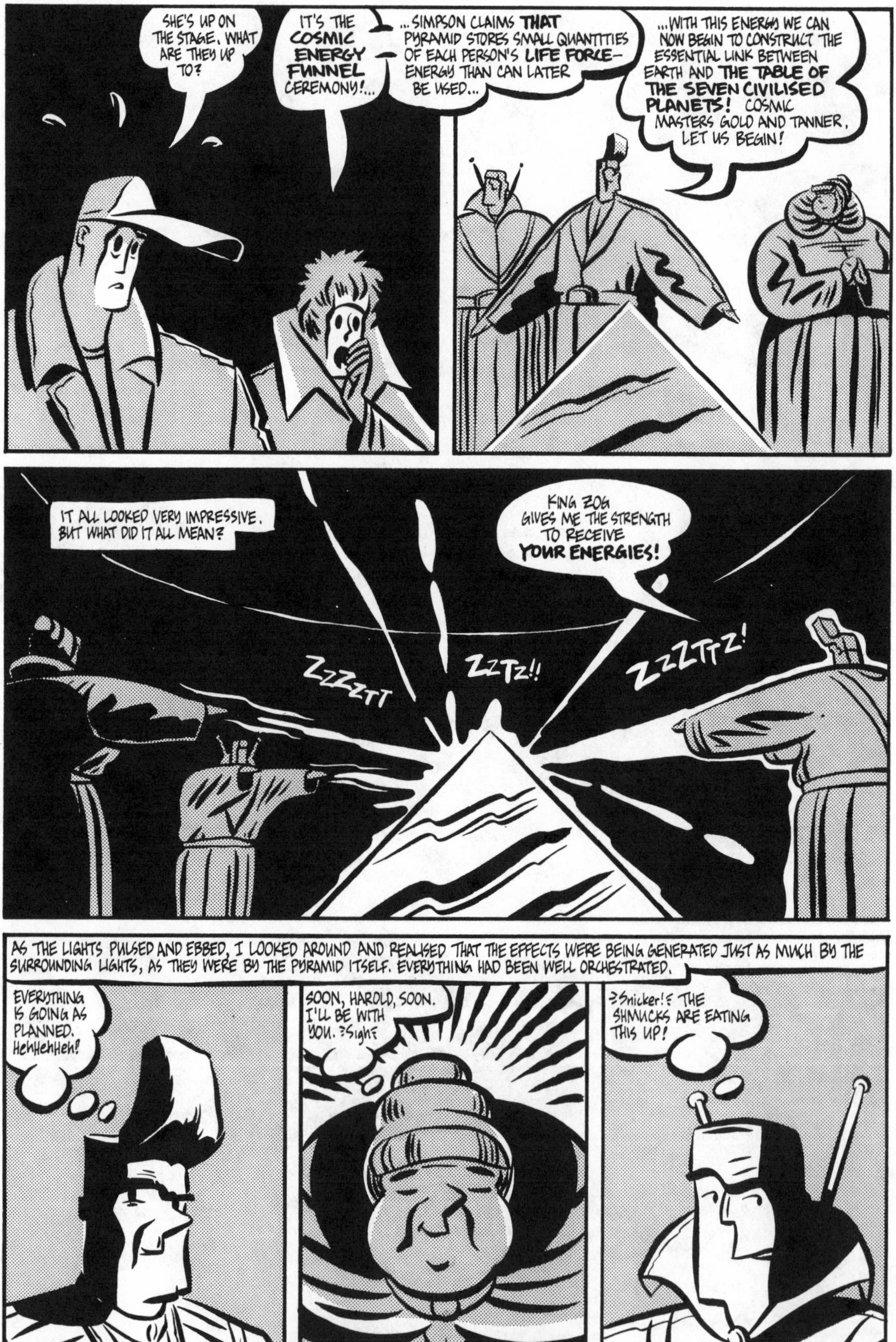
SHE'S UP ON THE STAGE. WHAT ARE THEY UP TO?
IT'S THE COSMIC ENERGY FUNNEL CEREMONY!...
...SIMPSON CLAIMS THAT PYRAMID STORES SMALL QUANTITIES OF EACH PERSON'S LIFE FORCE– ENERGY THAN CAN LATER BE USED...
...WITH THIS ENERGY WE CAN NOW BEGIN TO CONSTRUCT THE ESSENTIAL LINK BETWEEN EARTH AND THE TABLE OF THE SEVEN CIVILISED PLANETS! COSMIC MASTERS GOLD AND TANNER, LET US BEGIN!
IT ALL LOOKED VERY IMPRESSIVE. BUT WHAT DID IT ALL MEAN?
KING ZOG GIVES ME THE STRENGTH TO RECEIVE YOUR ENERGIES!
ZZZZTT
ZZTZ!!
ZZZTTZ!
AS THE LIGHTS PULSED AND EBBED, I LOOKED AROUND AND REALISED THAT THE EFFECTS WERE BEING GENERATED JUST AS MUCH BY THE SURROUNDING LIGHTS, AS THEY WERE BY THE PYRAMID ITSELF. EVERYTHING HAD BEEN WELL ORCHESTRATED.
EVERYTHING IS GOING AS PLANNED. HehHehHeh!
SOON, HAROLD, SOON. I'LL BE WITH YOU. ≷Sigh≶
≷Snicker!≶ THE SHMUCKS ARE EATING THIS UP!

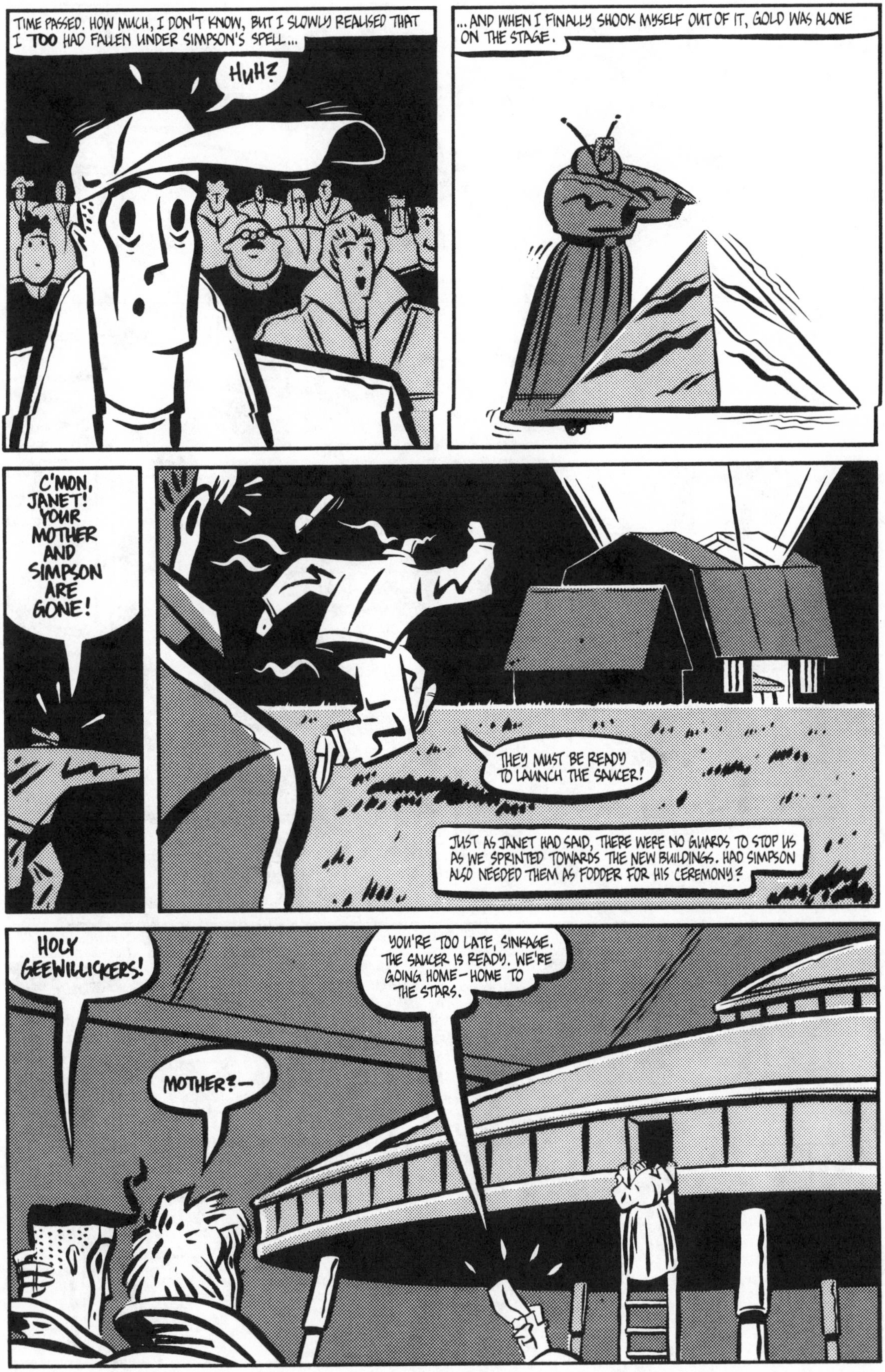

TIME PASSED. HOW MUCH, I DON'T KNOW, BUT I SLOWLY REALISED THAT I TOO HAD FALLEN UNDER SIMPSON'S SPELL...
HUH?
...AND WHEN I FINALLY SHOOK MYSELF OUT OF IT, GOLD WAS ALONE ON THE STAGE.
C'MON, JANET! YOUR MOTHER AND SIMPSON ARE GONE!
THEY MUST BE READY TO LAUNCH THE SAUCER!
JUST AS JANET HAD SAID, THERE WERE NO GUARDS TO STOP US AS WE SPRINTED TOWARDS THE NEW BUILDINGS. HAD SIMPSON ALSO NEEDED THEM AS FODDER FOR HIS CEREMONY?
HOLY GEEWILLICKERS!
YOU'RE TOO LATE, SINKAGE. THE SAUCER IS READY. WE'RE GOING HOME—HOME TO THE STARS.
MOTHER?—

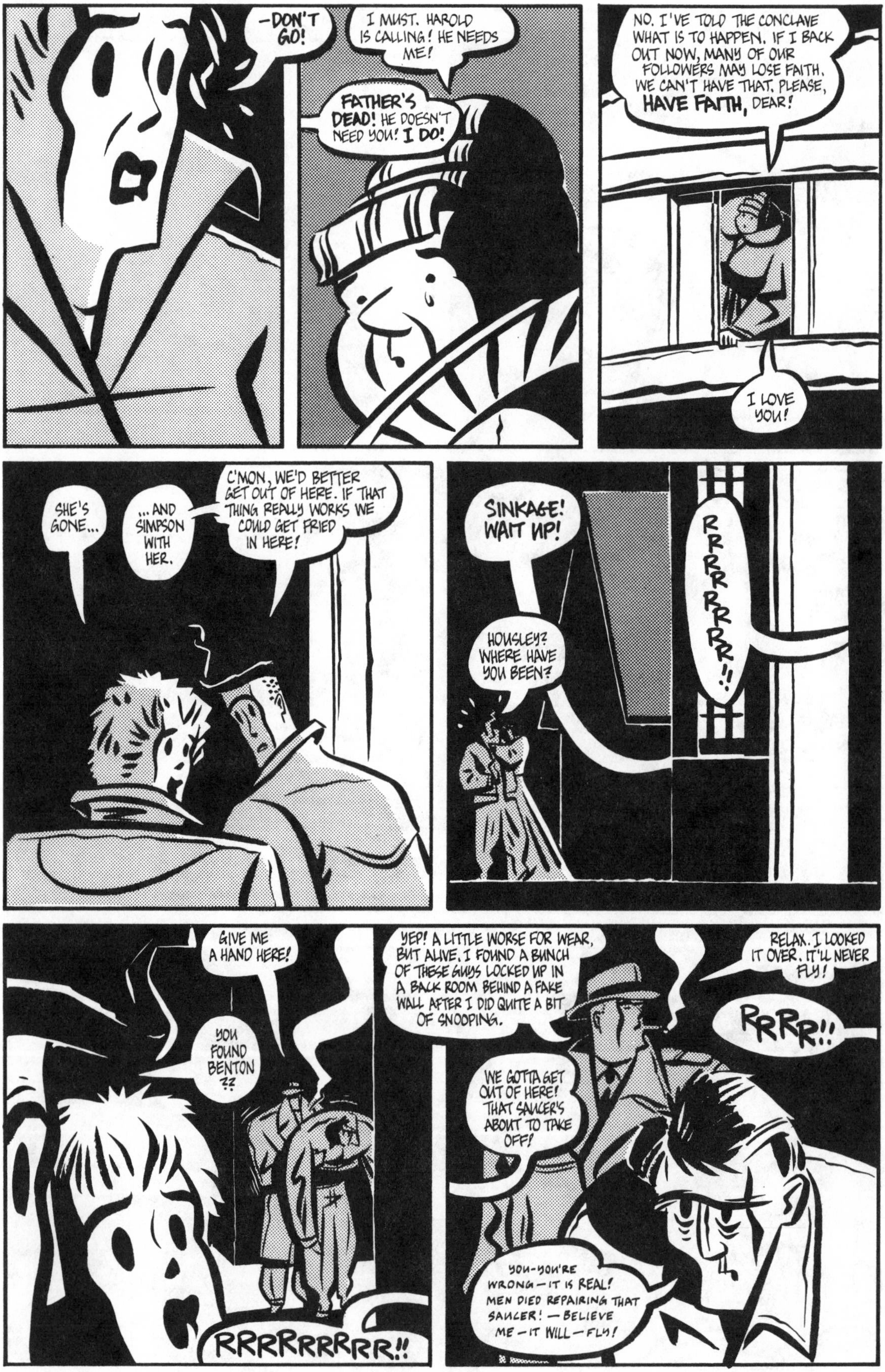
-DON'T GO!
I MUST. HAROLD IS CALLING! HE NEEDS ME!
FATHER'S DEAD! HE DOESN'T NEED YOU! I DO!
NO. I'VE TOLD THE CONCLAVE WHAT IS TO HAPPEN. IF I BACK OUT NOW, MANY OF OUR FOLLOWERS MAY LOSE FAITH. WE CAN'T HAVE THAT. PLEASE, HAVE FAITH, DEAR!
I LOVE YOU!
SHE'S GONE...
...AND SIMPSON WITH HER.
C'MON, WE'D BETTER GET OUT OF HERE. IF THAT THING REALLY WORKS WE COULD GET FRIED IN HERE!
SINKAGE! WAIT UP!
HOUSLEY? WHERE HAVE YOU BEEN?
RRRRRRR!!
GIVE ME A HAND HERE!
YOU FOUND BENTON ??
RRRRRRRRR!!
YEP! A LITTLE WORSE FOR WEAR, BUT ALIVE. I FOUND A BUNCH OF THESE GUYS LOCKED UP IN A BACK ROOM BEHIND A FAKE WALL AFTER I DID QUITE A BIT OF SNOOPING.
RELAX. I LOOKED IT OVER. IT'LL NEVER FLY!
RRRR!!
WE GOTTA GET OUT OF HERE! THAT SAUCER'S ABOUT TO TAKE OFF!
YOU-YOU'RE WRONG—IT IS REAL! MEN DIED REPAIRING THAT SAUCER! —BELIEVE ME—IT WILL—FLY!

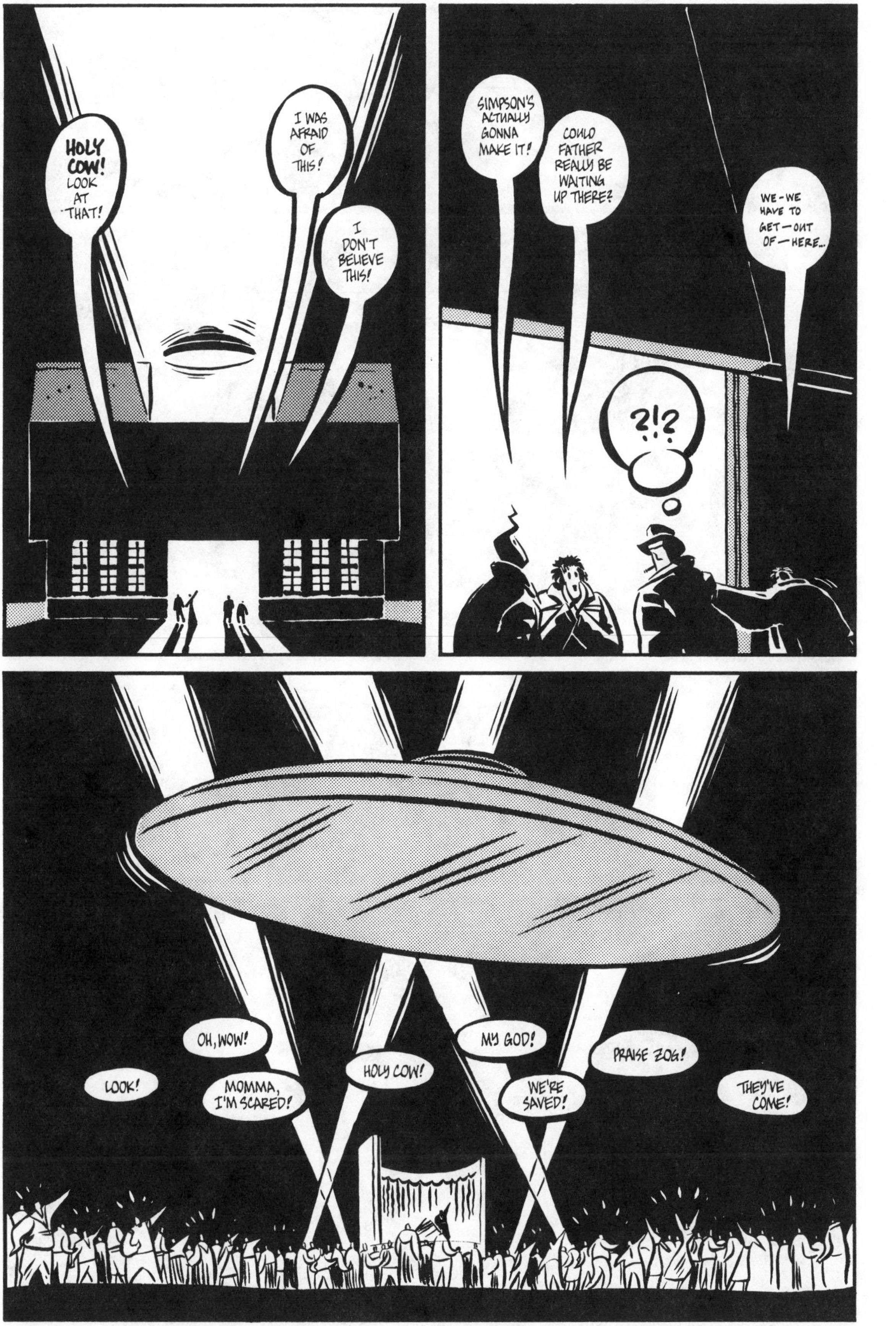
HOLY COW! LOOK AT THAT!
I WAS AFRAID OF THIS!
I DON'T BELIEVE THIS!
SIMPSON'S ACTUALLY GONNA MAKE IT!
COULD FATHER REALLY BE WAITING UP THERE?
WE-WE HAVE TO GET—OUT OF—HERE...
?!?
OH, WOW!
LOOK!
MOMMA, I'M SCARED!
HOLY COW!
MY GOD!
WE'RE SAVED!
PRAISE ZOG!
THEY'VE COME!

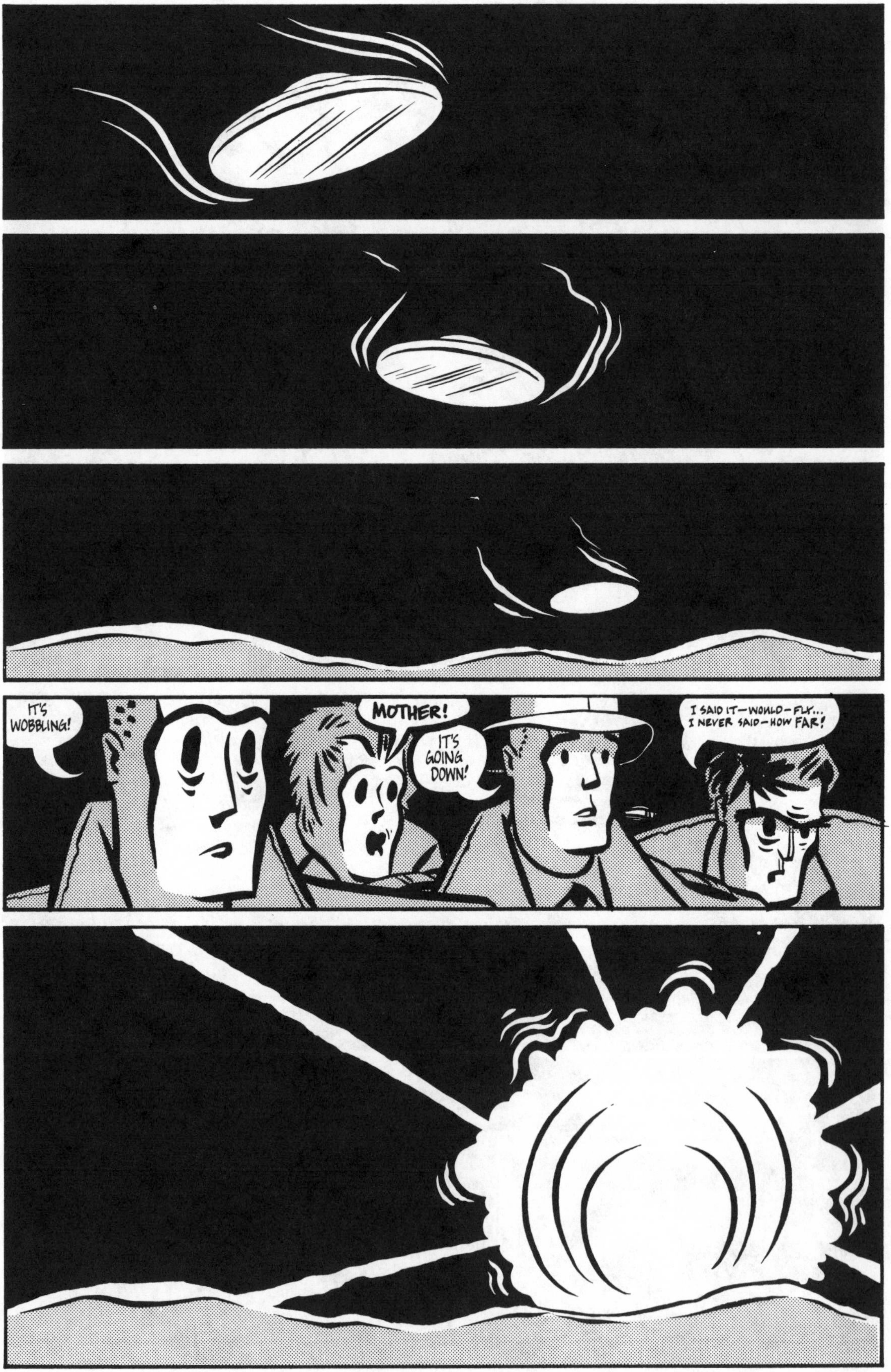
IT'S WOBBLING!
MOTHER!
IT'S GOING DOWN!
I SAID IT—WOULD—FLY...
I NEVER SAID—HOW FAR!

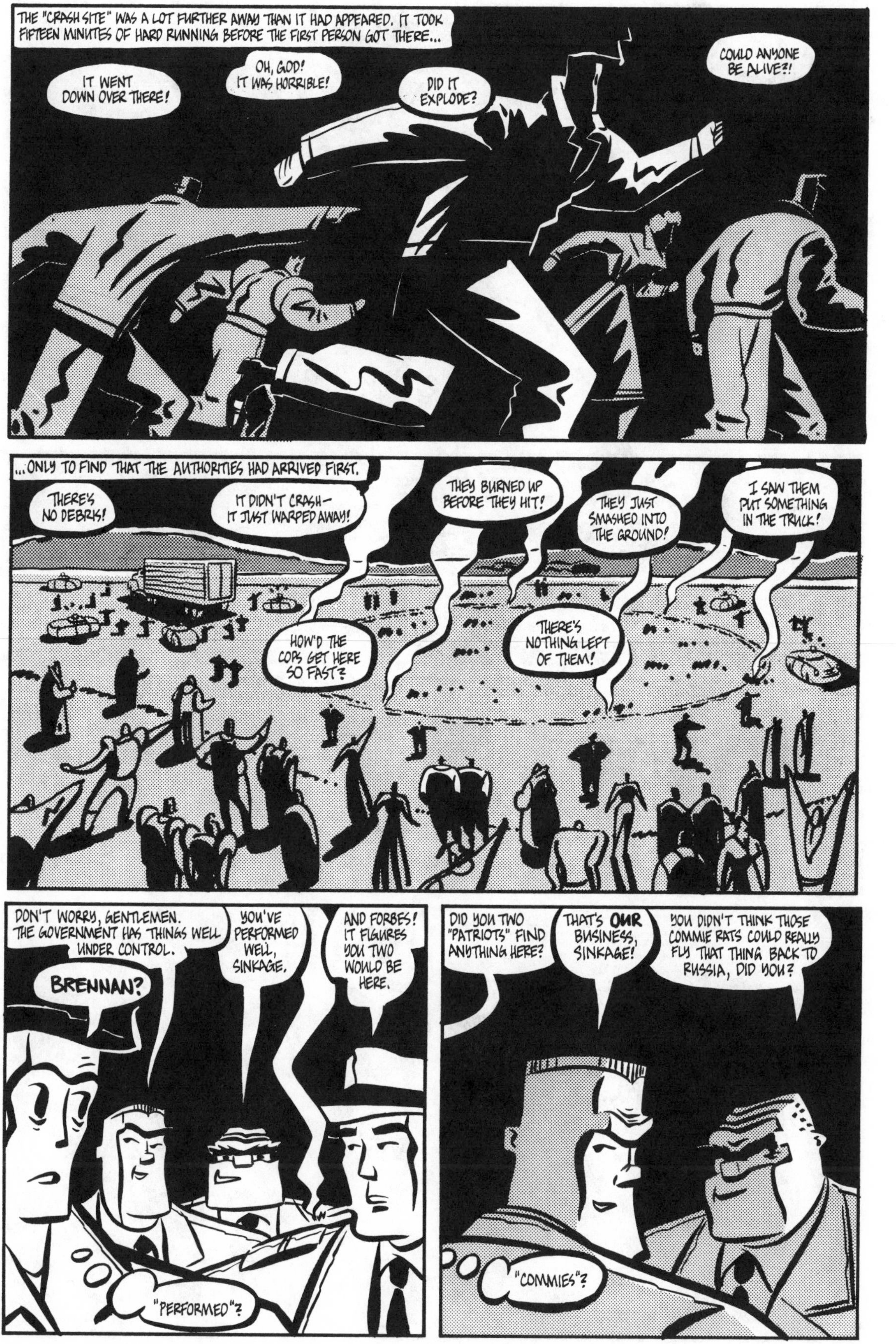
THE "CRASH SITE" WAS A LOT FURTHER AWAY THAN IT HAD APPEARED. IT TOOK FIFTEEN MINUTES OF HARD RUNNING BEFORE THE FIRST PERSON GOT THERE...
IT WENT DOWN OVER THERE!
OH, GOD! IT WAS HORRIBLE!
DID IT EXPLODE?
COULD ANYONE BE ALIVE?!
...ONLY TO FIND THAT THE AUTHORITIES HAD ARRIVED FIRST.
THERE'S NO DEBRIS!
IT DIDN'T CRASH— IT JUST WARPED AWAY!
THEY BURNED UP BEFORE THEY HIT!
THEY JUST SMASHED INTO THE GROUND!
I SAW THEM PUT SOMETHING IN THE TRUCK!
HOW'D THE COPS GET HERE SO FAST?
THERE'S NOTHING LEFT OF THEM!
DON'T WORRY, GENTLEMEN. THE GOVERNMENT HAS THINGS WELL UNDER CONTROL.
BRENNAN?
YOU'VE PERFORMED WELL, SINKAGE.
AND FORBES! IT FIGURES YOU TWO WOULD BE HERE.
"PERFORMED"?
DID YOU TWO "PATRIOTS" FIND ANYTHING HERE?
THAT'S OUR BUSINESS, SINKAGE!
YOU DIDN'T THINK THOSE COMMIE RATS COULD REALLY FLY THAT THING BACK TO RUSSIA, DID YOU?
"COMMIES"?

CAN WE HOLD THESE TWO?

NO—NOTHING TO HOLD THEM ON. AND THE LOCAL SHERIFF IS ALREADY MAD AT US FOR APPROPRIATING HIS MEN.

THINK WE COULD GET A LOOK IN THAT TRUCK?

NOPE! DOESN'T REALLY MATTER THOUGH, DO YOU **REALLY** THINK THEY COULD HAVE CLEANED UP ANY DEBRIS THIS QUICKLY?

SO WHAT DO YOU THINK HAPPENED?

EITHER THE SAUCER BURNED UP BEFORE IT HIT THE GROUND, OR THE EXPLOSION BLEW IT INTO A MILLION TINY BITS. EITHER WAY, THERE'S NOTHING LEFT.

EEEEEEEEEEEEEEEEEEEEEEEE

YOU— YOU'RE WRONG— THEY —THEY— GOT AWAY.

WHAT DID HE SAY?

NOTHING. HE'S DELIRIOUS. I'VE GOT TO GET HIM TO A HOSPITAL IN UNION CITY. C'MON I'LL DRIVE YOU HOME.

KING ZOG WATCHES OVER—HIS OWN...

MATT!

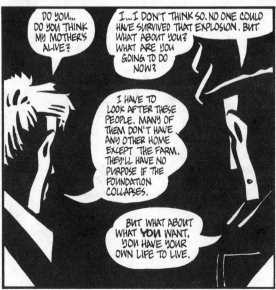

DO YOU... DO YOU THINK MY MOTHER'S ALIVE?

I...I DON'T THINK SO. NO ONE COULD HAVE SURVIVED THAT EXPLOSION. BUT WHAT ABOUT YOU? WHAT ARE YOU GOING TO DO NOW?

I HAVE TO LOOK AFTER THESE PEOPLE. MANY OF THEM DON'T HAVE ANY OTHER HOME EXCEPT THE FARM. THEY'LL HAVE NO PURPOSE IF THE FOUNDATION COLLAPSES.

BUT WHAT ABOUT WHAT **YOU** WANT. YOU HAVE YOUR OWN LIFE TO LIVE.

THIS **IS** MY LIFE. MAYBE— JUST MAYBE—MOTHER WAS RIGHT...MAYBE SHE HAS GONE TO JOIN MY FATHER... I HAVE TO CARRY ON ...FOR MY MOTHER...

...SHE ASKED ME TO.

HEY, SINKAGE! LET'S GO!

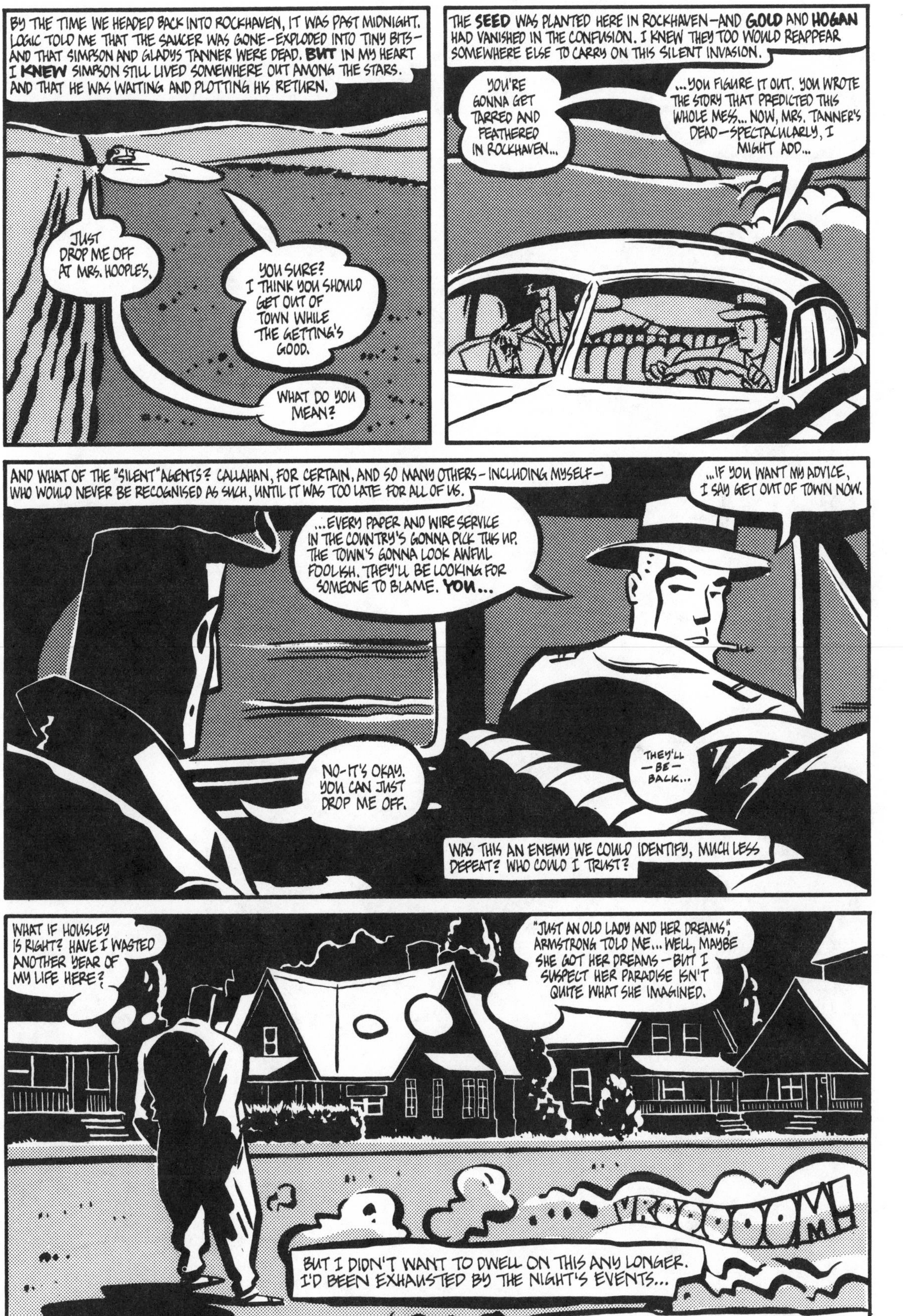

BY THE TIME WE HEADED BACK INTO ROCKHAVEN, IT WAS PAST MIDNIGHT. LOGIC TOLD ME THAT THE SAUCER WAS GONE—EXPLODED INTO TINY BITS—AND THAT SIMPSON AND GLADYS TANNER WERE DEAD. BUT IN MY HEART I KNEW SIMPSON STILL LIVED SOMEWHERE OUT AMONG THE STARS. AND THAT HE WAS WAITING AND PLOTTING HIS RETURN.
JUST DROP ME OFF AT MRS. HOOPLE'S.
YOU SURE? I THINK YOU SHOULD GET OUT OF TOWN WHILE THE GETTING'S GOOD.
WHAT DO YOU MEAN?
THE SEED WAS PLANTED HERE IN ROCKHAVEN—AND GOLD AND HOGAN HAD VANISHED IN THE CONFUSION. I KNEW THEY TOO WOULD REAPPEAR SOMEWHERE ELSE TO CARRY ON THIS SILENT INVASION.
YOU'RE GONNA GET TARRED AND FEATHERED IN ROCKHAVEN...
...YOU FIGURE IT OUT. YOU WROTE THE STORY THAT PREDICTED THIS WHOLE MESS... NOW, MRS. TANNER'S DEAD—SPECTACULARLY, I MIGHT ADD...
AND WHAT OF THE "SILENT" AGENTS? CALLAHAN, FOR CERTAIN, AND SO MANY OTHERS—INCLUDING MYSELF—WHO WOULD NEVER BE RECOGNISED AS SUCH, UNTIL IT WAS TOO LATE FOR ALL OF US.
...EVERY PAPER AND WIRE SERVICE IN THE COUNTRY'S GONNA PICK THIS UP. THE TOWN'S GONNA LOOK AWFUL FOOLISH. THEY'LL BE LOOKING FOR SOMEONE TO BLAME. YOU...
...IF YOU WANT MY ADVICE, I SAY GET OUT OF TOWN NOW.
NO—IT'S OKAY. YOU CAN JUST DROP ME OFF.
THEY'LL —BE— BACK...
WAS THIS AN ENEMY WE COULD IDENTIFY, MUCH LESS DEFEAT? WHO COULD I TRUST?
WHAT IF HOUSLEY IS RIGHT? HAVE I WASTED ANOTHER YEAR OF MY LIFE HERE?
"JUST AN OLD LADY AND HER DREAMS," ARMSTRONG TOLD ME... WELL, MAYBE SHE GOT HER DREAMS—BUT I SUSPECT HER PARADISE ISN'T QUITE WHAT SHE IMAGINED.
VROOOOOOM!
BUT I DIDN'T WANT TO DWELL ON THIS ANY LONGER. I'D BEEN EXHAUSTED BY THE NIGHT'S EVENTS...
...ALL I WANTED WAS A GOOD NIGHT'S SLEEP.

CHAPTER FOUR

A REAL AND EVER PRESENT DANGER

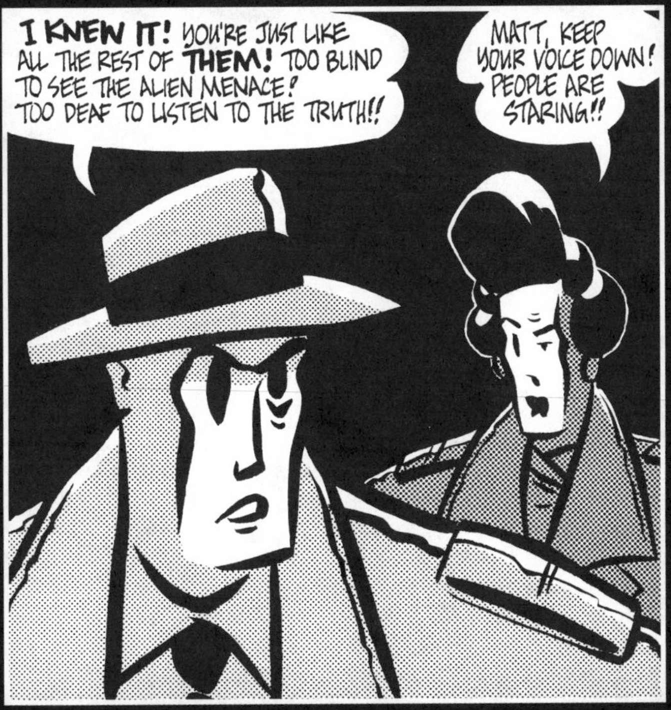
I KNEW IT! YOU'RE JUST LIKE ALL THE REST OF THEM! TOO BLIND TO SEE THE ALIEN MENACE! TOO DEAF TO LISTEN TO THE TRUTH!!
MATT, KEEP YOUR VOICE DOWN! PEOPLE ARE STARING!!

OCTOBER 1955.

IT WAS ALL FRESH IN MY MIND. THE EVENTS OF THE LAST FEW HOURS, THE LAST FEW DAYS— THE LAST FEW WEEKS, AND, IN ITS OWN TWISTED WAY, EVERYTHING MADE SENSE.

STUBBINSVILLE FILE

I SAW IT ALL WITH A CLARITY THAT HAD PREVIOUSLY ELUDED ME. I HAD TO GET IT ALL DOWN ON PAPER BEFORE—

—MISTER SINKAGE !?!

~~~~—WHA-?!?

MRS. HOOPLE?! YOU STARTLED ME. I THOUGHT YOU WERE ASLEEP—

TAP TAP TAP TAP TAP TAP TAP TAP TAP TAP TAP TAP TAP TAP TAP TAP TAP TAP TAPT

—NOBODY CAN SLEEP WITH ALL THAT RACKET! YOU'LL HAVE TO STOP THAT INFERNAL TYPING THIS INSTANT!

THERE ARE PEOPLE TRYING TO SLEEP! WE'VE ALL HAD A TRYING NIGHT— AS YOU WELL KNOW!

BUT—BUT I HAVE TO ORGANISE MY THOUGHTS ... MY NOTES ON THE UFO'S... TH-THE ALIENS—

—WHAT UTTER HOGWASH!

BUT YOU WERE THERE! YOU SAW—

—ALL FIGMENTS OF YOUR ALCOHOL-ADDLED BRAIN, MR. SINKAGE!

NOW, PLEASE KEEP THE NOISE DOWN!

JEEZ!

SLAM!

WHY DOESN'T ANYONE IN THIS TOWN BELIEVE WHAT THEY SAW TONIGHT?

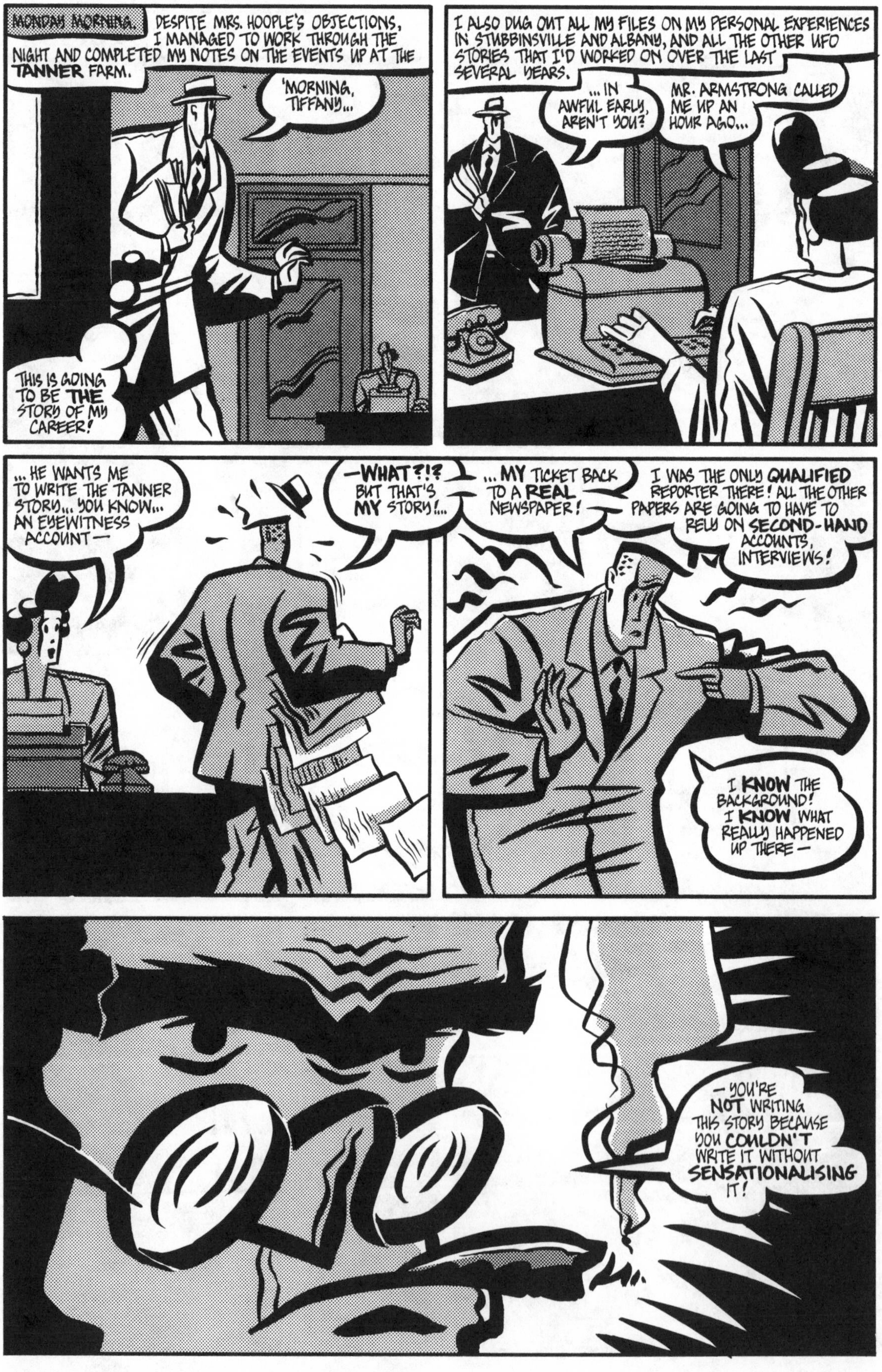
MONDAY MORNING.
DESPITE MRS. HOOPLE'S OBJECTIONS, I MANAGED TO WORK THROUGH THE NIGHT AND COMPLETED MY NOTES ON THE EVENTS UP AT THE TANNER FARM.
'MORNING, TIFFANY...
THIS IS GOING TO BE THE STORY OF MY CAREER!
I ALSO DUG OUT ALL MY FILES ON MY PERSONAL EXPERIENCES IN STUBBINSVILLE AND ALBANY, AND ALL THE OTHER UFO STORIES THAT I'D WORKED ON OVER THE LAST SEVERAL YEARS.
... IN AWFUL EARLY, AREN'T YOU?
MR. ARMSTRONG CALLED ME UP AN HOUR AGO...
... HE WANTS ME TO WRITE THE TANNER STORY... YOU KNOW... AN EYEWITNESS ACCOUNT —
— WHAT?!? BUT THAT'S MY STORY!...
... MY TICKET BACK TO A REAL NEWSPAPER!
I WAS THE ONLY QUALIFIED REPORTER THERE! ALL THE OTHER PAPERS ARE GOING TO HAVE TO RELY ON SECOND-HAND ACCOUNTS, INTERVIEWS!
I KNOW THE BACKGROUND! I KNOW WHAT REALLY HAPPENED UP THERE —
— YOU'RE NOT WRITING THIS STORY BECAUSE YOU COULDN'T WRITE IT WITHOUT SENSATIONALISING IT!

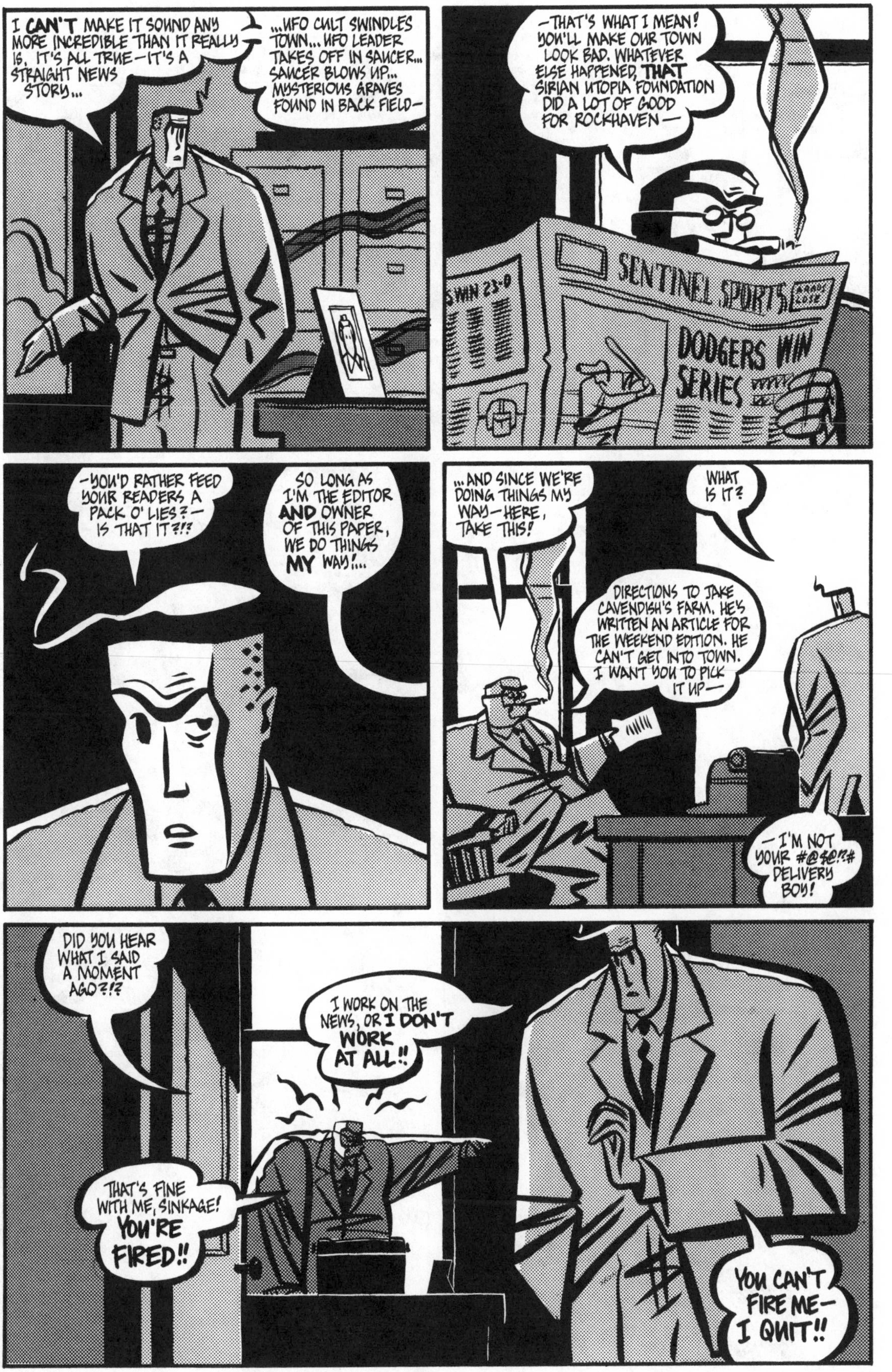
I CAN'T MAKE IT SOUND ANY MORE INCREDIBLE THAN IT REALLY IS. IT'S ALL TRUE—IT'S A STRAIGHT NEWS STORY...
...UFO CULT SWINDLES TOWN... UFO LEADER TAKES OFF IN SAUCER... SAUCER BLOWS UP... MYSTERIOUS GRAVES FOUND IN BACK FIELD—
—THAT'S WHAT I MEAN! YOU'LL MAKE OUR TOWN LOOK BAD. WHATEVER ELSE HAPPENED, THAT SIRIAN UTOPIA FOUNDATION DID A LOT OF GOOD FOR ROCKHAVEN—
SENTINEL SPORTS
S WIN 23-0
DODGERS WIN SERIES
—YOU'D RATHER FEED YOUR READERS A PACK O' LIES?—IS THAT IT?!?
SO LONG AS I'M THE EDITOR AND OWNER OF THIS PAPER, WE DO THINGS MY WAY!...
...AND SINCE WE'RE DOING THINGS MY WAY—HERE, TAKE THIS!
WHAT IS IT?
DIRECTIONS TO JAKE CAVENDISH'S FARM. HE'S WRITTEN AN ARTICLE FOR THE WEEKEND EDITION. HE CAN'T GET INTO TOWN. I WANT YOU TO PICK IT UP—
—I'M NOT YOUR #@$@!?# DELIVERY BOY!
DID YOU HEAR WHAT I SAID A MOMENT AGO?!?
I WORK ON THE NEWS, OR I DON'T WORK AT ALL!!
THAT'S FINE WITH ME, SINKAGE! YOU'RE FIRED!!
YOU CAN'T FIRE ME—I QUIT!!

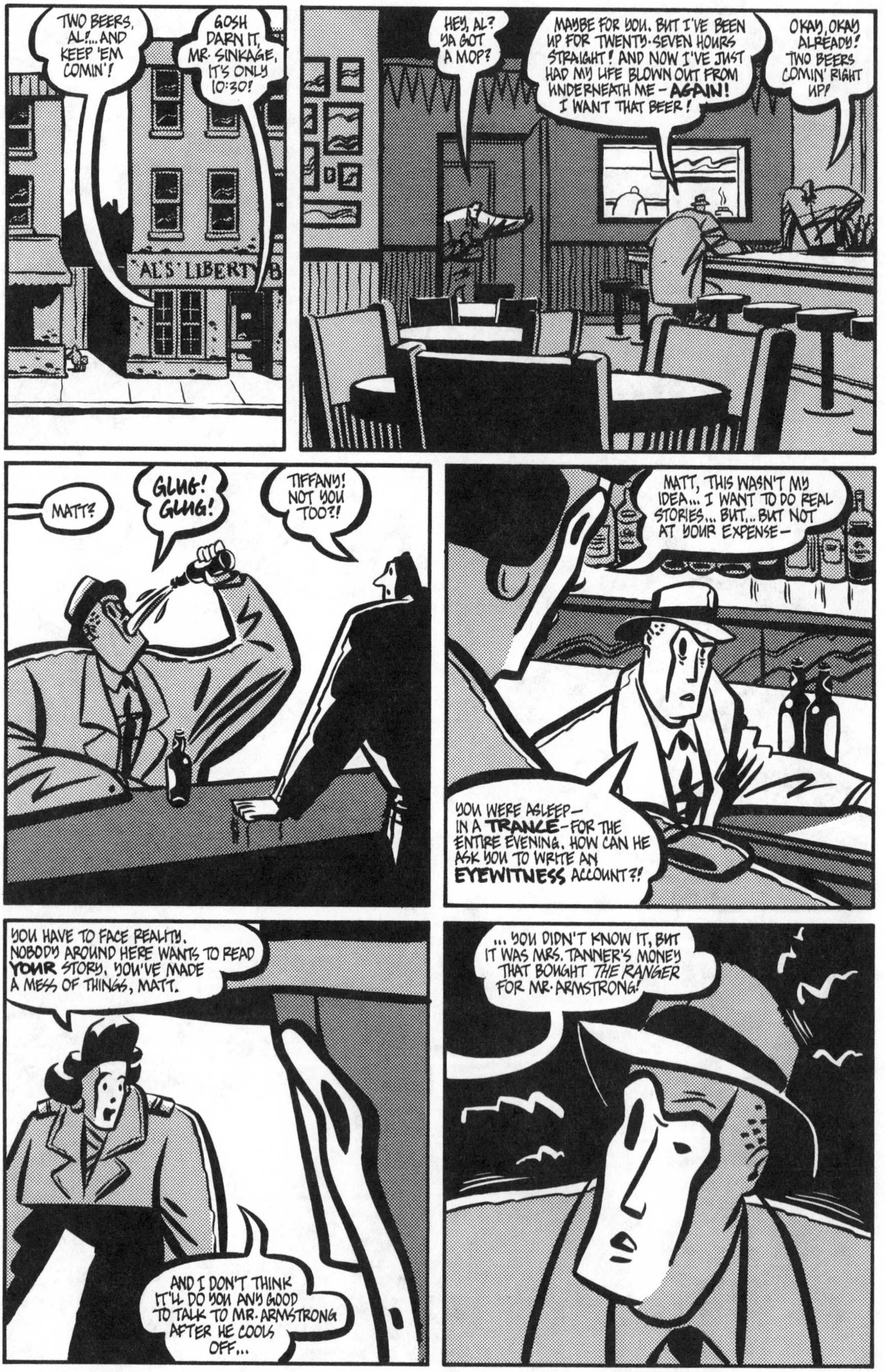
TWO BEERS, AL!... AND KEEP 'EM COMIN'!
GOSH DARN IT, MR. SINKAGE, IT'S ONLY 10:30!
"AL'S" LIBERTY B
HEY, AL? YA GOT A MOP?
MAYBE FOR YOU. BUT I'VE BEEN UP FOR TWENTY-SEVEN HOURS STRAIGHT! AND NOW I'VE JUST HAD MY LIFE BLOWN OUT FROM UNDERNEATH ME - AGAIN! I WANT THAT BEER!
OKAY, OKAY ALREADY! TWO BEERS COMIN' RIGHT UP!
MATT?
GLUG! GLUG!
TIFFANY! NOT YOU TOO?!
MATT, THIS WASN'T MY IDEA... I WANT TO DO REAL STORIES... BUT... BUT NOT AT YOUR EXPENSE-
YOU WERE ASLEEP- IN A TRANCE- FOR THE ENTIRE EVENING. HOW CAN HE ASK YOU TO WRITE AN EYEWITNESS ACCOUNT?!
YOU HAVE TO FACE REALITY. NOBODY AROUND HERE WANTS TO READ YOUR STORY. YOU'VE MADE A MESS OF THINGS, MATT.
AND I DON'T THINK IT'LL DO YOU ANY GOOD TO TALK TO MR. ARMSTRONG AFTER HE COOLS OFF...
... YOU DIDN'T KNOW IT, BUT IT WAS MRS. TANNER'S MONEY THAT BOUGHT THE RANGER FOR MR. ARMSTRONG!

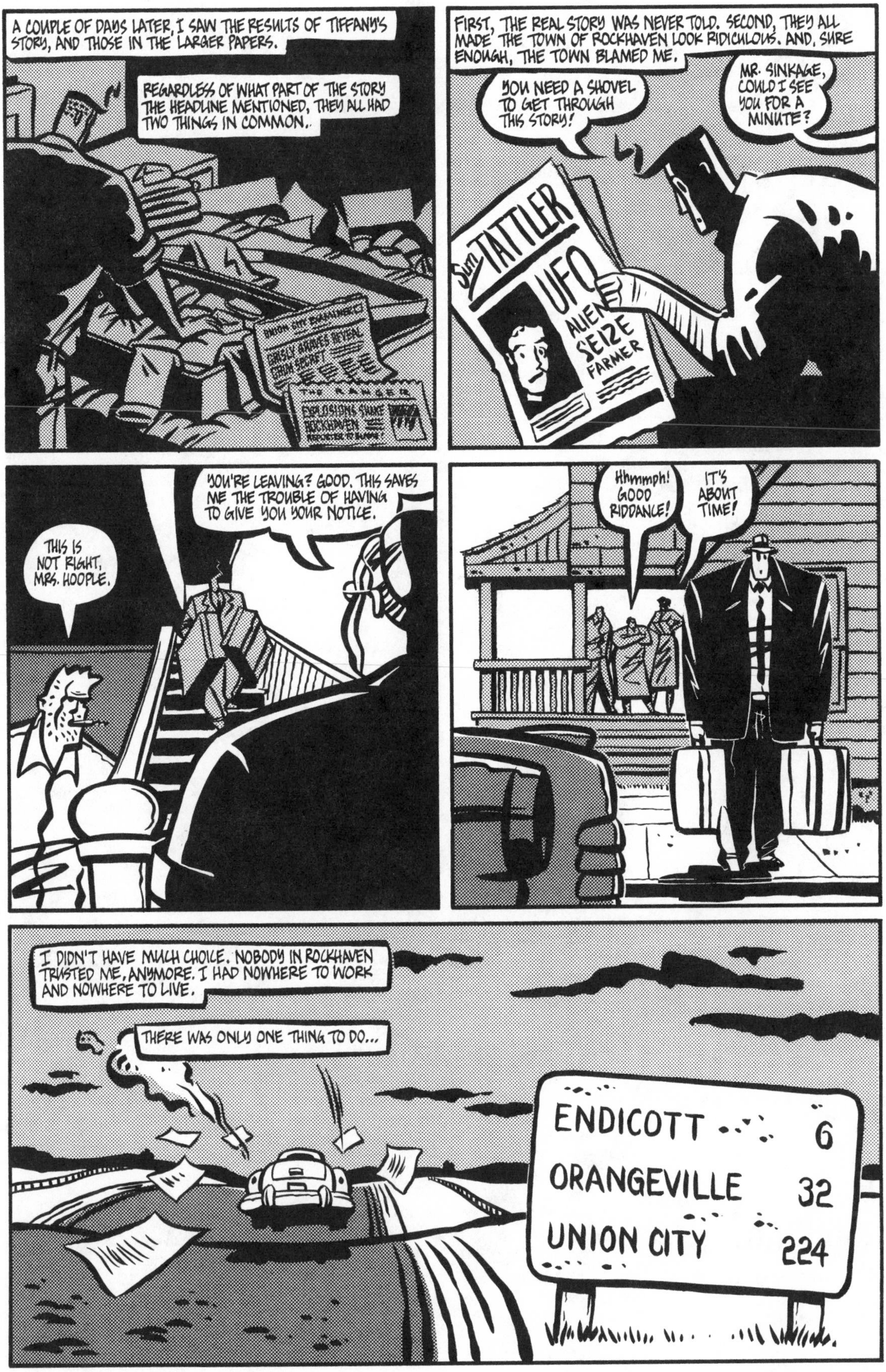
A COUPLE OF DAYS LATER, I SAW THE RESULTS OF TIFFANY'S STORY, AND THOSE IN THE LARGER PAPERS.
REGARDLESS OF WHAT PART OF THE STORY THE HEADLINE MENTIONED, THEY ALL HAD TWO THINGS IN COMMON.
GRISLY GRAVES REVEAL
THE RANGER
EXPLOSIONS SHAKE ROCKHAVEN
FIRST, THE REAL STORY WAS NEVER TOLD. SECOND, THEY ALL MADE THE TOWN OF ROCKHAVEN LOOK RIDICULOUS. AND, SURE ENOUGH, THE TOWN BLAMED ME.
YOU NEED A SHOVEL TO GET THROUGH THIS STORY!
MR. SINKAGE, COULD I SEE YOU FOR A MINUTE?
Sun TATTLER
UFO
ALIEN SEIZE FARMER
THIS IS NOT RIGHT, MRS. HOOPLE.
YOU'RE LEAVING? GOOD. THIS SAVES ME THE TROUBLE OF HAVING TO GIVE YOU YOUR NOTICE.
Hhmmph! GOOD RIDDANCE!
IT'S ABOUT TIME!
I DIDN'T HAVE MUCH CHOICE. NOBODY IN ROCKHAVEN TRUSTED ME, ANYMORE. I HAD NOWHERE TO WORK AND NOWHERE TO LIVE.
THERE WAS ONLY ONE THING TO DO...
ENDICOTT 6
ORANGEVILLE 32
UNION CITY 224

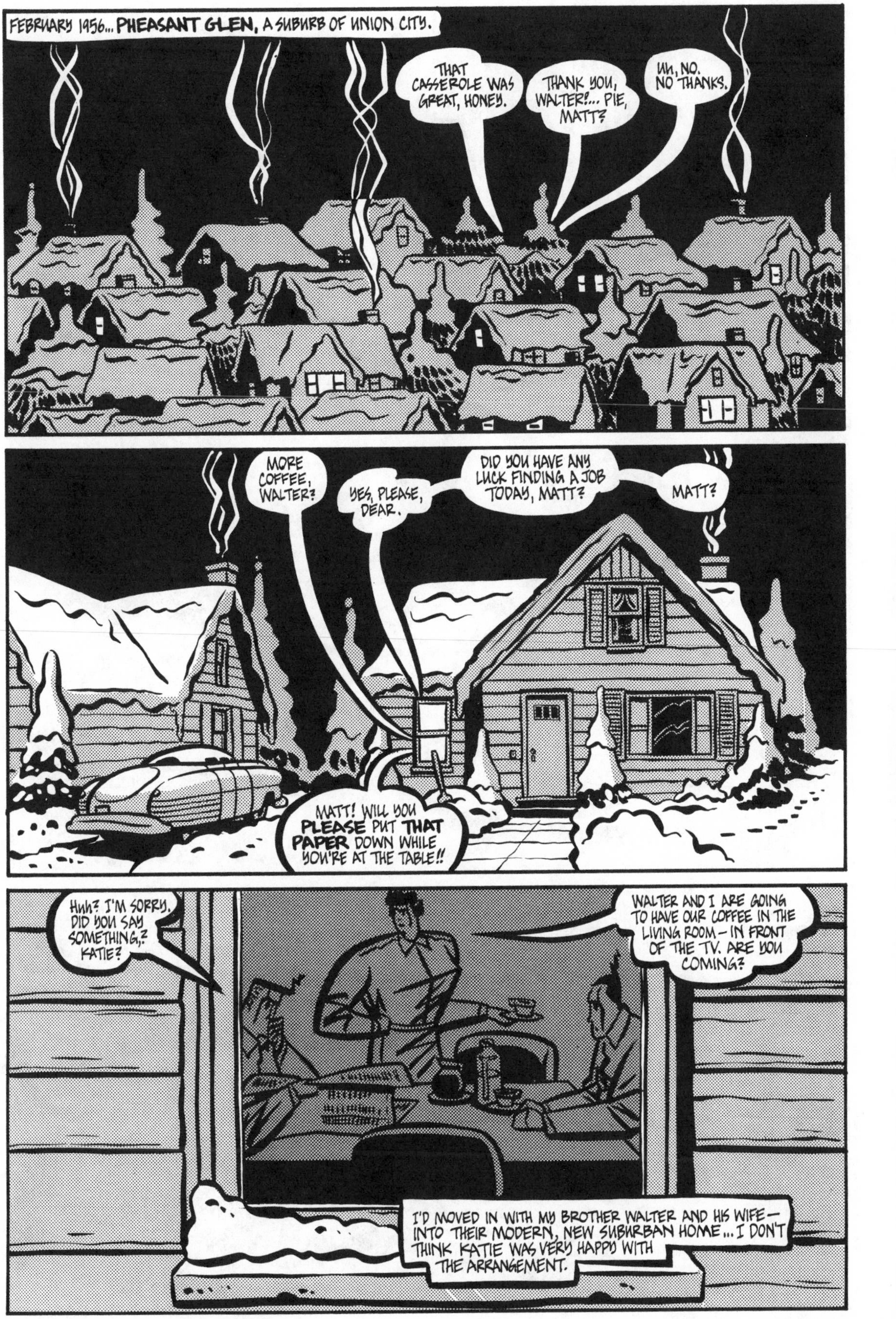
FEBRUARY 1956... PHEASANT GLEN, A SUBURB OF UNION CITY.
THAT CASSEROLE WAS GREAT, HONEY.
THANK YOU, WALTER!... PIE, MATT?
UH, NO. NO THANKS.
MORE COFFEE, WALTER?
YES, PLEASE, DEAR.
DID YOU HAVE ANY LUCK FINDING A JOB TODAY, MATT?
MATT?
MATT! WILL YOU PLEASE PUT THAT PAPER DOWN WHILE YOU'RE AT THE TABLE!!
HUH? I'M SORRY, DID YOU SAY SOMETHING, KATIE?
WALTER AND I ARE GOING TO HAVE OUR COFFEE IN THE LIVING ROOM – IN FRONT OF THE TV. ARE YOU COMING?
I'D MOVED IN WITH MY BROTHER WALTER AND HIS WIFE– INTO THEIR MODERN, NEW SUBURBAN HOME... I DON'T THINK KATIE WAS VERY HAPPY WITH THE ARRANGEMENT.

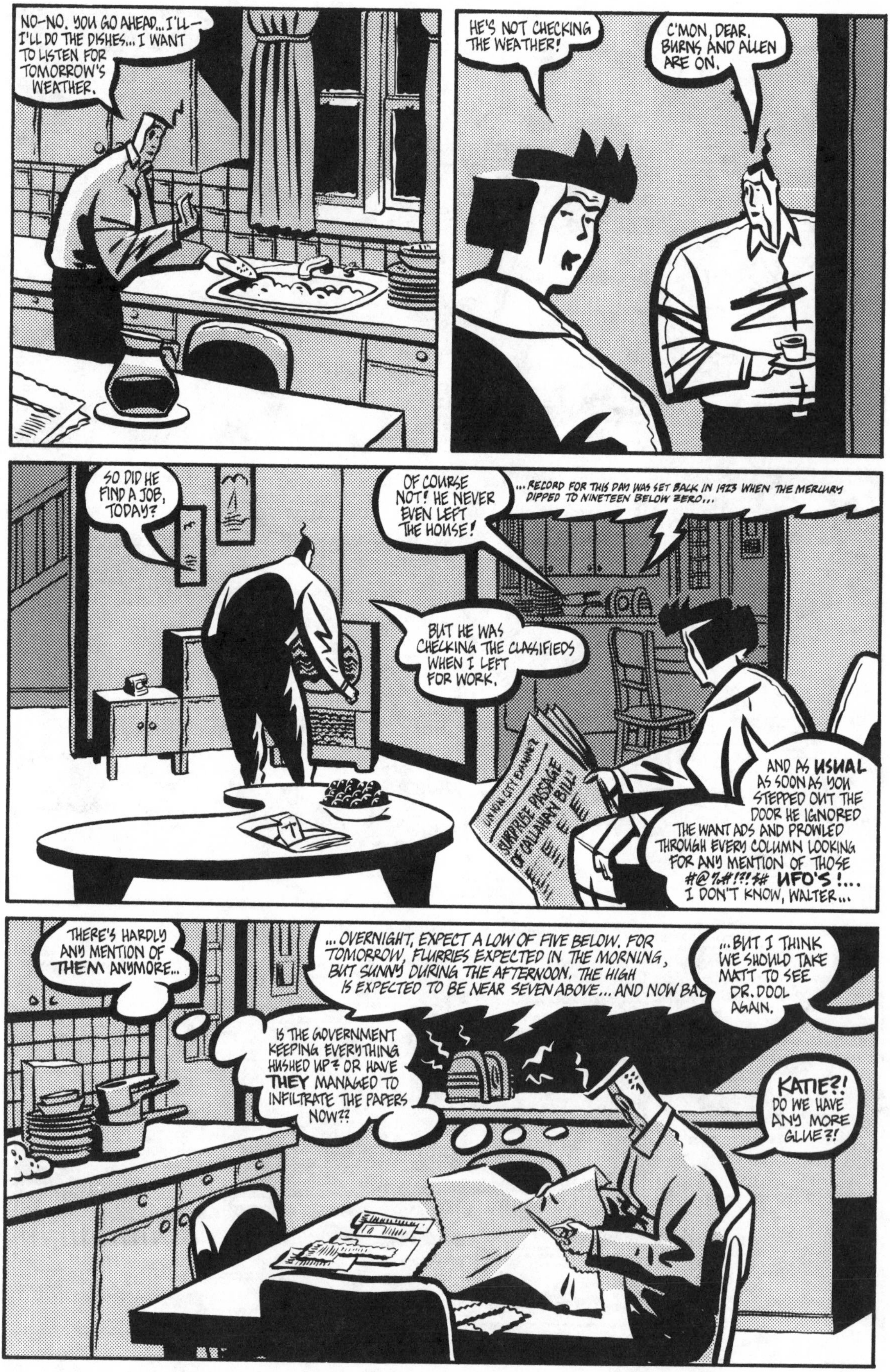
NO-NO. YOU GO AHEAD... I'LL— I'LL DO THE DISHES... I WANT TO LISTEN FOR TOMORROW'S WEATHER.
HE'S NOT CHECKING THE WEATHER!
C'MON, DEAR. BURNS AND ALLEN ARE ON.
SO DID HE FIND A JOB, TODAY?
OF COURSE NOT! HE NEVER EVEN LEFT THE HOUSE!
...RECORD FOR THIS DAY WAS SET BACK IN 1923 WHEN THE MERCURY DIPPED TO NINETEEN BELOW ZERO...
BUT HE WAS CHECKING THE CLASSIFIEDS WHEN I LEFT FOR WORK.
SURPRISE PASSAGE OF CALLAHAN BILL
AND AS USUAL AS SOON AS YOU STEPPED OUT THE DOOR HE IGNORED THE WANT ADS AND PROWLED THROUGH EVERY COLUMN LOOKING FOR ANY MENTION OF THOSE #@%#!?!$# UFO'S!... I DON'T KNOW, WALTER...
THERE'S HARDLY ANY MENTION OF THEM ANYMORE...
...OVERNIGHT, EXPECT A LOW OF FIVE BELOW. FOR TOMORROW, FLURRIES EXPECTED IN THE MORNING, BUT SUNNY DURING THE AFTERNOON. THE HIGH IS EXPECTED TO BE NEAR SEVEN ABOVE... AND NOW BA
...BUT I THINK WE SHOULD TAKE MATT TO SEE DR. DOOL AGAIN.
IS THE GOVERNMENT KEEPING EVERYTHING HUSHED UP?? OR HAVE THEY MANAGED TO INFILTRATE THE PAPERS NOW??
KATIE?! DO WE HAVE ANY MORE GLUE?!

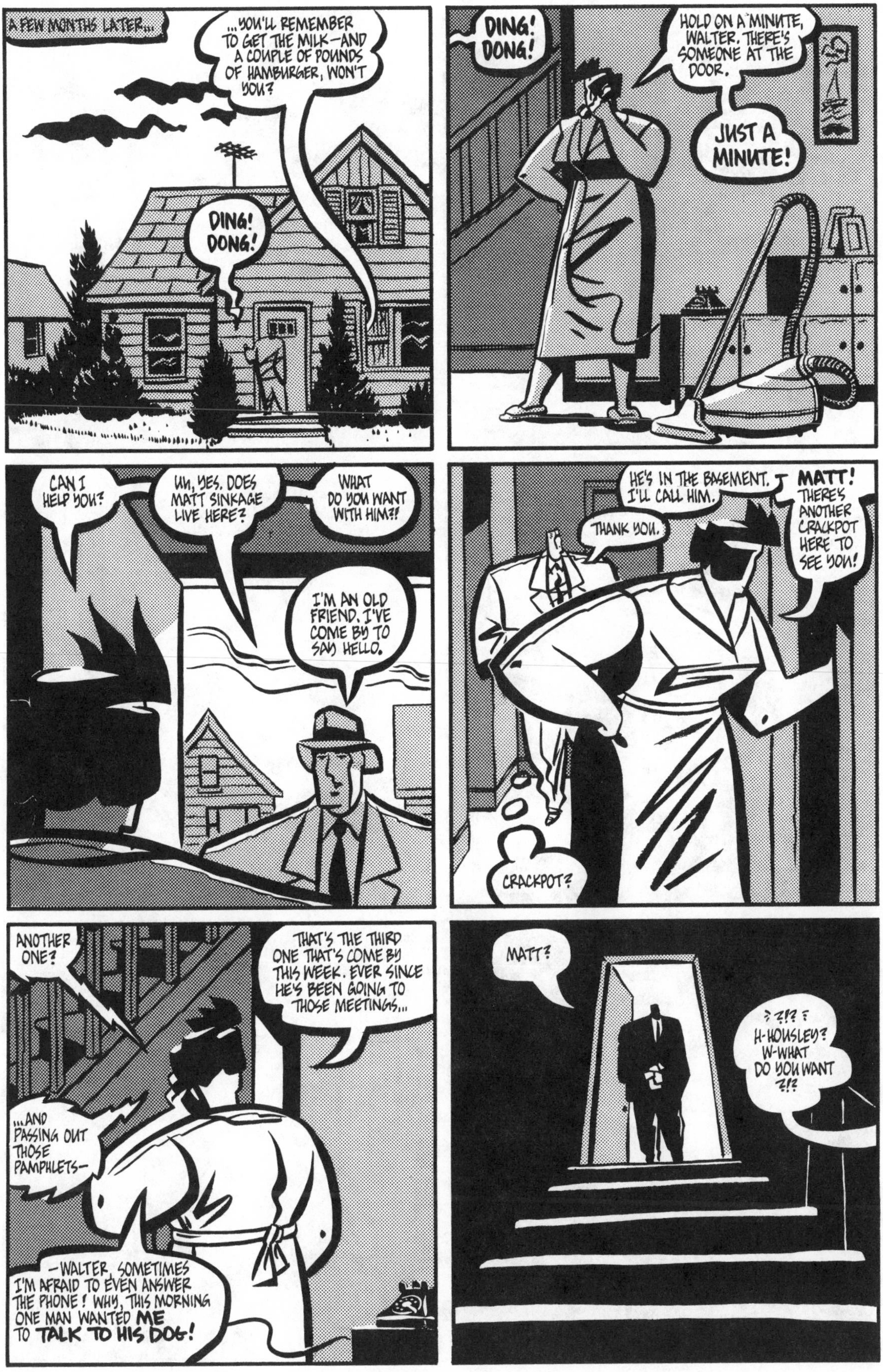
A FEW MONTHS LATER...
...YOU'LL REMEMBER TO GET THE MILK—AND A COUPLE OF POUNDS OF HAMBURGER, WON'T YOU?
DING! DONG!
DING! DONG!
HOLD ON A MINUTE, WALTER. THERE'S SOMEONE AT THE DOOR.
JUST A MINUTE!
CAN I HELP YOU?
UH, YES. DOES MATT SINKAGE LIVE HERE?
WHAT DO YOU WANT WITH HIM?!
I'M AN OLD FRIEND. I'VE COME BY TO SAY HELLO.
HE'S IN THE BASEMENT. I'LL CALL HIM.
MATT! THERE'S ANOTHER CRACKPOT HERE TO SEE YOU!
THANK YOU.
CRACKPOT?
ANOTHER ONE?
THAT'S THE THIRD ONE THAT'S COME BY THIS WEEK. EVER SINCE HE'S BEEN GOING TO THOSE MEETINGS...
...AND PASSING OUT THOSE PAMPHLETS—
—WALTER, SOMETIMES I'M AFRAID TO EVEN ANSWER THE PHONE! WHY, THIS MORNING ONE MAN WANTED ME TO TALK TO HIS DOG!
MATT?
?!?!?
H-HOUSLEY? W-WHAT DO YOU WANT ?!?

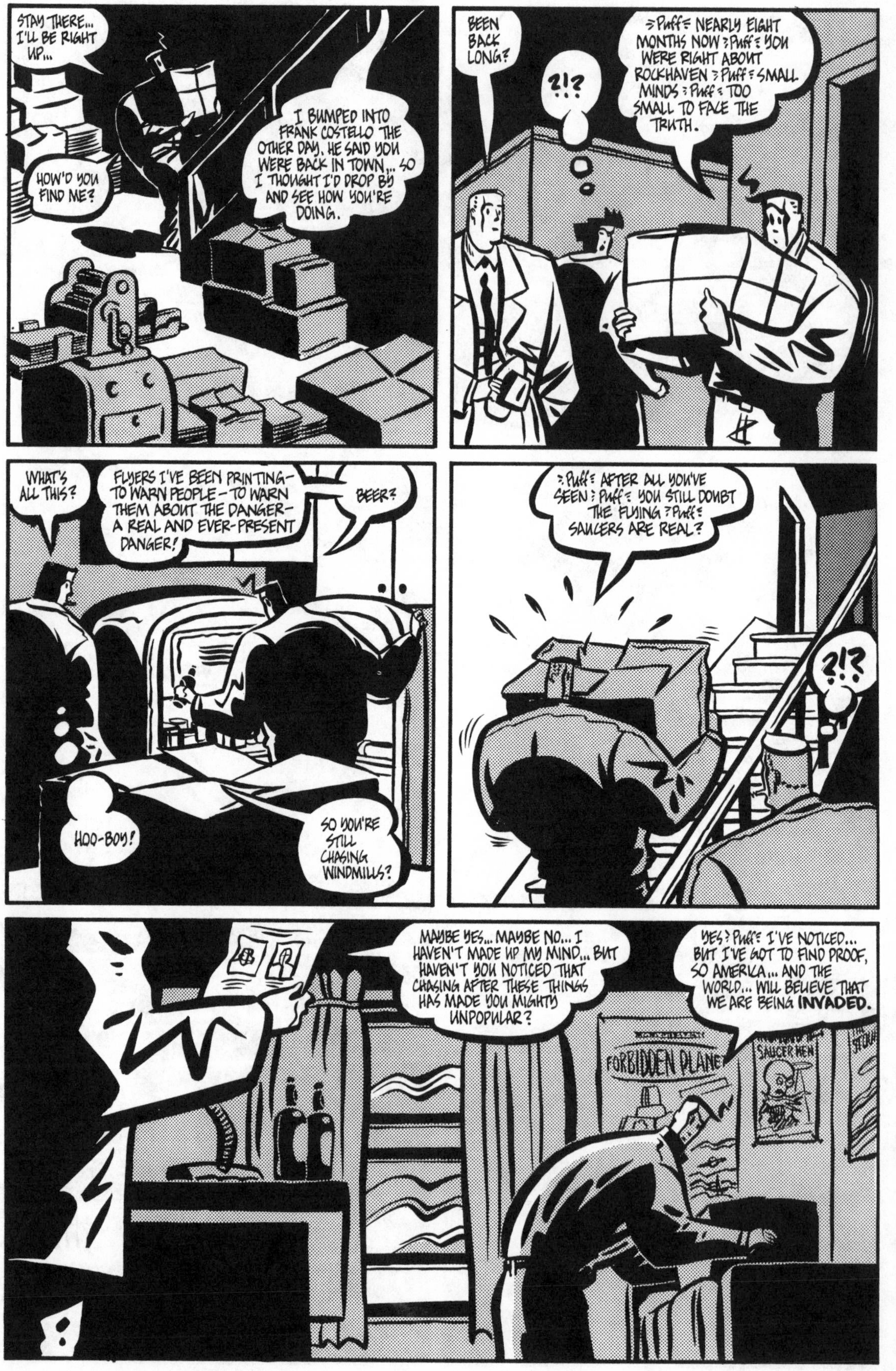
STAY THERE... I'LL BE RIGHT UP...
HOW'D YOU FIND ME?
I BUMPED INTO FRANK COSTELLO THE OTHER DAY. HE SAID YOU WERE BACK IN TOWN... SO I THOUGHT I'D DROP BY AND SEE HOW YOU'RE DOING.
BEEN BACK LONG?
?!?
≥Puff≤ NEARLY EIGHT MONTHS NOW ≥Puff≤ YOU WERE RIGHT ABOUT ROCKHAVEN ≥Puff≤ SMALL MINDS ≥Puff≤ TOO SMALL TO FACE THE TRUTH.
WHAT'S ALL THIS?
FLYERS I'VE BEEN PRINTING– TO WARN PEOPLE– TO WARN THEM ABOUT THE DANGER– A REAL AND EVER-PRESENT DANGER!
BEER?
HOO-BOY!
SO YOU'RE STILL CHASING WINDMILLS?
≥Puff≤ AFTER ALL YOU'VE SEEN ≥Puff≤ YOU STILL DOUBT THE FLYING ≥Puff≤ SAUCERS ARE REAL?
?!?
MAYBE YES... MAYBE NO... I HAVEN'T MADE UP MY MIND... BUT HAVEN'T YOU NOTICED THAT CHASING AFTER THESE THINGS HAS MADE YOU MIGHTY UNPOPULAR?
YES? ≥Puff≤ I'VE NOTICED... BUT I'VE GOT TO FIND PROOF, SO AMERICA... AND THE WORLD... WILL BELIEVE THAT WE ARE BEING **INVADED.**
FORBIDDEN PLANET
SAUCER MEN

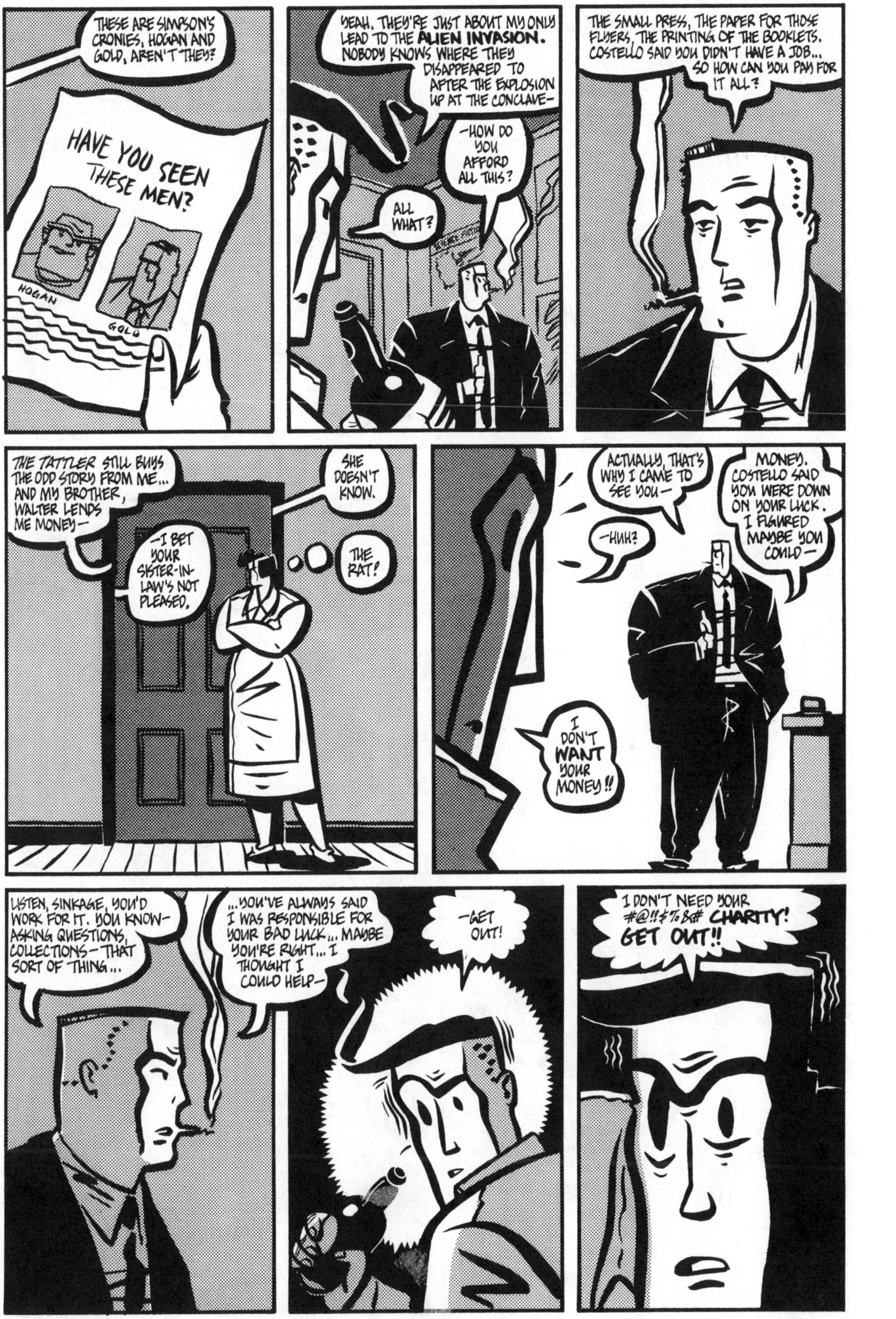
THESE ARE SIMPSON'S CRONIES, HOGAN AND GOLD, AREN'T THEY?
HAVE YOU SEEN THESE MEN?
HOGAN
GOLD
YEAH. THEY'RE JUST ABOUT MY ONLY LEAD TO THE ALIEN INVASION. NOBODY KNOWS WHERE THEY DISAPPEARED TO AFTER THE EXPLOSION UP AT THE CONCLAVE-
-HOW DO YOU AFFORD ALL THIS?
ALL WHAT?
THE SMALL PRESS, THE PAPER FOR THOSE FLYERS, THE PRINTING OF THE BOOKLETS. COSTELLO SAID YOU DIDN'T HAVE A JOB... SO HOW CAN YOU PAY FOR IT ALL?
THE TATTLER STILL BUYS THE ODD STORY FROM ME... AND MY BROTHER, WALTER LENDS ME MONEY-
-I BET YOUR SISTER-IN-LAW'S NOT PLEASED.
SHE DOESN'T KNOW.
THE RAT!
ACTUALLY, THAT'S WHY I CAME TO SEE YOU-
-HUH?
MONEY. COSTELLO SAID YOU WERE DOWN ON YOUR LUCK. I FIGURED MAYBE YOU COULD-
I DON'T WANT YOUR MONEY!!
LISTEN, SINKAGE, YOU'D WORK FOR IT. YOU KNOW- ASKING QUESTIONS, COLLECTIONS- THAT SORT OF THING...
...YOU'VE ALWAYS SAID I WAS RESPONSIBLE FOR YOUR BAD LUCK... MAYBE YOU'RE RIGHT... I THOUGHT I COULD HELP-
-GET OUT!
I DON'T NEED YOUR #@!!$%&# CHARITY! GET OUT!!

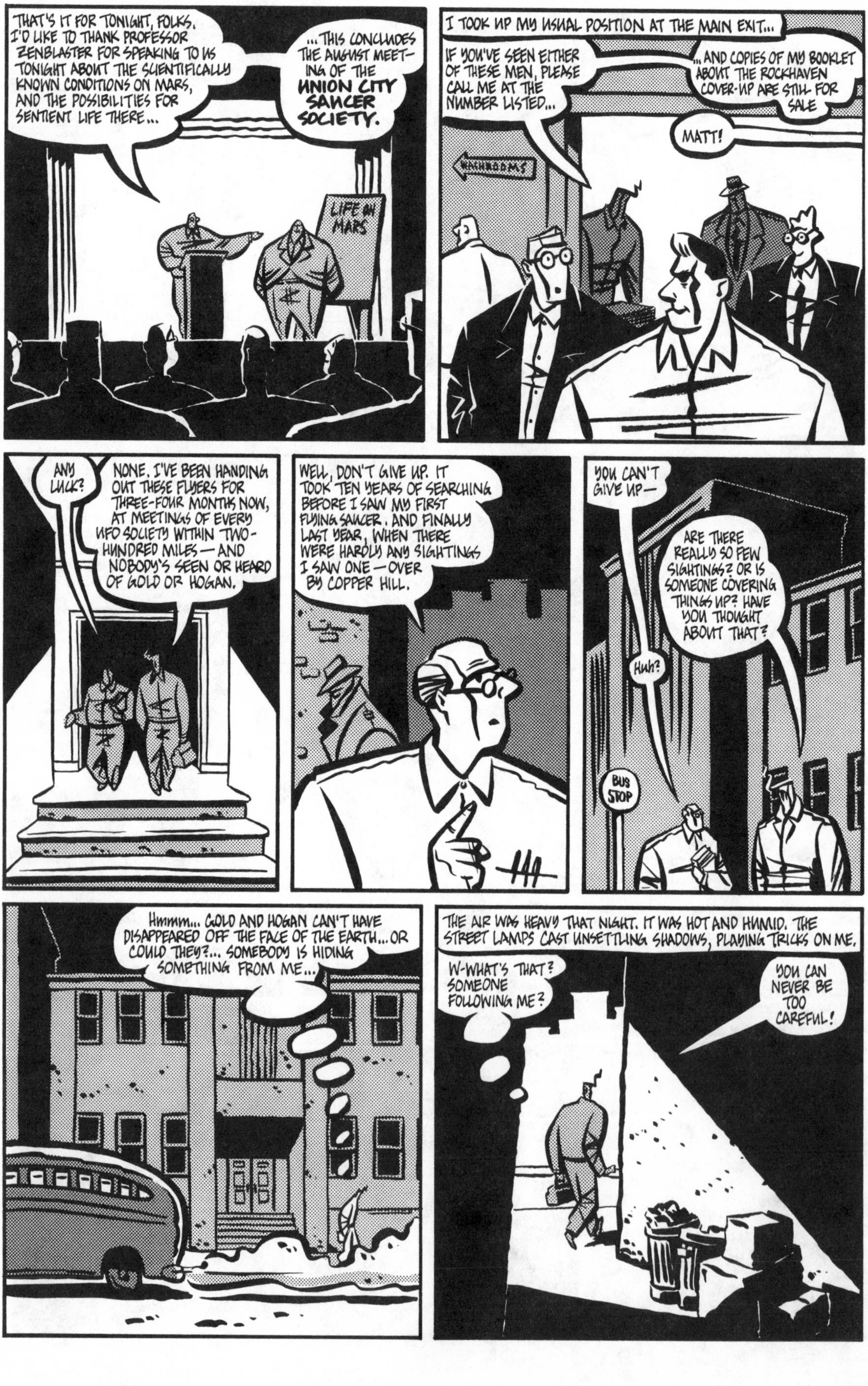
THAT'S IT FOR TONIGHT, FOLKS. I'D LIKE TO THANK PROFESSOR ZENBLASTER FOR SPEAKING TO US TONIGHT ABOUT THE SCIENTIFICALLY KNOWN CONDITIONS ON MARS, AND THE POSSIBILITIES FOR SENTIENT LIFE THERE...
...THIS CONCLUDES THE AUGUST MEETING OF THE UNION CITY SAUCER SOCIETY.
LIFE ON MARS
I TOOK UP MY USUAL POSITION AT THE MAIN EXIT...
IF YOU'VE SEEN EITHER OF THESE MEN, PLEASE CALL ME AT THE NUMBER LISTED...
...AND COPIES OF MY BOOKLET ABOUT THE ROCKHAVEN COVER-UP ARE STILL FOR SALE
MATT!
WASHROOMS
ANY LUCK?
NONE. I'VE BEEN HANDING OUT THESE FLYERS FOR THREE-FOUR MONTHS NOW, AT MEETINGS OF EVERY UFO SOCIETY WITHIN TWO-HUNDRED MILES — AND NOBODY'S SEEN OR HEARD OF GOLD OR HOGAN.
WELL, DON'T GIVE UP. IT TOOK TEN YEARS OF SEARCHING BEFORE I SAW MY FIRST FLYING SAUCER. AND FINALLY LAST YEAR, WHEN THERE WERE HARDLY ANY SIGHTINGS I SAW ONE — OVER BY COPPER HILL.
YOU CAN'T GIVE UP—
ARE THERE REALLY SO FEW SIGHTINGS? OR IS SOMEONE COVERING THINGS UP? HAVE YOU THOUGHT ABOUT THAT?
Huh?
BUS STOP
Hmmm... GOLD AND HOGAN CAN'T HAVE DISAPPEARED OFF THE FACE OF THE EARTH... OR COULD THEY?... SOMEBODY IS HIDING SOMETHING FROM ME...
THE AIR WAS HEAVY THAT NIGHT. IT WAS HOT AND HUMID. THE STREET LAMPS CAST UNSETTLING SHADOWS, PLAYING TRICKS ON ME.
W-WHAT'S THAT? SOMEONE FOLLOWING ME?
YOU CAN NEVER BE TOO CAREFUL!

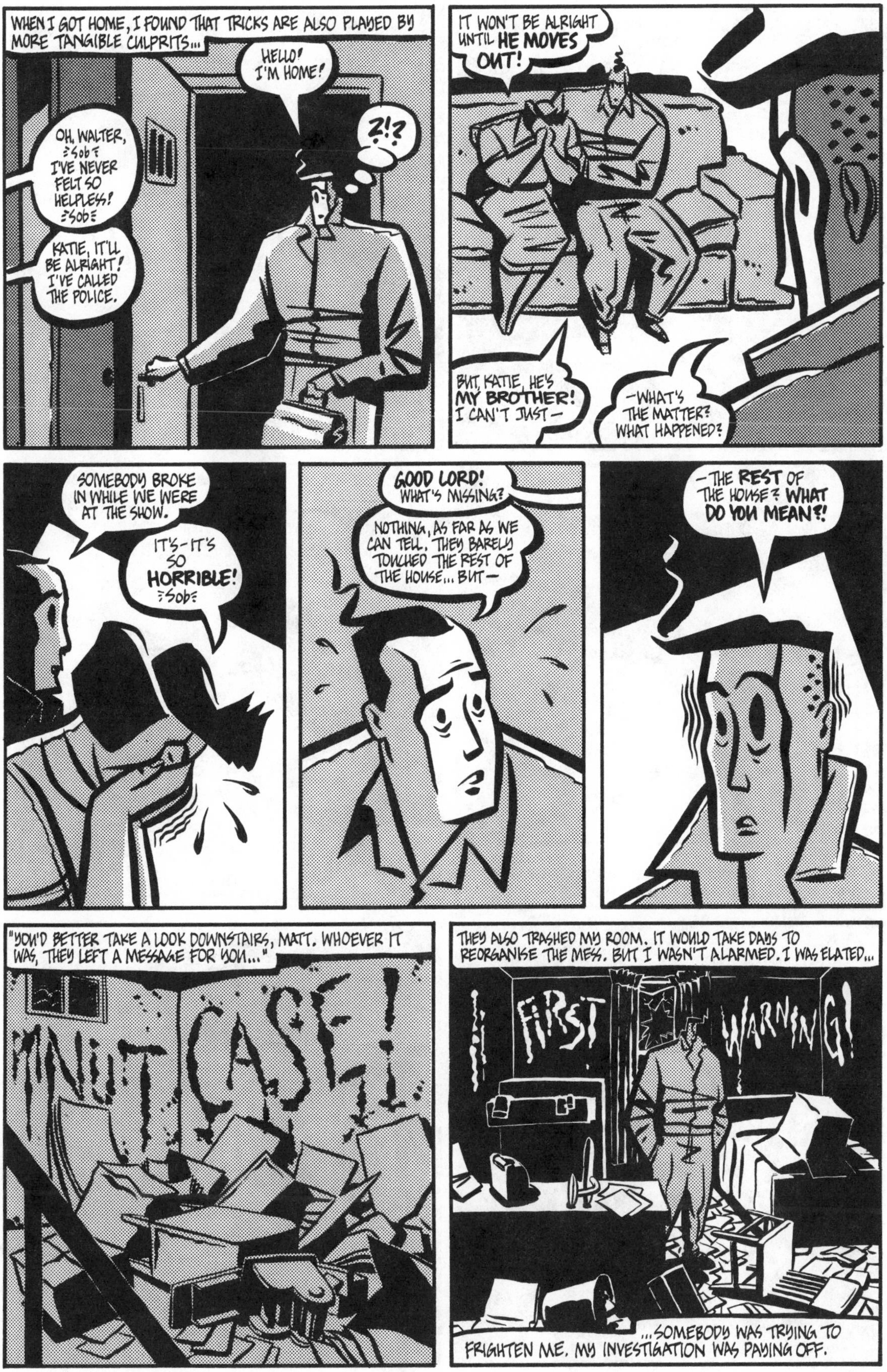

WHEN I GOT HOME, I FOUND THAT TRICKS ARE ALSO PLAYED BY MORE TANGIBLE CULPRITS...
HELLO! I'M HOME!
Z!?
OH, WALTER, =SOB= I'VE NEVER FELT SO HELPLESS! =SOB=
KATIE, IT'LL BE ALRIGHT! I'VE CALLED THE POLICE.
IT WON'T BE ALRIGHT UNTIL HE MOVES OUT!
BUT, KATIE, HE'S MY BROTHER! I CAN'T JUST—
—WHAT'S THE MATTER? WHAT HAPPENED?
SOMEBODY BROKE IN WHILE WE WERE AT THE SHOW.
IT'S—IT'S SO HORRIBLE! =SOB=
GOOD LORD! WHAT'S MISSING?
NOTHING, AS FAR AS WE CAN TELL. THEY BARELY TOUCHED THE REST OF THE HOUSE... BUT—
—THE REST OF THE HOUSE? WHAT DO YOU MEAN?!
"YOU'D BETTER TAKE A LOOK DOWNSTAIRS, MATT. WHOEVER IT WAS, THEY LEFT A MESSAGE FOR YOU..."
NUT CASE!
THEY ALSO TRASHED MY ROOM. IT WOULD TAKE DAYS TO REORGANISE THE MESS. BUT I WASN'T ALARMED. I WAS ELATED...
FIRST WARNING!
...SOMEBODY WAS TRYING TO FRIGHTEN ME. MY INVESTIGATION WAS PAYING OFF.

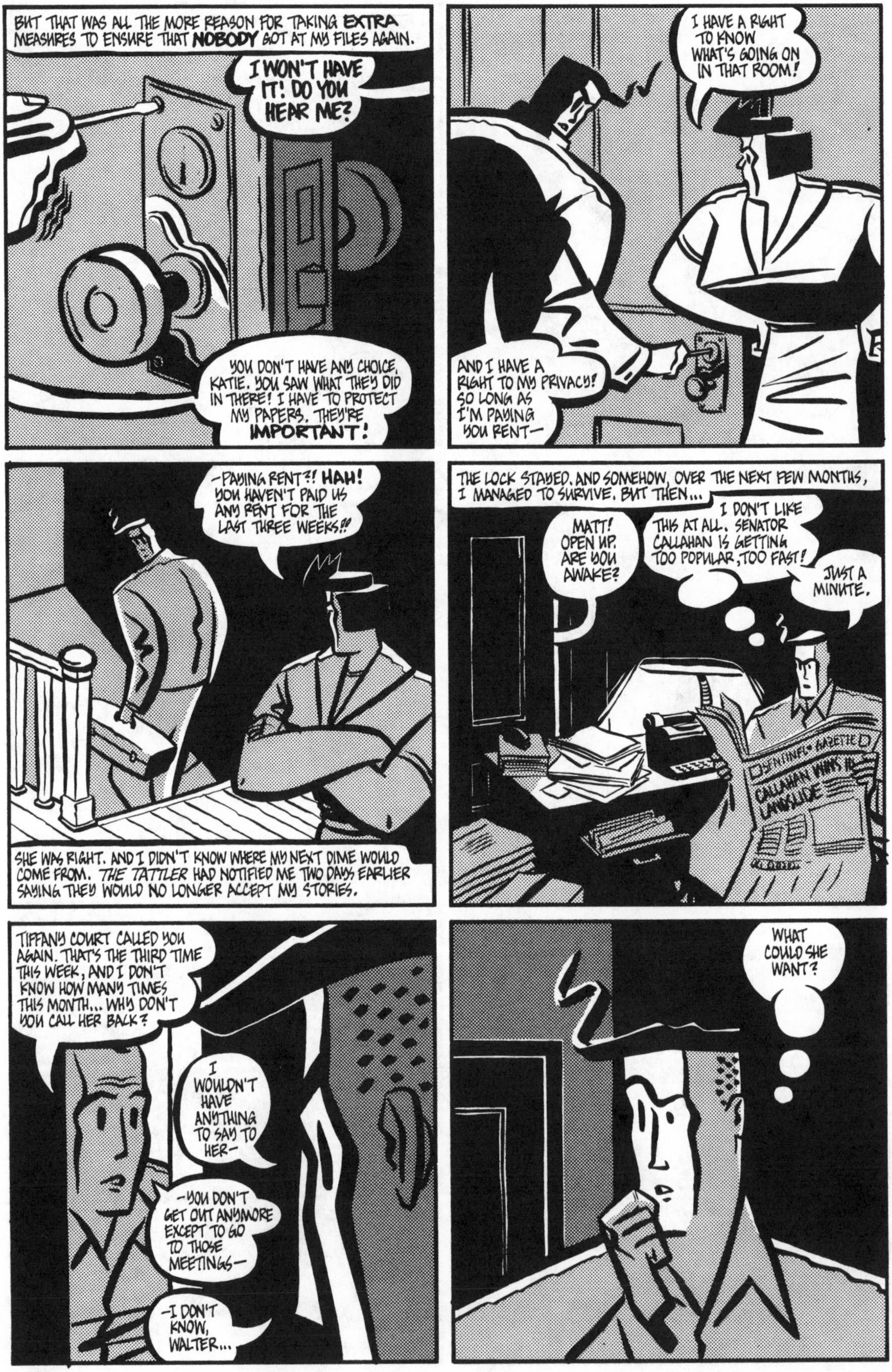

BUT THAT WAS ALL THE MORE REASON FOR TAKING **EXTRA** MEASURES TO ENSURE THAT **NOBODY** GOT AT MY FILES AGAIN.
I WON'T HAVE IT! DO YOU HEAR ME?
YOU DON'T HAVE ANY CHOICE, KATIE. YOU SAW WHAT THEY DID IN THERE! I HAVE TO PROTECT MY PAPERS. THEY'RE **IMPORTANT!**
I HAVE A RIGHT TO KNOW WHAT'S GOING ON IN THAT ROOM!
AND I HAVE A RIGHT TO MY PRIVACY! SO LONG AS I'M PAYING YOU RENT—
—PAYING RENT?! **HAH!** YOU HAVEN'T PAID US ANY RENT FOR THE LAST THREE WEEKS?!?
SHE WAS RIGHT. AND I DIDN'T KNOW WHERE MY NEXT DIME WOULD COME FROM. *THE TATTLER* HAD NOTIFIED ME TWO DAYS EARLIER SAYING THEY WOULD NO LONGER ACCEPT MY STORIES.
THE LOCK STAYED. AND SOMEHOW, OVER THE NEXT FEW MONTHS, I MANAGED TO SURVIVE. BUT THEN...
MATT! OPEN UP. ARE YOU AWAKE?
I DON'T LIKE THIS AT ALL. SENATOR CALLAHAN IS GETTING TOO POPULAR, TOO FAST!
JUST A MINUTE.
CALLAHAN WINS IN LANDSLIDE
TIFFANY COURT CALLED YOU AGAIN. THAT'S THE THIRD TIME THIS WEEK, AND I DON'T KNOW HOW MANY TIMES THIS MONTH... WHY DON'T YOU CALL HER BACK?
I WOULDN'T HAVE ANYTHING TO SAY TO HER—
—YOU DON'T GET OUT ANYMORE EXCEPT TO GO TO THOSE MEETINGS—
—I DON'T KNOW, WALTER...
WHAT COULD SHE WANT?

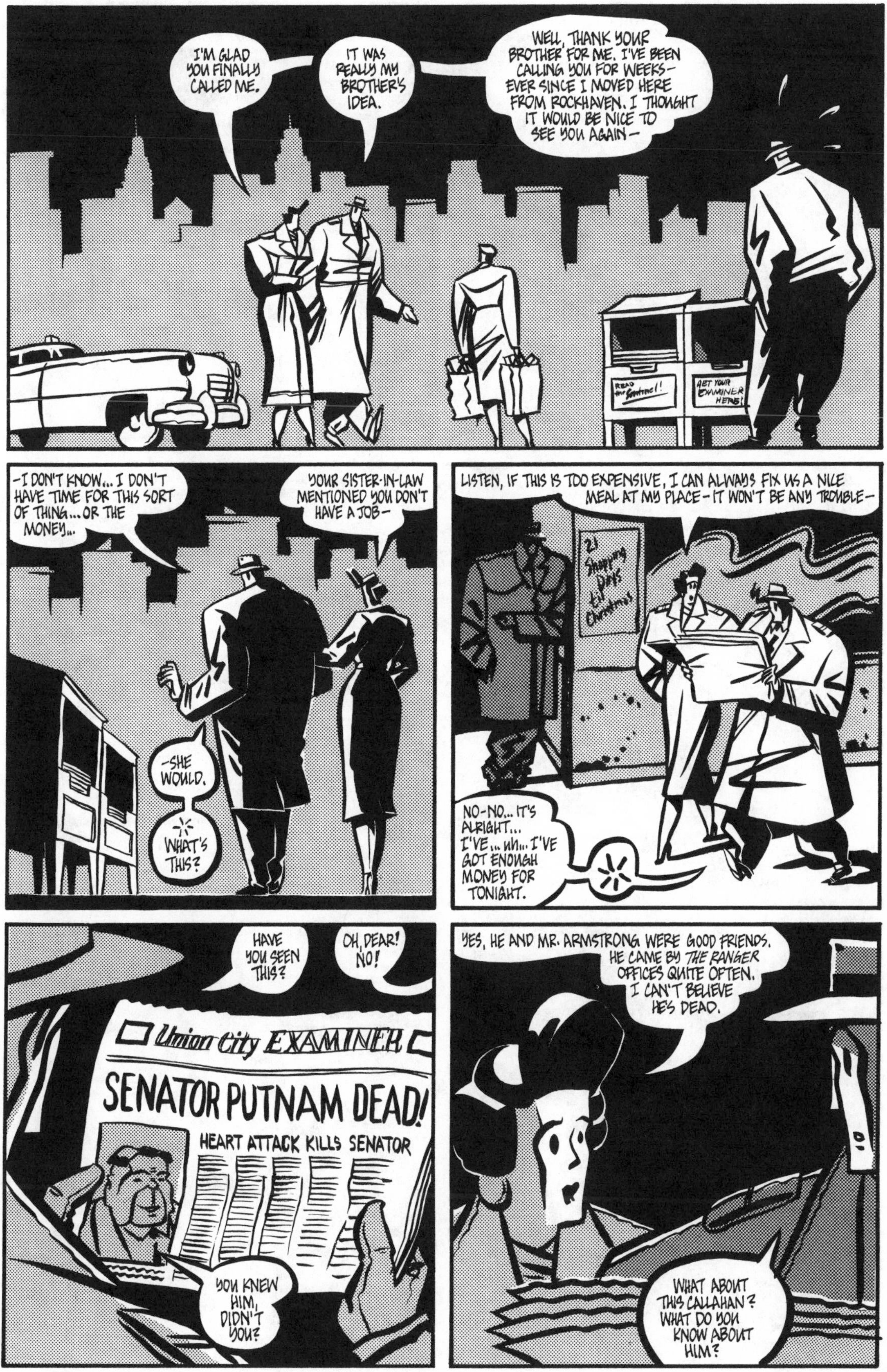
I'M GLAD YOU FINALLY CALLED ME.
IT WAS REALLY MY BROTHER'S IDEA.
WELL, THANK YOUR BROTHER FOR ME. I'VE BEEN CALLING YOU FOR WEEKS— EVER SINCE I MOVED HERE FROM ROCKHAVEN. I THOUGHT IT WOULD BE NICE TO SEE YOU AGAIN—
READ the Sentinel!
GET YOUR EXAMINER HERE!
—I DON'T KNOW... I DON'T HAVE TIME FOR THIS SORT OF THING... OR THE MONEY...
YOUR SISTER-IN-LAW MENTIONED YOU DON'T HAVE A JOB—
—SHE WOULD.
WHAT'S THIS?
LISTEN, IF THIS IS TOO EXPENSIVE, I CAN ALWAYS FIX US A NICE MEAL AT MY PLACE— IT WON'T BE ANY TROUBLE—
21 Shopping Days til Christmas
NO-NO... IT'S ALRIGHT... I'VE... uh... I'VE GOT ENOUGH MONEY FOR TONIGHT.
HAVE YOU SEEN THIS?
OH, DEAR! NO!
Union City EXAMINER
SENATOR PUTNAM DEAD!
HEART ATTACK KILLS SENATOR
YOU KNEW HIM, DIDN'T YOU?
YES, HE AND MR. ARMSTRONG WERE GOOD FRIENDS. HE CAME BY THE RANGER OFFICES QUITE OFTEN. I CAN'T BELIEVE HE'S DEAD.
WHAT ABOUT THIS CALLAHAN? WHAT DO YOU KNOW ABOUT HIM?

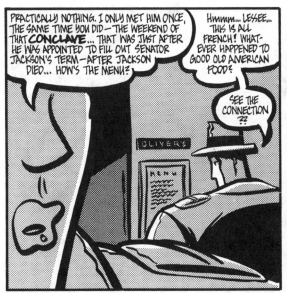

PRACTICALLY NOTHING. I ONLY MET HIM ONCE, THE SAME TIME YOU DID—THE WEEKEND OF THAT **CONCLAVE**... THAT WAS JUST AFTER HE WAS APPOINTED TO FILL OUT SENATOR JACKSON'S TERM—AFTER JACKSON DIED... HOW'S THE MENU?

Hmmm... LESSEE... THIS IS ALL FRENCH! WHAT-EVER HAPPENED TO GOOD OLD AMERICAN FOOD?

SEE THE CONNECTION??

JUST AFTER CALLAHAN'S BEEN ELECTED TO THE SENATE, PUTNAM DIES—MYSTERIOUSLY, I MIGHT ADD!

WHAT'S SO MYSTERIOUS ABOUT A HEART ATTACK???

"I'VE GOT MY SUSPICIONS THAT SENATOR CALLAHAN ISN'T WHAT HE APPEARS TO BE..."

WHAT **ARE** YOU TALKING ABOUT?

CALLAHAN DOESN'T KNOW IT, BUT HE'S AN **ALIEN** AGENT—A SLEEPER!

WHAT?!

I **SAW** HIM BEING **PROCESSED**, TIFFANY—JUST AS I WAS! SOME DAY, HIS ALIEN MASTERS WILL ACTIVATE HIS ALIEN MIND AND HE WILL **BETRAY** US ALL!

MATT, THIS IS NONSENSE. CAN WE FORGET THIS AND HAVE A NICE QUIET DIN—

I KNEW IT! YOU'RE JUST LIKE ALL THE REST OF **THEM!** TOO BLIND TO SEE THE ALIEN MENACE! TOO DEAF TO LISTEN TO THE TRUTH!!

MATT, KEEP YOUR VOICE DOWN! PEOPLE ARE STARING!!

LET THEM STARE! YOU'LL HAVE TO EXCUSE ME! I HAVE IMPORTANT WORK WAITING TO BE DONE!!

MATT?!?

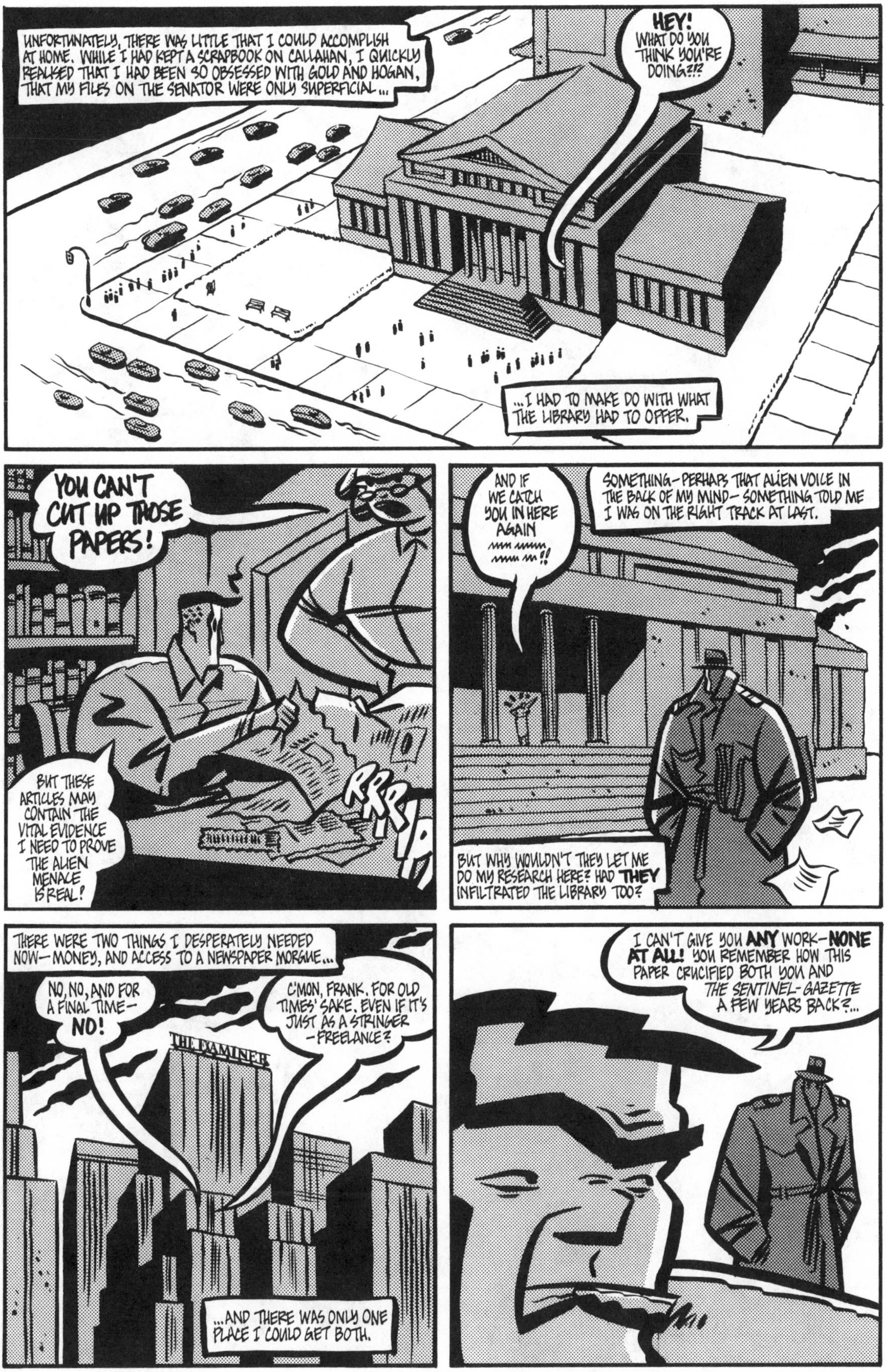
UNFORTUNATELY, THERE WAS LITTLE THAT I COULD ACCOMPLISH AT HOME. WHILE I HAD KEPT A SCRAPBOOK ON CALLAHAN, I QUICKLY REALISED THAT I HAD BEEN SO OBSESSED WITH GOLD AND HOGAN, THAT MY FILES ON THE SENATOR WERE ONLY SUPERFICIAL...
HEY! WHAT DO YOU THINK YOU'RE DOING?!?
...I HAD TO MAKE DO WITH WHAT THE LIBRARY HAD TO OFFER.
YOU CAN'T CUT UP THOSE PAPERS!
BUT THESE ARTICLES MAY CONTAIN THE VITAL EVIDENCE I NEED TO PROVE THE ALIEN MENACE IS REAL!
RRRIP
AND IF WE CATCH YOU IN HERE AGAIN
SOMETHING—PERHAPS THAT ALIEN VOICE IN THE BACK OF MY MIND—SOMETHING TOLD ME I WAS ON THE RIGHT TRACK AT LAST.
BUT WHY WOULDN'T THEY LET ME DO MY RESEARCH HERE? HAD THEY INFILTRATED THE LIBRARY TOO?
THERE WERE TWO THINGS I DESPERATELY NEEDED NOW—MONEY, AND ACCESS TO A NEWSPAPER MORGUE...
NO, NO, AND FOR A FINAL TIME—NO!
C'MON, FRANK. FOR OLD TIMES' SAKE. EVEN IF IT'S JUST AS A STRINGER—FREELANCE?
THE EXAMINER
...AND THERE WAS ONLY ONE PLACE I COULD GET BOTH.
I CAN'T GIVE YOU ANY WORK—NONE AT ALL! YOU REMEMBER HOW THIS PAPER CRUCIFIED BOTH YOU AND THE SENTINEL-GAZETTE A FEW YEARS BACK?...

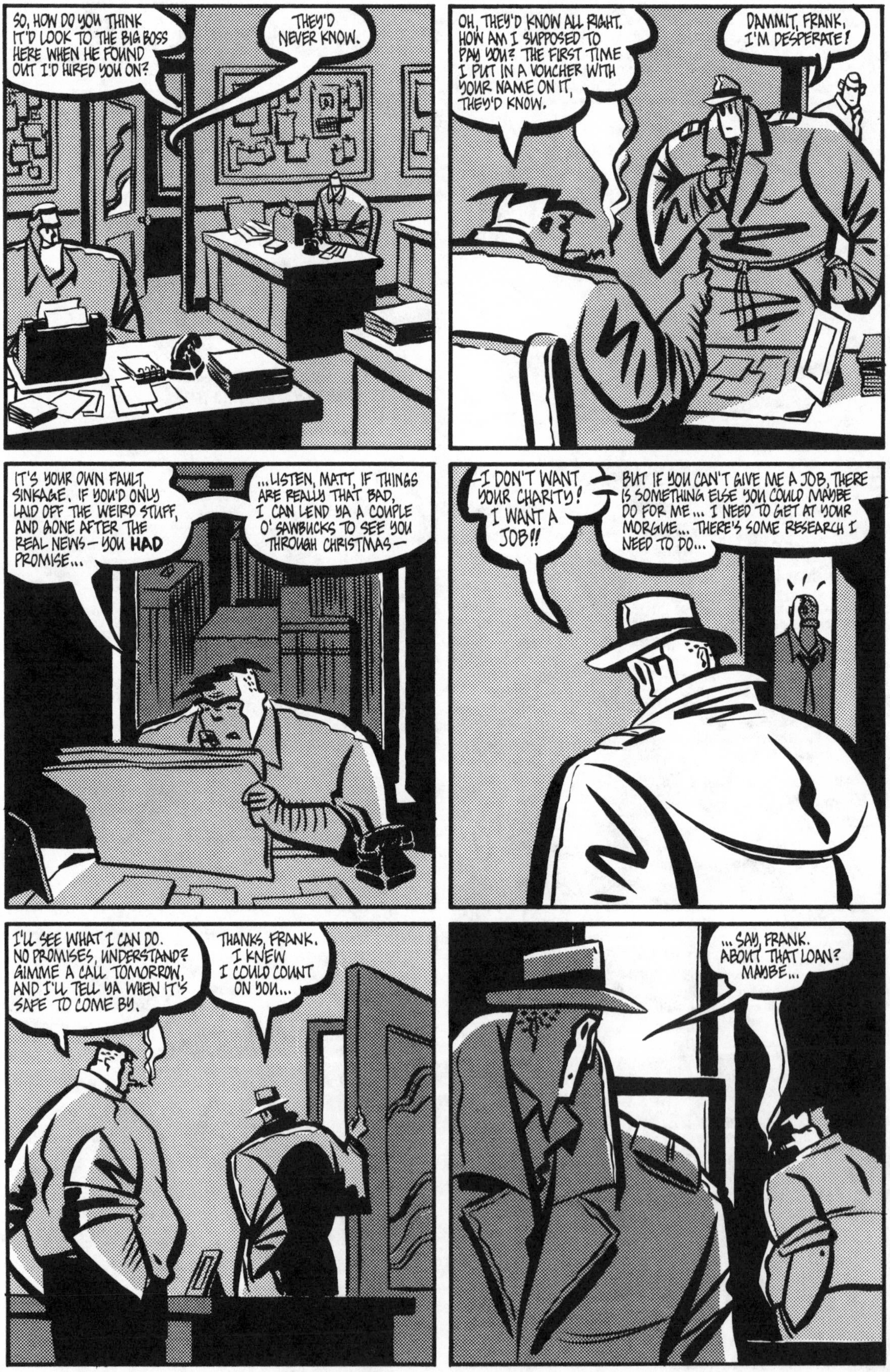
SO, HOW DO YOU THINK IT'D LOOK TO THE BIG BOSS HERE WHEN HE FOUND OUT I'D HIRED YOU ON?
THEY'D NEVER KNOW.
OH, THEY'D KNOW ALL RIGHT. HOW AM I SUPPOSED TO PAY YOU? THE FIRST TIME I PUT IN A VOUCHER WITH YOUR NAME ON IT, THEY'D KNOW.
DAMMIT, FRANK, I'M DESPERATE!
IT'S YOUR OWN FAULT, SINKAGE. IF YOU'D ONLY LAID OFF THE WEIRD STUFF, AND GONE AFTER THE REAL NEWS— YOU **HAD** PROMISE...
...LISTEN, MATT, IF THINGS ARE REALLY THAT BAD, I CAN LEND YA A COUPLE O' SAWBUCKS TO SEE YOU THROUGH CHRISTMAS—
I DON'T WANT YOUR CHARITY! I WANT A JOB!!
BUT IF YOU CAN'T GIVE ME A JOB, THERE IS SOMETHING ELSE YOU COULD MAYBE DO FOR ME... I NEED TO GET AT YOUR MORGUE... THERE'S SOME RESEARCH I NEED TO DO...
I'LL SEE WHAT I CAN DO. NO PROMISES, UNDERSTAND? GIMME A CALL TOMORROW, AND I'LL TELL YA WHEN IT'S SAFE TO COME BY.
THANKS, FRANK. I KNEW I COULD COUNT ON YOU...
...SAY, FRANK. ABOUT THAT LOAN? MAYBE...

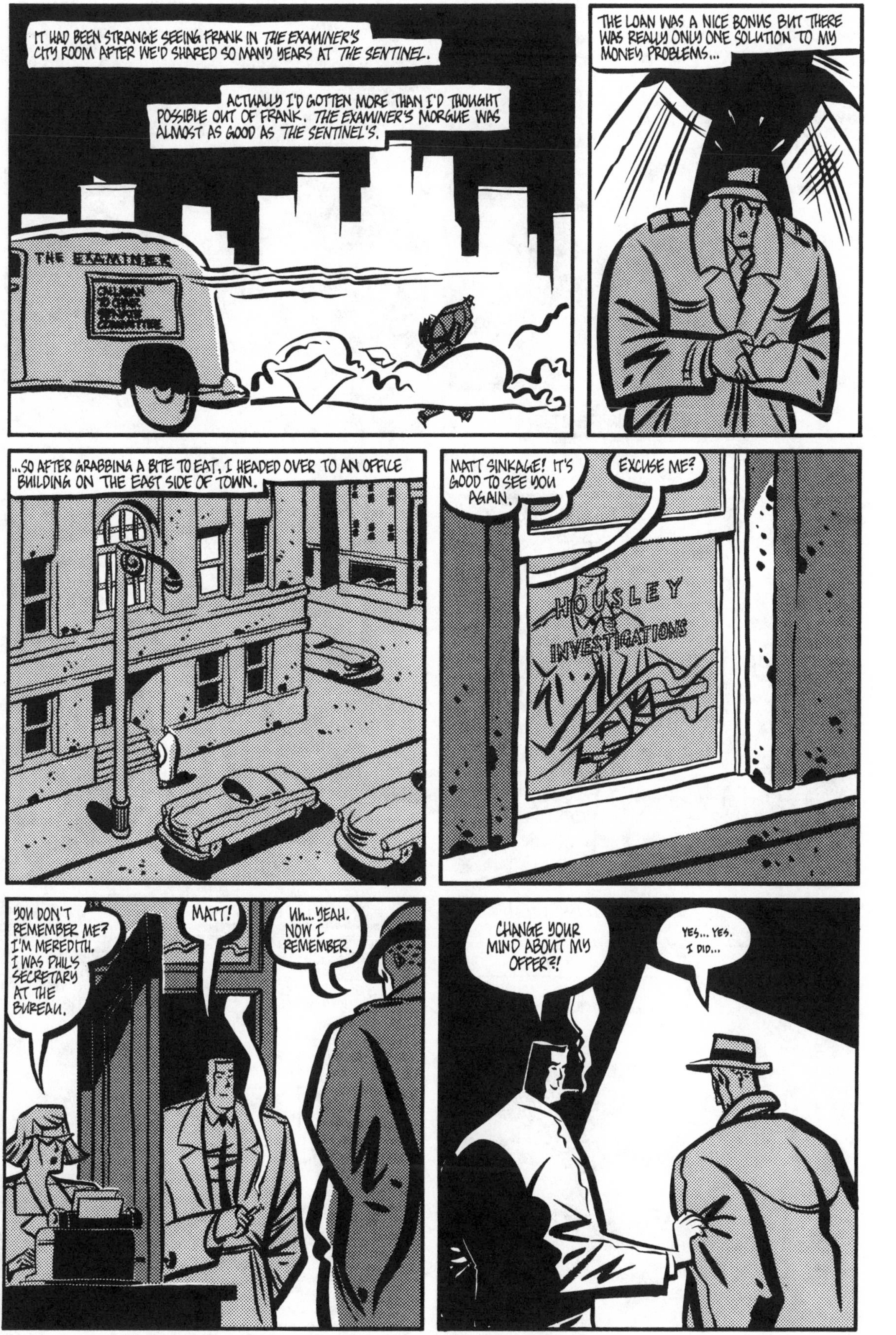
IT HAD BEEN STRANGE SEEING FRANK IN THE EXAMINER'S CITY ROOM AFTER WE'D SHARED SO MANY YEARS AT THE SENTINEL.
ACTUALLY I'D GOTTEN MORE THAN I'D THOUGHT POSSIBLE OUT OF FRANK. THE EXAMINER'S MORGUE WAS ALMOST AS GOOD AS THE SENTINEL'S.
THE EXAMINER
THE LOAN WAS A NICE BONUS BUT THERE WAS REALLY ONLY ONE SOLUTION TO MY MONEY PROBLEMS...
...SO AFTER GRABBING A BITE TO EAT, I HEADED OVER TO AN OFFICE BUILDING ON THE EAST SIDE OF TOWN.
MATT SINKAGE! IT'S GOOD TO SEE YOU AGAIN.
EXCUSE ME?
HOUSLEY INVESTIGATIONS
YOU DON'T REMEMBER ME? I'M MEREDITH. I WAS PHIL'S SECRETARY AT THE BUREAU.
MATT!
UH... YEAH. NOW I REMEMBER.
CHANGE YOUR MIND ABOUT MY OFFER?!
YES... YES. I DID...

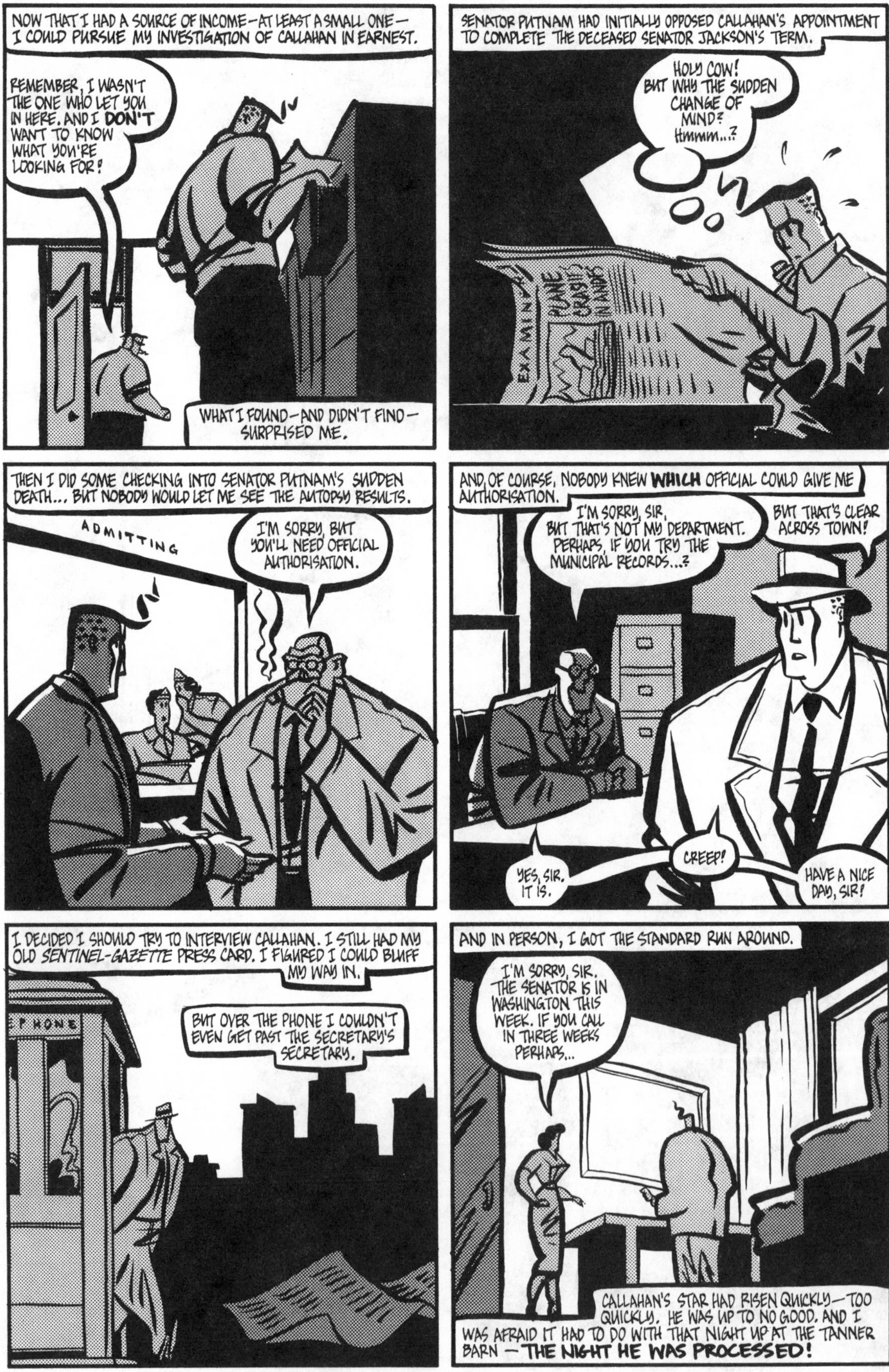
NOW THAT I HAD A SOURCE OF INCOME—AT LEAST A SMALL ONE—I COULD PURSUE MY INVESTIGATION OF CALLAHAN IN EARNEST.
REMEMBER, I WASN'T THE ONE WHO LET YOU IN HERE. AND I **DON'T** WANT TO KNOW WHAT YOU'RE LOOKING FOR!
WHAT I FOUND—AND DIDN'T FIND—SURPRISED ME.
SENATOR PUTNAM HAD INITIALLY OPPOSED CALLAHAN'S APPOINTMENT TO COMPLETE THE DECEASED SENATOR JACKSON'S TERM.
HOLY COW! BUT WHY THE SUDDEN CHANGE OF MIND? Hmmm...?
EXAMINER
PLANE CRASH IN ANDES
THEN I DID SOME CHECKING INTO SENATOR PUTNAM'S SUDDEN DEATH... BUT NOBODY WOULD LET ME SEE THE AUTOPSY RESULTS.
ADMITTING
I'M SORRY, BUT YOU'LL NEED OFFICIAL AUTHORISATION.
AND, OF COURSE, NOBODY KNEW **WHICH** OFFICIAL COULD GIVE ME AUTHORISATION.
I'M SORRY, SIR, BUT THAT'S NOT MY DEPARTMENT. PERHAPS, IF YOU TRY THE MUNICIPAL RECORDS...?
BUT THAT'S CLEAR ACROSS TOWN!
YES, SIR. IT IS.
CREEP!
HAVE A NICE DAY, SIR!
I DECIDED I SHOULD TRY TO INTERVIEW CALLAHAN. I STILL HAD MY OLD SENTINEL-GAZETTE PRESS CARD. I FIGURED I COULD BLUFF MY WAY IN.
PHONE
BUT OVER THE PHONE I COULDN'T EVEN GET PAST THE SECRETARY'S SECRETARY.
AND IN PERSON, I GOT THE STANDARD RUN AROUND.
I'M SORRY, SIR. THE SENATOR IS IN WASHINGTON THIS WEEK. IF YOU CALL IN THREE WEEKS PERHAPS...
CALLAHAN'S STAR HAD RISEN QUICKLY—TOO QUICKLY. HE WAS UP TO NO GOOD. AND I WAS AFRAID IT HAD TO DO WITH THAT NIGHT UP AT THE TANNER BARN — **THE NIGHT HE WAS PROCESSED!**

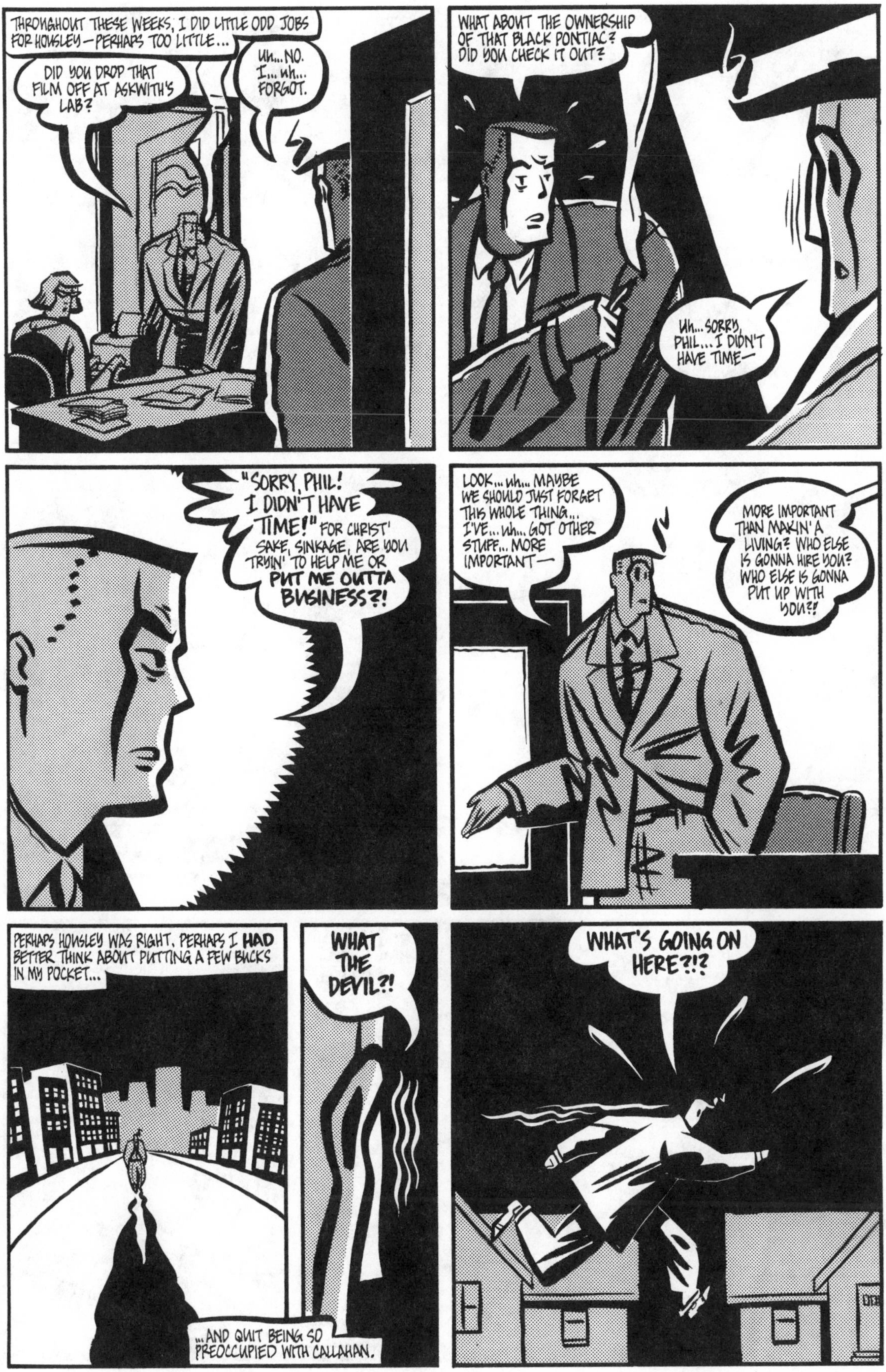
THROUGHOUT THESE WEEKS, I DID LITTLE ODD JOBS FOR HOUSLEY—PERHAPS TOO LITTLE...
DID YOU DROP THAT FILM OFF AT ASKWITH'S LAB?
UH... NO. I... UH... FORGOT.
WHAT ABOUT THE OWNERSHIP OF THAT BLACK PONTIAC? DID YOU CHECK IT OUT?
UH... SORRY, PHIL... I DIDN'T HAVE TIME—
"SORRY, PHIL! I DIDN'T HAVE TIME!" FOR CHRIST' SAKE, SINKAGE, ARE YOU TRYIN' TO HELP ME OR PUT ME OUTTA BUSINESS?!
LOOK... UH... MAYBE WE SHOULD JUST FORGET THIS WHOLE THING... I'VE... UH... GOT OTHER STUFF... MORE IMPORTANT—
MORE IMPORTANT THAN MAKIN' A LIVING? WHO ELSE IS GONNA HIRE YOU? WHO ELSE IS GONNA PUT UP WITH YOU?!
PERHAPS HOUSLEY WAS RIGHT. PERHAPS I HAD BETTER THINK ABOUT PUTTING A FEW BUCKS IN MY POCKET...
...AND QUIT BEING SO PREOCCUPIED WITH CALLAHAN.
WHAT THE DEVIL?!
WHAT'S GOING ON HERE?!?

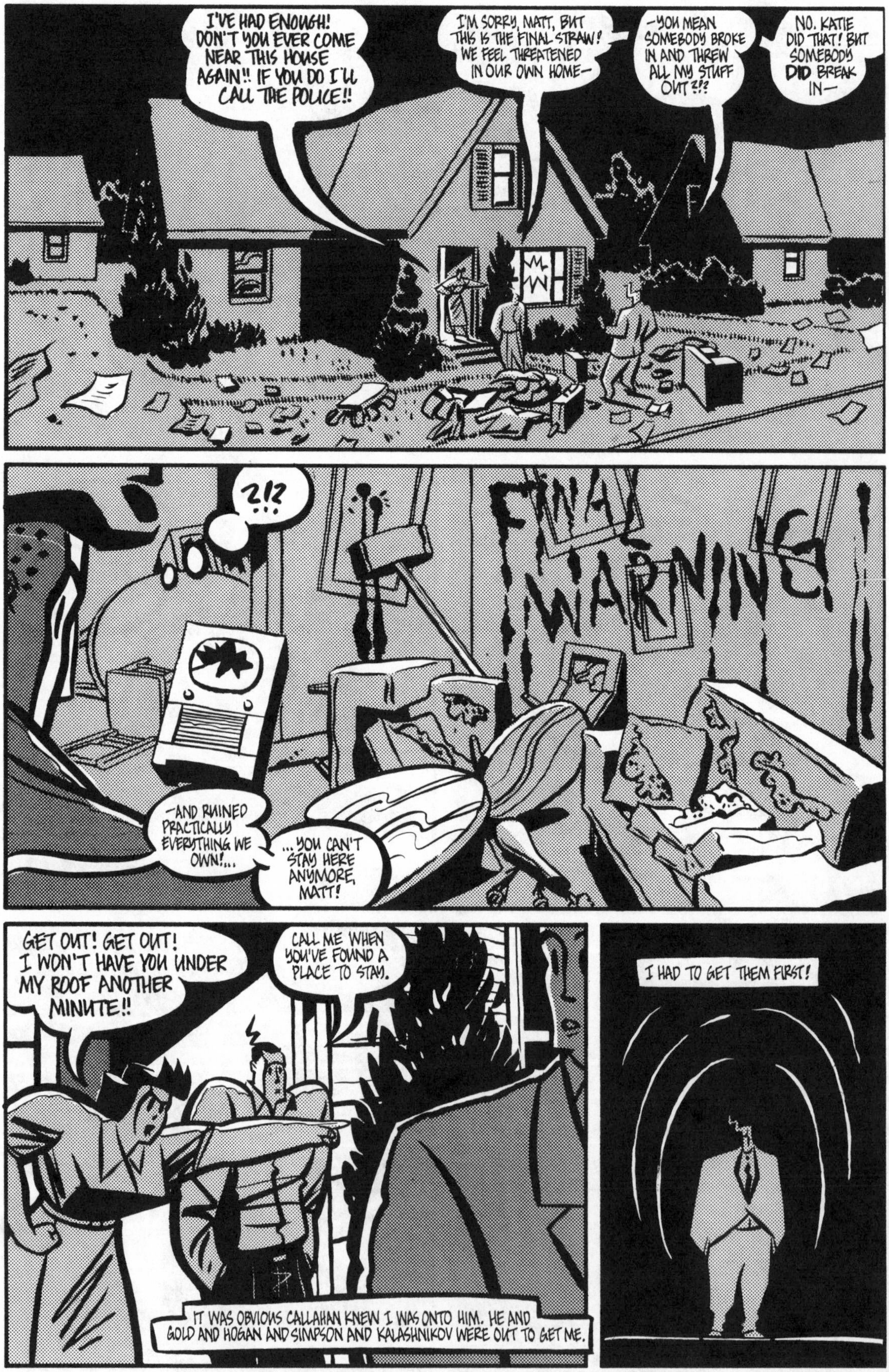
I'VE HAD ENOUGH! DON'T YOU EVER COME NEAR THIS HOUSE AGAIN!! IF YOU DO I'LL CALL THE POLICE!!
I'M SORRY, MATT, BUT THIS IS THE FINAL STRAW! WE FEEL THREATENED IN OUR OWN HOME—
—YOU MEAN SOMEBODY BROKE IN AND THREW ALL MY STUFF OUT?!?
NO. KATIE DID THAT! BUT SOMEBODY **DID** BREAK IN—
?!?
FINAL WARNING
—AND RUINED PRACTICALLY EVERYTHING WE OWN!...
...YOU CAN'T STAY HERE ANYMORE, MATT!
GET OUT! GET OUT! I WON'T HAVE YOU UNDER MY ROOF ANOTHER MINUTE!!
CALL ME WHEN YOU'VE FOUND A PLACE TO STAY.
IT WAS OBVIOUS CALLAHAN KNEW I WAS ONTO HIM. HE AND GOLD AND HOGAN AND SIMPSON AND KALASHNIKOV WERE OUT TO GET ME.
I HAD TO GET THEM FIRST!

CHAPTER FIVE

FORCES BEYOND OUR CONTROL

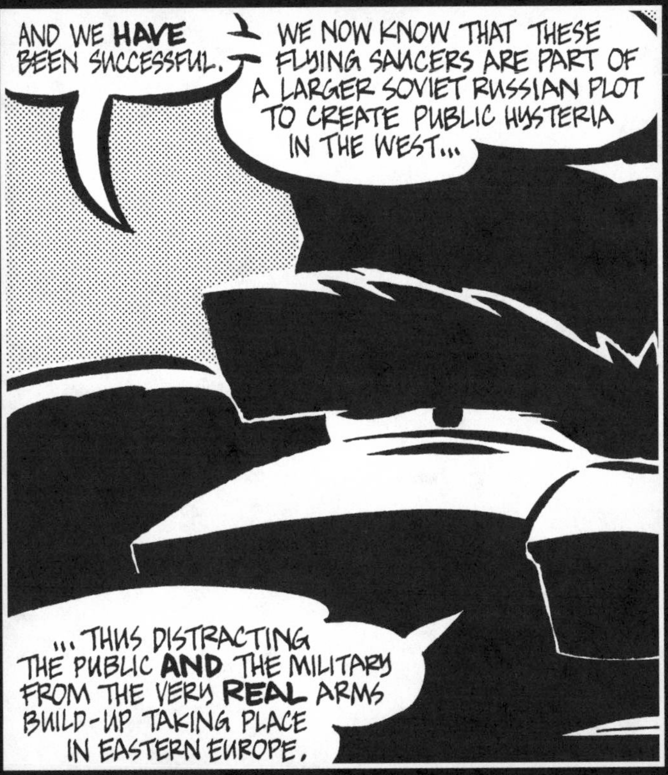
AND WE **HAVE** BEEN SUCCESSFUL.
WE NOW KNOW THAT THESE FLYING SAUCERS ARE PART OF A LARGER SOVIET RUSSIAN PLOT TO CREATE PUBLIC HYSTERIA IN THE WEST...
... THUS DISTRACTING THE PUBLIC **AND** THE MILITARY FROM THE VERY **REAL** ARMS BUILD-UP TAKING PLACE IN EASTERN EUROPE.

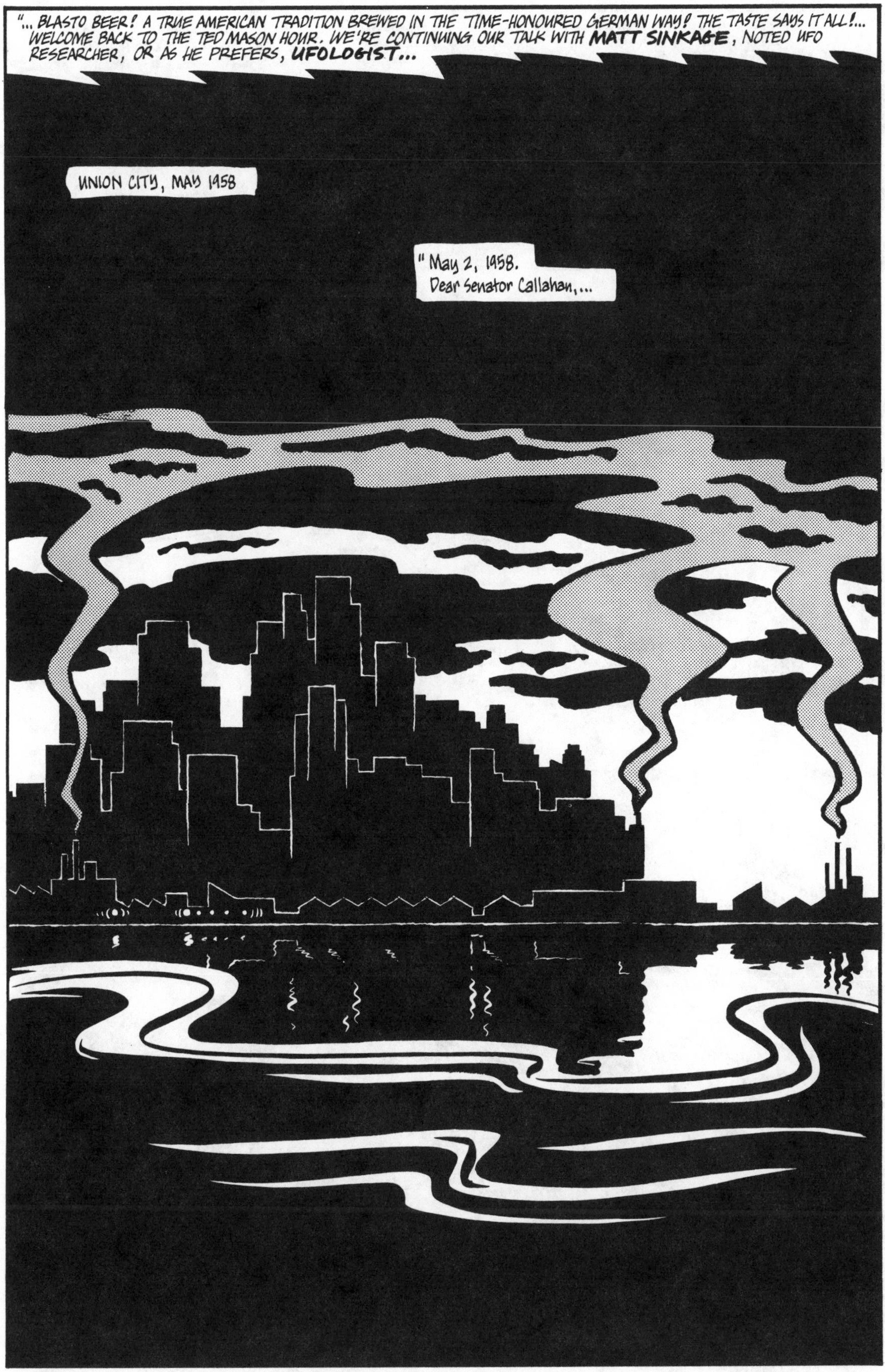
"... BLASTO BEER! A TRUE AMERICAN TRADITION BREWED IN THE TIME-HONOURED GERMAN WAY! THE TASTE SAYS IT ALL!... WELCOME BACK TO THE TED MASON HOUR. WE'RE CONTINUING OUR TALK WITH **MATT SINKAGE**, NOTED UFO RESEARCHER, OR AS HE PREFERS, **UFOLOGIST...**
UNION CITY, MAY 1958
"May 2, 1958.
Dear Senator Callahan,...

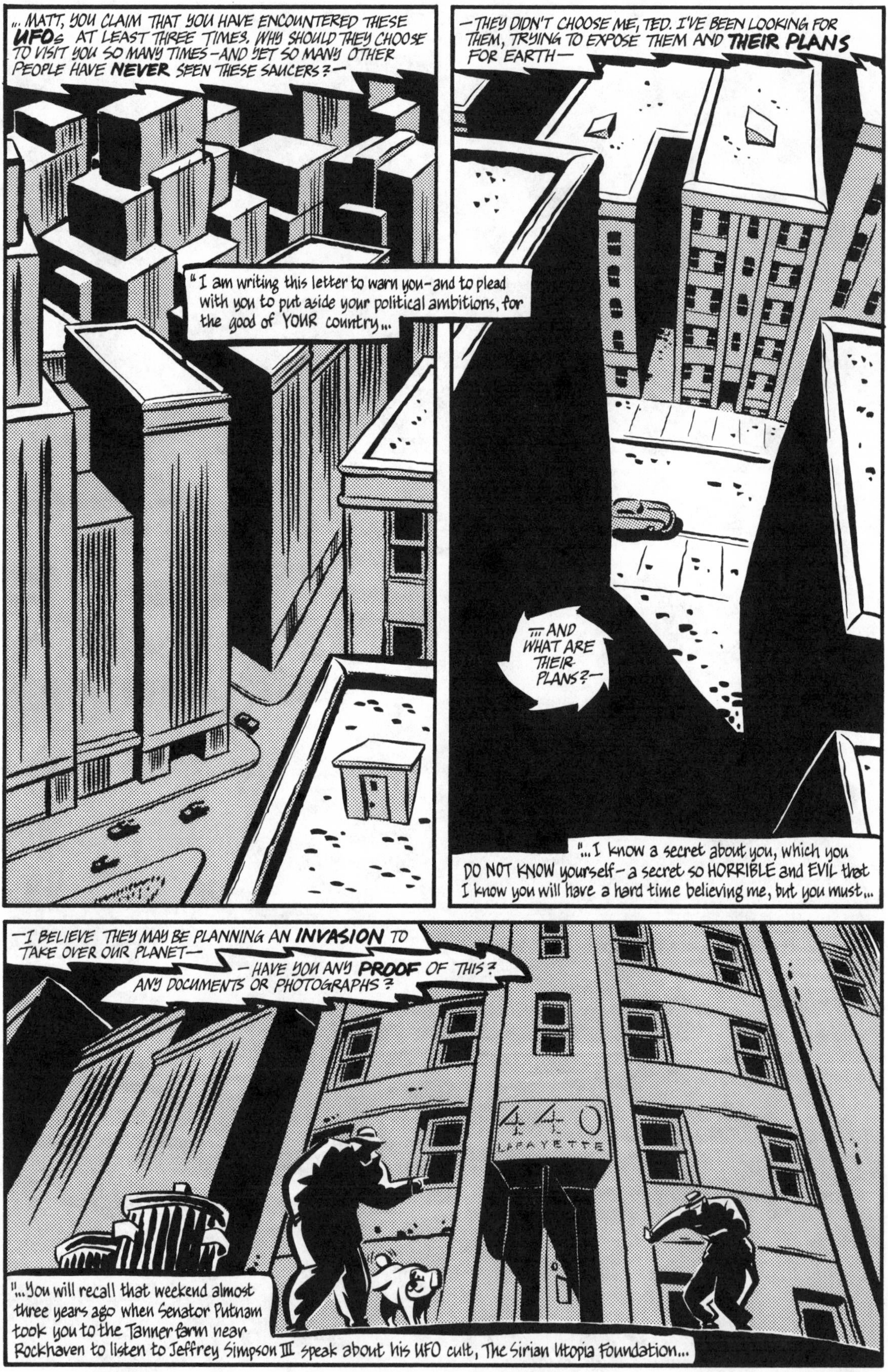

...MATT, YOU CLAIM THAT YOU HAVE ENCOUNTERED THESE UFOs AT LEAST THREE TIMES. WHY SHOULD THEY CHOOSE TO VISIT YOU SO MANY TIMES—AND YET SO MANY OTHER PEOPLE HAVE NEVER SEEN THESE SAUCERS?—
"I am writing this letter to warn you—and to plead with you to put aside your political ambitions, for the good of YOUR country...
—THEY DIDN'T CHOOSE ME, TED. I'VE BEEN LOOKING FOR THEM, TRYING TO EXPOSE THEM AND THEIR PLANS FOR EARTH—
...AND WHAT ARE THEIR PLANS?—
"...I know a secret about you, which you DO NOT KNOW yourself—a secret so HORRIBLE and EVIL that I know you will have a hard time believing me, but you must...
—I BELIEVE THEY MAY BE PLANNING AN INVASION TO TAKE OVER OUR PLANET—
—HAVE YOU ANY PROOF OF THIS? ANY DOCUMENTS OR PHOTOGRAPHS?
440 LAFAYETTE
"...You will recall that weekend almost three years ago when Senator Putnam took you to the Tanner farm near Rockhaven to listen to Jeffrey Simpson III speak about his UFO cult, The Sirian Utopia Foundation...

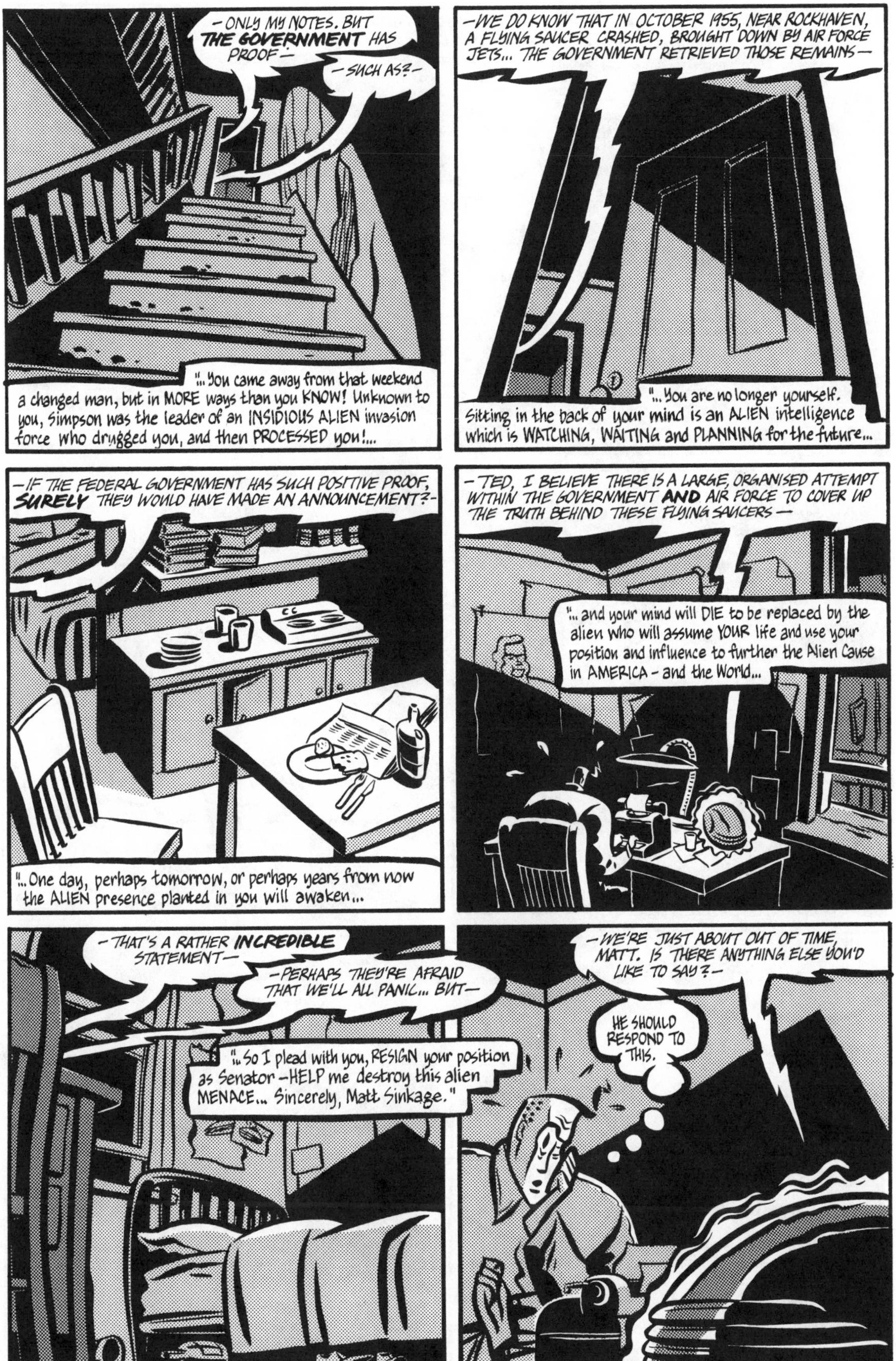
–ONLY MY NOTES. BUT THE GOVERNMENT HAS PROOF–
–SUCH AS?–
"...You came away from that weekend a changed man, but in MORE ways than you KNOW! Unknown to you, Simpson was the leader of an INSIDIOUS ALIEN invasion force who drugged you, and then PROCESSED you!...
–WE DO KNOW THAT IN OCTOBER 1955, NEAR ROCKHAVEN, A FLYING SAUCER CRASHED, BROUGHT DOWN BY AIR FORCE JETS... THE GOVERNMENT RETRIEVED THOSE REMAINS–
"...You are no longer yourself. Sitting in the back of your mind is an ALIEN intelligence which is WATCHING, WAITING and PLANNING for the future...
–IF THE FEDERAL GOVERNMENT HAS SUCH POSITIVE PROOF, SURELY THEY WOULD HAVE MADE AN ANNOUNCEMENT?–
"...One day, perhaps tomorrow, or perhaps years from now the ALIEN presence planted in you will awaken...
–TED, I BELIEVE THERE IS A LARGE, ORGANISED ATTEMPT WITHIN THE GOVERNMENT AND AIR FORCE TO COVER UP THE TRUTH BEHIND THESE FLYING SAUCERS–
"...and your mind will DIE to be replaced by the alien who will assume YOUR life and use your position and influence to further the Alien Cause in AMERICA – and the World...
–THAT'S A RATHER INCREDIBLE STATEMENT–
–PERHAPS THEY'RE AFRAID THAT WE'LL ALL PANIC... BUT–
"...So I plead with you, RESIGN your position as Senator –HELP me destroy this alien MENACE... Sincerely, Matt Sinkage."
–WE'RE JUST ABOUT OUT OF TIME, MATT. IS THERE ANYTHING ELSE YOU'D LIKE TO SAY?–
HE SHOULD RESPOND TO THIS.

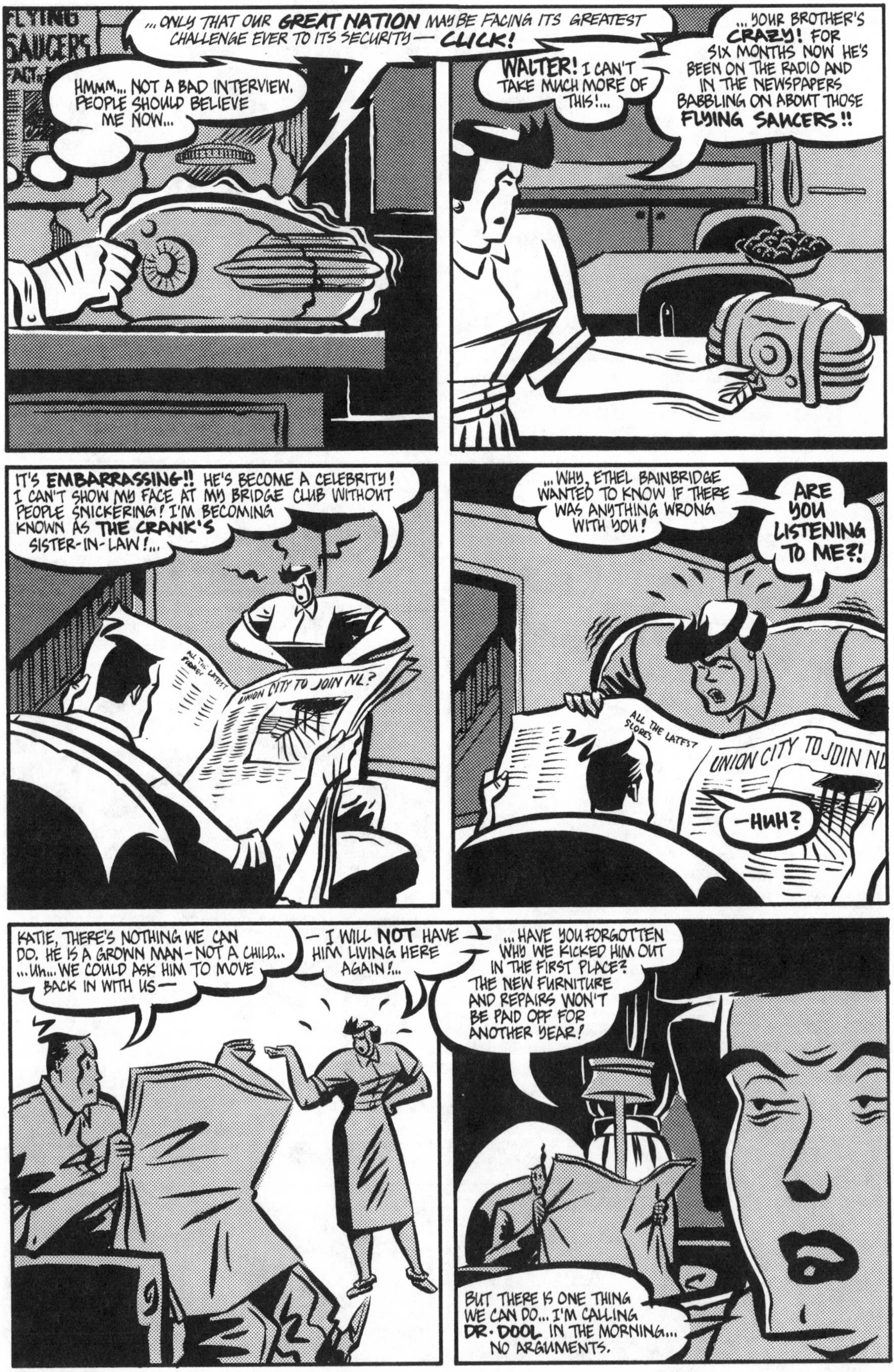
FLYING SAUCERS FACT
...ONLY THAT OUR GREAT NATION MAYBE FACING ITS GREATEST CHALLENGE EVER TO ITS SECURITY— CLICK!
HMMM... NOT A BAD INTERVIEW. PEOPLE SHOULD BELIEVE ME NOW...
WALTER! I CAN'T TAKE MUCH MORE OF THIS!...
...YOUR BROTHER'S CRAZY! FOR SIX MONTHS NOW HE'S BEEN ON THE RADIO AND IN THE NEWSPAPERS BABBLING ON ABOUT THOSE FLYING SAUCERS!!
IT'S EMBARRASSING!! HE'S BECOME A CELEBRITY! I CAN'T SHOW MY FACE AT MY BRIDGE CLUB WITHOUT PEOPLE SNICKERING! I'M BECOMING KNOWN AS THE CRANK'S SISTER-IN-LAW!...
UNION CITY TO JOIN NL?
...WHY, ETHEL BAINBRIDGE WANTED TO KNOW IF THERE WAS ANYTHING WRONG WITH YOU!
ARE YOU LISTENING TO ME?!
ALL THE LATEST STORES
UNION CITY TO JOIN NL
-HUH?
KATIE, THERE'S NOTHING WE CAN DO. HE IS A GROWN MAN—NOT A CHILD... ...UH... WE COULD ASK HIM TO MOVE BACK IN WITH US—
—I WILL NOT HAVE HIM LIVING HERE AGAIN!...
...HAVE YOU FORGOTTEN WHY WE KICKED HIM OUT IN THE FIRST PLACE? THE NEW FURNITURE AND REPAIRS WON'T BE PAID OFF FOR ANOTHER YEAR!
BUT THERE IS ONE THING WE CAN DO... I'M CALLING DR. DOOL IN THE MORNING... NO ARGUMENTS.

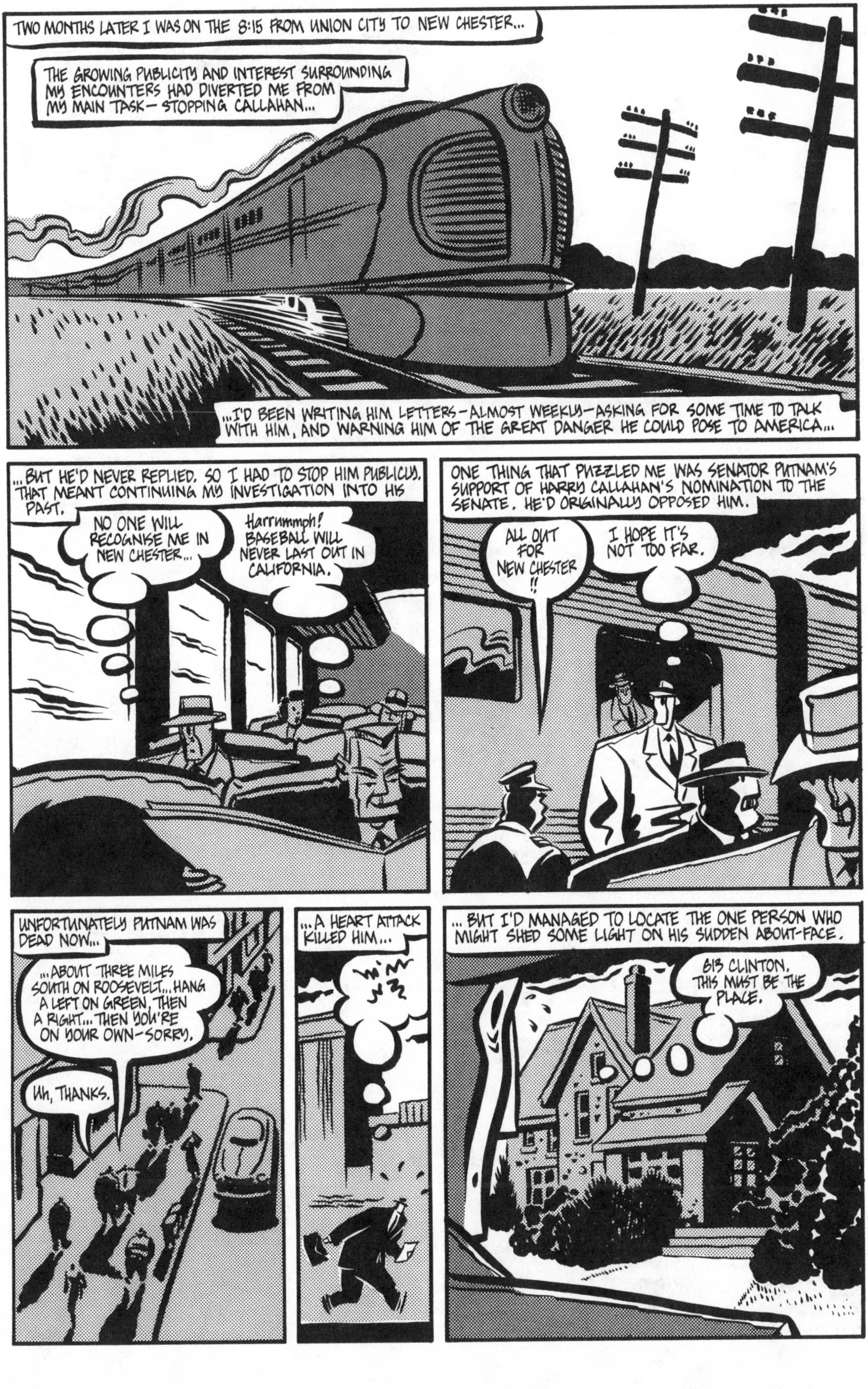

TWO MONTHS LATER I WAS ON THE 8:15 FROM UNION CITY TO NEW CHESTER...
THE GROWING PUBLICITY AND INTEREST SURROUNDING MY ENCOUNTERS HAD DIVERTED ME FROM MY MAIN TASK— STOPPING CALLAHAN...
...I'D BEEN WRITING HIM LETTERS—ALMOST WEEKLY—ASKING FOR SOME TIME TO TALK WITH HIM, AND WARNING HIM OF THE GREAT DANGER HE COULD POSE TO AMERICA...
...BUT HE'D NEVER REPLIED. SO I HAD TO STOP HIM PUBLICLY. THAT MEANT CONTINUING MY INVESTIGATION INTO HIS PAST.
NO ONE WILL RECOGNISE ME IN NEW CHESTER...
Harrummph! BASEBALL WILL NEVER LAST OUT IN CALIFORNIA.
ONE THING THAT PUZZLED ME WAS SENATOR PUTNAM'S SUPPORT OF HARRY CALLAHAN'S NOMINATION TO THE SENATE. HE'D ORIGINALLY OPPOSED HIM.
ALL OUT FOR NEW CHESTER !!
I HOPE IT'S NOT TOO FAR.
UNFORTUNATELY PUTNAM WAS DEAD NOW...
...ABOUT THREE MILES SOUTH ON ROOSEVELT... HANG A LEFT ON GREEN, THEN A RIGHT... THEN YOU'RE ON YOUR OWN-SORRY.
Uh, THANKS.
...A HEART ATTACK KILLED HIM...
...BUT I'D MANAGED TO LOCATE THE ONE PERSON WHO MIGHT SHED SOME LIGHT ON HIS SUDDEN ABOUT-FACE.
613 CLINTON. THIS MUST BE THE PLACE.

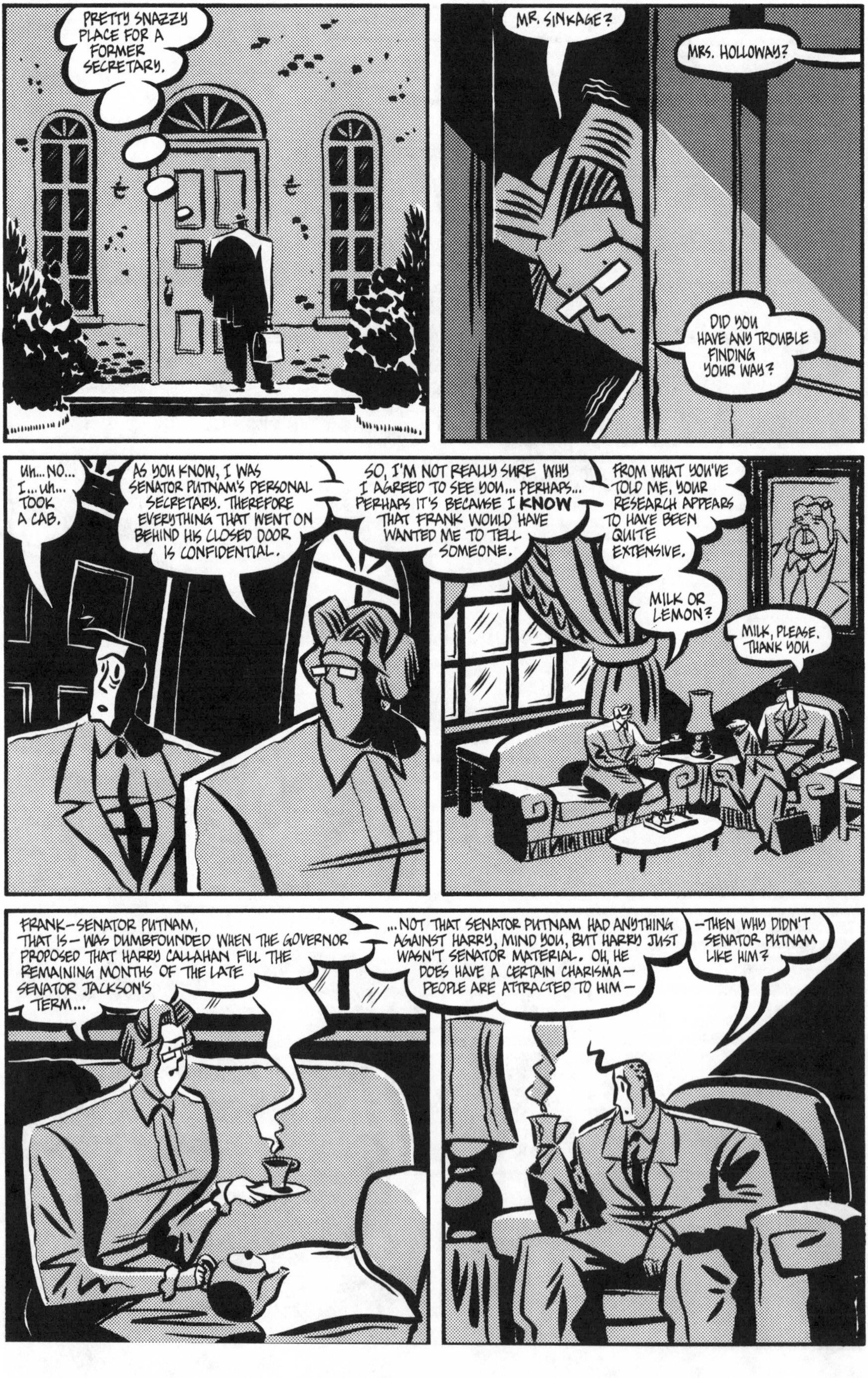
PRETTY SNAZZY PLACE FOR A FORMER SECRETARY.
MR. SINKAGE?
MRS. HOLLOWAY?
DID YOU HAVE ANY TROUBLE FINDING YOUR WAY?
UH... NO... I... UH... TOOK A CAB.
AS YOU KNOW, I WAS SENATOR PUTNAM'S PERSONAL SECRETARY. THEREFORE EVERYTHING THAT WENT ON BEHIND HIS CLOSED DOOR IS CONFIDENTIAL.
SO, I'M NOT REALLY SURE WHY I AGREED TO SEE YOU... PERHAPS... PERHAPS IT'S BECAUSE I KNOW THAT FRANK WOULD HAVE WANTED ME TO TELL SOMEONE.
FROM WHAT YOU'VE TOLD ME, YOUR RESEARCH APPEARS TO HAVE BEEN QUITE EXTENSIVE.
MILK OR LEMON?
MILK, PLEASE. THANK YOU.
FRANK—SENATOR PUTNAM, THAT IS—WAS DUMBFOUNDED WHEN THE GOVERNOR PROPOSED THAT HARRY CALLAHAN FILL THE REMAINING MONTHS OF THE LATE SENATOR JACKSON'S TERM...
...NOT THAT SENATOR PUTNAM HAD ANYTHING AGAINST HARRY, MIND YOU, BUT HARRY JUST WASN'T SENATOR MATERIAL. OH, HE DOES HAVE A CERTAIN CHARISMA—PEOPLE ARE ATTRACTED TO HIM—
—THEN WHY DIDN'T SENATOR PUTNAM LIKE HIM?

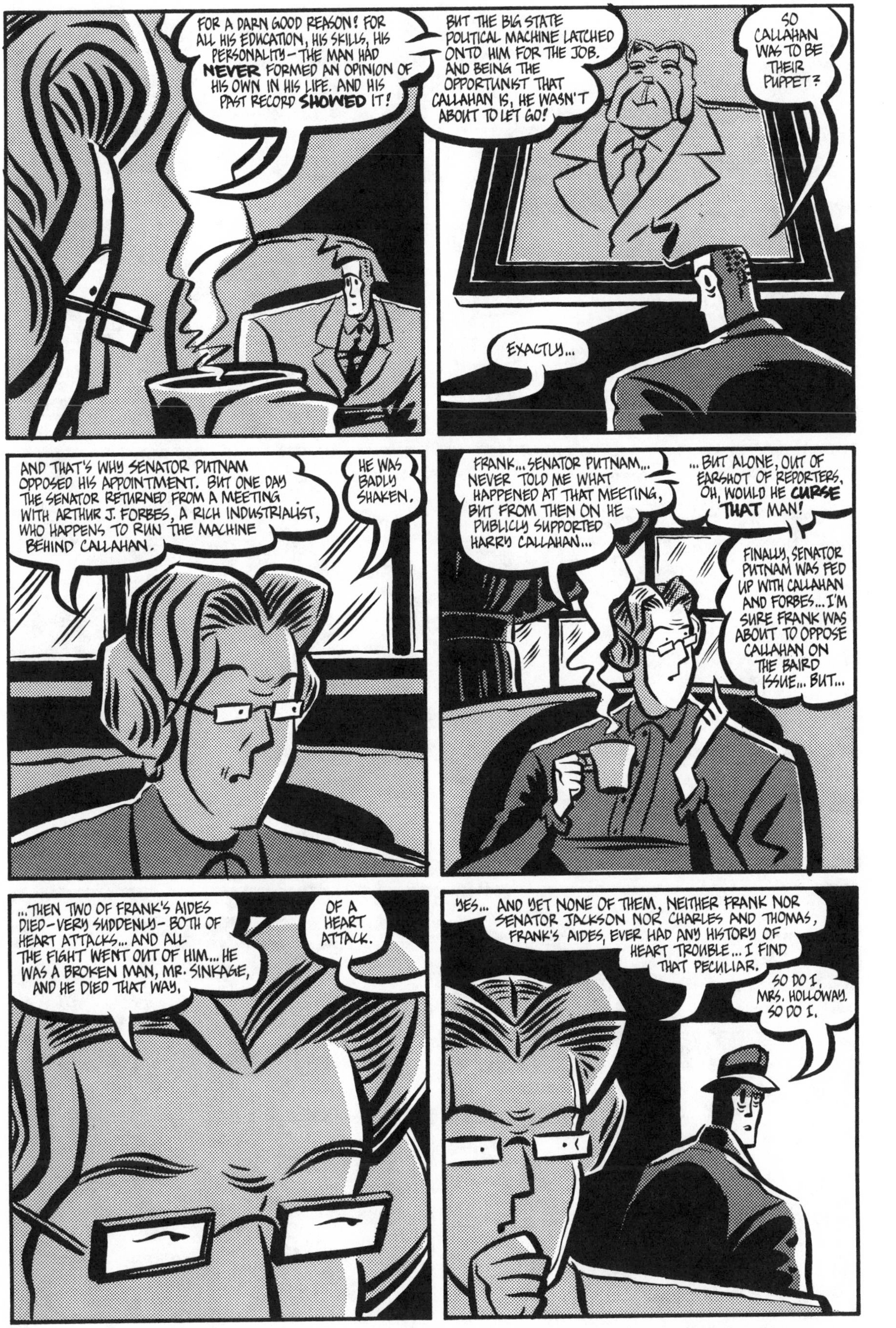
FOR A DARN GOOD REASON! FOR ALL HIS EDUCATION, HIS SKILLS, HIS PERSONALITY—THE MAN HAD NEVER FORMED AN OPINION OF HIS OWN IN HIS LIFE. AND HIS PAST RECORD SHOWED IT!
BUT THE BIG STATE POLITICAL MACHINE LATCHED ONTO HIM FOR THE JOB. AND BEING THE OPPORTUNIST THAT CALLAHAN IS, HE WASN'T ABOUT TO LET GO!
SO CALLAHAN WAS TO BE THEIR PUPPET?
EXACTLY...
AND THAT'S WHY SENATOR PUTNAM OPPOSED HIS APPOINTMENT. BUT ONE DAY THE SENATOR RETURNED FROM A MEETING WITH ARTHUR J. FORBES, A RICH INDUSTRIALIST, WHO HAPPENS TO RUN THE MACHINE BEHIND CALLAHAN.
HE WAS BADLY SHAKEN.
FRANK... SENATOR PUTNAM... NEVER TOLD ME WHAT HAPPENED AT THAT MEETING, BUT FROM THEN ON HE PUBLICLY SUPPORTED HARRY CALLAHAN...
...BUT ALONE, OUT OF EARSHOT OF REPORTERS, OH, WOULD HE CURSE THAT MAN!
FINALLY, SENATOR PUTNAM WAS FED UP WITH CALLAHAN AND FORBES... I'M SURE FRANK WAS ABOUT TO OPPOSE CALLAHAN ON THE BAIRD ISSUE... BUT...
...THEN TWO OF FRANK'S AIDES DIED—VERY SUDDENLY—BOTH OF HEART ATTACKS... AND ALL THE FIGHT WENT OUT OF HIM... HE WAS A BROKEN MAN, MR. SINKAGE, AND HE DIED THAT WAY,
OF A HEART ATTACK.
YES... AND YET NONE OF THEM, NEITHER FRANK NOR SENATOR JACKSON NOR CHARLES AND THOMAS, FRANK'S AIDES, EVER HAD ANY HISTORY OF HEART TROUBLE... I FIND THAT PECULIAR.
SO DO I, MRS. HOLLOWAY, SO DO I.

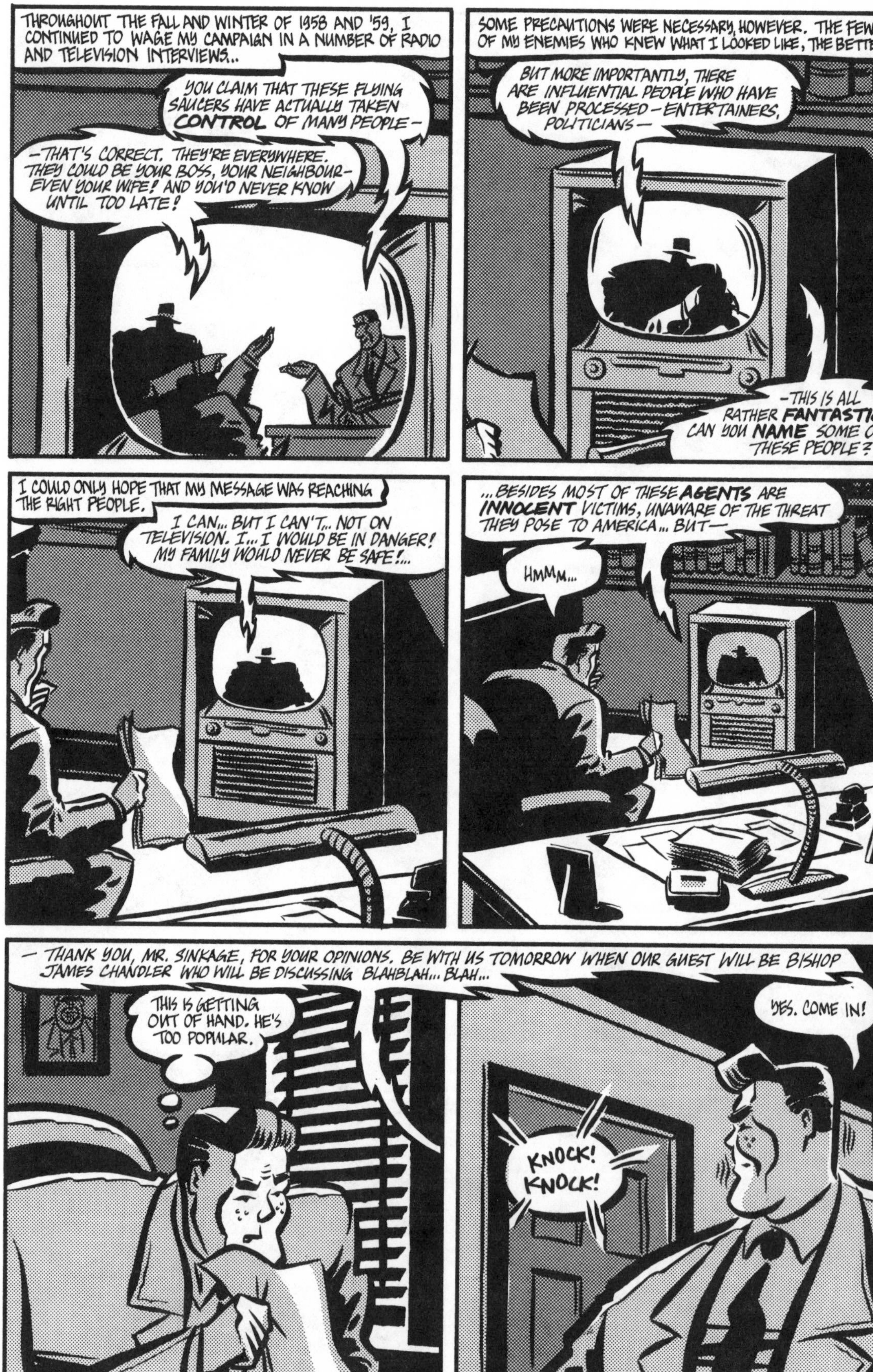
THROUGHOUT THE FALL AND WINTER OF 1958 AND '59, I CONTINUED TO WAGE MY CAMPAIGN IN A NUMBER OF RADIO AND TELEVISION INTERVIEWS..
YOU CLAIM THAT THESE FLYING SAUCERS HAVE ACTUALLY TAKEN CONTROL OF MANY PEOPLE—
—THAT'S CORRECT. THEY'RE EVERYWHERE. THEY COULD BE YOUR BOSS, YOUR NEIGHBOUR—EVEN YOUR WIFE! AND YOU'D NEVER KNOW UNTIL TOO LATE!
SOME PRECAUTIONS WERE NECESSARY, HOWEVER. THE FEWER OF MY ENEMIES WHO KNEW WHAT I LOOKED LIKE, THE BETTER.
BUT MORE IMPORTANTLY, THERE ARE INFLUENTIAL PEOPLE WHO HAVE BEEN PROCESSED—ENTERTAINERS, POLITICIANS—
—THIS IS ALL RATHER FANTASTIC! CAN YOU NAME SOME OF THESE PEOPLE?
I COULD ONLY HOPE THAT MY MESSAGE WAS REACHING THE RIGHT PEOPLE.
I CAN... BUT I CAN'T... NOT ON TELEVISION. I... I WOULD BE IN DANGER! MY FAMILY WOULD NEVER BE SAFE!...
...BESIDES MOST OF THESE AGENTS ARE INNOCENT VICTIMS, UNAWARE OF THE THREAT THEY POSE TO AMERICA... BUT—
HMMM...
— THANK YOU, MR. SINKAGE, FOR YOUR OPINIONS. BE WITH US TOMORROW WHEN OUR GUEST WILL BE BISHOP JAMES CHANDLER WHO WILL BE DISCUSSING BLAHBLAH... BLAH...
THIS IS GETTING OUT OF HAND. HE'S TOO POPULAR.
YES. COME IN!
KNOCK! KNOCK!

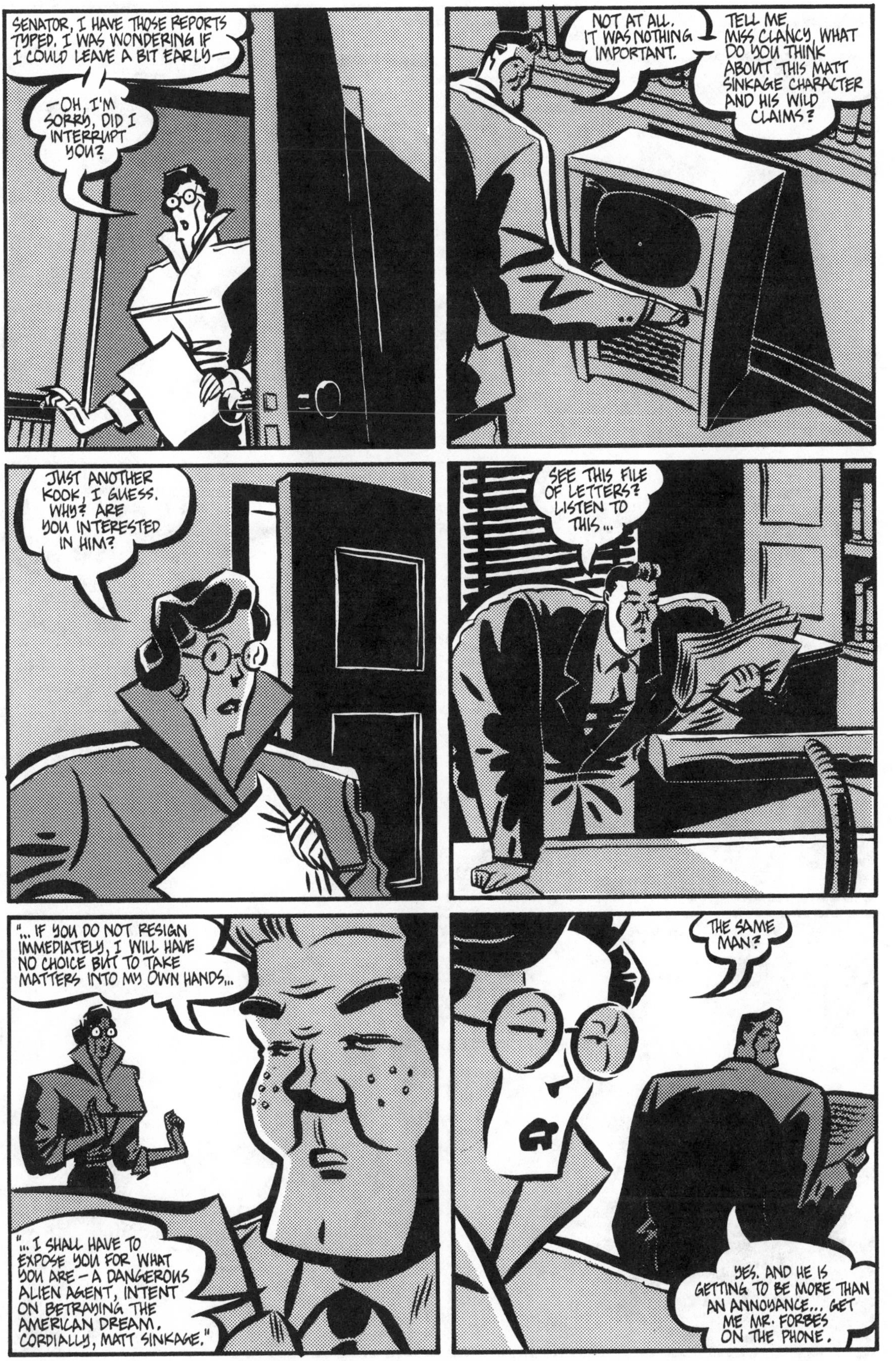
SENATOR, I HAVE THOSE REPORTS TYPED. I WAS WONDERING IF I COULD LEAVE A BIT EARLY—
—OH, I'M SORRY, DID I INTERRUPT YOU?
NOT AT ALL. IT WAS NOTHING IMPORTANT.
TELL ME, MISS CLANCY, WHAT DO YOU THINK ABOUT THIS MATT SINKAGE CHARACTER AND HIS WILD CLAIMS?
JUST ANOTHER KOOK, I GUESS. WHY? ARE YOU INTERESTED IN HIM?
SEE THIS FILE OF LETTERS? LISTEN TO THIS...
"... IF YOU DO NOT RESIGN IMMEDIATELY, I WILL HAVE NO CHOICE BUT TO TAKE MATTERS INTO MY OWN HANDS...
"... I SHALL HAVE TO EXPOSE YOU FOR WHAT YOU ARE—A DANGEROUS ALIEN AGENT, INTENT ON BETRAYING THE AMERICAN DREAM. CORDIALLY, MATT SINKAGE."
THE SAME MAN?
YES. AND HE IS GETTING TO BE MORE THAN AN ANNOYANCE... GET ME MR. FORBES ON THE PHONE.

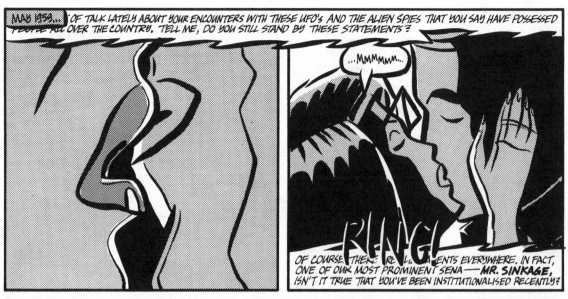

MAY 1959... OF TALK LATELY ABOUT YOUR ENCOUNTERS WITH THESE UFO's AND THE ALIEN SPIES THAT YOU SAY HAVE POSSESSED PEOPLE ALL OVER THE COUNTRY. TELL ME, DO YOU STILL STAND BY THESE STATEMENTS?

...MMMMMM...

RING!

OF COURSE, THERE ARE ALIEN AGENTS EVERYWHERE. IN FACT, ONE OF OUR MOST PROMINENT SENA— **MR. SINKAGE**, ISN'T IT TRUE THAT YOU'VE BEEN INSTITUTIONALISED RECENTLY?

YES, BUT— IN FACT, HAVEN'T YOU BEEN COMMITTED **TWICE** IN THE LAST SIX YEARS? — I'M **NOT** HIDING THAT! MY ENEMIES TRIED TO BURY ME AND THE EVIDENCE I'VE GATHERED. **BUT I WON!** I WAS RELEASED BOTH TIMES. THE ISSUE ISN'T MY SANITY. THE REAL ISSUE HERE IS THE SLOW INFILTRATION OF OUR CIVILISATION BY ALIEN FORCES.

RING! RING! RING

UH, PHIL?

DAMN! I BETTER GET THAT

...THESE FORCES HAVE BEGUN TO UNDERMINE THE **AMERICAN WAY OF LIFE!** YOU CAN SEE IT IN THE FASHIONS, YOU CAN HEAR IT IN THE MUSIC! WHY, I KNOW FOR A FACT THAT THERE ARE SEVENTY-EIGHT ALIENS IN CONGRESS! — SINKAGE, THAT'S A SERIOUS STATEMENT TO MAKE WITH NO EVIDENCE TO —— CLICK!

RING!

COULD YOU TURN OFF THAT RADIO? IF THERE'S ONE THING I DON'T NEED, IT'S ANOTHER INTERVIEW WITH SINKAGE.

IS THAT BETTER, HONEY?

YEAH... HELLO?... UH-HUH... UH-HUH... YEAH, ALL RIGHT. IN TWENTY MINUTES. BYE.

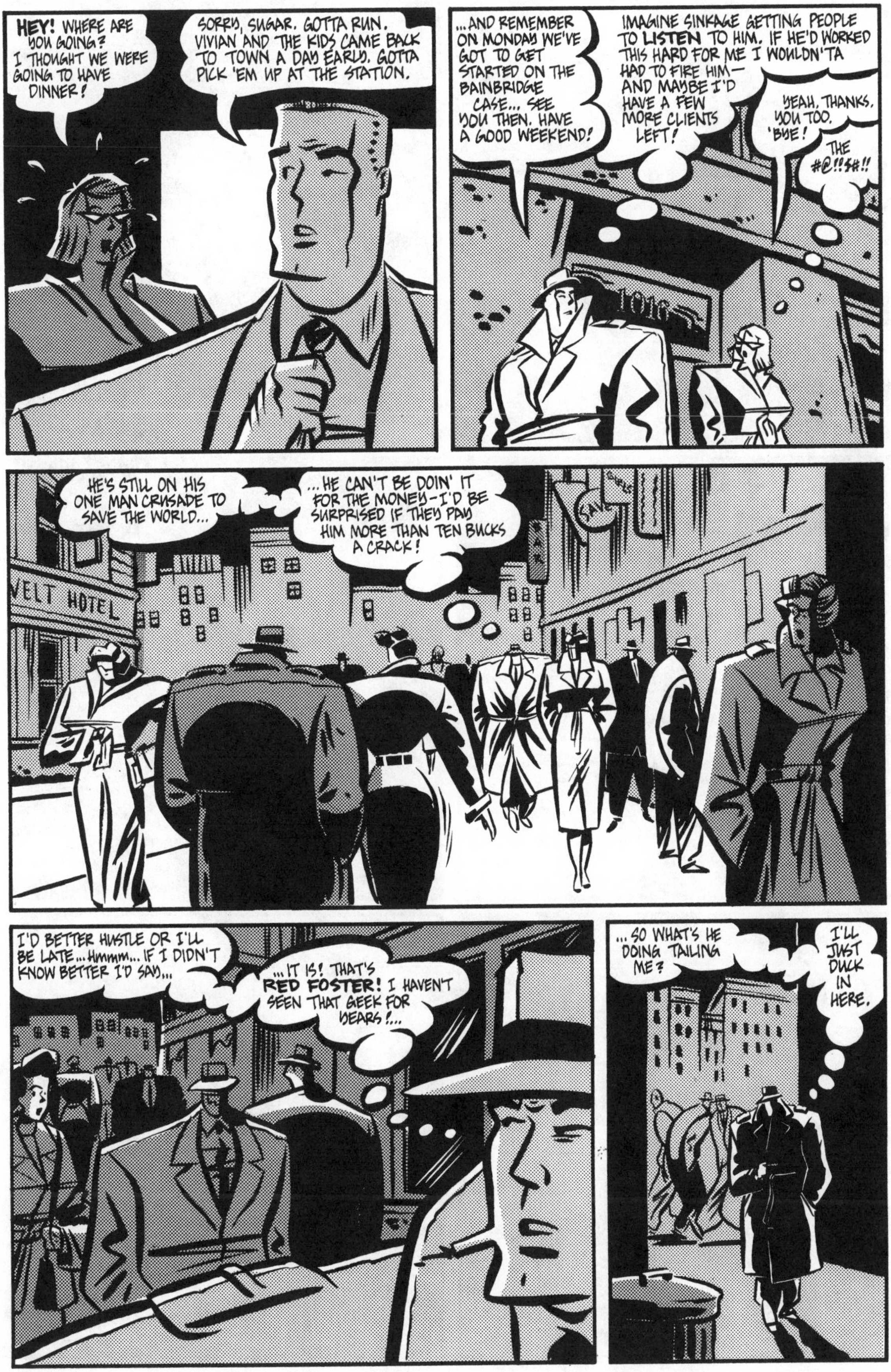
HEY! WHERE ARE YOU GOING? I THOUGHT WE WERE GOING TO HAVE DINNER!
SORRY, SUGAR. GOTTA RUN. VIVIAN AND THE KIDS CAME BACK TO TOWN A DAY EARLY. GOTTA PICK 'EM UP AT THE STATION.
...AND REMEMBER ON MONDAY WE'VE GOT TO GET STARTED ON THE BAINBRIDGE CASE... SEE YOU THEN. HAVE A GOOD WEEKEND!
IMAGINE SINKAGE GETTING PEOPLE TO LISTEN TO HIM. IF HE'D WORKED THIS HARD FOR ME I WOULDN'TA HAD TO FIRE HIM— AND MAYBE I'D HAVE A FEW MORE CLIENTS LEFT!
YEAH, THANKS. YOU TOO. 'BYE!
THE #@!!$#!!
1016
HE'S STILL ON HIS ONE MAN CRUSADE TO SAVE THE WORLD...
...HE CAN'T BE DOIN' IT FOR THE MONEY—I'D BE SURPRISED IF THEY PAY HIM MORE THAN TEN BUCKS A CRACK!
VELT HOTEL
I'D BETTER HUSTLE OR I'LL BE LATE...HMMM... IF I DIDN'T KNOW BETTER I'D SAY...
...IT IS! THAT'S RED FOSTER! I HAVEN'T SEEN THAT GEEK FOR YEARS!...
...SO WHAT'S HE DOING TAILING ME?
I'LL JUST DUCK IN HERE.

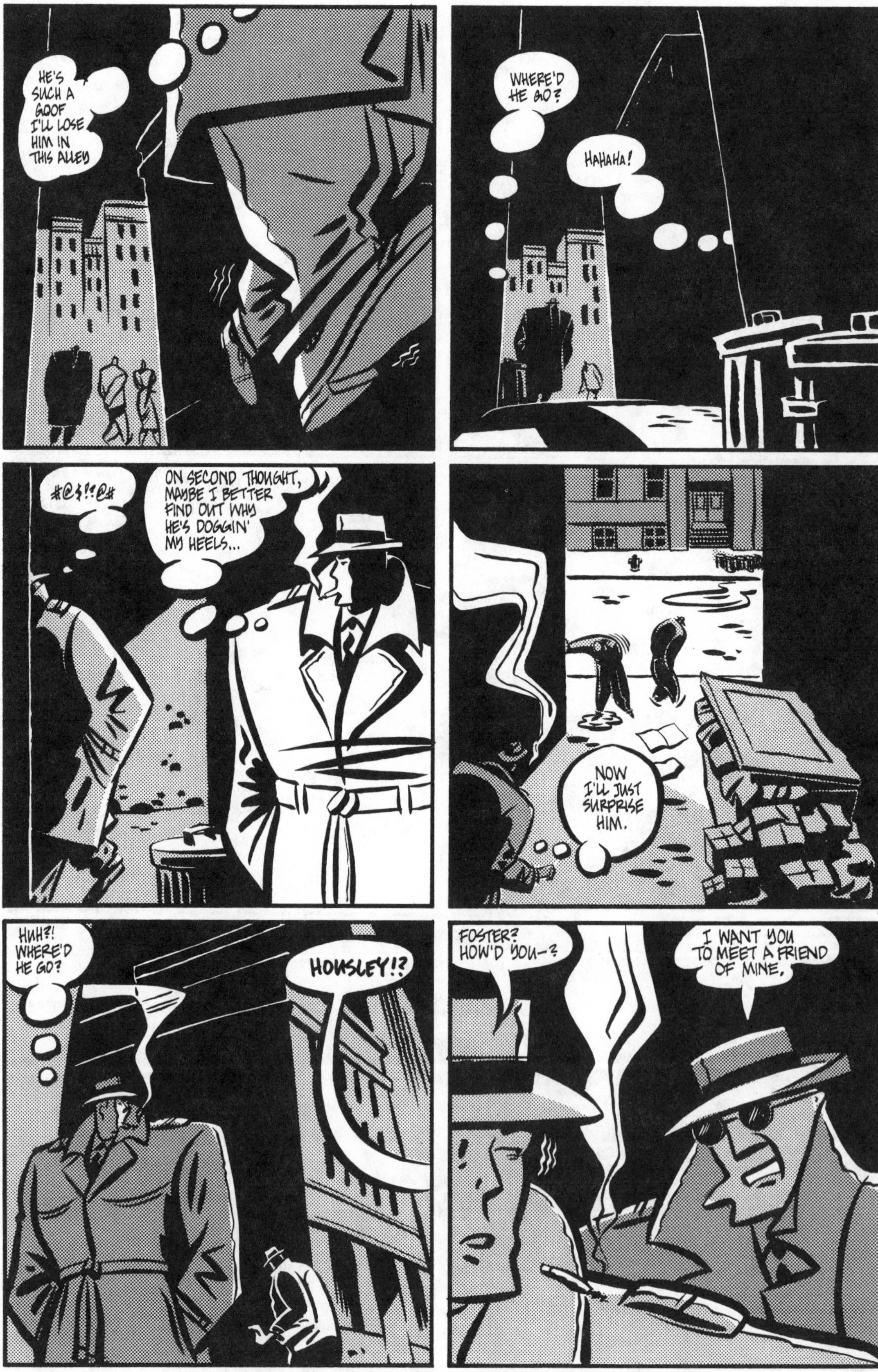
HE'S SUCH A GOOF I'LL LOSE HIM IN THIS ALLEY
WHERE'D HE GO?
HAHAHA!
#@$!!@#
ON SECOND THOUGHT, MAYBE I BETTER FIND OUT WHY HE'S DOGGIN' MY HEELS...
NOW I'LL JUST SURPRISE HIM.
HUH?! WHERE'D HE GO?
HOUSLEY!?
FOSTER? HOW'D YOU-?
I WANT YOU TO MEET A FRIEND OF MINE.

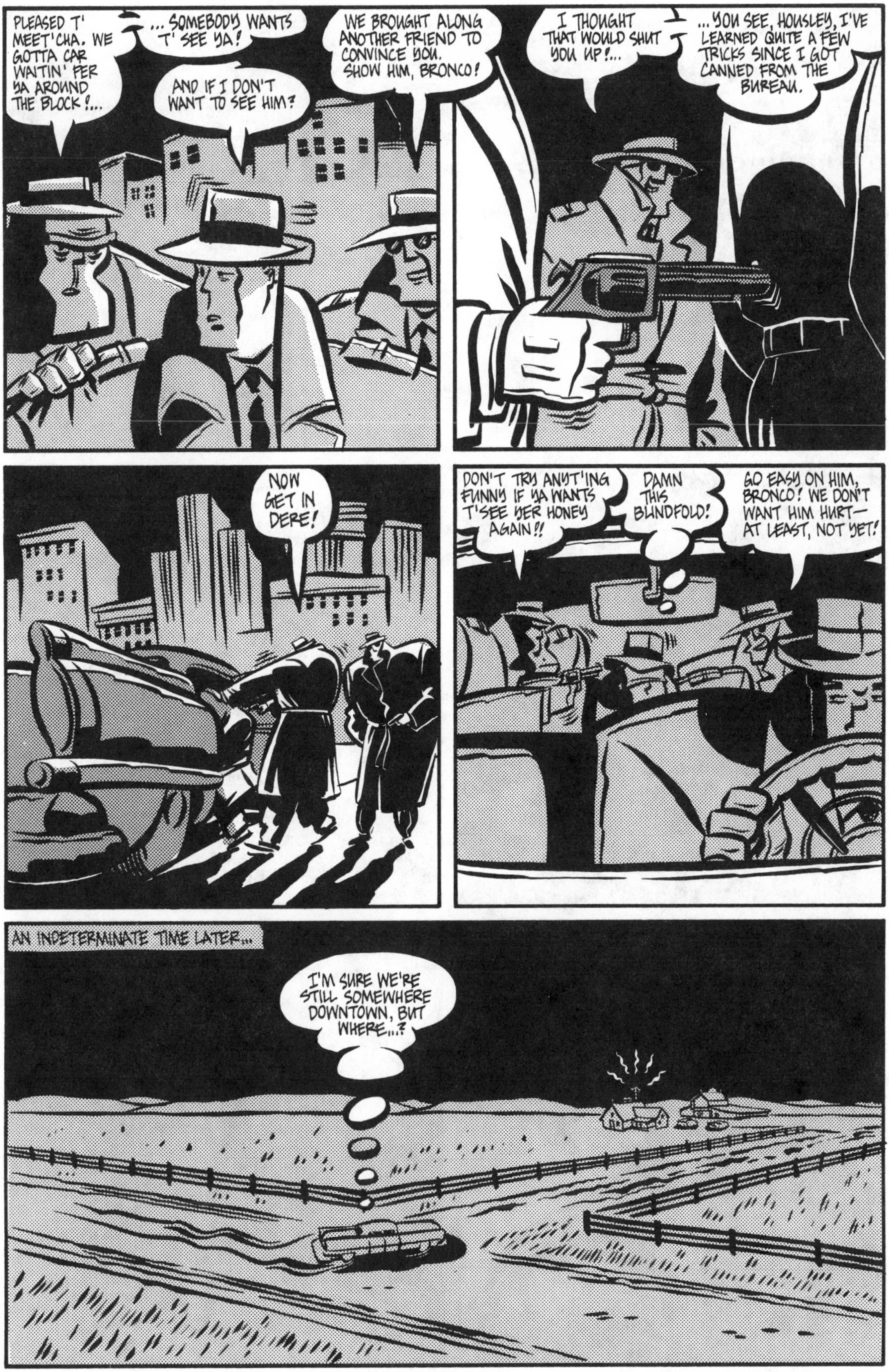

PLEASED T' MEET'CHA. WE GOTTA CAR WAITIN' FER YA AROUND THE BLOCK!...
...SOMEBODY WANTS T' SEE YA!
AND IF I DON'T WANT TO SEE HIM?
WE BROUGHT ALONG ANOTHER FRIEND TO CONVINCE YOU. SHOW HIM, BRONCO!
I THOUGHT THAT WOULD SHUT YOU UP!...
...YOU SEE, HOUSLEY, I'VE LEARNED QUITE A FEW TRICKS SINCE I GOT CANNED FROM THE BUREAU.
NOW GET IN DERE!
DON'T TRY ANYT'ING FUNNY IF YA WANTS T'SEE YER HONEY AGAIN!!
DAMN THIS BLINDFOLD!
GO EASY ON HIM, BRONCO! WE DON'T WANT HIM HURT—AT LEAST, NOT YET!
AN INDETERMINATE TIME LATER...
I'M SURE WE'RE STILL SOMEWHERE DOWNTOWN, BUT WHERE...?

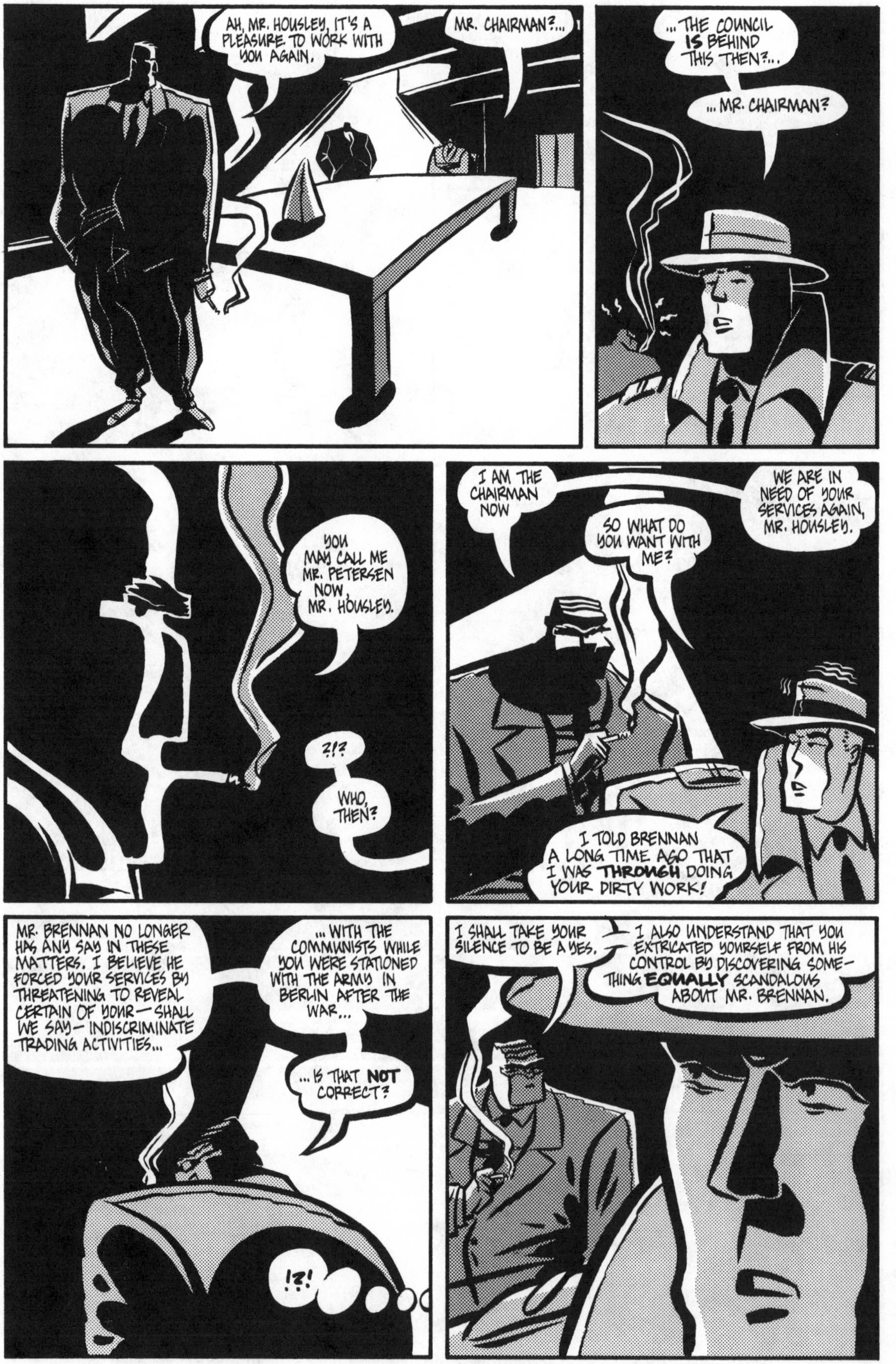
AH, MR. HOUSLEY, IT'S A PLEASURE TO WORK WITH YOU AGAIN.
MR. CHAIRMAN?...
... THE COUNCIL IS BEHIND THIS THEN?...
... MR. CHAIRMAN?
YOU MAY CALL ME MR. PETERSEN NOW, MR. HOUSLEY.
?!?
WHO, THEN?
I AM THE CHAIRMAN NOW
WE ARE IN NEED OF YOUR SERVICES AGAIN, MR. HOUSLEY.
SO WHAT DO YOU WANT WITH ME?
I TOLD BRENNAN A LONG TIME AGO THAT I WAS THROUGH DOING YOUR DIRTY WORK!
MR. BRENNAN NO LONGER HAS ANY SAY IN THESE MATTERS. I BELIEVE HE FORCED YOUR SERVICES BY THREATENING TO REVEAL CERTAIN OF YOUR— SHALL WE SAY— INDISCRIMINATE TRADING ACTIVITIES...
... WITH THE COMMUNISTS WHILE YOU WERE STATIONED WITH THE ARMY IN BERLIN AFTER THE WAR...
... IS THAT NOT CORRECT?
!?!
I SHALL TAKE YOUR SILENCE TO BE A YES.
I ALSO UNDERSTAND THAT YOU EXTRICATED YOURSELF FROM HIS CONTROL BY DISCOVERING SOMETHING EQUALLY SCANDALOUS ABOUT MR. BRENNAN.

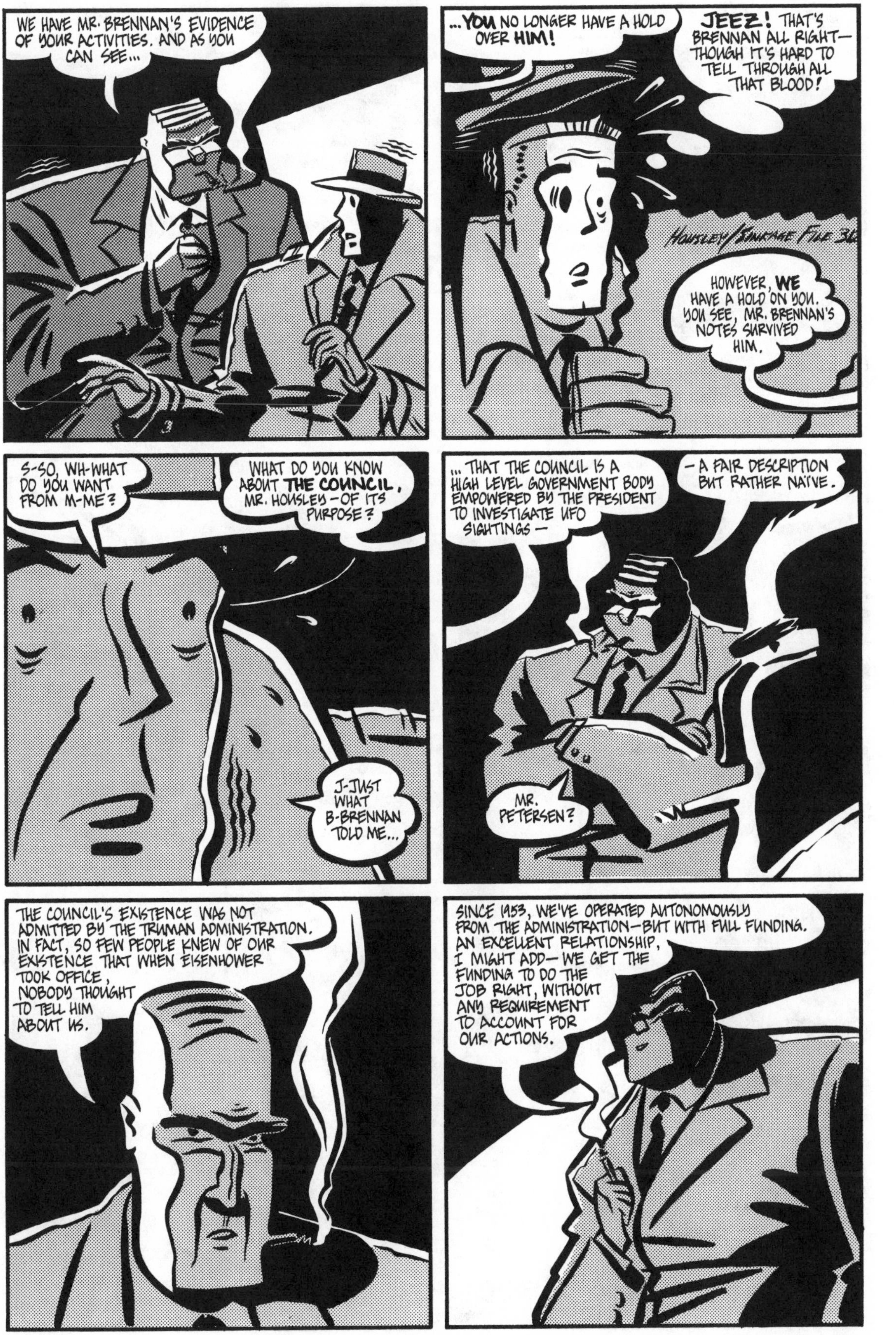
WE HAVE MR. BRENNAN'S EVIDENCE OF YOUR ACTIVITIES. AND AS YOU CAN SEE...
...YOU NO LONGER HAVE A HOLD OVER HIM!
JEEZ! THAT'S BRENNAN ALL RIGHT— THOUGH IT'S HARD TO TELL THROUGH ALL THAT BLOOD!
HOWEVER, WE HAVE A HOLD ON YOU. YOU SEE, MR. BRENNAN'S NOTES SURVIVED HIM.
S-SO, WH-WHAT DO YOU WANT FROM M-ME?
WHAT DO YOU KNOW ABOUT THE COUNCIL, MR. HOUSLEY—OF ITS PURPOSE?
J-JUST WHAT B-BRENNAN TOLD ME...
...THAT THE COUNCIL IS A HIGH LEVEL GOVERNMENT BODY EMPOWERED BY THE PRESIDENT TO INVESTIGATE UFO SIGHTINGS—
—A FAIR DESCRIPTION BUT RATHER NAÏVE.
MR. PETERSEN?
THE COUNCIL'S EXISTENCE WAS NOT ADMITTED BY THE TRUMAN ADMINISTRATION. IN FACT, SO FEW PEOPLE KNEW OF OUR EXISTENCE THAT WHEN EISENHOWER TOOK OFFICE, NOBODY THOUGHT TO TELL HIM ABOUT US.
SINCE 1953, WE'VE OPERATED AUTONOMOUSLY FROM THE ADMINISTRATION—BUT WITH FULL FUNDING. AN EXCELLENT RELATIONSHIP, I MIGHT ADD—WE GET THE FUNDING TO DO THE JOB RIGHT, WITHOUT ANY REQUIREMENT TO ACCOUNT FOR OUR ACTIONS.

AND WE **HAVE** BEEN SUCCESSFUL.

WE NOW KNOW THAT THESE FLYING SAUCERS ARE PART OF A LARGER SOVIET RUSSIAN PLOT TO CREATE PUBLIC HYSTERIA IN THE WEST...

... THUS DISTRACTING THE PUBLIC **AND** THE MILITARY FROM THE VERY **REAL** ARMS BUILD-UP TAKING PLACE IN EASTERN EUROPE.

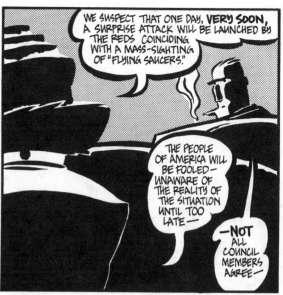

WE SUSPECT THAT ONE DAY, **VERY SOON,** A SURPRISE ATTACK WILL BE LAUNCHED BY THE REDS COINCIDING WITH A MASS-SIGHTING OF "FLYING SAUCERS."

THE PEOPLE OF AMERICA WILL BE FOOLED— UNAWARE OF THE REALITY OF THE SITUATION UNTIL TOO LATE—

—**NOT** ALL COUNCIL MEMBERS AGREE—

—THE **MAJORITY** AGREE WITH ME, **MR. PETERSEN.**

AND NOW THE COUNCIL HAS A NEW TASK—TO STOP THE SPREAD OF LIES ABOUT THE UFO'S, AND THE FIFTH COLUMNISTS BEHIND THOSE LIES.

LIKE I SAID BEFORE, WHERE DO I FIT INTO ALL OF THIS?

YOU WILL CONTINUE WITH YOUR PRIVATE INVESTIGATION "GAMES". BUT WE **WILL** BE CALLING UPON YOU FOR YOUR SERVICES AND KNOWLEDGE FROM TIME TO TIME...

... YOUR FIRST ASSIGNMENT IS TO REPORT TO SENATOR CALLAHAN'S OFFICE MONDAY MORNING!

CALLAHAN?! WHY?

?!?

THAT IS NOT YOUR CONCERN, MR. HOUSLEY! JUST DO AS I SAY...

...GENTLEMEN, YOU MAY NOW LEAVE.

HE TREATS ME LIKE AN OFFICE BOY.

SO WHAT DOES THAT MAKE ME?

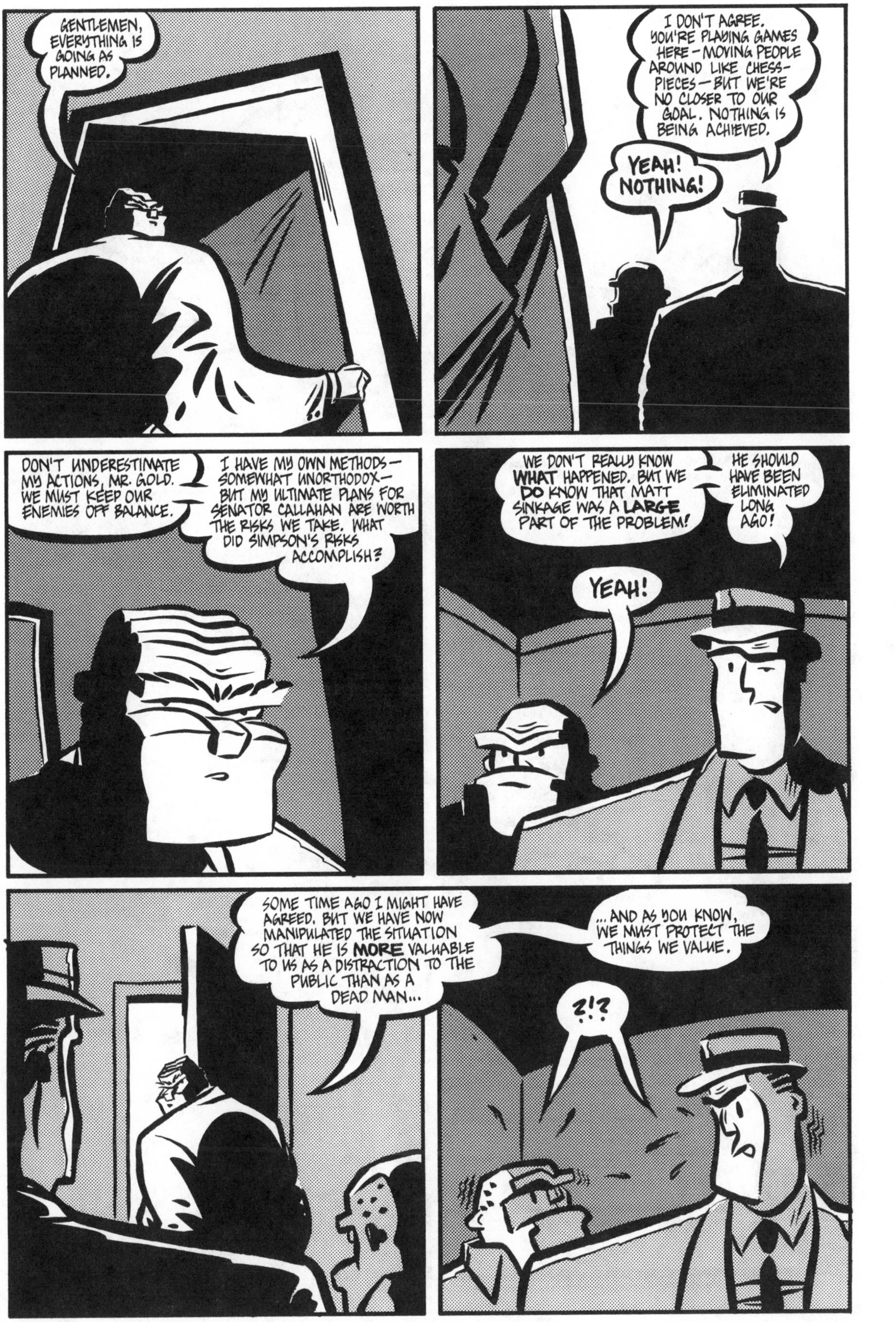
GENTLEMEN, EVERYTHING IS GOING AS PLANNED.
I DON'T AGREE. YOU'RE PLAYING GAMES HERE—MOVING PEOPLE AROUND LIKE CHESS-PIECES—BUT WE'RE NO CLOSER TO OUR GOAL. NOTHING IS BEING ACHIEVED.
YEAH! NOTHING!
DON'T UNDERESTIMATE MY ACTIONS, MR. GOLD. WE MUST KEEP OUR ENEMIES OFF BALANCE.
I HAVE MY OWN METHODS—SOMEWHAT UNORTHODOX—BUT MY ULTIMATE PLANS FOR SENATOR CALLAHAN ARE WORTH THE RISKS WE TAKE. WHAT DID SIMPSON'S RISKS ACCOMPLISH?
WE DON'T REALLY KNOW **WHAT** HAPPENED. BUT WE **DO** KNOW THAT MATT SINKAGE WAS A **LARGE** PART OF THE PROBLEM!
HE SHOULD HAVE BEEN ELIMINATED LONG AGO!
YEAH!
SOME TIME AGO I MIGHT HAVE AGREED. BUT WE HAVE NOW MANIPULATED THE SITUATION SO THAT HE IS **MORE** VALUABLE TO US AS A DISTRACTION TO THE PUBLIC THAN AS A DEAD MAN...
...AND AS YOU KNOW, WE MUST PROTECT THE THINGS WE VALUE.
?!?

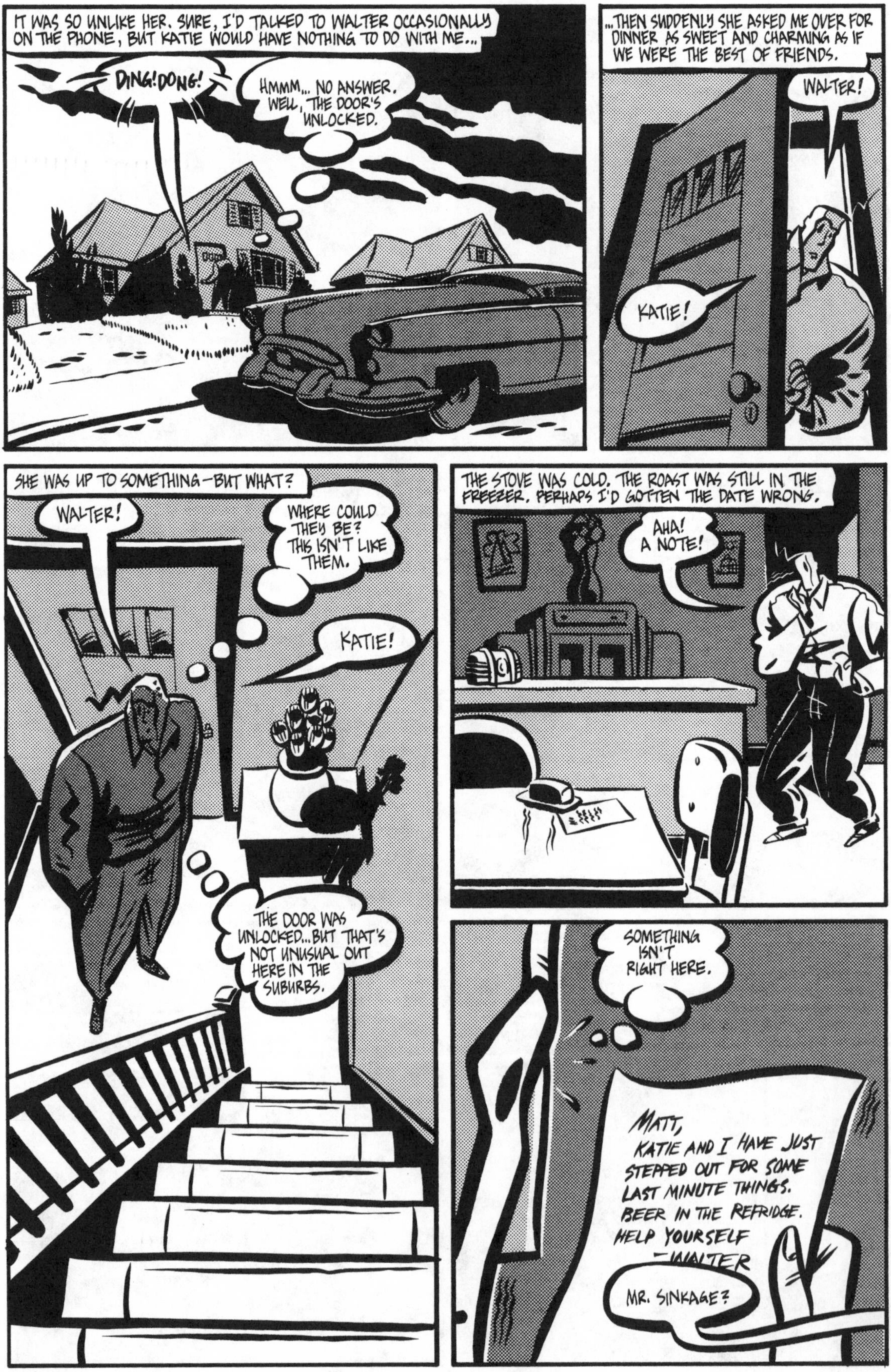
IT WAS SO UNLIKE HER. SURE, I'D TALKED TO WALTER OCCASIONALLY ON THE PHONE, BUT KATIE WOULD HAVE NOTHING TO DO WITH ME...
DING! DONG!
HMMM... NO ANSWER. WELL, THE DOOR'S UNLOCKED.
...THEN SUDDENLY SHE ASKED ME OVER FOR DINNER AS SWEET AND CHARMING AS IF WE WERE THE BEST OF FRIENDS.
WALTER!
KATIE!
SHE WAS UP TO SOMETHING—BUT WHAT?
WALTER!
WHERE COULD THEY BE? THIS ISN'T LIKE THEM.
KATIE!
THE DOOR WAS UNLOCKED...BUT THAT'S NOT UNUSUAL OUT HERE IN THE SUBURBS.
THE STOVE WAS COLD. THE ROAST WAS STILL IN THE FREEZER. PERHAPS I'D GOTTEN THE DATE WRONG.
AHA! A NOTE!
SOMETHING ISN'T RIGHT HERE.
MATT,
KATIE AND I HAVE JUST STEPPED OUT FOR SOME LAST MINUTE THINGS. BEER IN THE REFRIDGE. HELP YOURSELF
—WALTER
MR. SINKAGE?

DR. DOOL!? WH-WHAT ARE YOU D-DOING HERE?!

YOUR SISTER-IN-LAW HAS ASKED ME TO EXAMINE YOU AGAIN. SHE FEELS THAT YOU MAY HAVE HAD A RELAPSE—

—IN OTHER WORDS, SHE WANTS ME OUT OF HER HAIR ONCE AND FOR ALL.

SHE ONLY WANTS WHAT IS BEST FOR YOU. PLEASE, SIT DOWN.

THAT OTHER MAN... I KNOW I'VE SEEN HIM SOMEWHERE BEFORE. WHO IS HE?

DR. WATSON—MY COLLEAGUE. DON'T WORRY. I'LL BE ASKING ALL THE QUESTIONS...

DOOL HAD BEEN THE DOCTOR WHO SIGNED MY COMMITMENT PAPERS THE SECOND TIME—AFTER THE INCIDENT IN UNION CITY...

...NOW, SHALL WE BEGIN?

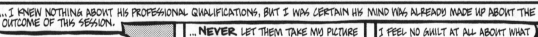

...I KNEW NOTHING ABOUT HIS PROFESSIONAL QUALIFICATIONS, BUT I WAS CERTAIN HIS MIND WAS ALREADY MADE UP ABOUT THE OUTCOME OF THIS SESSION.

...OF COURSE I BELIEVE FLYING SAUCERS EXIST! WHAT DO YOU THINK I'VE BEEN CHASING THE LAST FIVE YEARS— MARSH GAS?!?...

...NEVER LET THEM TAKE MY PICTURE OR SHOW MY FACE ON CAMERA...THERE ARE PEOPLE OUT THERE WHO'D LOVE TO SEE ME DEAD...

I FEEL NO GUILT AT ALL ABOUT WHAT KATIE IS GOING THROUGH. SHE BRINGS IT ON HERSELF...

...IF YOU ASK ME, SHE'S THE ONE WHO SHOULD BE LOCKED AWAY!

TWO HOURS OF RIDICULOUS QUESTIONS LATER...

WELL, AM I CRAZY?

I SHALL NEED A FEW MOMENTS TO CONSULT MY COLLEAGUE. I'LL BE BACK IN A MOMENT.

WELL, DOCTOR?

HIS CONDITION APPEARS MARGINAL, BUT I'M WILLING TO SIGN THE PAPERS IF HIS BROTHER WILL—

—I DON'T THINK SO, DOCTOR.

THEN WHY DID YOU JUST WASTE OVER TWO HOURS OF MY TIME?

THOSE HOURS WERE **NOT** WASTED, DOCTOR. I NEEDED TO HEAR HIS ANSWERS—TO JUDGE HIS STATE OF MIND FOR **MYSELF.**

WELL, THEN, IF YOU DON'T WANT THOSE PAPERS SIGNED, LET'S TALK ABOUT THAT ADDITIONAL FUNDING YOU PROMISED MY CLINIC—

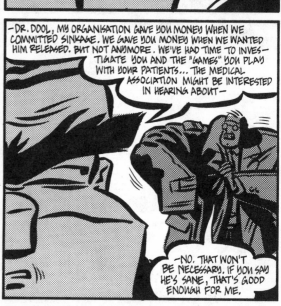

—DR. DOOL, MY ORGANISATION GAVE YOU MONEY WHEN WE COMMITTED SINKAGE. WE GAVE YOU MONEY WHEN WE WANTED HIM RELEASED. BUT NOT ANYMORE. WE'VE HAD TIME TO INVES- TIGATE YOU AND THE "GAMES" YOU PLAY WITH YOUR PATIENTS... THE MEDICAL ASSOCIATION MIGHT BE INTERESTED IN HEARING ABOUT—

—NO. THAT WON'T BE NECESSARY. IF YOU SAY HE'S SANE, THAT'S GOOD ENOUGH FOR ME.

WE HAVE NO CAUSE TO HOLD YOU, MATT. I SHALL INFORM YOUR SISTER-IN-LAW IN THE MORNING.

BUT I DON'T UNDERSTAND—

—JUST BE THANKFUL THAT YOU DON'T, MR. SINKAGE. GOOD DAY.

NERVOUS ENERGY HAD MADE ME FAMISHED. I FIXED UP A SANDWICH AND WAITED FOR WALTER AND KATIE...

WHA—?! WHAT ARE YOU STILL—?! THEY WERE SUPPOSED TO TAKE—! WALTER!

?!?

HI, KATIE!

I KNEW KATIE WOULD BE GLAD TO SEE ME.

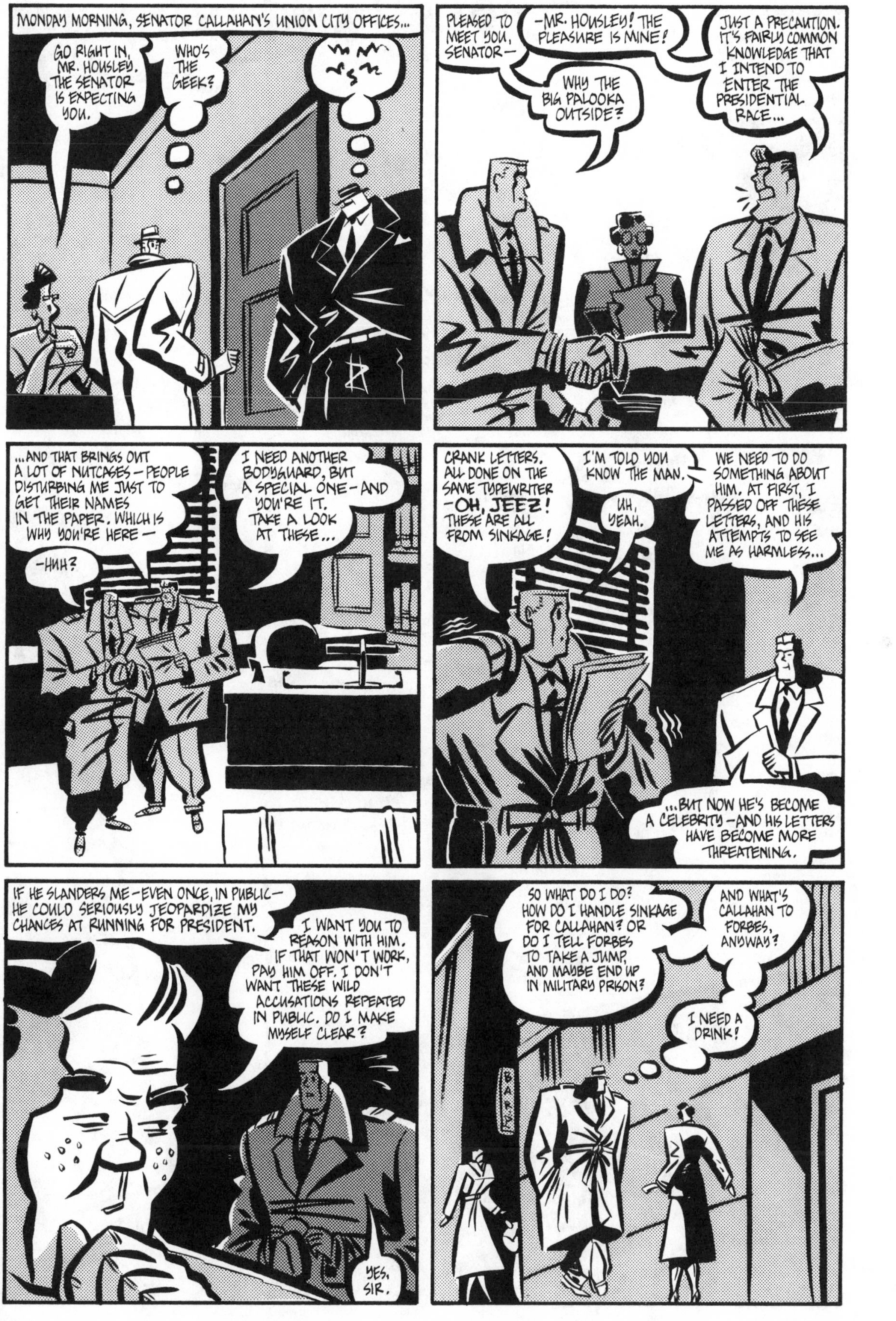
MONDAY MORNING, SENATOR CALLAHAN'S UNION CITY OFFICES...
GO RIGHT IN, MR. HOUSLEY. THE SENATOR IS EXPECTING YOU.
WHO'S THE GEEK?
PLEASED TO MEET YOU, SENATOR—
—MR. HOUSLEY! THE PLEASURE IS MINE!
WHY THE BIG PALOOKA OUTSIDE?
JUST A PRECAUTION. IT'S FAIRLY COMMON KNOWLEDGE THAT I INTEND TO ENTER THE PRESIDENTIAL RACE...
...AND THAT BRINGS OUT A LOT OF NUTCASES—PEOPLE DISTURBING ME JUST TO GET THEIR NAMES IN THE PAPER. WHICH IS WHY YOU'RE HERE—
—HUH?
I NEED ANOTHER BODYGUARD, BUT A SPECIAL ONE—AND YOU'RE IT. TAKE A LOOK AT THESE...
CRANK LETTERS. ALL DONE ON THE SAME TYPEWRITER —OH, JEEZ! THESE ARE ALL FROM SINKAGE!
I'M TOLD YOU KNOW THE MAN.
UH, YEAH.
WE NEED TO DO SOMETHING ABOUT HIM. AT FIRST, I PASSED OFF THESE LETTERS, AND HIS ATTEMPTS TO SEE ME AS HARMLESS...
...BUT NOW HE'S BECOME A CELEBRITY—AND HIS LETTERS HAVE BECOME MORE THREATENING.
IF HE SLANDERS ME—EVEN ONCE, IN PUBLIC—HE COULD SERIOUSLY JEOPARDIZE MY CHANCES AT RUNNING FOR PRESIDENT.
I WANT YOU TO REASON WITH HIM. IF THAT WON'T WORK, PAY HIM OFF. I DON'T WANT THESE WILD ACCUSATIONS REPEATED IN PUBLIC. DO I MAKE MYSELF CLEAR?
YES, SIR.
SO WHAT DO I DO? HOW DO I HANDLE SINKAGE FOR CALLAHAN? OR DO I TELL FORBES TO TAKE A JUMP, AND MAYBE END UP IN MILITARY PRISON?
AND WHAT'S CALLAHAN TO FORBES, ANYWAY?
I NEED A DRINK!
BAR

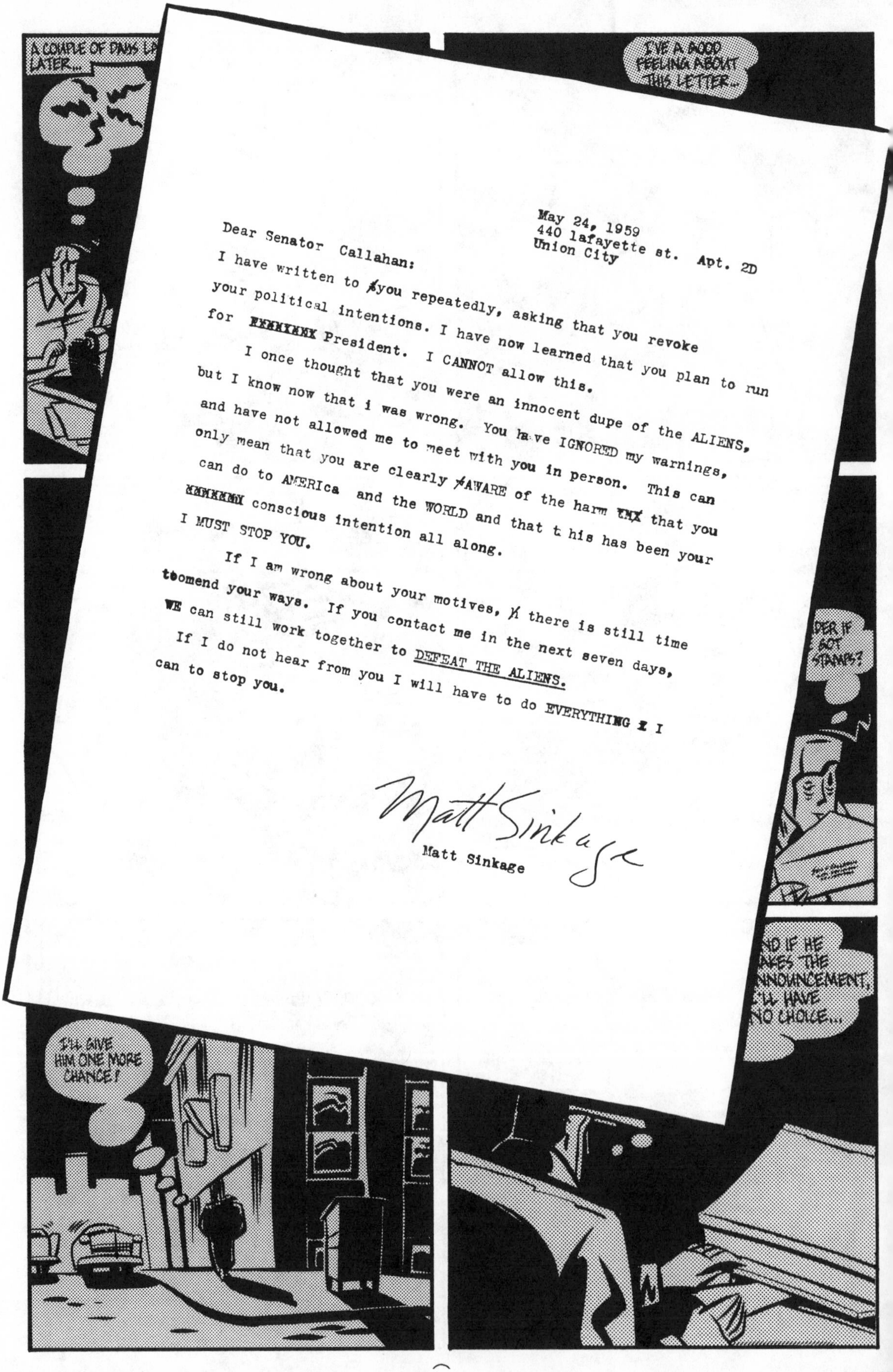
A COUPLE OF DAYS LA
LATER...
I'VE A GOOD FEELING ABOUT THIS LETTER...
May 24, 1959
440 lafayette st. Apt. 2D
Union City
Dear Senator Callahan:
I have written to you repeatedly, asking that you revoke your political intentions. I have now learned that you plan to run for XXXXXXXX President. I CANNOT allow this.
I once thought that you were an innocent dupe of the ALIENS, but I know now that i was wrong. You have IGNORED my warnings, and have not allowed me to meet with you in person. This can only mean that you are clearly AWARE of the harm that you can do to AMERICa and the WORLD and that this has been your XXXXXXX conscious intention all along.
I MUST STOP YOU.
If I am wrong about your motives, there is still time to mend your ways. If you contact me in the next seven days, WE can still work together to DEFEAT THE ALIENS.
If I do not hear from you I will have to do EVERYTHING I can to stop you.
Matt Sinkage
Matt Sinkage
DER IF
GOT STAMPS?
ND IF HE
AKES THE
NNOUNCEMENT,
'LL HAVE
NO CHOICE...
I'LL GIVE HIM ONE MORE CHANCE!

CHAPTER SIX
THE WILL OF THE PEOPLE

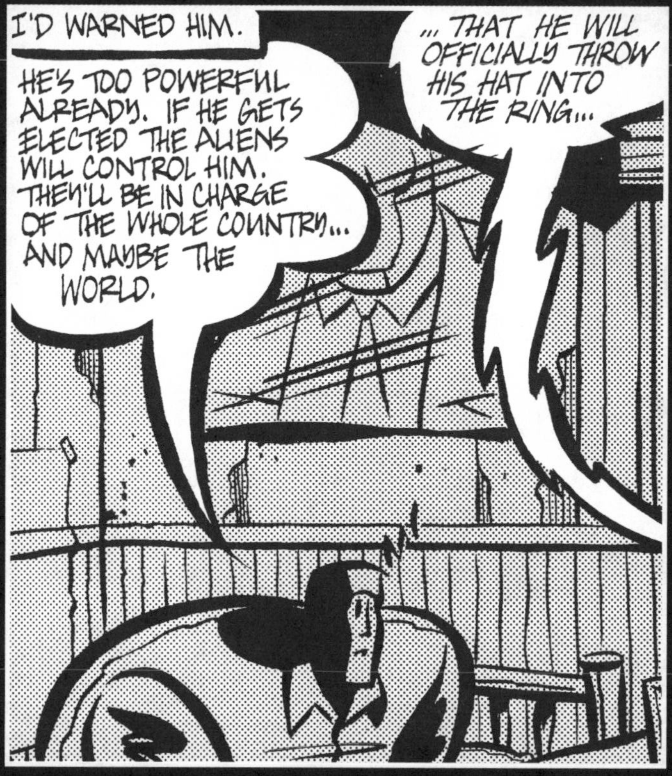
I'D WARNED HIM.
HE'S TOO POWERFUL ALREADY. IF HE GETS ELECTED THE ALIENS WILL CONTROL HIM. THEY'LL BE IN CHARGE OF THE WHOLE COUNTRY... AND MAYBE THE WORLD.
...THAT HE WILL OFFICIALLY THROW HIS HAT INTO THE RING...

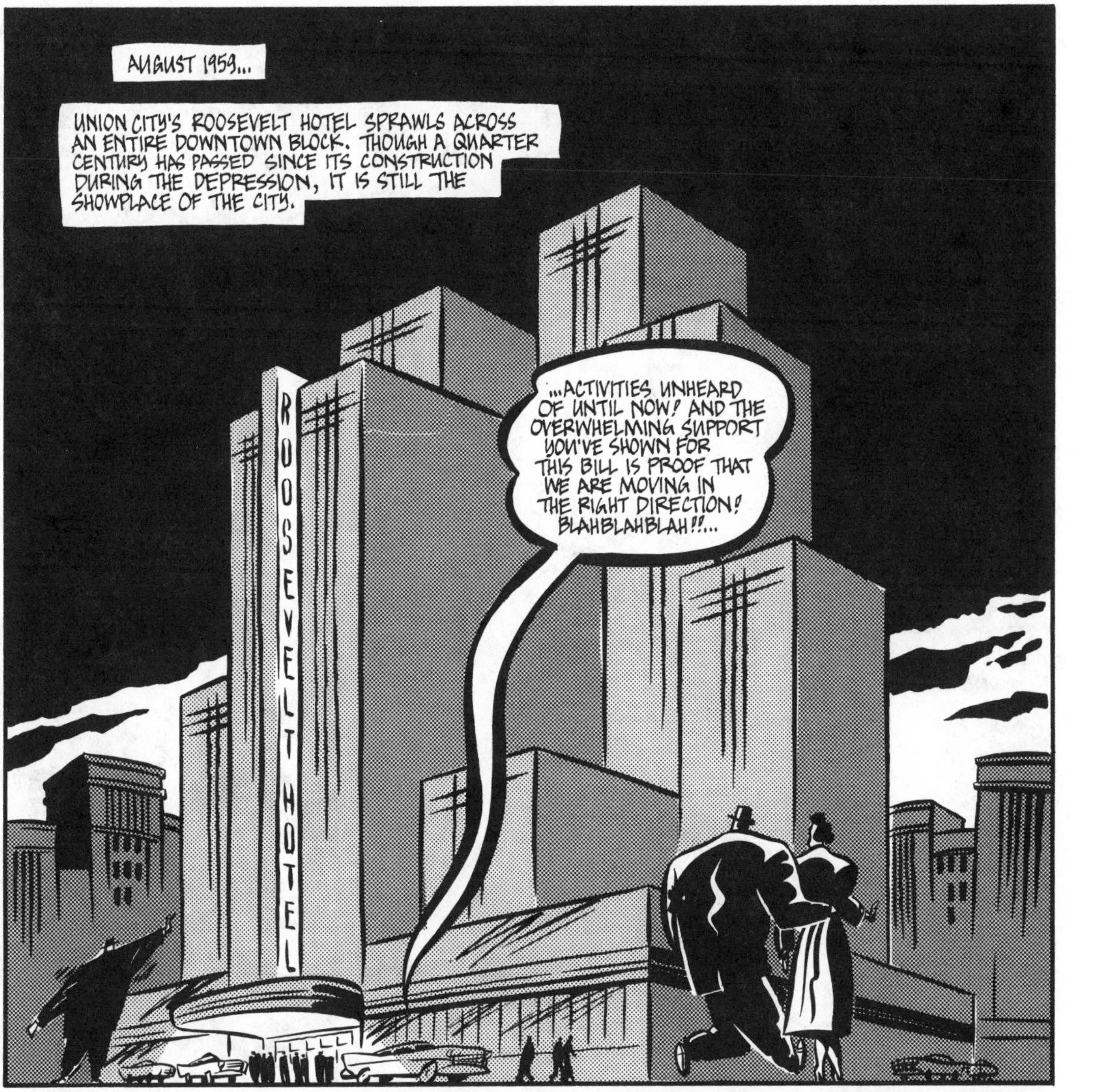
AUGUST 1959...
UNION CITY'S ROOSEVELT HOTEL SPRAWLS ACROSS AN ENTIRE DOWNTOWN BLOCK. THOUGH A QUARTER CENTURY HAS PASSED SINCE ITS CONSTRUCTION DURING THE DEPRESSION, IT IS STILL THE SHOWPLACE OF THE CITY.
...ACTIVITIES UNHEARD OF UNTIL NOW! AND THE OVERWHELMING SUPPORT YOU'VE SHOWN FOR THIS BILL IS PROOF THAT WE ARE MOVING IN THE RIGHT DIRECTION! BLAHBLAHBLAH!!...
ROOSEVELT HOTEL

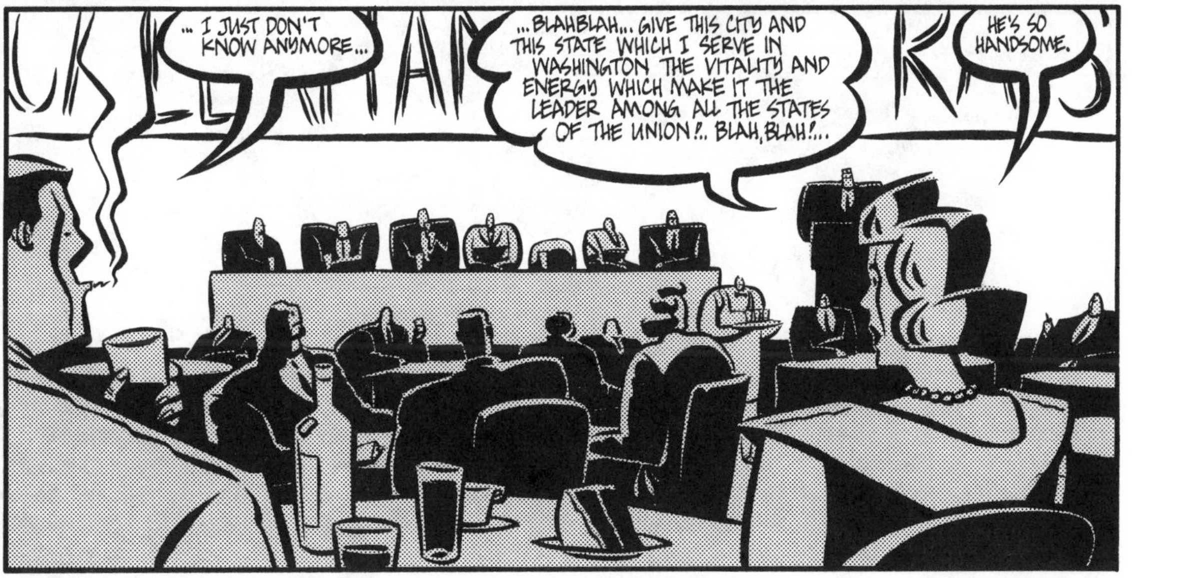
... I JUST DON'T KNOW ANYMORE...
...BLAHBLAH... GIVE THIS CITY AND THIS STATE WHICH I SERVE IN WASHINGTON THE VITALITY AND ENERGY WHICH MAKE IT THE LEADER AMONG ALL THE STATES OF THE UNION!.. BLAH,BLAH!...
HE'S SO HANDSOME.

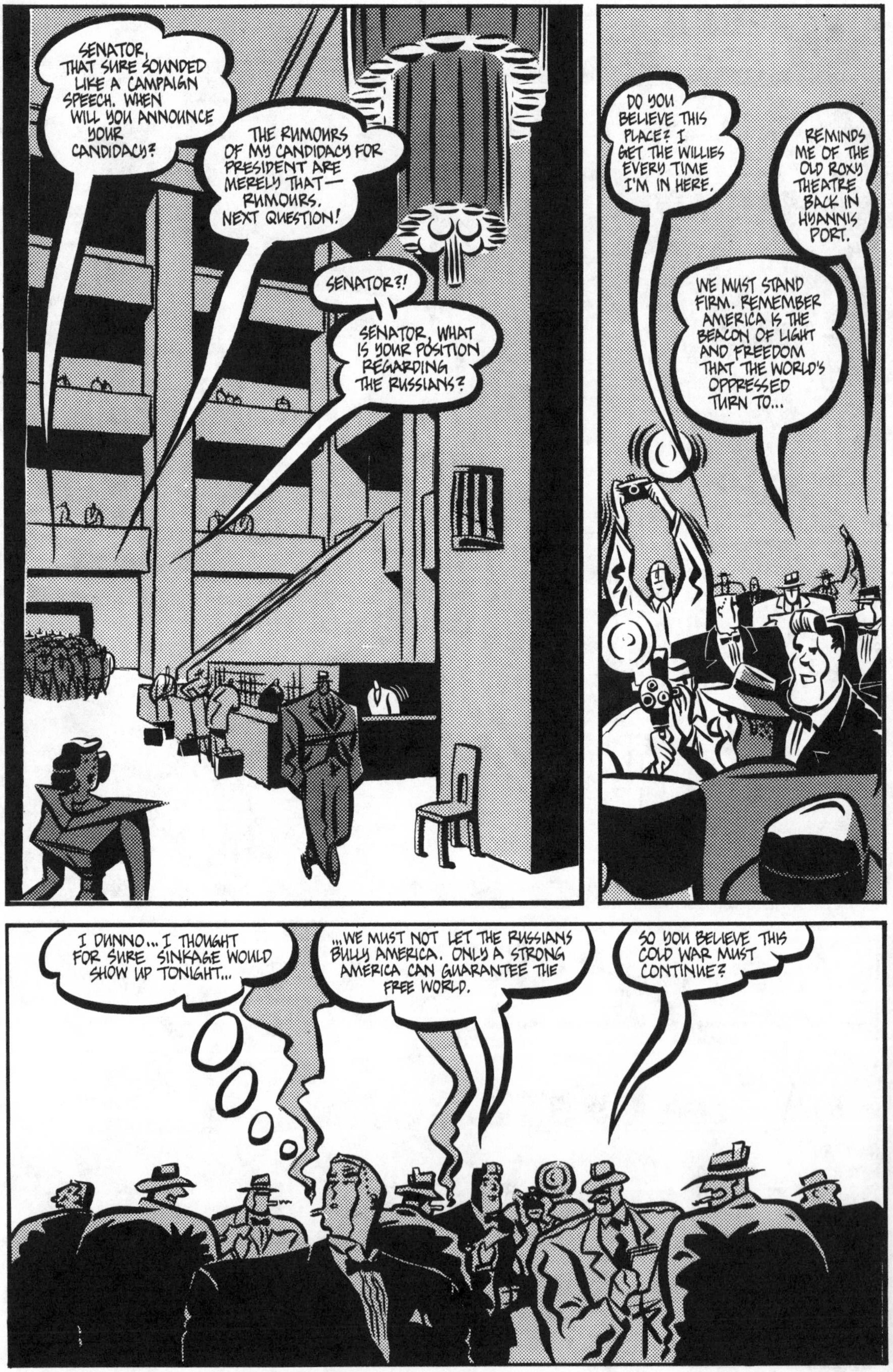
SENATOR, THAT SURE SOUNDED LIKE A CAMPAIGN SPEECH. WHEN WILL YOU ANNOUNCE YOUR CANDIDACY?
THE RUMOURS OF MY CANDIDACY FOR PRESIDENT ARE MERELY THAT— RUMOURS. NEXT QUESTION!
SENATOR?!
SENATOR, WHAT IS YOUR POSITION REGARDING THE RUSSIANS?
DO YOU BELIEVE THIS PLACE? I GET THE WILLIES EVERY TIME I'M IN HERE.
REMINDS ME OF THE OLD ROXY THEATRE BACK IN HYANNIS PORT.
WE MUST STAND FIRM. REMEMBER AMERICA IS THE BEACON OF LIGHT AND FREEDOM THAT THE WORLD'S OPPRESSED TURN TO...
I DUNNO... I THOUGHT FOR SURE SINKAGE WOULD SHOW UP TONIGHT...
...WE MUST NOT LET THE RUSSIANS BULLY AMERICA. ONLY A STRONG AMERICA CAN GUARANTEE THE FREE WORLD.
SO YOU BELIEVE THIS COLD WAR MUST CONTINUE?

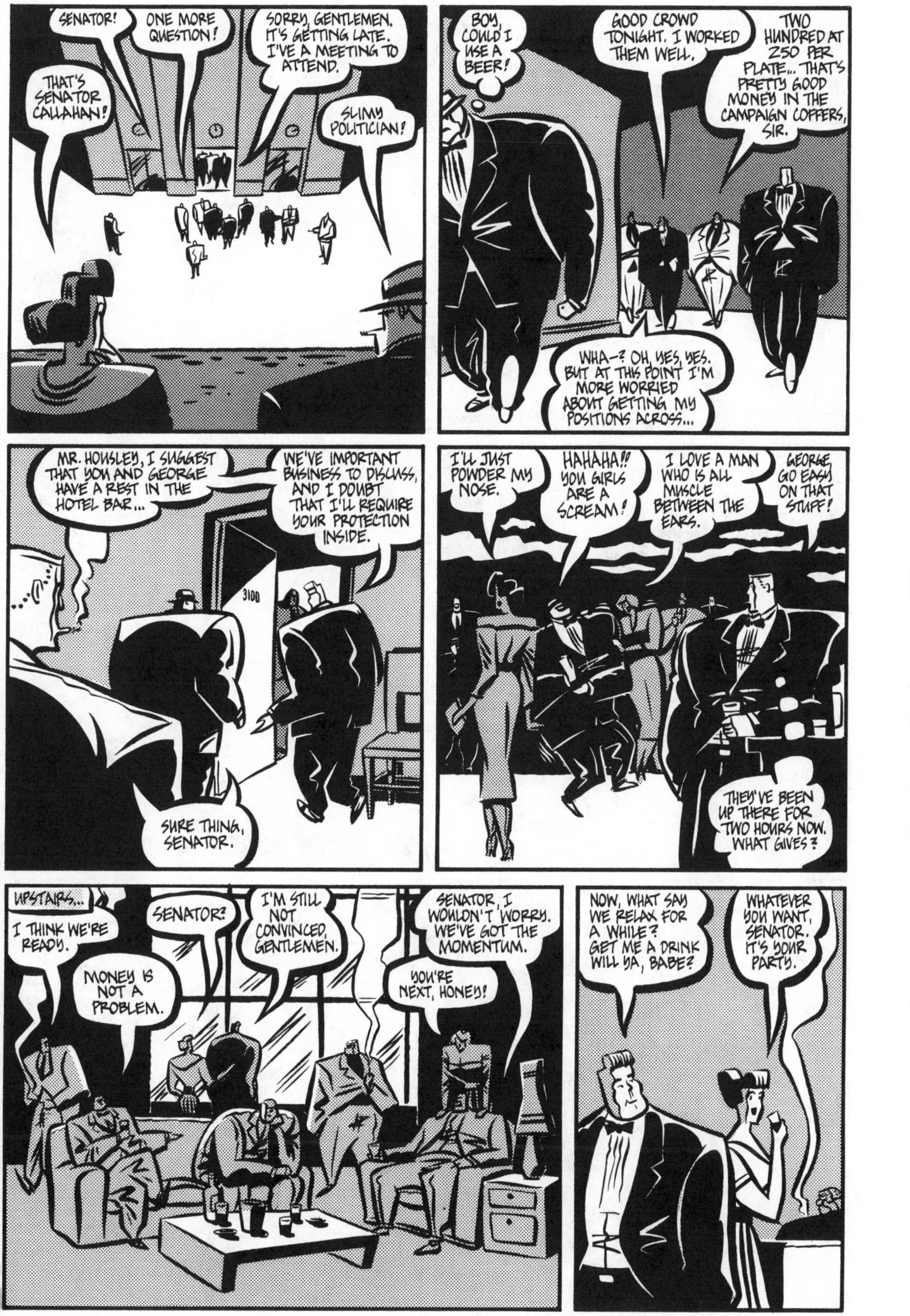
SENATOR!
ONE MORE QUESTION!
THAT'S SENATOR CALLAHAN!
SORRY, GENTLEMEN. IT'S GETTING LATE. I'VE A MEETING TO ATTEND.
SLIMY POLITICIAN!
BOY, COULD I USE A BEER!
GOOD CROWD TONIGHT. I WORKED THEM WELL.
TWO HUNDRED AT 250 PER PLATE... THAT'S PRETTY GOOD MONEY IN THE CAMPAIGN COFFERS, SIR.
WHA-? OH, YES, YES. BUT AT THIS POINT I'M MORE WORRIED ABOUT GETTING MY POSITIONS ACROSS...
MR. HOUSLEY, I SUGGEST THAT YOU AND GEORGE HAVE A REST IN THE HOTEL BAR...
WE'VE IMPORTANT BUSINESS TO DISCUSS, AND I DOUBT THAT I'LL REQUIRE YOUR PROTECTION INSIDE.
3100
SURE THING, SENATOR.
I'LL JUST POWDER MY NOSE.
HAHAHA!! YOU GIRLS ARE A SCREAM!
I LOVE A MAN WHO IS ALL MUSCLE BETWEEN THE EARS.
GEORGE, GO EASY ON THAT STUFF!
THEY'VE BEEN UP THERE FOR TWO HOURS NOW. WHAT GIVES?
UPSTAIRS...
I THINK WE'RE READY.
SENATOR?
MONEY IS NOT A PROBLEM.
I'M STILL NOT CONVINCED, GENTLEMEN.
SENATOR, I WOULDN'T WORRY. WE'VE GOT THE MOMENTUM.
YOU'RE NEXT, HONEY!
NOW, WHAT SAY WE RELAX FOR A WHILE? GET ME A DRINK WILL YA, BABE?
WHATEVER YOU WANT, SENATOR. IT'S YOUR PARTY.

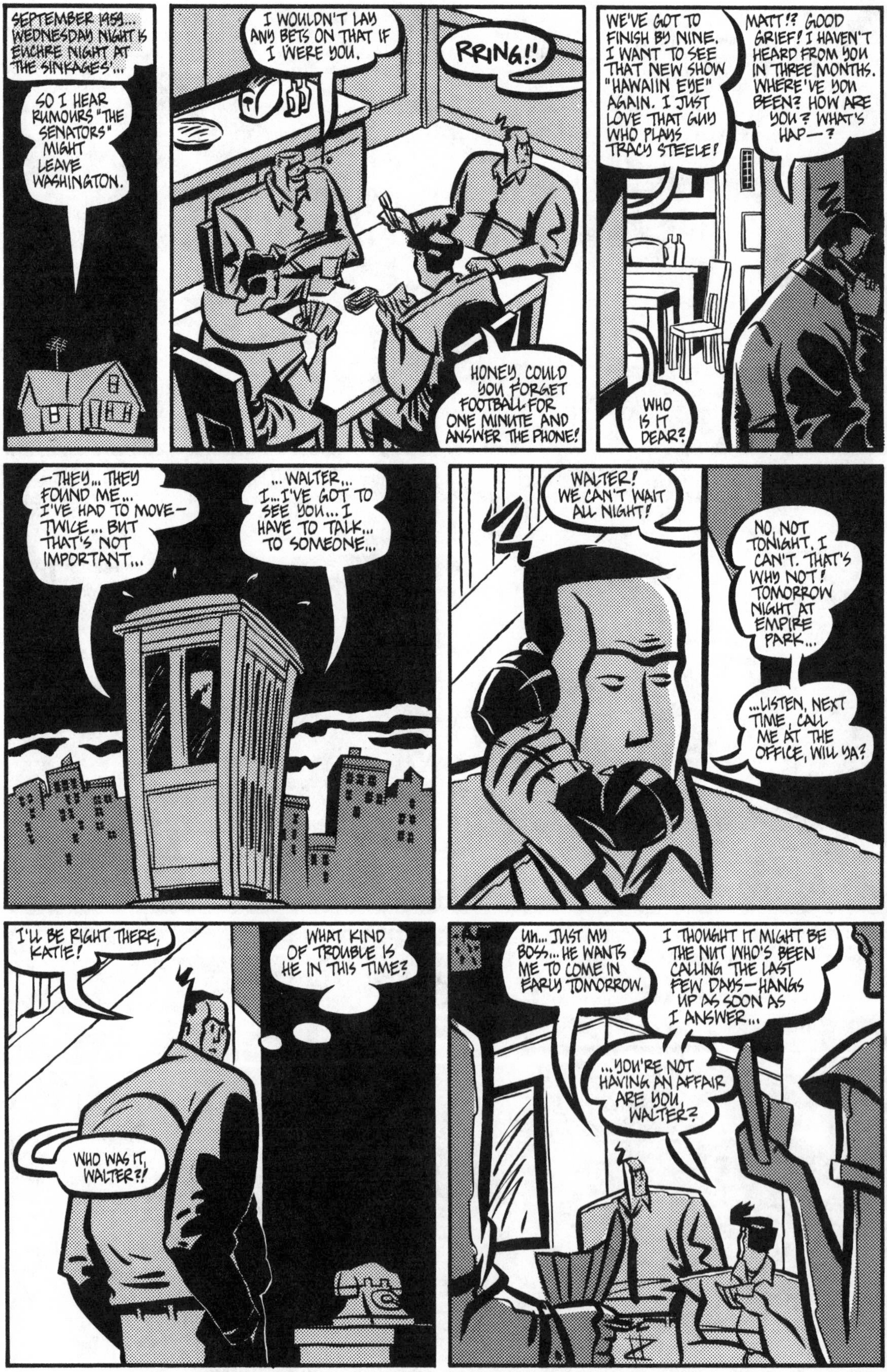
SEPTEMBER 1959... WEDNESDAY NIGHT IS EUCHRE NIGHT AT THE SINKAGES'...
SO I HEAR RUMOURS "THE SENATORS" MIGHT LEAVE WASHINGTON.
I WOULDN'T LAY ANY BETS ON THAT IF I WERE YOU.
RRING!!
HONEY, COULD YOU FORGET FOOTBALL FOR ONE MINUTE AND ANSWER THE PHONE!
WE'VE GOT TO FINISH BY NINE. I WANT TO SEE THAT NEW SHOW "HAWAIIN EYE" AGAIN. I JUST LOVE THAT GUY WHO PLAYS TRACY STEELE!
MATT!? GOOD GRIEF! I HAVEN'T HEARD FROM YOU IN THREE MONTHS. WHERE'VE YOU BEEN? HOW ARE YOU? WHAT'S HAP—?
WHO IS IT DEAR?
—THEY... THEY FOUND ME... I'VE HAD TO MOVE— TWICE... BUT THAT'S NOT IMPORTANT...
...WALTER... I...I'VE GOT TO SEE YOU... I HAVE TO TALK... TO SOMEONE...
WALTER! WE CAN'T WAIT ALL NIGHT!
NO, NOT TONIGHT. I CAN'T. THAT'S WHY NOT! TOMORROW NIGHT AT EMPIRE PARK...
...LISTEN, NEXT TIME, CALL ME AT THE OFFICE, WILL YA?
I'LL BE RIGHT THERE, KATIE!
WHAT KIND OF TROUBLE IS HE IN THIS TIME?
WHO WAS IT, WALTER?!
UH... JUST MY BOSS... HE WANTS ME TO COME IN EARLY TOMORROW.
I THOUGHT IT MIGHT BE THE NUT WHO'S BEEN CALLING THE LAST FEW DAYS—HANGS UP AS SOON AS I ANSWER...
...YOU'RE NOT HAVING AN AFFAIR ARE YOU, WALTER?

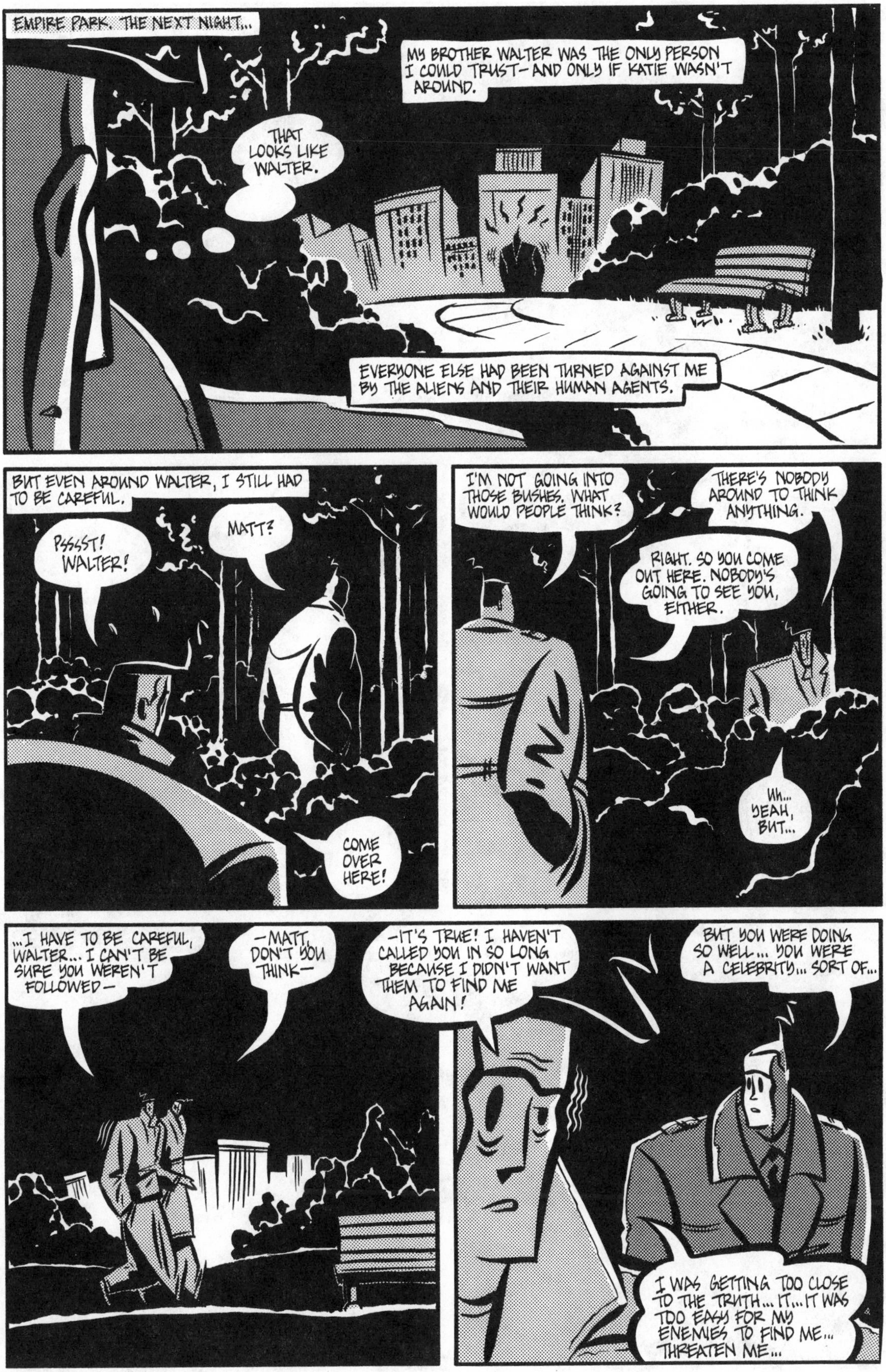
EMPIRE PARK. THE NEXT NIGHT...
MY BROTHER WALTER WAS THE ONLY PERSON I COULD TRUST— AND ONLY IF KATIE WASN'T AROUND.
THAT LOOKS LIKE WALTER.
EVERYONE ELSE HAD BEEN TURNED AGAINST ME BY THE ALIENS AND THEIR HUMAN AGENTS.
BUT EVEN AROUND WALTER, I STILL HAD TO BE CAREFUL.
PSSSST! WALTER!
MATT?
COME OVER HERE!
I'M NOT GOING INTO THOSE BUSHES. WHAT WOULD PEOPLE THINK?
THERE'S NOBODY AROUND TO THINK ANYTHING.
RIGHT. SO YOU COME OUT HERE. NOBODY'S GOING TO SEE YOU, EITHER.
UH... YEAH, BUT...
...I HAVE TO BE CAREFUL, WALTER... I CAN'T BE SURE YOU WEREN'T FOLLOWED—
—MATT, DON'T YOU THINK—
—IT'S TRUE! I HAVEN'T CALLED YOU IN SO LONG BECAUSE I DIDN'T WANT THEM TO FIND ME AGAIN!
BUT YOU WERE DOING SO WELL... YOU WERE A CELEBRITY... SORT OF...
I WAS GETTING TOO CLOSE TO THE TRUTH... IT... IT WAS TOO EASY FOR MY ENEMIES TO FIND ME... THREATEN ME...

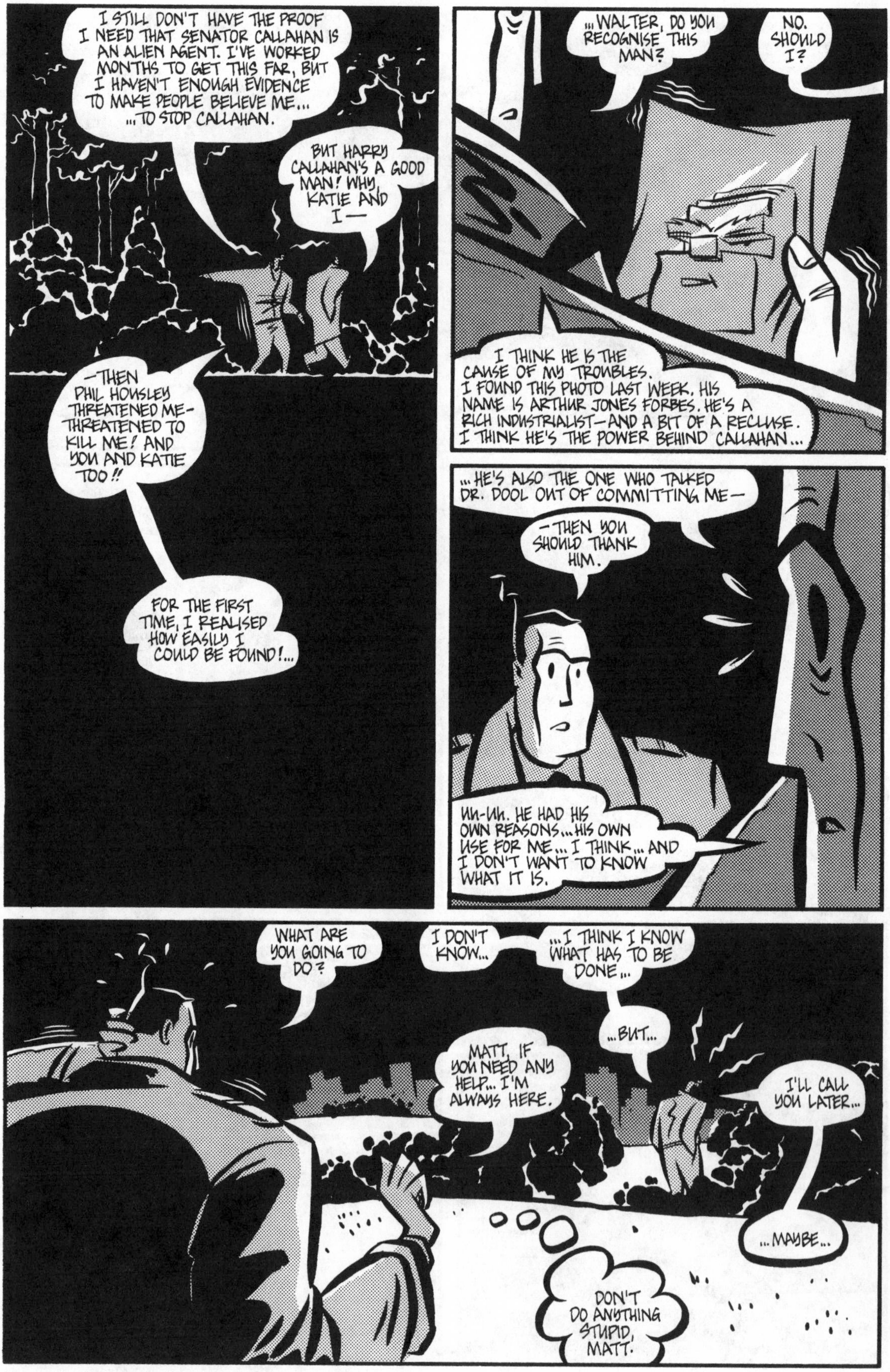
I STILL DON'T HAVE THE PROOF I NEED THAT SENATOR CALLAHAN IS AN ALIEN AGENT. I'VE WORKED MONTHS TO GET THIS FAR, BUT I HAVEN'T ENOUGH EVIDENCE TO MAKE PEOPLE BELIEVE ME...
...TO STOP CALLAHAN.
BUT HARRY CALLAHAN'S A GOOD MAN! WHY, KATIE AND I—
—THEN PHIL HOUSLEY THREATENED ME—THREATENED TO KILL ME! AND YOU AND KATIE TOO!!
FOR THE FIRST TIME, I REALISED HOW EASILY I COULD BE FOUND!...
...WALTER, DO YOU RECOGNISE THIS MAN?
NO. SHOULD I?
I THINK HE IS THE CAUSE OF MY TROUBLES. I FOUND THIS PHOTO LAST WEEK. HIS NAME IS ARTHUR JONES FORBES. HE'S A RICH INDUSTRIALIST—AND A BIT OF A RECLUSE. I THINK HE'S THE POWER BEHIND CALLAHAN...
...HE'S ALSO THE ONE WHO TALKED DR. DOOL OUT OF COMMITTING ME—
—THEN YOU SHOULD THANK HIM.
UH-UH. HE HAD HIS OWN REASONS...HIS OWN USE FOR ME... I THINK... AND I DON'T WANT TO KNOW WHAT IT IS.
WHAT ARE YOU GOING TO DO?
I DON'T KNOW...
...I THINK I KNOW WHAT HAS TO BE DONE...
...BUT...
MATT, IF YOU NEED ANY HELP... I'M ALWAYS HERE.
I'LL CALL YOU LATER...
...MAYBE...
DON'T DO ANYTHING STUPID, MATT.

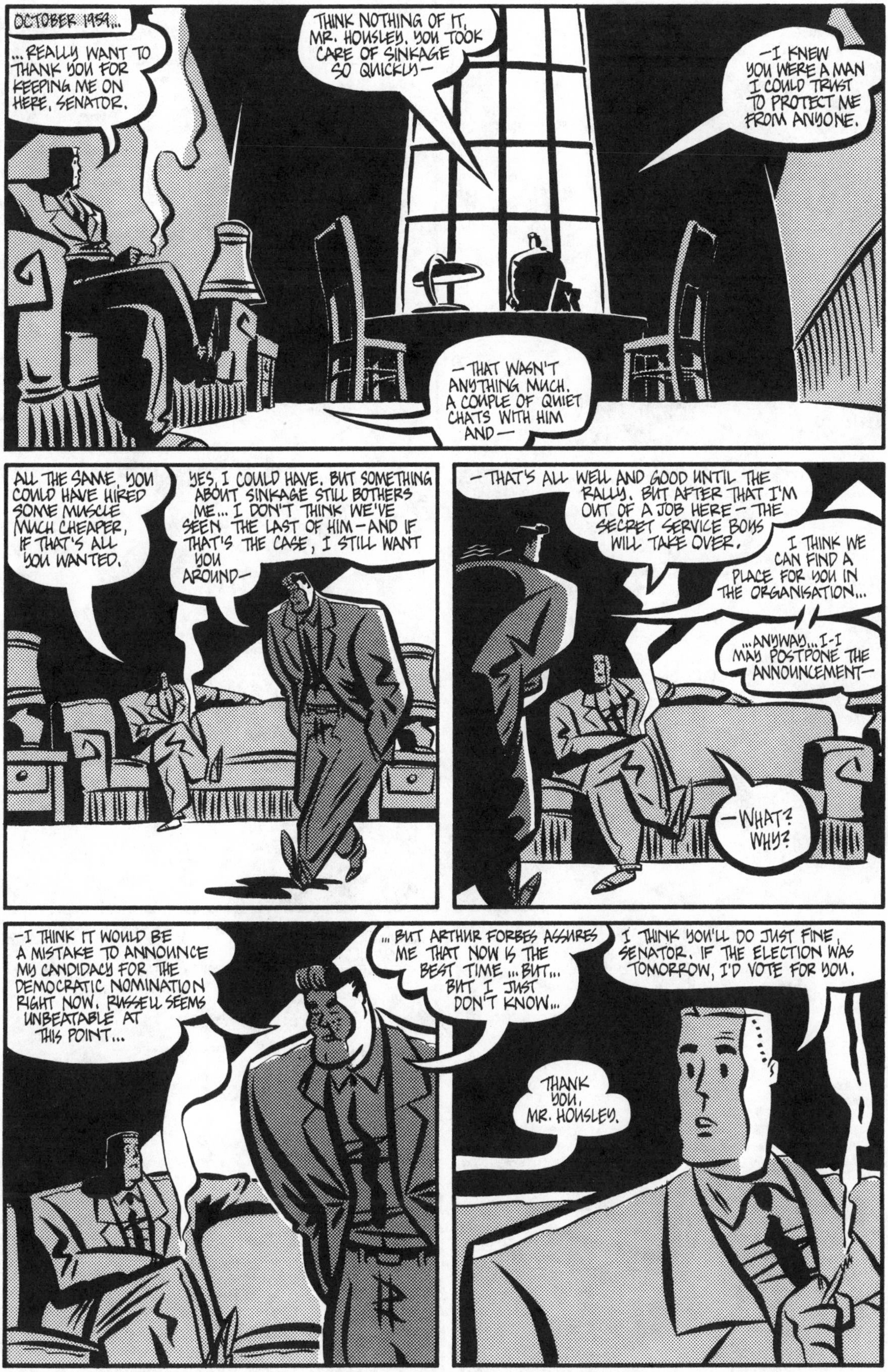
OCTOBER 1959...
...REALLY WANT TO THANK YOU FOR KEEPING ME ON HERE, SENATOR.
THINK NOTHING OF IT, MR. HOUSLEY. YOU TOOK CARE OF SINKAGE SO QUICKLY—
—I KNEW YOU WERE A MAN I COULD TRUST TO PROTECT ME FROM ANYONE.
—THAT WASN'T ANYTHING MUCH. A COUPLE OF QUIET CHATS WITH HIM AND—
ALL THE SAME, YOU COULD HAVE HIRED SOME MUSCLE MUCH CHEAPER, IF THAT'S ALL YOU WANTED.
YES, I COULD HAVE. BUT SOMETHING ABOUT SINKAGE STILL BOTHERS ME... I DON'T THINK WE'VE SEEN THE LAST OF HIM—AND IF THAT'S THE CASE, I STILL WANT YOU AROUND—
—THAT'S ALL WELL AND GOOD UNTIL THE RALLY. BUT AFTER THAT I'M OUT OF A JOB HERE—THE SECRET SERVICE BOYS WILL TAKE OVER.
I THINK WE CAN FIND A PLACE FOR YOU IN THE ORGANISATION...
...ANYWAY... I-I MAY POSTPONE THE ANNOUNCEMENT—
—WHAT? WHY?
—I THINK IT WOULD BE A MISTAKE TO ANNOUNCE MY CANDIDACY FOR THE DEMOCRATIC NOMINATION RIGHT NOW. RUSSELL SEEMS UNBEATABLE AT THIS POINT...
...BUT ARTHUR FORBES ASSURES ME THAT NOW IS THE BEST TIME ...BUT... BUT I JUST DON'T KNOW...
I THINK YOU'LL DO JUST FINE, SENATOR. IF THE ELECTION WAS TOMORROW, I'D VOTE FOR YOU.
THANK YOU, MR. HOUSLEY.

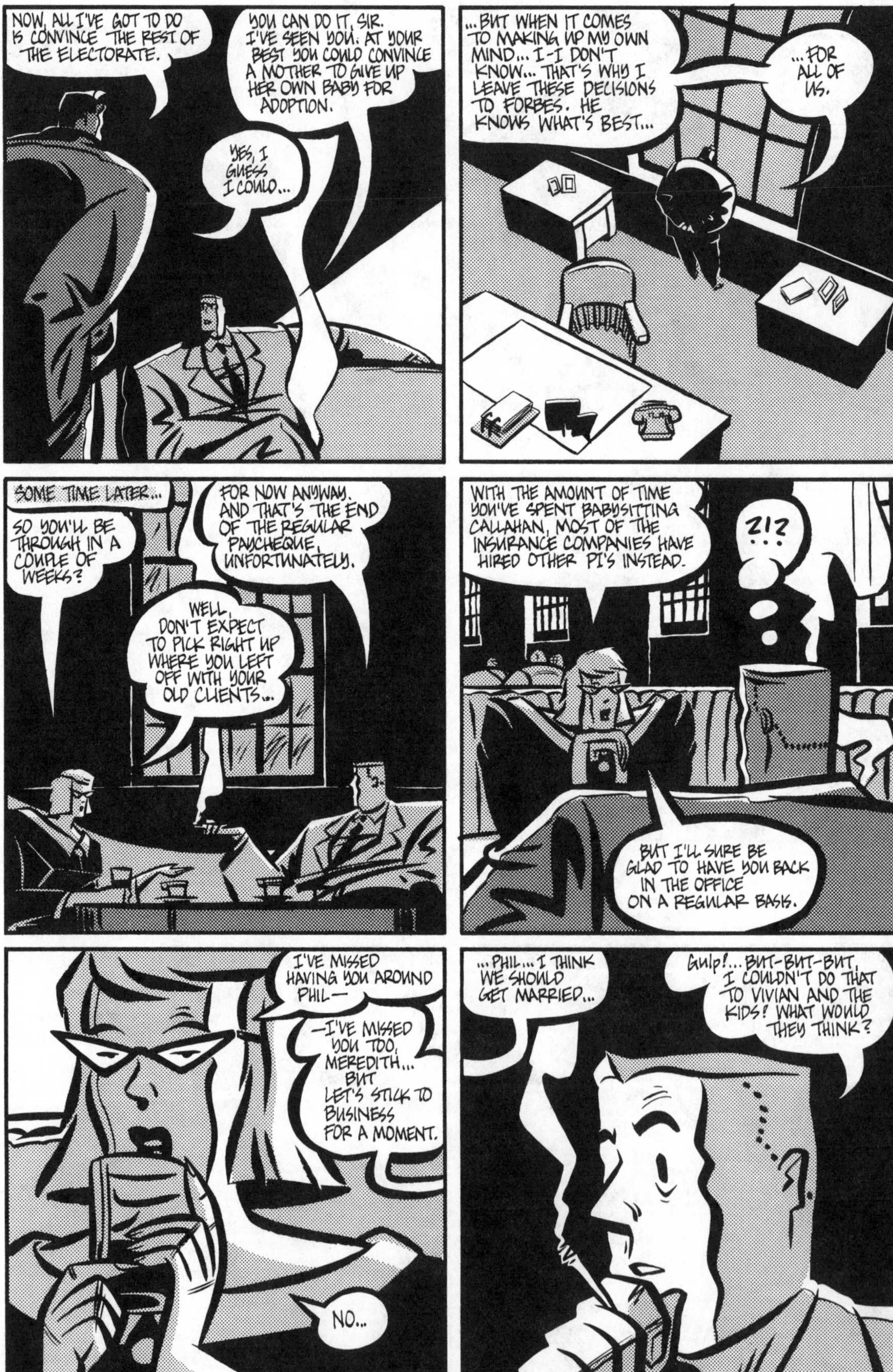
NOW, ALL I'VE GOT TO DO IS CONVINCE THE REST OF THE ELECTORATE.
YOU CAN DO IT, SIR. I'VE SEEN YOU: AT YOUR BEST YOU COULD CONVINCE A MOTHER TO GIVE UP HER OWN BABY FOR ADOPTION.
YES, I GUESS I COULD...
...BUT WHEN IT COMES TO MAKING UP MY OWN MIND... I-I DON'T KNOW... THAT'S WHY I LEAVE THESE DECISIONS TO FORBES. HE KNOWS WHAT'S BEST...
...FOR ALL OF US.
SOME TIME LATER...
SO YOU'LL BE THROUGH IN A COUPLE OF WEEKS?
FOR NOW ANYWAY. AND THAT'S THE END OF THE REGULAR PAYCHEQUE, UNFORTUNATELY.
WELL, DON'T EXPECT TO PICK RIGHT UP WHERE YOU LEFT OFF WITH YOUR OLD CLIENTS...
WITH THE AMOUNT OF TIME YOU'VE SPENT BABYSITTING CALLAHAN, MOST OF THE INSURANCE COMPANIES HAVE HIRED OTHER PI'S INSTEAD.
?!?
BUT I'LL SURE BE GLAD TO HAVE YOU BACK IN THE OFFICE ON A REGULAR BASIS.
I'VE MISSED HAVING YOU AROUND PHIL—
—I'VE MISSED YOU TOO, MEREDITH... BUT LET'S STICK TO BUSINESS FOR A MOMENT.
NO...
...PHIL... I THINK WE SHOULD GET MARRIED...
Gulp!... BUT-BUT-BUT, I COULDN'T DO THAT TO VIVIAN AND THE KIDS! WHAT WOULD THEY THINK?

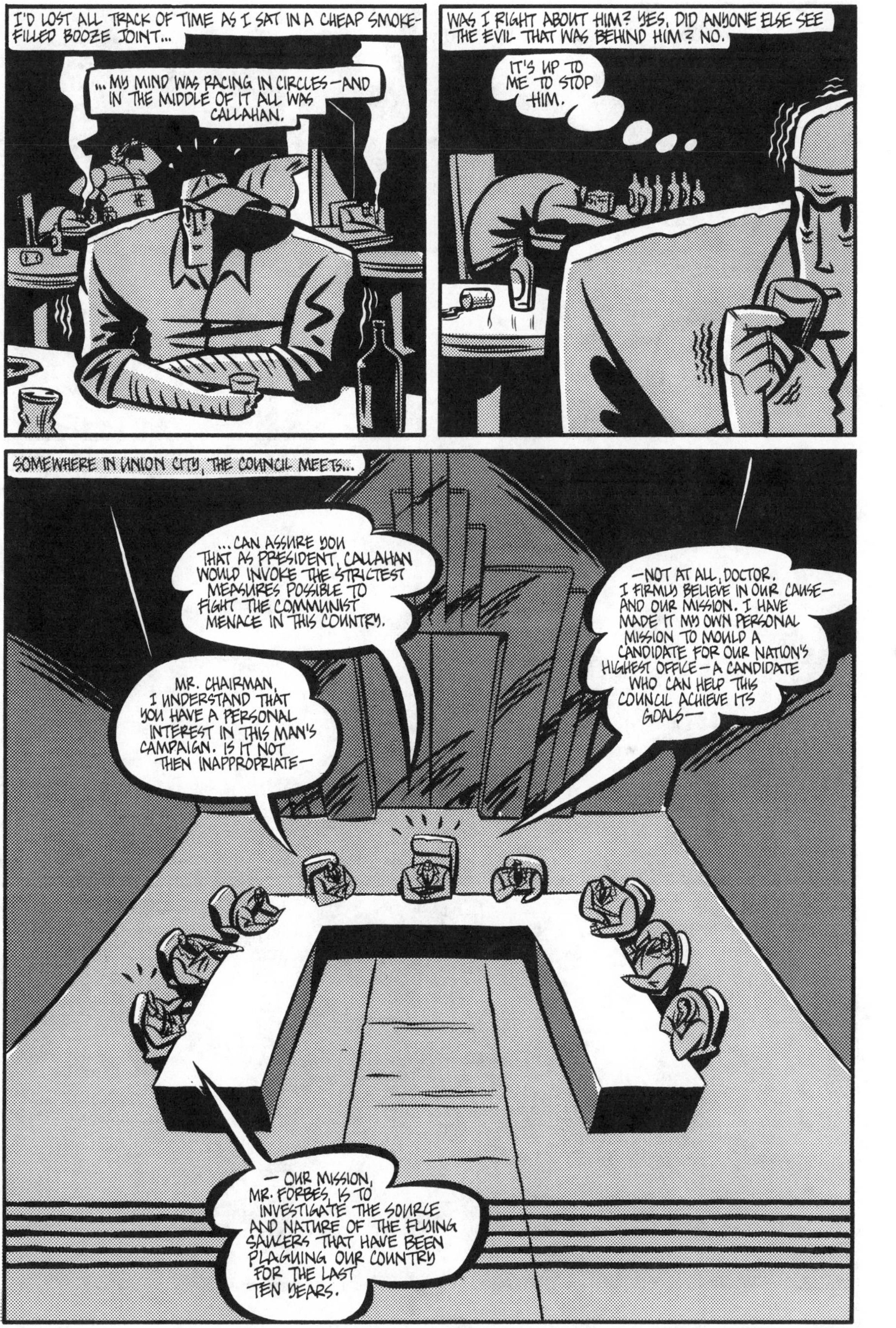
I'D LOST ALL TRACK OF TIME AS I SAT IN A CHEAP SMOKE-FILLED BOOZE JOINT...
... MY MIND WAS RACING IN CIRCLES—AND IN THE MIDDLE OF IT ALL WAS CALLAHAN.
WAS I RIGHT ABOUT HIM? YES. DID ANYONE ELSE SEE THE EVIL THAT WAS BEHIND HIM? NO.
IT'S UP TO ME TO STOP HIM.
SOMEWHERE IN UNION CITY, THE COUNCIL MEETS...
...CAN ASSURE YOU THAT AS PRESIDENT, CALLAHAN WOULD INVOKE THE STRICTEST MEASURES POSSIBLE TO FIGHT THE COMMUNIST MENACE IN THIS COUNTRY.
MR. CHAIRMAN, I UNDERSTAND THAT YOU HAVE A PERSONAL INTEREST IN THIS MAN'S CAMPAIGN. IS IT NOT THEN INAPPROPRIATE—
—NOT AT ALL, DOCTOR. I FIRMLY BELIEVE IN OUR CAUSE—AND OUR MISSION. I HAVE MADE IT MY OWN PERSONAL MISSION TO MOULD A CANDIDATE FOR OUR NATION'S HIGHEST OFFICE—A CANDIDATE WHO CAN HELP THIS COUNCIL ACHIEVE ITS GOALS—
— OUR MISSION, MR. FORBES, IS TO INVESTIGATE THE SOURCE AND NATURE OF THE FLYING SAUCERS THAT HAVE BEEN PLAGUING OUR COUNTRY FOR THE LAST TEN YEARS.

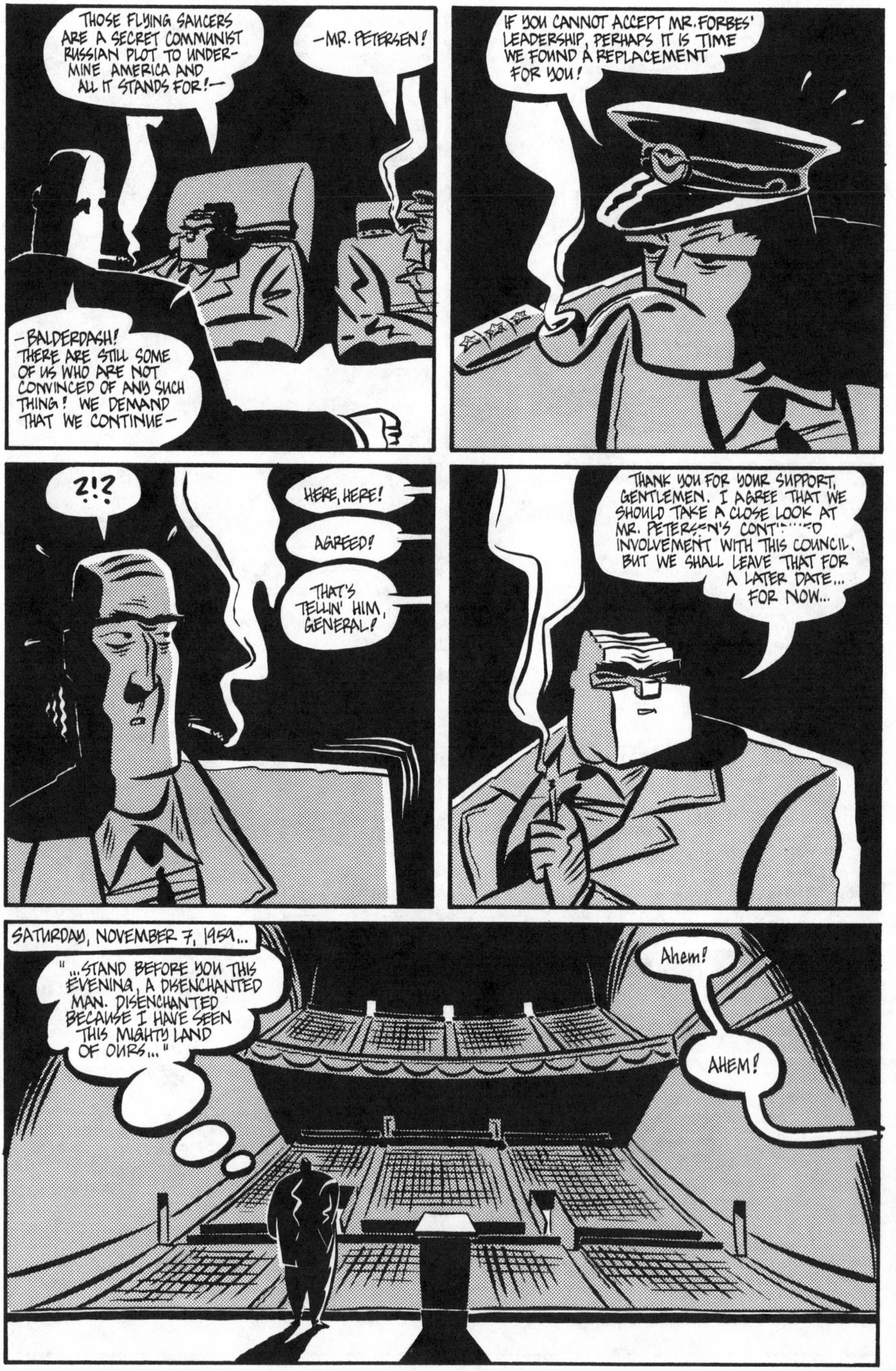

THOSE FLYING SAUCERS ARE A SECRET COMMUNIST RUSSIAN PLOT TO UNDERMINE AMERICA AND ALL IT STANDS FOR!—
—MR. PETERSEN!
—BALDERDASH! THERE ARE STILL SOME OF US WHO ARE NOT CONVINCED OF ANY SUCH THING! WE DEMAND THAT WE CONTINUE—
IF YOU CANNOT ACCEPT MR. FORBES' LEADERSHIP, PERHAPS IT IS TIME WE FOUND A REPLACEMENT FOR YOU!
?!?
HERE, HERE!
AGREED!
THAT'S TELLIN' HIM, GENERAL!
THANK YOU FOR YOUR SUPPORT, GENTLEMEN. I AGREE THAT WE SHOULD TAKE A CLOSE LOOK AT MR. PETERSEN'S CONTINUED INVOLVEMENT WITH THIS COUNCIL. BUT WE SHALL LEAVE THAT FOR A LATER DATE... FOR NOW...
SATURDAY, NOVEMBER 7, 1959...
"...STAND BEFORE YOU THIS EVENING, A DISENCHANTED MAN. DISENCHANTED BECAUSE I HAVE SEEN THIS MIGHTY LAND OF OURS..."
Ahem!
AHEM!

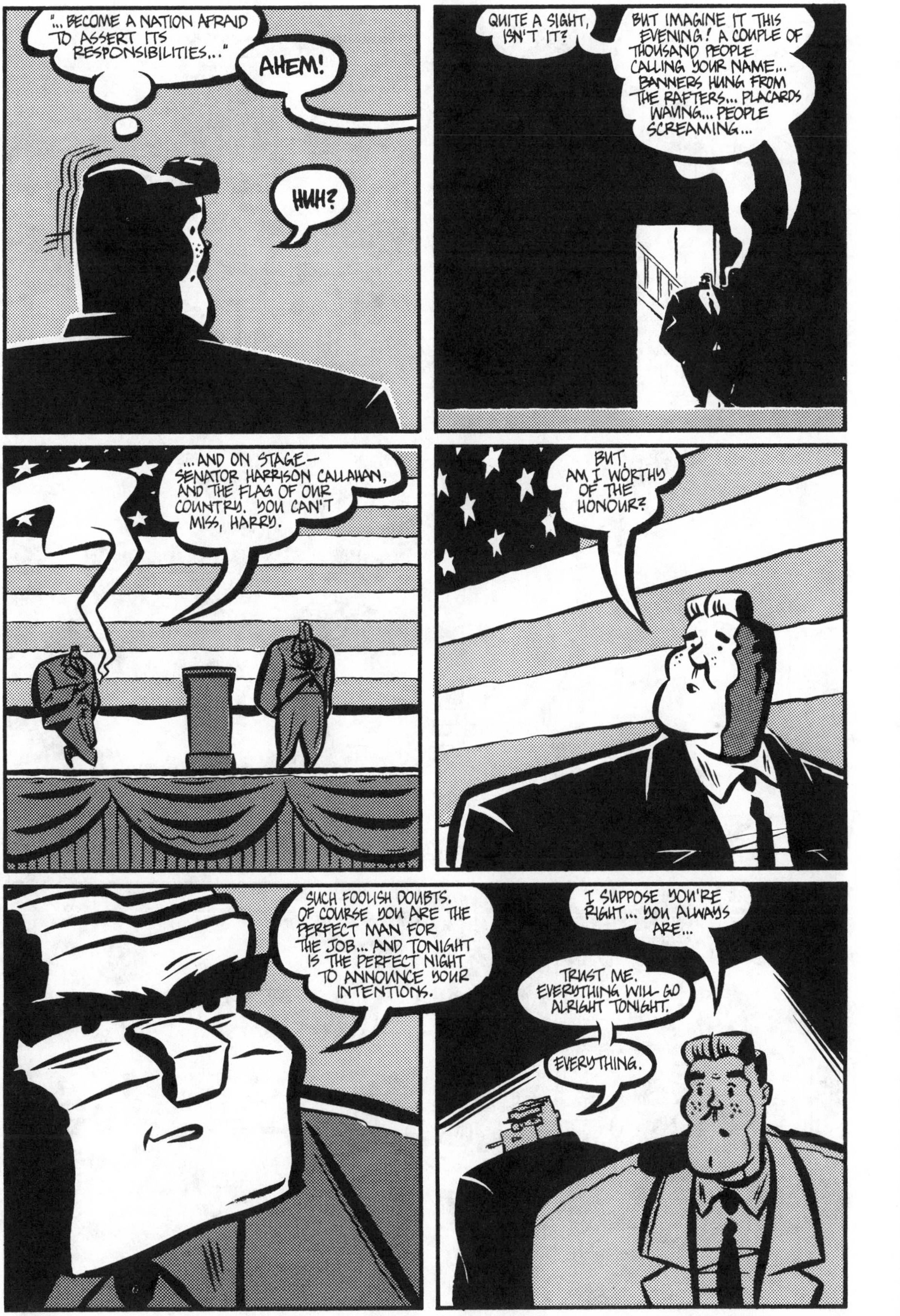
"... BECOME A NATION AFRAID TO ASSERT ITS RESPONSIBILITIES..."
AHEM!
HUH?
QUITE A SIGHT, ISN'T IT?
BUT IMAGINE IT THIS EVENING! A COUPLE OF THOUSAND PEOPLE CALLING YOUR NAME... BANNERS HUNG FROM THE RAFTERS... PLACARDS WAVING... PEOPLE SCREAMING...
...AND ON STAGE—SENATOR HARRISON CALLAHAN, AND THE FLAG OF OUR COUNTRY. YOU CAN'T MISS, HARRY.
BUT, AM I WORTHY OF THE HONOUR?
SUCH FOOLISH DOUBTS. OF COURSE YOU ARE THE PERFECT MAN FOR THE JOB... AND TONIGHT IS THE PERFECT NIGHT TO ANNOUNCE YOUR INTENTIONS.
I SUPPOSE YOU'RE RIGHT... YOU ALWAYS ARE...
TRUST ME. EVERYTHING WILL GO ALRIGHT TONIGHT.
EVERYTHING.

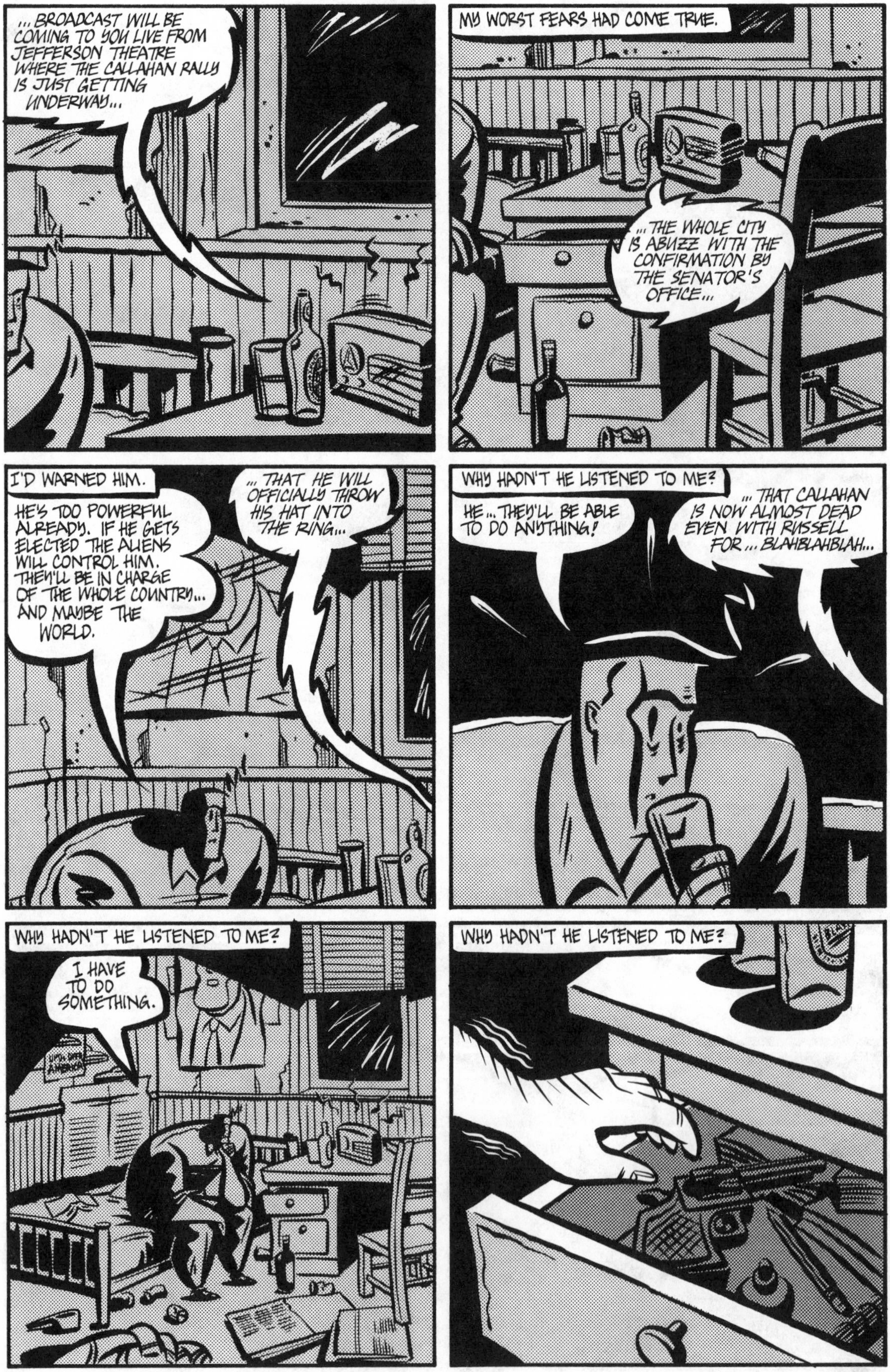
...BROADCAST WILL BE COMING TO YOU LIVE FROM JEFFERSON THEATRE WHERE THE CALLAHAN RALLY IS JUST GETTING UNDERWAY...
MY WORST FEARS HAD COME TRUE.
...THE WHOLE CITY IS ABUZZ WITH THE CONFIRMATION BY THE SENATOR'S OFFICE...
I'D WARNED HIM.
HE'S TOO POWERFUL ALREADY. IF HE GETS ELECTED THE ALIENS WILL CONTROL HIM. THEY'LL BE IN CHARGE OF THE WHOLE COUNTRY... AND MAYBE THE WORLD.
...THAT HE WILL OFFICIALLY THROW HIS HAT INTO THE RING...
WHY HADN'T HE LISTENED TO ME?
HE... THEY'LL BE ABLE TO DO ANYTHING!
...THAT CALLAHAN IS NOW ALMOST DEAD EVEN WITH RUSSELL FOR... BLAHBLAHBLAH...
WHY HADN'T HE LISTENED TO ME?
I HAVE TO DO SOMETHING.
WHY HADN'T HE LISTENED TO ME?

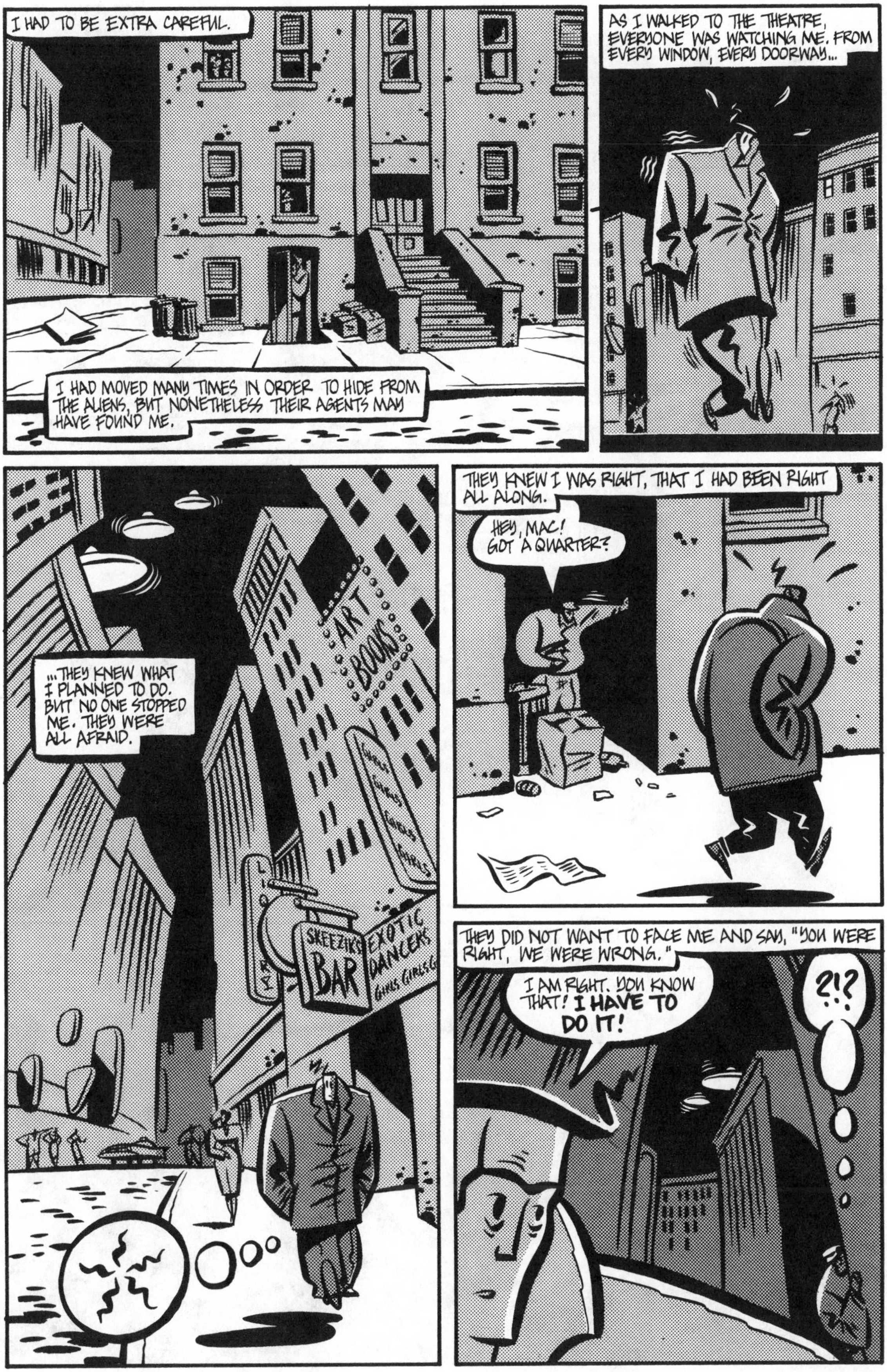

I HAD TO BE EXTRA CAREFUL.
I HAD MOVED MANY TIMES IN ORDER TO HIDE FROM THE ALIENS, BUT NONETHELESS THEIR AGENTS MAY HAVE FOUND ME.
AS I WALKED TO THE THEATRE, EVERYONE WAS WATCHING ME. FROM EVERY WINDOW, EVERY DOORWAY...
...THEY KNEW WHAT I PLANNED TO DO. BUT NO ONE STOPPED ME. THEY WERE ALL AFRAID.
ART BOOKS
GIRLS GIRLS GIRLS GIRLS
SKEEZIKS BAR
EXOTIC DANCERS
GIRLS GIRLS G
THEY KNEW I WAS RIGHT, THAT I HAD BEEN RIGHT ALL ALONG.
HEY, MAC! GOT A QUARTER?
THEY DID NOT WANT TO FACE ME AND SAY, "YOU WERE RIGHT, WE WERE WRONG."
I AM RIGHT. YOU KNOW THAT! I HAVE TO DO IT!
?!?

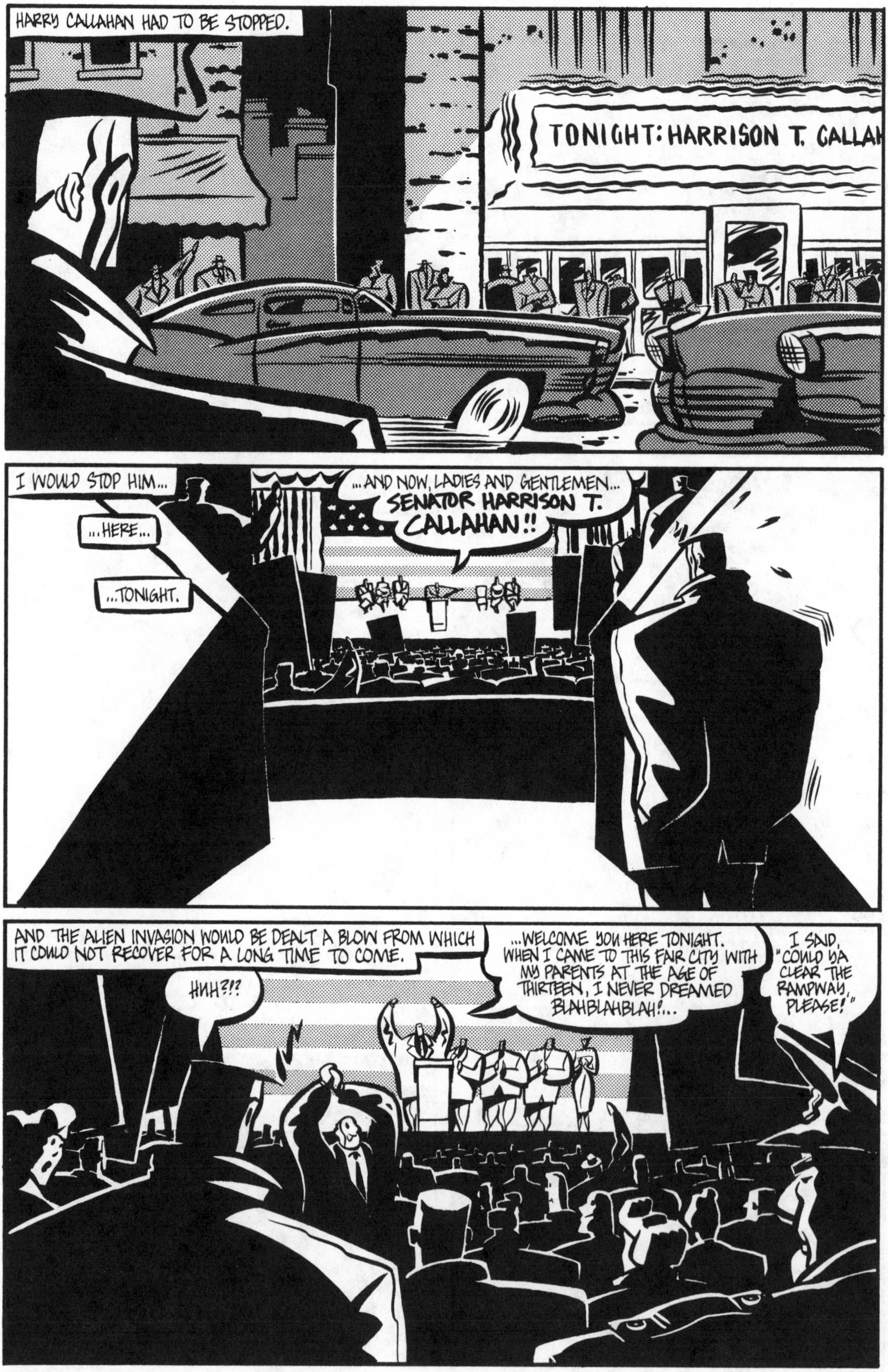
HARRY CALLAHAN HAD TO BE STOPPED.
TONIGHT: HARRISON T. CALLAH
I WOULD STOP HIM...
...HERE...
...TONIGHT.
...AND NOW, LADIES AND GENTLEMEN... SENATOR HARRISON T. CALLAHAN!!
AND THE ALIEN INVASION WOULD BE DEALT A BLOW FROM WHICH IT COULD NOT RECOVER FOR A LONG TIME TO COME.
HNH?!?
...WELCOME YOU HERE TONIGHT. WHEN I CAME TO THIS FAIR CITY WITH MY PARENTS AT THE AGE OF THIRTEEN, I NEVER DREAMED BLAHBLAHBLAH!...
I SAID, "COULD YA CLEAR THE RAMPWAY, PLEASE!"

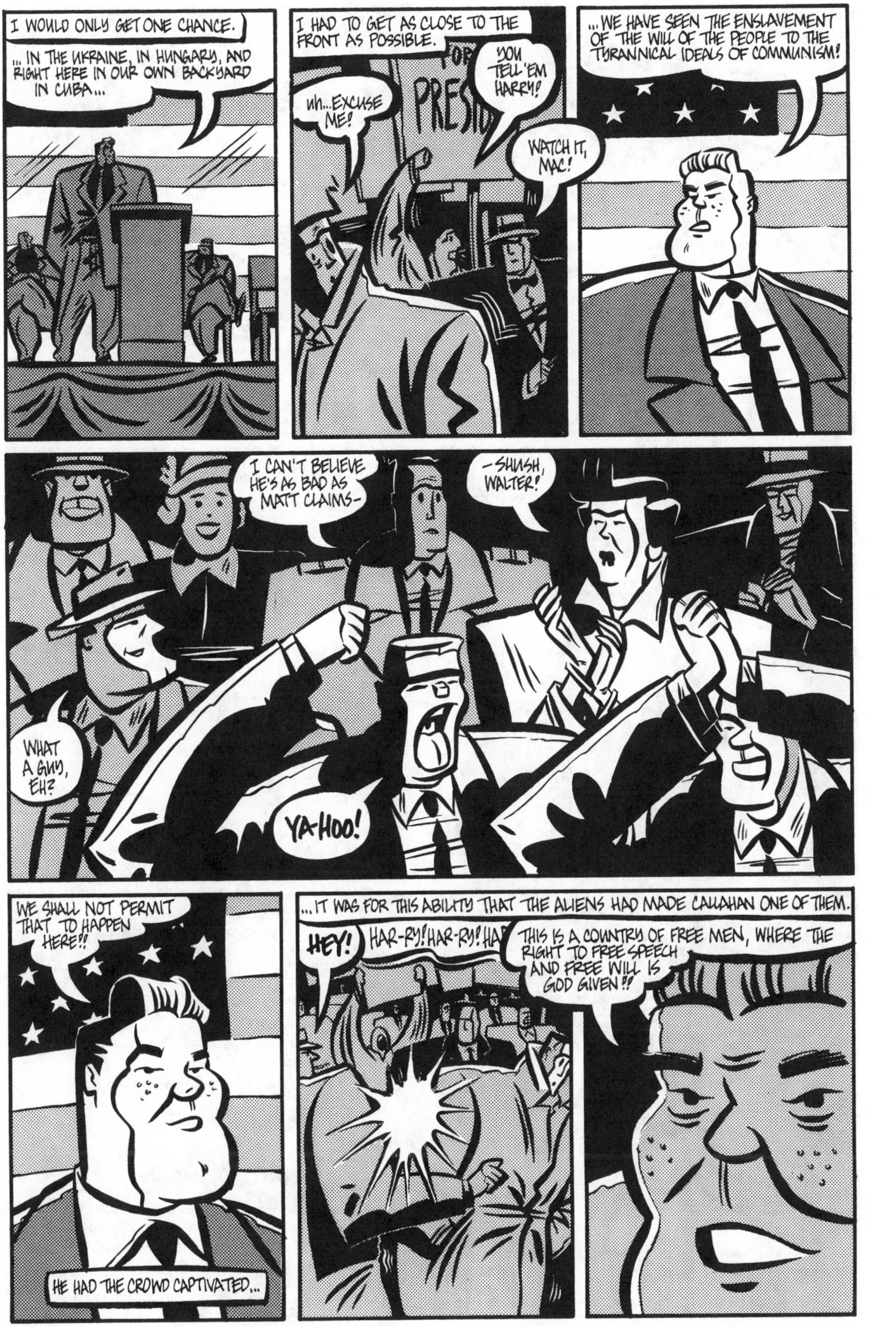

I WOULD ONLY GET ONE CHANCE.
...IN THE UKRAINE, IN HUNGARY, AND RIGHT HERE IN OUR OWN BACKYARD IN CUBA...
I HAD TO GET AS CLOSE TO THE FRONT AS POSSIBLE.
uh...EXCUSE ME!
YOU TELL 'EM HARRY!
WATCH IT, MAC!
...WE HAVE SEEN THE ENSLAVEMENT OF THE WILL OF THE PEOPLE TO THE TYRANNICAL IDEALS OF COMMUNISM!
I CAN'T BELIEVE HE'S AS BAD AS MATT CLAIMS-
-SHUSH, WALTER!
WHAT A GUY, EH?
YA-HOO!
WE SHALL NOT PERMIT THAT TO HAPPEN HERE!!
HE HAD THE CROWD CAPTIVATED...
...IT WAS FOR THIS ABILITY THAT THE ALIENS HAD MADE CALLAHAN ONE OF THEM.
HEY!
HAR-RY! HAR-RY! HAR
THIS IS A COUNTRY OF FREE MEN, WHERE THE RIGHT TO FREE SPEECH AND FREE WILL IS GOD GIVEN!!

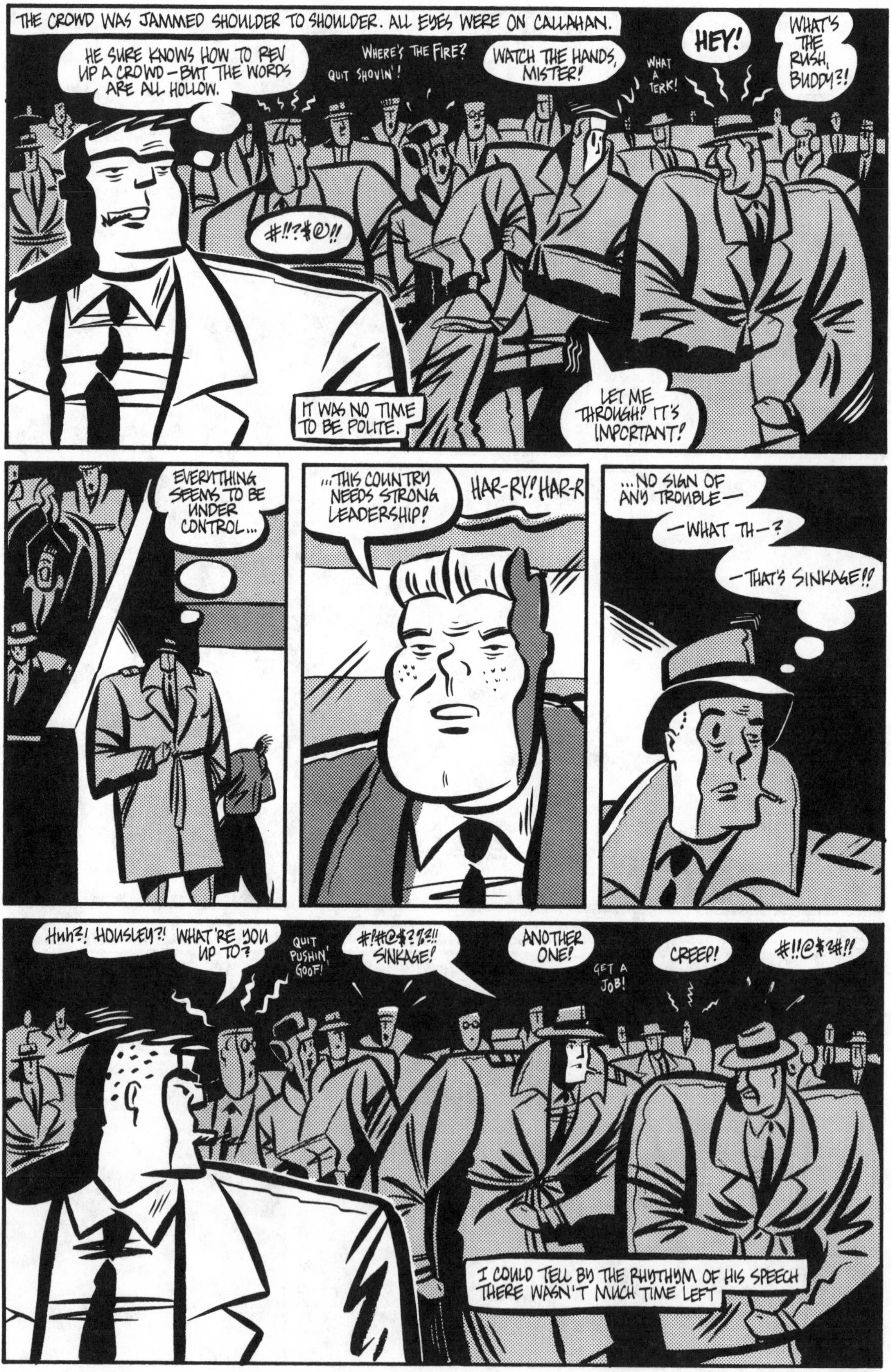
THE CROWD WAS JAMMED SHOULDER TO SHOULDER. ALL EYES WERE ON CALLAHAN.
HE SURE KNOWS HOW TO REV UP A CROWD — BUT THE WORDS ARE ALL HOLLOW.
WHERE'S THE FIRE?
QUIT SHOVIN'!
WATCH THE HANDS, MISTER!
WHAT A JERK!
HEY!
WHAT'S THE RUSH, BUDDY?!
#!!?$@!!
IT WAS NO TIME TO BE POLITE.
LET ME THROUGH! IT'S IMPORTANT!
EVERYTHING SEEMS TO BE UNDER CONTROL...
...THIS COUNTRY NEEDS STRONG LEADERSHIP!
HAR-RY! HAR-R
...NO SIGN OF ANY TROUBLE—
—WHAT TH—?
—THAT'S SINKAGE!!
Huh?! HOUSLEY?! WHAT'RE YOU UP TO?
QUIT PUSHIN', GOOF!
#!#@$?%?!! SINKAGE!
ANOTHER ONE!
GET A JOB!
CREEP!
#!!@$?#!!
I COULD TELL BY THE RHYTHYM OF HIS SPEECH THERE WASN'T MUCH TIME LEFT

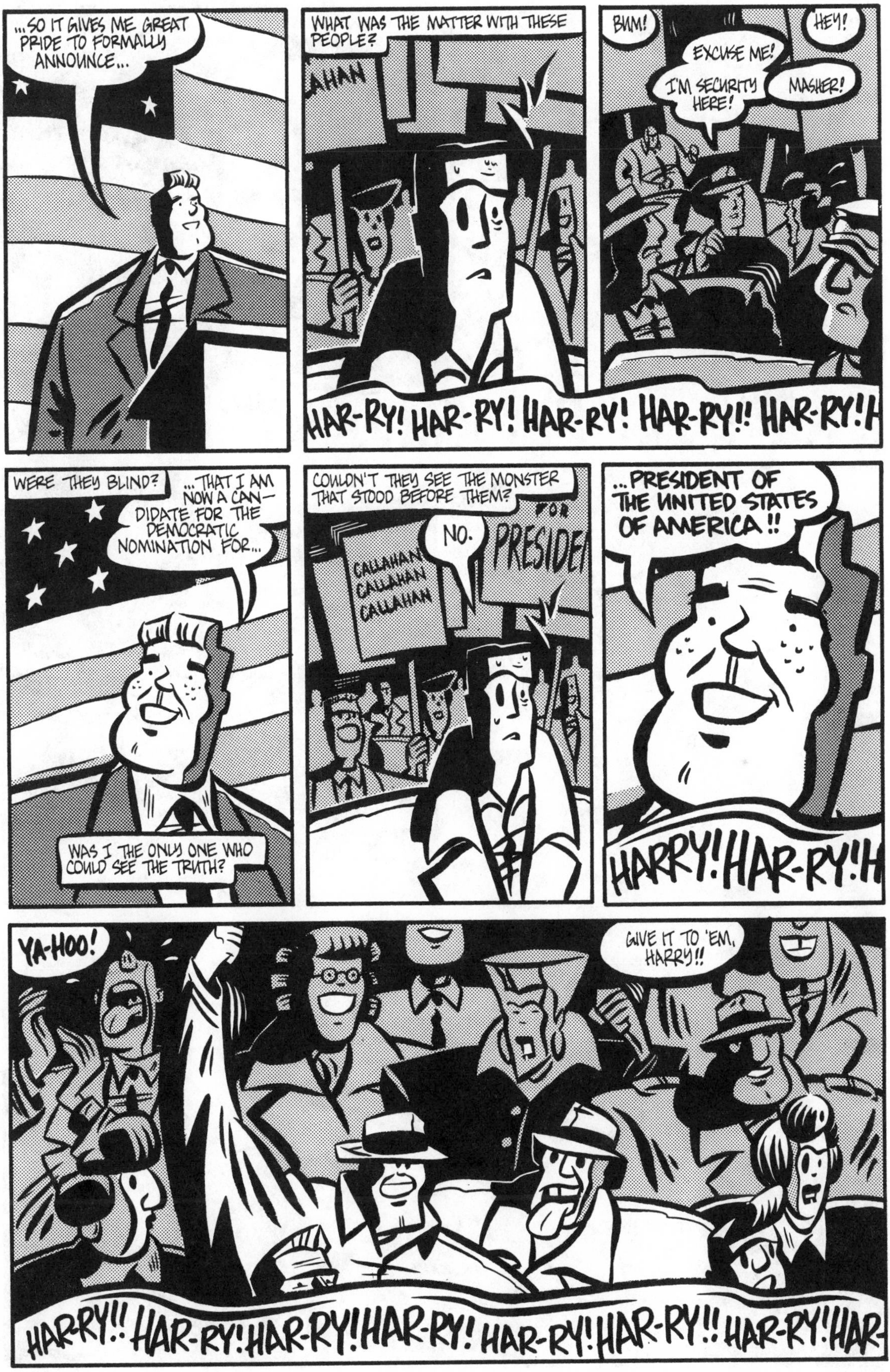
...SO IT GIVES ME GREAT PRIDE TO FORMALLY ANNOUNCE...
WHAT WAS THE MATTER WITH THESE PEOPLE?
BUM!
HEY!
EXCUSE ME!
I'M SECURITY HERE!
MASHER!
HAR-RY! HAR-RY! HAR-RY! HAR-RY!! HAR-RY!
WERE THEY BLIND?
...THAT I AM NOW A CAN-DIDATE FOR THE DEMOCRATIC NOMINATION FOR...
WAS I THE ONLY ONE WHO COULD SEE THE TRUTH?
COULDN'T THEY SEE THE MONSTER THAT STOOD BEFORE THEM?
NO.
CALLAHAN CALLAHAN CALLAHAN
PRESIDEN
...PRESIDENT OF THE UNITED STATES OF AMERICA!!
HARRY! HAR-RY!
YA-HOO!
GIVE IT TO 'EM, HARRY!!
HAR-RY!! HAR-RY! HAR-RY! HAR-RY! HAR-RY! HAR-RY!! HAR-RY! HAR-

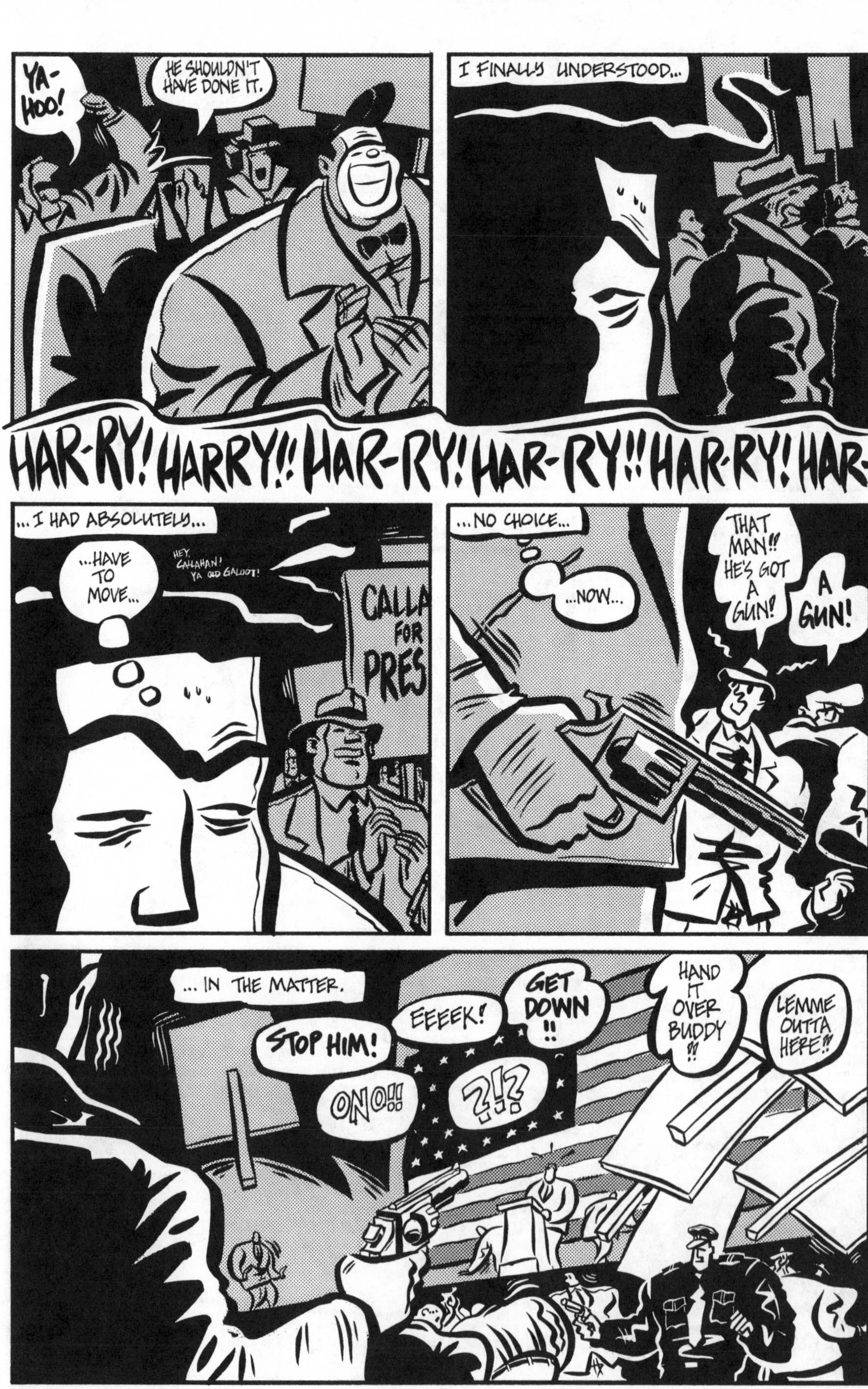
YA-HOO!
HE SHOULDN'T HAVE DONE IT.
I FINALLY UNDERSTOOD...
HAR-RY! HARRY!! HAR-RY! HAR-RY!! HAR-RY! HAR-
... I HAD ABSOLUTELY...
...HAVE TO MOVE...
HEY, CALLAHAN! YA OLD GALOOT!
CALLA
FOR
PRES
... NO CHOICE...
...NOW...
THAT MAN!! HE'S GOT A GUN!
A GUN!
... IN THE MATTER.
STOP HIM!
EEEEK!
GET DOWN !!
HAND IT OVER BUDDY !!
LEMME OUTTA HERE!!
ONO!!
?!?

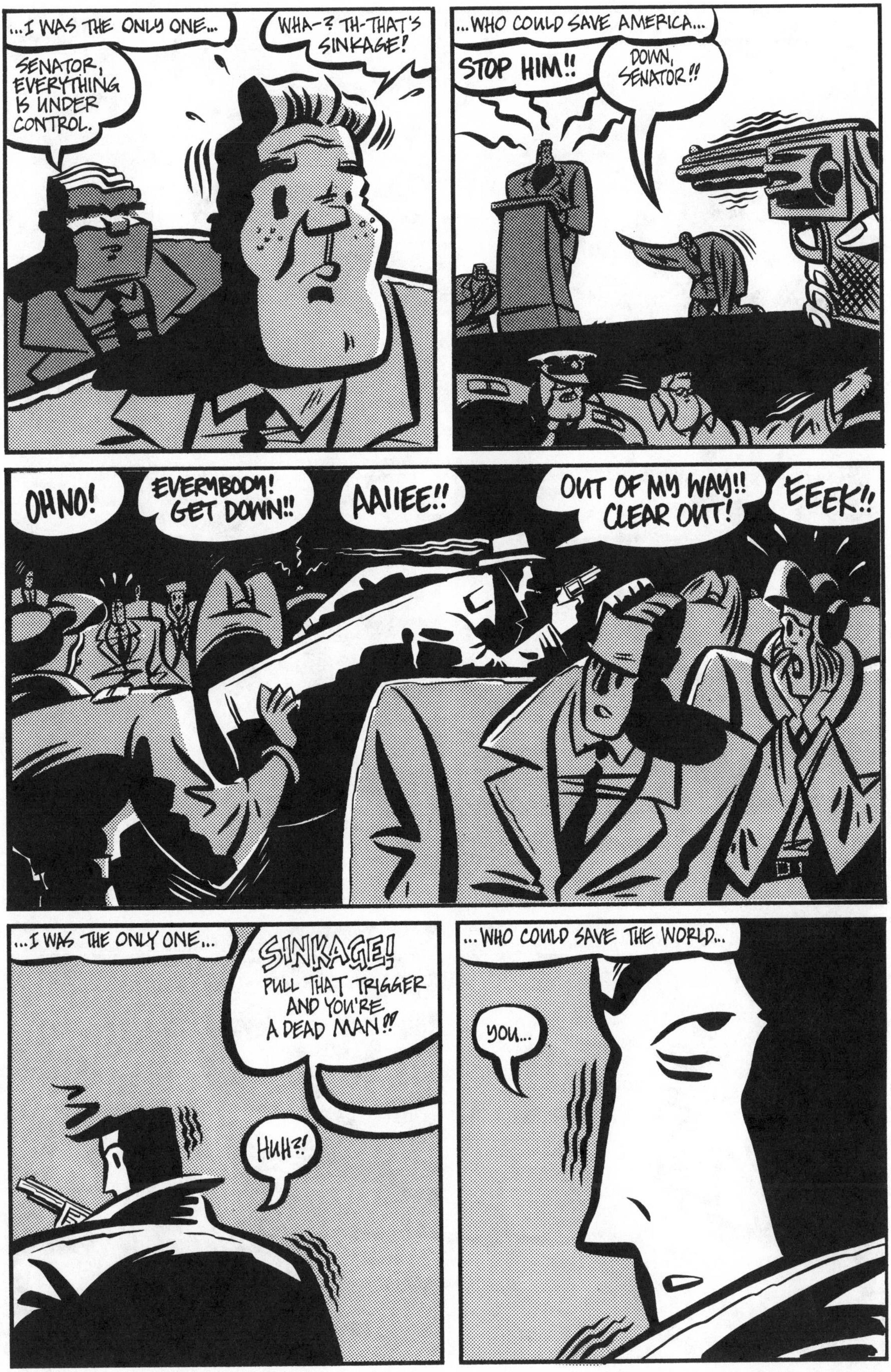
...I WAS THE ONLY ONE...
SENATOR, EVERYTHING IS UNDER CONTROL.
WHA-? TH-THAT'S SINKAGE!
...WHO COULD SAVE AMERICA...
STOP HIM!!
DOWN, SENATOR!!
OHNO!
EVERYBODY! GET DOWN!!
AAIIEE!!
OUT OF MY WAY!! CLEAR OUT!
EEEK!!
...I WAS THE ONLY ONE...
SINKAGE! PULL THAT TRIGGER AND YOU'RE A DEAD MAN!!
HUH?!
...WHO COULD SAVE THE WORLD...
YOU...

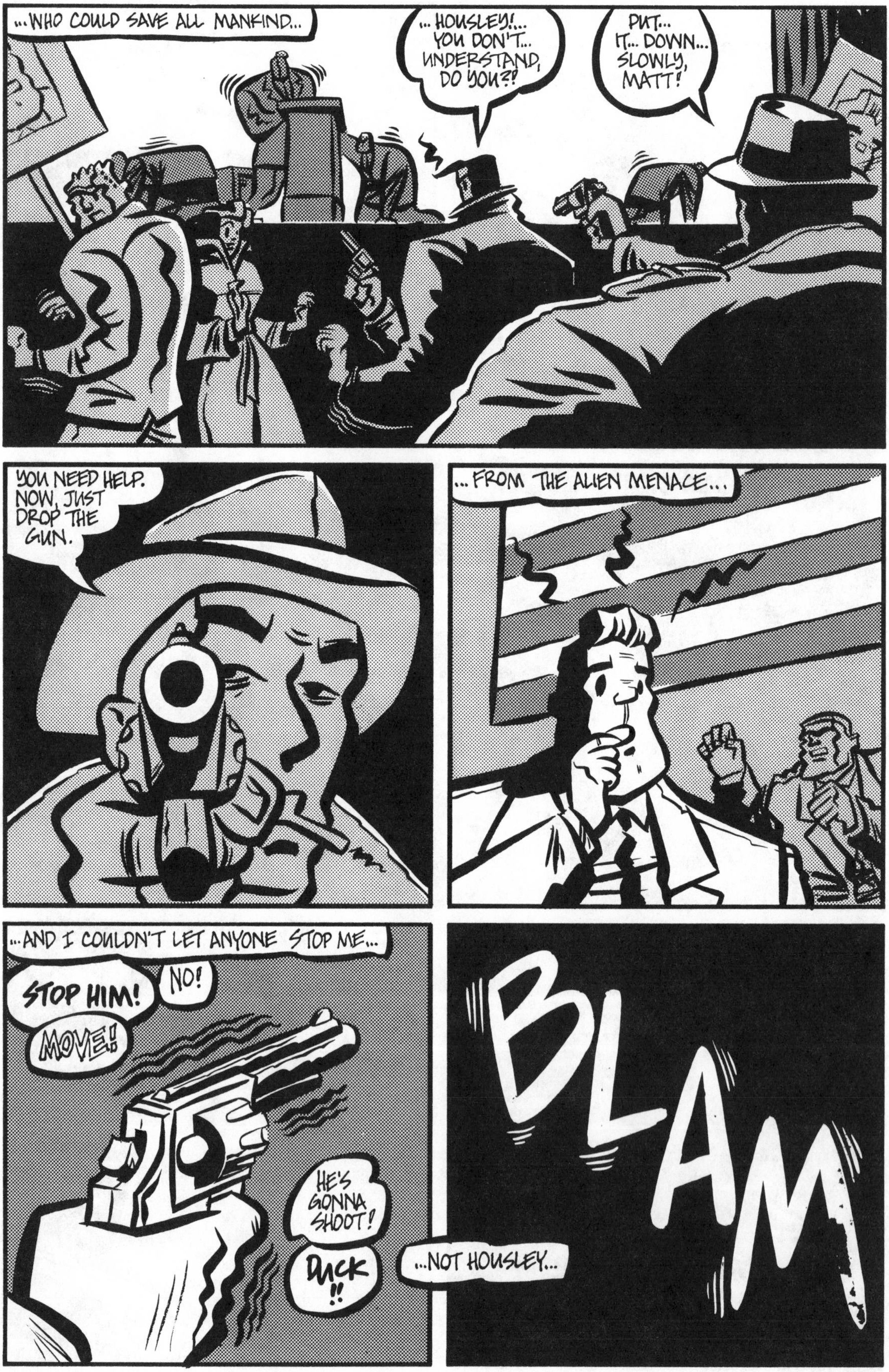
...WHO COULD SAVE ALL MANKIND...
...HOUSLEY!... YOU DON'T... UNDERSTAND, DO YOU?!
PUT... IT... DOWN... SLOWLY, MATT!
YOU NEED HELP. NOW, JUST DROP THE GUN.
...FROM THE ALIEN MENACE...
...AND I COULDN'T LET ANYONE STOP ME...
STOP HIM!
NO!
MOVE!
HE'S GONNA SHOOT!
DUCK!!
...NOT HOUSLEY...
BLAM

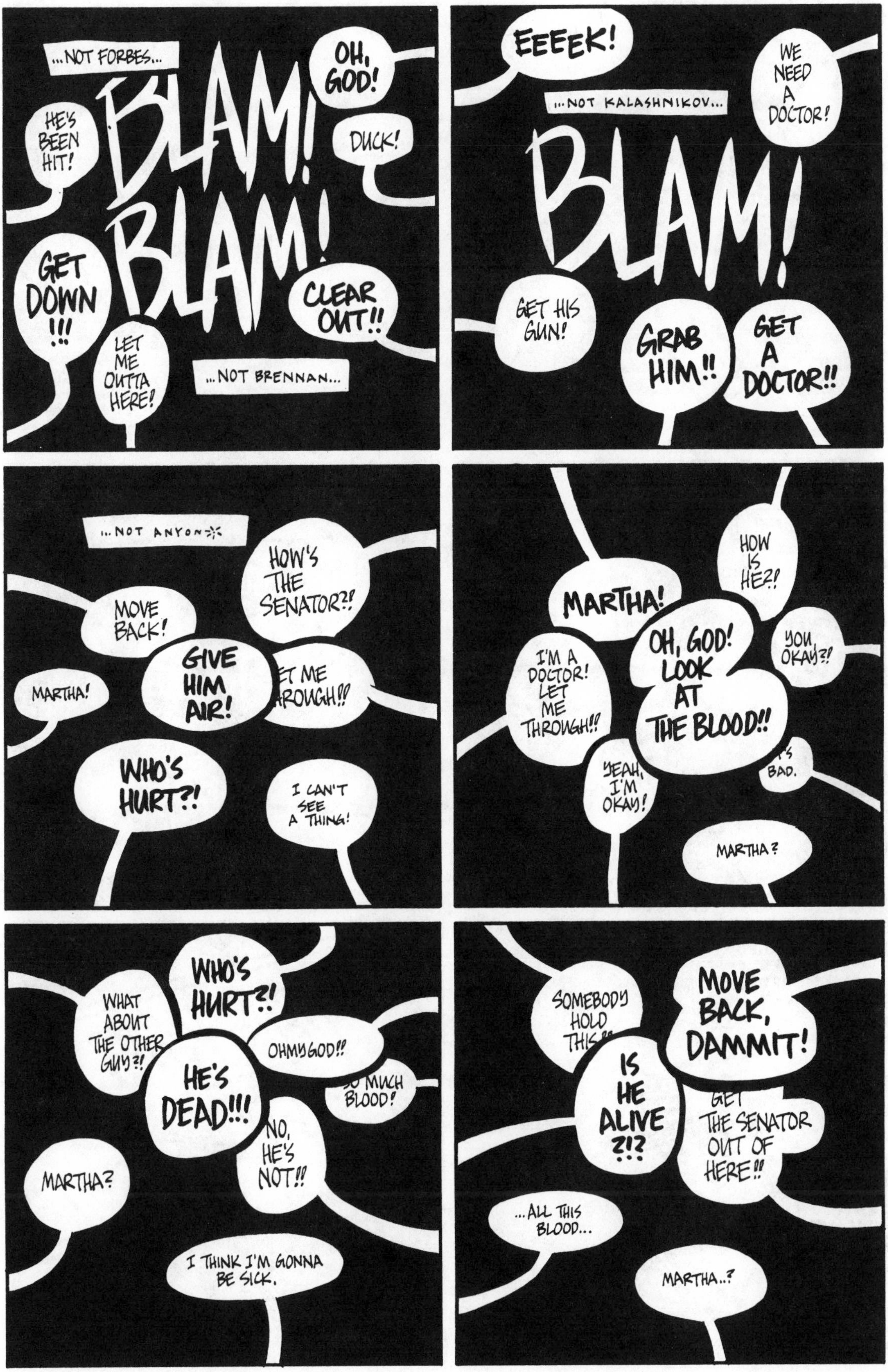
...NOT FORBES...
OH, GOD!
BLAM!
HE'S BEEN HIT!
DUCK!
BLAM!
GET DOWN!!!
CLEAR OUT!!
LET ME OUTTA HERE!
...NOT BRENNAN...
EEEEK!
WE NEED A DOCTOR!
...NOT KALASHNIKOV...
BLAM!
GET HIS GUN!
GRAB HIM!!
GET A DOCTOR!!
...NOT ANYON
HOW'S THE SENATOR?!
MOVE BACK!
GIVE HIM AIR!
MARTHA!
WHO'S HURT?!
I CAN'T SEE A THING!
HOW IS HE?!
MARTHA!
OH, GOD! LOOK AT THE BLOOD!!
I'M A DOCTOR! LET ME THROUGH!!
YOU OKAY?!
YEAH, I'M OKAY!
MARTHA?
WHAT ABOUT THE OTHER GUY?!
WHO'S HURT?!
OHMYGOD!!
HE'S DEAD!!!
NO, HE'S NOT!!
MARTHA?
I THINK I'M GONNA BE SICK.
MOVE BACK, DAMMIT!
IS HE ALIVE?!?
THE SENATOR OUT OF HERE!!
...ALL THIS BLOOD...
MARTHA...?

WEDNESDAY, NOVEMBER 9, 1960...

PHIL?

I'LL BE RIGHT WITH YOU, MEREDITH. JUST LOOKING OVER THE FINAL RESULTS.

WELL?

I CAN'T HELP BUT WONDER HOW DIFFERENTLY EVERYTHING MIGHT HAVE TURNED OUT IF SINKAGE HADN'T SHOT THE SENATOR...

I'VE A SNEAKING SUSPICION THAT BY SURVIVING THE ASSASSINATION ATTEMPT, CALLAHAN GAINED A LOT OF SUPPORT—

SAY, DID WALTER SINKAGE EVER GET THE COURT ORDER TO HAVE HIS BROTHER'S BODY RELEASED?

YEAH... BUT THE AUTHORITIES SAID THERE WASN'T ENOUGH LEFT AFTER THE CORONER GOT FINISHED WITH HIM.

IF ONLY MATT WOULD HAVE LISTENED... I DIDN'T WANT TO KILL HIM...

Sentinel-Gazette

CALLAHAN WINS IN 32 STATES

Sentinel-Gaz

CALLAHAN WINS IN

PRESIDENT

THE END.

ABOUT THE AUTHORS

MICHAEL CHERKAS has worked for over 30 years as a graphic designer, art director, cartoonist and illustrator. He still enjoys using non-repro blue pencils, brushes, India ink and paper when making comics. His other comics include *Suburban Nightmares* (with Larry Hancock and John van Bruggen), *The Purple Ray* (with Larry Hancock) and *The New Frontier* (with John Sabljic). He's been watching the skies for UFOs since he was a wonder-struck boy and looks forward to his first sighting.

LARRY HANCOCK was born in Toronto, Ontario in 1954. He graduated from the University of Waterloo with a Bachelor of Mathematics and since then has toiled in Toronto as a Chartered Accountant. However, counter to the view of accountants as boring, he has written *The Silent Invasion* and *The Purple Ray* with Michael Cherkas and *Suburban Nightmares* with Cherkas and John van Bruggen. He enjoys reading mysteries, science fiction and comic books (as if you could not guess!).

THE SILENT INVASION SERIES

Red Shadows
The Great Fear
Abductions
Dark Matter

WATCH FOR ABDUCTIONS!
THE NEXT VOLUME IN THE SILENT INVASION

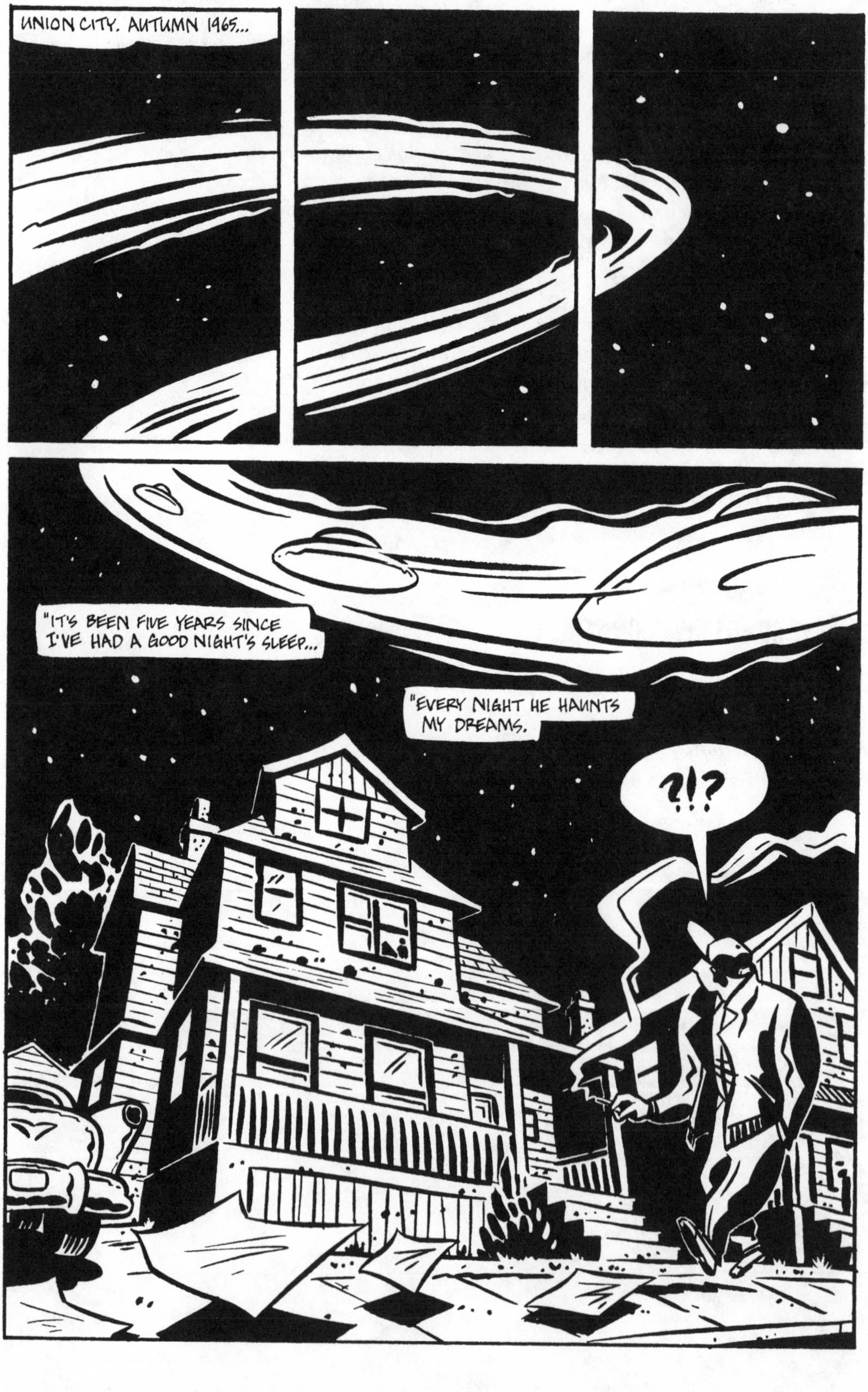

UNION CITY. AUTUMN 1965...
"IT'S BEEN FIVE YEARS SINCE I'VE HAD A GOOD NIGHT'S SLEEP...
"EVERY NIGHT HE HAUNTS MY DREAMS.
?!?

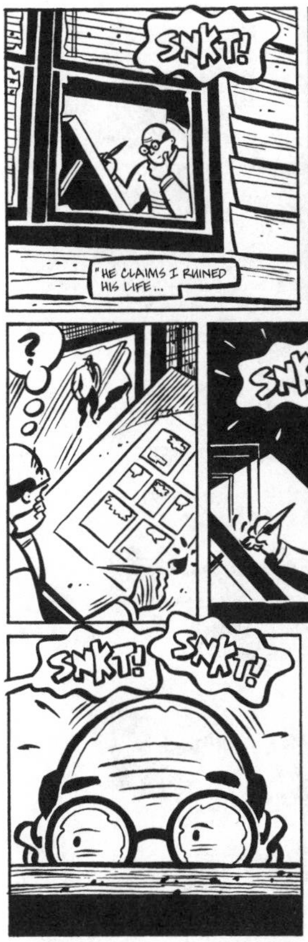
SNKT!
SNKT!
"HE CLAIMS I RUINED HIS LIFE...
?
SNKT!
!!
SNKT!
SNKT!
MRS. B-BORNSTEIN?
"...AND NOW HE'S GOING TO RUIN MINE.

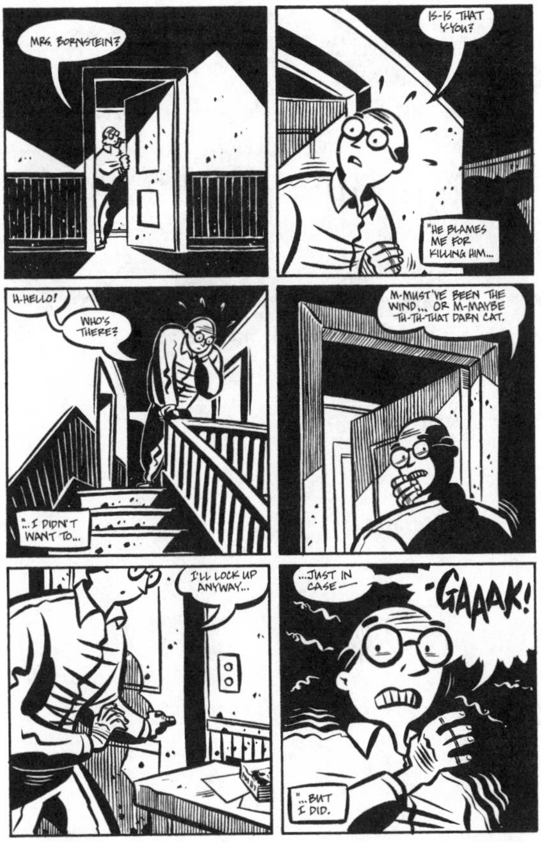
MRS. BORNSTEIN?
IS-IS THAT Y-YOU?
"HE BLAMES ME FOR KILLING HIM...
H-HELLO!
WHO'S THERE?
"...I DIDN'T WANT TO...
M-MUST'VE BEEN THE WIND... OR M-MAYBE TH-TH-THAT DARN CAT.
I'LL LOCK UP ANYWAY...
...JUST IN CASE—
-GAAAK!
"...BUT I DID.

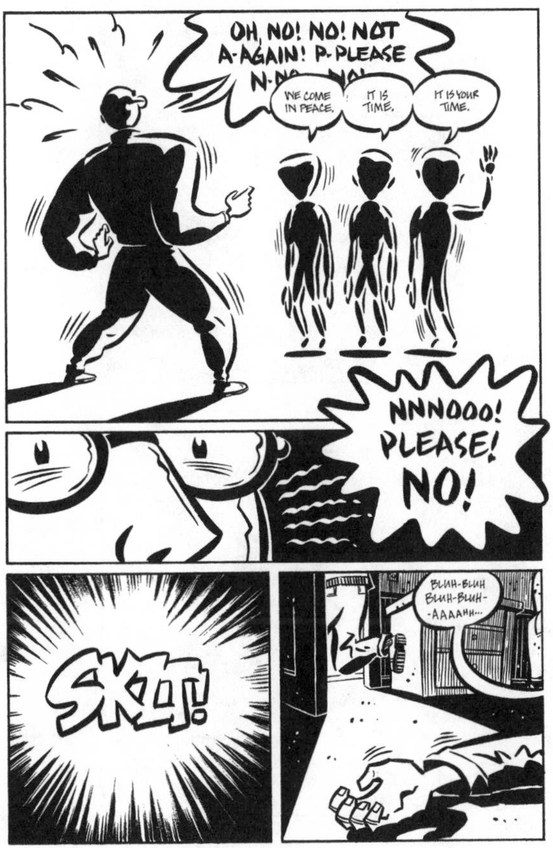
OH, NO! NO! NOT A-AGAIN! P-PLEASE
WE COME IN PEACE.
IT IS TIME.
IT IS YOUR TIME.
NNNOOO! PLEASE! NO!
SKLT!
BLUH-BLUH BLUH-BLUH -AAAAHH...

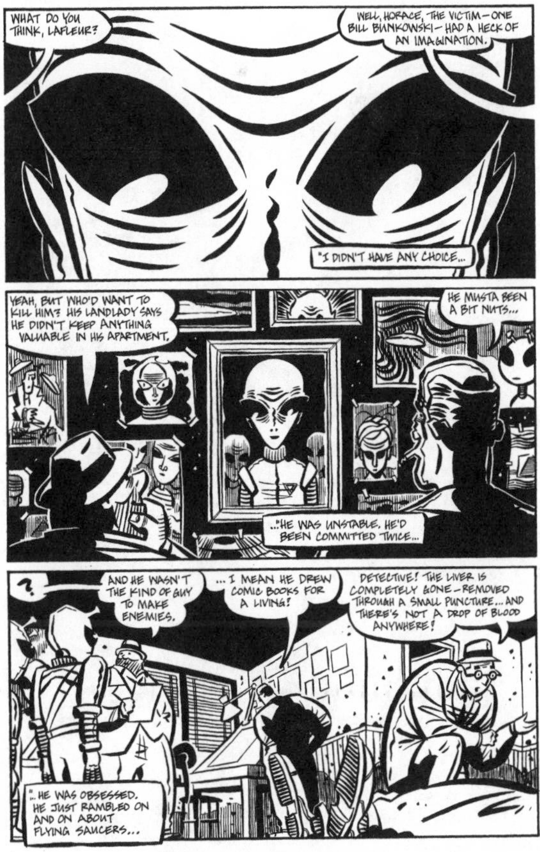
WHAT DO YOU THINK, LAFLEUR?
WELL, HORACE, THE VICTIM—ONE BILL BLINKOWSKI—HAD A HECK OF AN IMAGINATION.
"I DIDN'T HAVE ANY CHOICE...
YEAH, BUT WHO'D WANT TO KILL HIM? HIS LANDLADY SAYS HE DIDN'T KEEP ANYTHING VALUABLE IN HIS APARTMENT.
HE MUSTA BEEN A BIT NUTS...
"...HE WAS UNSTABLE. HE'D BEEN COMMITTED TWICE...
?
AND HE WASN'T THE KIND OF GUY TO MAKE ENEMIES.
...I MEAN HE DREW COMIC BOOKS FOR A LIVING!
DETECTIVE! THE LIVER IS COMPLETELY GONE—REMOVED THROUGH A SMALL PUNCTURE... AND THERE'S NOT A DROP OF BLOOD ANYWHERE!
"...HE WAS OBSESSED. HE JUST RAMBLED ON AND ON ABOUT FLYING SAUCERS...

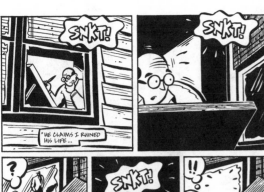

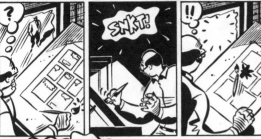

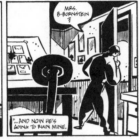

Already available in The Silent Invasion:
Vol. 1: Red Shadows
If you liked this you might also like these from NBM:
The DUNGEON Series
Lewis Trondheim, Joann Sfar, and assorted artists
LOOK
Jon Nielsen
Philip K. DICK
A Comics Biography
Laurent Queyssi, writer, Mauro Marchesi, artist

THE SILENT INVASION
SEE AMERICA TORN APART BY FEAR AND PARANOIA!
MICHAEL CHERKAS AND LARRY HANCOCK
Introduction by MAX ALLAN COLLINS
RED SHADOWS

Joann SFAR & Lewis TRONDHEIM
Dungeon
Zenith
Vol. 2: The Barbarian Princess

LOOK
JON NIELSEN

THE IMPROBABLE LIFE OF THE AUTHOR OF MINORITY REPORT, BLADE RUNNER, ELECTRIC DREAMS AND TOTAL RECALL!
PHILIP K. DICK
A COMICS BIOGRAPHY
LAURENT QUEYSSI / MAURO MARCHESI

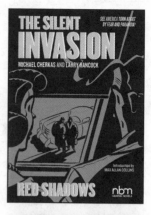

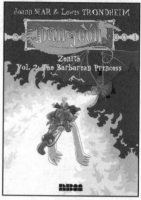

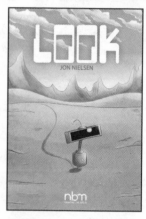

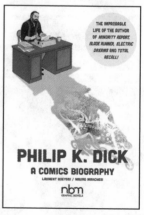